Group Work with
Populations at Risk

Group Work with Populations at Risk

Edited by

Geoffrey L. Greif

Paul H. Ephross

New York   Oxford
OXFORD UNIVERSITY PRESS
1997

Oxford University Press

Oxford   New York
Athens   Aukland   Bangkok
Bogota   Bombay   Buenos Aires   Calcutta
Cape Town   Dar es Salaam   Delhi
Florence   Hong Kong   Istanbul   Karachi
Kuala Lumpur   Madras   Madrid   Melbourne
Mexico City   Nairobi   Paris   Singapore
Taipei   Tokyo   Toronto

and associated companies in
Berlin   Ibadan

Copyright © 1997 by Oxford University Press, Inc.

Published by Oxford University Press, Inc.
198 Madison Avenue, New York, New York 10016

Oxford is a registered trademark of Oxford University Press

Library of Congress Cataloging-in-Publication Data

Group work with populations at risk/edited by
Geoffrey L. Greif and Paul H. Ephross.
p.   cm.   Includes bibliographical references and index.
ISBN 0-19-509519-7   ISBN 0-19-509520-0 (pbk.)
1. Social group work.   2. Marginality, Social.
I. Greif, Geoffrey L.   II. Ephross, Paul H.
HV45.G73165   1997
361.4—dc20   95-25900

3 5 7 9 8 6 4

Printed in the United States of America
on acid-free paper

Contents

Part II Adjusting to Change

Part III   Violence: Victims and Perpetrators

Part IV   Substance Abuse

Part V   Gay Men and Lesbian Issues

Part VI   Schools and the Workplace

Preface

The genesis of this book was our belief that beginning social workers need concrete suggestions for managing and guiding their forays into group work. Newcomers entering an agency, for example, are often asked to start or take over a group that serves members of a particular population. Where should the worker begin in trying to understand the group's members and their shared condition? Publications about work with the target population may focus on individual needs, policy proposals, social action agendas, or important findings from research. Literature on group work with that population may be available periodically but is not always up-to-date or easily accessible to the worker. It may also not be geared toward guiding a novice through the beginning stages of helping.

Social work with groups has become an orphan in many departments and schools over the last few decades, relegated to part of a practice course or ignored altogether (Birnbaum & Auerbach, 1994). As fewer schools taught group work as a separate subject, fewer group work specialists were developed and the supply of group work teachers, prepared both academically and by practice experience with groups, declined sharply. It is only recently, with the hard work of the Association for the Advancement of Social Work with Groups and recognition by the Council on Social Work Education of the necessity of strengthening education in group work, that the trend toward marginalizing group work has been reversed. The teaching and practice of social work with groups are again starting to proliferate (as they did 50 years ago) both in undergraduate and graduate social work curricula and in the field. This expansion stems from the recognition that group work is often the method of choice to meet the needs of the client and community; is financially viable, given the increased pressure on resources, both organizational and third party; and is often a wise use of the worker's time. Group work can also help meet deeply felt personal and social needs at a time when alienation, a sense of disenfranchisement, and experiences of oppression and fragmentation characterize the lives of many people who seek help from social workers and others.

Learning group work methods in the broadest sense—including the phases of group life, the demands of the worker in each phase, the uses of authority, the opportunities and constraints of agency contexts, and the value of limits, among others—is one important aspect of dealing with the rising demand for groups. Another is learning how to work with the specific population from which group members are drawn. With the rapidly changing nature of practice and its increasing focus on the particular needs of specific populations (a reflection of American society), we believe that proficiency and specificity of skills are in great demand. People seeking help are more likely to be wary consumers. They want to be understood as individuals and will seek help elsewhere if the worker does not help them achieve their goals and reach the outcomes they seek.

The purpose of this book is to provide social workers with a practice-oriented source that describes specific ways of working with a variety of populations in groups. The focus is on populations at risk, those most likely to need social work services in groups. The phrase *at risk* refers to people who have experienced life-changing events; who are at crossroads where prevention would be helpful in staving off undesirable consequences; or who, through their own actions, may represent a risk to others and themselves unless they are helped to change.

To achieve our goal, we approached practitioners who had extensive experience either with populations that have frequently been served by social workers in the past or with populations that we anticipate will need many services in the near future. It is not only their experience that makes these contributors experts; it is also their ability to see themselves in a helping role with the sometimes stigmatized population they serve. Each contributor was asked to write a chapter that would answer the following questions:

1. What does the professional literature say about this population?
2. What particular principles should guide a social worker beginning to work with this population?
3. What common themes have you seen in working with groups composed of members of this particular population?
4. What are some of the methods that you have found successful and that you recommend for working with this population?
5. What evaluation measures are being used to judge whether the members are benefiting from their experiences in these groups?
6. Are there any national sources of information that can be tapped by social workers for further information?

We were especially interested in the common themes that are raised by the groups being served. Social workers often know how to recruit members for groups, screen them, and start the first session. But once all members have introduced themselves, the usual first step, the worker may not know how to proceed. The contributors to this book offer that information by focusing on the areas of concern they have most frequently heard identified by group members. The worker is thus prepared to raise, respond to, or reinforce issues related to potential topics or areas of concern that are known to have been relevant to other such groups.

We begin with an introductory chapter that summarizes the generic practice principles of social work with groups. Then, because it is impossible for one book to encompass all of the populations at risk—our initial survey listed almost 50—the book includes a chapter on each of the following populations: persons being treated for cancer, abused children, parents in the urban public schools, seriously mentally ill people, children of divorce, incarcerated offenders, grieving adults, parents being treated for substance abuse, African-American youth who have had contact with the legal system, gay men, lesbian women, substance-abusing teenagers, men who have committed family violence, HIV-positive men, head-injured people, men who have sexually abused children, noncustodial parents, victims of hate crimes (a growing population), unemployed workers, and workers connected to employee assistance programs. Because of the complexity of the work site, this last chapter presents an overview of groups offered in that setting.

Some contributors have offered detailed explanations of step-by-step programs that they offer. Others are more general in their approach. We believe there is much to be learned from these experts and have left their views and opinions in place, regardless of whether we agree with their points of view. It is our hope that this text will be useful to social workers in a variety of settings and that it will demystify what can be the frightening experience of sitting in a group of strangers and not knowing where to begin.

We would like to thank Renée Forbes for her secretarial assistance, Gioia Stevens of Oxford University Press for her editorial support, and Dean Jesse J. Harris for helping bring about an atmosphere at the School of Social Work, University of Maryland at Baltimore, that makes writing a pleasure. When the entire manuscript had been completed, we realized that we had never decided the order in which the editors should be listed. We flipped a coin to solve this problem. Would that all problems could be solved so easily.

Baltimore, Maryland　　　　　　　　　　　　　　　　　　　　G.L.G.
May 1996　　　　　　　　　　　　　　　　　　　　　　　　　P.H.E.

REFERENCE

Birnbaum, M., & Auerbach, C. (1994). Group work in graduate social work education: The price of neglect. *Journal of Social Work Education, 30*(4), 325–334.

About the Contributors

Steven Ball, ACSW, is a private practitioner and consultant to Gay Men's Health Crisis in New York City.

Sara Bonkowski, Ph.D., is a professor at George Williams College, School of Social Work, Aurora University.

Margot Breton, MSW, is a professor, Faculty of Social Work, University of Toronto, Toronto, Ontario.

Barry M. Daste, is a professor, School of Social Work, Louisiana State University.

Sharon England, MSW, J.D., conducted groups for the Baltimore City and Anne Arundel County Departments of Social Services and was the founding executive director of the Court-Appointed Special Advocate Program, Baltimore.

Bonnie J. Englehardt, ACSW, LICSW, is a social group worker in private practice in Needham, Massachusetts.

Paul H. Ephross, Ph.D., is a professor, School of Social Work, University of Maryland at Baltimore.

Susan T. Futeral, Ph.D., is on the faculty of Towson State University in sociology and is engaged in private practice and consulting.

Charles Garvin, Ph.D., is a professor and director of the doctoral program, School of Social Work, University of Michigan.

George S. Getzel, Ph.D., is a professor, Hunter College School of Social Work.

Muriel Gray, Ph.D., is an associate professor, School of Social Work, University of Maryland at Baltimore.

Geoffrey L. Greif, D.S.W., is an associate dean and professor, School of Social Work, University of Maryland at Baltimore.

Aminifu R. Harvey, D.S.W., is an assistant professor, School of Social Work, University of Maryland at Baltimore.

Benjamin Lipton, CSW, is clinical supervisor, Gay Men's Health Crisis and in private practice in New York City.

Jane E. Lytle-Vieira, MSW, is clinical director, Family Life Center, Columbia, Maryland.

Andrew Malekoff, ACSW, CAC, is director of program development for North Shore Child and Family Guidance Center, Roslyn Heights, New York, and co-editor of *Social Work with Groups*.

Anna Nosko, MSW, is a social worker at Family Services Association of Toronto.

Susan Rice, DSW, is a professor, department of Social Work, and director of the Peace Studies Certificate Program at California State University at Long Beach.

Steven Stosny, Ph.D., is director of Community Outreach Service in Silver Spring, Maryland.

Joan C. Weiss, MSW, is executive director of the Justice Research and Statistics Association, Washington, DC.

Carolyn Ambler Walter, Ph.D., is associate professor and director of the baccalaureate social work program, Center for Social Work Education, Widener University, Chester, Pennsylvania.

Margaret M. Wright, Ph.D., is a professor, School of Social Work, Ryerson Polytechnic University, Toronto, Ontario.

Group Work with
Populations at Risk

Introduction

Social Work with Groups: Practice Principles

Paul H. Ephross

This book is about the practice of group work with a wide variety of people who are at risk. The populations are defined by a particular physical or psychological condition, a social identity, a condition that causes them to be stigmatized or discriminated against by society or social institutions, or by a challenge that arises from their stage of life or personal history. Many are affected by more than one of these situations. What unites the people described in the following chapters is that they share two characteristics. They are at risk for continued, intensified harm, pain, and dysfunction. They can also benefit from participating in a group experience through which they can gain skills, understanding, and emotional learnings that can reduce their level of vulnerability.

Each chapter author was asked to note ways in which the particular needs of his or her population may necessitate modifications or adaptations of traditional or mainstream social work practice in groups. This instruction, and the chapter authors' responses, suggest that there is a body of knowledge and skills, supported by a cluster of perceptions and attitudes, undergirded by a set of values and commitments about the nature of human beings and society, that constitute mainstream group work. Each chapter assumes that the reader understands the bases of group work and uses those bases as a starting point. The purpose of this chapter is to provide an introduction to concepts that are generic to social group work, including the nature of group experience, values, perceptions, purposes and goals, and methods.

Defining *group* is not a simple matter.

The word *group* has met with difficulties of definition, both in the social sciences and in social work literature. In one sense, it is defined by size, i.e., the "small group" or such large units as legislative committees or assemblies. In a second sense, group is linked to collectivity. In still another sense, group is tied to the term *social*, thereby contrasting the group with individuals. Yet all writers suggest that groups, organizations, and collectivities consist of individuals. (Falck, 1988, p. 3)

THE NATURE OF GROUP EXPERIENCE

Human beings are born into groups, and their lives may be viewed as experiences in group memberships. As Falck has noted:

Every person is a member. A member is a human being characterized by body, personality, sociality, and the ability to comprehend human experience. Every member is an element in the community of men and women. . . .

He proceeds to characterize a member as a "social being in continuous interaction with others who are both seen and unseen . . . and . . . a psychological being capable of private experience." Falck drew several inferences from the "fact that in speaking of a member one implicitly speaks of others, who are also members."

The term *member* refers to a person who is:
1. A physical being bounded by semipermeable membranes and cavities;
2. A social being in continuous interaction with others who are both seen and unseen . . . and
3. A psychological being capable of private experience. The fact that in speaking of member one implicitly speaks of others, who are also members, leads to the following inferences:
1. A member's actions are socially derived and contributory;
2. The identity of each member is bound up with that of others through social involvement;
3. A member is a person whose differences from others create tensions that lead to growth, group cohesion, and group conflict; and
4. Human freedom is defined by simultaneous concern for oneself and others. . . . (1988, p. 30)

Membership, in this view, is such an essential aspect of humanness that the one is virtually indistinguishable from the other. It is little wonder, then, that groups have been described as microcosms (Ephross & Vassil, 1988), participation in which can lead toward growth, healing, expanded and enhanced social functioning, learning, the expression of democratic citizenship, the practice of self-determination, mutual aid, mutual support, and progress toward achieving social justice.

What can be mobilized in a group that can give group experiences power to affect the group's members? Northen lists 11 that she labels *dynamic forces*: mutual support, cohesiveness, quality of relationships, universalization, instillation of hope, altruism, acquisition of knowledge and skills, catharsis, corrective emotional experiences, reality testing, and group control. She proceeds to make some important observations about these forces:

> Findings . . . suggest that some factors are more important than others for different types of groups and even for different members of the same group. . . . Furthermore, these dynamic forces need to be viewed as potential benefits; they are not present automatically in groups but need to be fostered by the practitioner. (1988, pp. 11–13)

In this view, though groups are naturally occurring phenomena, the benefits of participation ought not to be taken for granted but rather need to be nurtured by the social worker/practitioner.

Other writers may name the influential aspects of group life differently, but they agree both on the power of group experience and generally on those aspects that generate groups' power to affect members. For example, one list highlights nine *mutual aid processes* as follows: "sharing data, the dialectical process, entering taboo areas, the 'all-in-the-same-boat' phenomenon, mutual support, mutual demand, individual problem solving, rehearsal, and the strength-in-numbers phenomenon" (Gitterman & Shulman, 1994, p. 14).

Focusing on "the group as an entity," Garvin has developed a

> classification of the dimensions of group process. . . . [T]hese dimensions are the (1) goal oriented activities of the group, and the (2) quality of the interactions among the members.

This list includes goal determination, goal pursuit, the development of values and norms, role differentiation, communication-interaction, conflict resolution and behavior control, changes in emotions, group culture, group resources, extragroup transactions, group boundaries, and group climate (Garvin, 1987, pp. 113–121).

Henry first notes conflict between those who prefer analytic and organic approaches, respectively, to the question of what goes on in a group. She bases her answers on those identified by many early group work writers. She identifies as important criteria aspects of group life that by now are familiar to the reader: group composition and criteria for membership; some level of consensus on group goals; the external structure, which consists of time, space, and size; time, or the time framework within which the groups meets; internal structure; cohesion, communication and decision making, norms, values, and group culture; and group control and influence (1992, pp. 3–16).

GROUP WORK: VALUES AND PERCEPTIONS

"What a social worker does in practice is for a purpose. It reflects values and is based on knowledge" (Northen, 1988, p. 4). Group work is part of social work. As such, it shares many values and perceptions with the social work profession. It has been pointed out with both truth and wit, however, that contemporary group work stems from a symbolic total of no fewer than three parents (Weiner, 1964). One understands well the permutations and distortions of identity that can arise from interacting with only one or two parents. Imagine those that can arise from inter-acting with three! The "three parents" referred to are recreation, infor-mal education, and social work. Each has left an inheritance of great value to group work.

From its recreational sources, group work has acquired an understand-ing of and a respect for the power of participation in activity, only one form of which is talking. Unlike other methods, which assume that talking is the highest form of interaction, group work understands that doing, in inter-action with others, can have wonderful outcomes for individual group members, for groups, and for the society of which the group is part.

Related to this is both a positive valuation and a perception that it is important for people to do, to act, to interact with their environments. Group work has never even seriously considered a view of humans as essentially passive recipients of external influences. In group work, em-powering group members to speak, to express opinions, to interact, to decide, and to act on their external environments are seen as essential purposes, always depending, of course, on the capacities of the group members. While assessment—especially self-assessment—is an important part of groups' lives, social work with groups emphasizes the assessment of strengths in addition to, indeed sometimes instead of, the assessment of weaknesses.

Partly for this reason, clinical diagnoses tend not to be seen as helpful by many group work practitioners. A great deal of practice experience teaches that categorical diagnoses are often inaccurate predictors of how people can and will act in groups. Also, although individual "intake" inter-views are recommended by many of the authors in this book, some skep-ticism about the yield of such interviews may be warranted, primarily because individual interviews do not always predict behavior in a group.

From its early years, group work has valued differences, whether of race, class, sex, ethnicity, citizenship status, religious identity, age, or dis-ability. Much group work took place in agencies and organizational set-tings identified with minority communities and/or with economically deprived and sometimes societally oppressed communities. A contempo-rary statement of perspective can be found, for example, in Toseland and Rivas (1995, pp. 131–135). Among the traditional sources of group work theory and practice, one of the two most influential theorists of group dynamics was himself a refugee from totalitarian oppression, and was therefore keenly aware of the potential for bigotry and intergroup vio-lence (Lewin, 1948). An awareness both of women's needs and of various aspects of ethnicity can be found in very early writings from the settle-ment house field (e.g., Addams, 1909).

As is true of other methods and fields of social work, group workers sometimes work with people with whom they quickly come to feel empathy. Sometimes, one feels admiration for group members who struggle with handicaps, who are the victims of injustice, or who face difficult processes of rehabilitation. By contrast, with other populations, it may be difficult or even painful for a worker to attempt to relate helpfully to group members whose past or present behavior is personally abhorrent, or is a reminder of painful experiences in the worker's own life, or violates deeply held personal convictions of the worker. Supervisors, peers, and consultants may all be helpful in dealing with one's feelings about working with such groups.

In the extreme case, it may be impossible for a particular worker at a particular stage of life to work effectively with a particular population. The pain involved may be too great and the blocks to working with a group within the framework of "empathy, genuineness and warmth" (Garvin, 1987, p. 87) or "humanistic values and democratic norms" (Glassman & Kates, 1990, pp. 21–22) too intense. For example, a worker who has recently lost a family member to cancer may not be able, at this time, to work with a group of cancer patients or their relatives. Recognizing such a limitation is a sign of maturity and ethical decision making on the part of the worker and agency, not of incompetence or weakness.

Experience teaches that such situations are rare. Social workers often establish helping, empathic, genuine, and warm relationships with groups whose members have committed deeply antisocial acts. This certainly does not mean that workers approve of these acts. It means that, in groups, members' humanity tends to have more impact on group workers than their past, or even present, misdeeds and pathologies. The principle of unconditional positive regard for the worth of each person, at the same time that one disapproves of specific behaviors—sometimes stated in a religious context as "loving the sinner even when one hates the sin"—is an important component of group work.

GROUP WORK: PURPOSES AND GOALS

At one level, the purposes of group work are those of the social work profession, given the particular perspectives just sketched: providing the best possible services to clients in order to achieve the three purposes of social work: prevention of dysfunction, provision of resources for enhanced social functioning, and rehabilitation. At a suitably high level of abstraction, it is difficult to argue with these purposes. However, at a higher level of specificity, we have found it useful to take into account the typology of agency purposes and the emphasis on the importance of organizational factors introduced by Garvin (1996).

While emphasizing that no agency can be considered to have only one purpose, this typology views the major categories of purpose as being *socialization* and *resocialization*. Each category contains two subpurposes: *identity development* and *skill attainment* in the case of socialization and *social control* and *rehabilitation* in the case of resocialization. By emphasizing the importance of agency processes and structure to what happens with groups within that agency, Garvin's discussion, which is based on those of several organizational theorists, provides a useful perspective for the group work practitioner.

Many health care and social agencies seek to sponsor group work programs but are less receptive to the idea that their organizational structure, their emotional climate, how they are perceived by the community, their policies, or even their physical facilities operate in ways that can undercut or oppose the thrusts of the program. For this reason, conducting a group work program within an organizational context requires a group worker to have a broad vision: one that encompasses the organizational sponsor as well as the members of the groups within the broader context of client systems. In keeping with the general principle that group work always involves work with the group *and* work with the environment, the worker has an ongoing responsibility to address, and sometimes to help the group address, organizational factors such as those mentioned that can interfere with the accomplishment of the group's purposes.

GROUP WORK METHOD: AN OVERVIEW

Alissi (1982) has defined what he referred to as a "reaffirmation of essentials" regarding group work method. It remains a useful platform from which to look at group work methods. He identified relationships, contracts, and programming as essential elements and as elements that distinguish social work with groups from other group methods.

By *relationships*, Alissi meant those that are authentic, that involve an atmosphere in which "genuine feelings can be expressed and shared and by which members can be encouraged to relate in similar ways within as well as beyond the group. . . . The fundamental question to be asked throughout the process is what kinds of relationships are best suited for what kinds of ends?" (1982, p. 13).

The worker's relationship with group members and with the group as a whole needs to be simultaneously conscious and spontaneous, a considerable challenge. The principle of conscious use of self—knowing what one is doing and why one is doing it—is basic. The countervailing principle of being oneself, of being spontaneous, of expressing feelings in a warm and accepting way, may seem like a contradiction to the first. In this writer's view, the bridging concept is one of focus on whose needs are being met primarily. The relationship between worker and group needs to be a disciplined and focused one, and, of course, a nonexploitive one that helps to provide an atmosphere of safety, both physical and emotional, within the group.

That exploitation and boundary violations are less often problems in group work than in the one-to-one situation is due to the greater availability of support for group members from each other. This in no way relieves the worker from observing the boundaries set by ethics, by prevailing social standards, and by the sensitivities of the members of a particular group or community.

Alissi's second aspect of method is that of *contracts*, or "working agreements" between worker and group. "Unless members are involved in clarifying and setting their own personal and common group goals, they cannot be expected to be active participants in their own behalf" (1982, p. 13). There is an egalitarian flavor—a sense of worker and members working together to accomplish a common goal that is overt and understood—that distinguishes social work with groups from other therapeutic methods. Naturally, the capacity of group members to understand the common goals often sets significant limitations on this part of group work method.

The third aspect, *programming*, refers to the point made above, about the ability of activities of various kinds, levels of intensity and skill, and media, to influence both interpersonal and intrapsychic processes within a group. With many of the populations discussed in this book, not only is verbal discussion not the only medium of communication, but it is often far from the best.

GROUP WORK: SPECIFIC TECHNIQUES

Many of the specific techniques and skills of group work practice are discussed in the chapters of this book as they relate to the population under discussion. As is often the case, terminology can pose a problem. What one author calls *techniques* another calls *skills, technologies, worker behaviors,* or *interventions*. Despite the popularity of the last term, we think it is limited as a description of what social workers do in groups. Somehow *intervention* connotes entering group process from the outside and therefore portrays the worker as external to the group, at least most of the time. We think that the social worker is best understood as a person who is a member of the group, although a member with a difference: one with a specialized, disciplined, professionally and ethically bounded role. This role is defined in part by the structure and purpose of the sponsoring organization, in part by the personality and style of the worker, and in large part by the needs and developmental stage of group and members.

Many writers have attempted to list techniques. It is often useful to review these lists, both to free one's creativity and to remind oneself of the great range of possibilities open to a worker in a group. Among the useful lists of techniques are those developed by Balgopal and Vassil (1983), Garvin (1987), Northen (1988), Glassman and Kates (1990), Brown (1991), Middleman and Goldberg Wood (1991), Bertcher (1994), and Toseland and Rivas (1995). Although Ephross and Vassil's list (1988) was originally intended for use with working groups, its contents are suitable for work with many other kinds of groups as well. Shulman's book on skills of helping (1992) contains a great deal of discussion of techniques.

Brown's (1991) list of 11 specific techniques may be particularly useful to beginning workers. Clearly referring primarily to verbal group processes, his typology is organized under three major headings:

Information Sharing

1. Giving information, advice, or suggestion; directing;
2. Seeking information or reactions about (a) individual, group, or significant others, or (b) agency policies and procedures.

Support and Involvement

1. Accepting and reassuring, showing interest;
2. Encouraging the expression of ideas and feelings;
3. Involving the individuals or group in activity or discussion.

Self-Awareness and Task Accomplishment

1. Exploring with the individual or group the meaning of individual or group behavior, as well as life experiences;
2. Reflecting on individual or group behavior;
3. Reframing an issue or problem;
4. Partializing and prioritizing an issue or problem;
5. Clarifying or interpreting individual or group behavior, as well as life experiences;
6. Confronting an individual or the group. (1991, p. 113)

Each of these techniques, of course, can be further subdivided and needs to be adapted to work with particular groups at particular stages of development in particular settings.

What may be useful to add to the various lists are some techniques and principles of practice that are so basic that they are often overlooked. The first is the *ability to keep still*, sometimes referred to as the *ability not to interfere with group process and group development*. The problem here is not just that social workers in general and group workers in particular tend to be verbal people, but rather a more serious, more or less conscious misunderstanding of the purposes of helping to form a group. The issue is one of the locus of the helping dynamic. Contrary to the (more or less conscious) fantasies of beginning group workers, help in groups comes *from the group, not just from the worker*. For the group to develop and to provide members with the support, learning, growth, and healing referred to earlier in the chapter and throughout this book, the group needs "air time," room for members to talk and act, and silences that can represent reflective pauses for groups or can stimulate participation by members.

Of course, workers need to be more active at the beginning of groups, with groups whose members have limited capacities, and in particular situations. After a while, though, we offer the following rough estimate: if the social worker is occupying more than 20% of the group's talking time—and with some groups this proportion is high—the situation needs analysis and reflection. This figure, not to be taken too literally, is meant to apply over a period of time. But the technique of *not responding verbally*, which is really an expression of a participative and group nurturing skill, is an important one.

A second technique is that of *summarizing and bridging*. Often akin to the technique of *framing and reframing*, noted by other writers, summarizing consists of sharing an assessment of what the group has done and the point it has reached, while bridging consists of suggesting the work that lies ahead and assigning it a time frame. Nothing sounds simpler or demands greater concentration on the part of the social worker. Because of the possibility that one may summarize inaccurately, social workers often will "ask" a summary rather than "tell" it, inviting correction and the expression of different views. Some experienced group workers refer to the summarizing-and-bridging process as serving as a road map for the group, helping its members see where it has arrived and where it has to go.

A third important technique is *the use of limits*. In group life as for individuals, the absence of limits equals madness. Skill in the use of limits is, in part, a willingness on the part of social workers to accept and feel comfortable with the authority they often have in groups. But skill in the use of limits means much more than comfort with the realities of administrative (and sometimes legal) authority as an internal process within the worker. Its other components include an ability to form clear and easily understood contracts with groups and an ability to help groups focus on why they exist and what they are about. Effective limits are those that have been internalized by group members and those that are defined by the reality of the group's situation, rather than merely those imposed by the social worker or agency, seemingly for arbitrary or irrelevant reasons.

Skilled group workers employ a range of approaches to developing consensual limits. Some people, situations, and matches between workers and groups seem to minimize conflicts concerning limits; others seem to intensify them. Also, one needs to recognize that there may be situations—as in a group in which attendance is legally mandated, for example—in which simply stating and enforcing a rule is the path to effective limits. One principle to keep in mind is that, for most members, most groups, and most sponsoring organizations, groups are transitory realities. The goal is for members to gain from their group participation knowledge and growth that they can take with them into the other areas of their lives and into future memberships, not merely to become the "best" possible members of the groups in which they participate with professional social work leadership.

Considerations of space limit us to a brief reference to the development of practice theory linked especially to the concept of stages of group development (Garland, Jones, & Kolodny, 1965). One of the most useful developments is the connection that can be drawn between stage theory and specific worker roles and behaviors in the group. Particularly, one should note that often the worker needs to be considerably more active in the beginning stages of a group than later, when the group has developed some momentum (and some norms and structure) of its own.

Let us turn now to some specific considerations about the behavior of the worker. First, the reader should note the use of the singular. In our view, the basis for professional helping in groups is one worker, one group. This is not to imply that there is no place for coleadership. In an era of concern about resources, for one thing, and given the nature of group work, for another, there needs to be a positive reason for having more than one worker in a group. Several good reasons come quickly to mind. They include:

1. Physical safety. In a group that contains people with a tendency to act out, there may need to be two workers, one of whom can go for help, leave the group with a disruptive member, and the like.
2. Situations in which the coleader is really a trainee. It is often very helpful for a student or an inexperienced worker to colead with a senior colleague. At other times, however, students and beginning workers can do very well in a solo worker situation.
3. Groups in which it is important to model differences, whether sexual, racial, ethnic, or any other kind. A male–female team may be effective in working with a group of heterosexual couples, for example.

Other situations that justify coleadership can be described. In the absence of a positive reason, however, solo leadership is much less expensive and causes fewer logistical problems. Of equal importance is the fact that coleadership can provide a fertile ground for various interpersonal processes that can impede group progress. These can be minimized in a solo worker format.

The basic reason for doing group work is the power of the group, *not the worker*. As long as one can keep this point clearly in mind and recognize that the worker in a group is the orchestra's conductor, not its concertmaster or principal bassist, the situation of solo worker will make greater sense, in the absence of a positive reason for having more than one worker.

A variety of texts are available that supplement the brief overview given in this chapter. Many are listed in the "References" at the end of this chapter. All agree that no specific techniques equal in importance the commitment of a group worker to enabling a group to form, allowing it to operate, and joining with the members in celebrating the individual and group growth which is the raison d'être of group work.

REFERENCES

Addams, J. (1909). *The spirit of youth and the city streets.* New York: Macmillan.

Alissi, A. S. (1982). The social group work method: Towards a reaffirmation of essentials. *Social Work with Groups,* 5(3), 3–17.

Balgopal, P., & Vassil, T.V. (1983). *Groups in social work.* New York: Macmillan.

Bertcher, H. J. (1994). *Group participation: Techniques for leaders and members* (2nd ed.). Thousand Oaks, CA: Sage.

Brown, L. N. (1991). *Groups for growth and change.* New York: Longman.

Ephross, P. H., & Vassil, T.V. (1988). *Groups that work: Structure and process.* New York: Columbia University Press.

Falck, H. S. (1988). *Social work: The membership perspective.* New York: Springer.

Fatout, M., & Rose, S. R. (1995). *Task groups in the social services.* Thousand Oaks, CA: Sage.

Galinsky, M., & Schopler, J. (1989). Developmental patterns in open-ended groups. *Social Work with Groups. 12*(2), 99–104.

Garland, J., Jones, H., & Kolodny, R. L. (1965). A model of stages of group development in social work groups. In S. Bernstein (Ed.), *Explorations in group work* (pp. 21–30). Boston: Boston University School of Social Work.

Garvin, C. D. (1987). *Contemporary group work* (2nd ed.). Englewood Cliffs, NJ: Prentice-Hall.

Garvin, C. D. (1996). *Contemporary group work* (3rd ed.). Boston: Allyn & Bacon.

Garvin, C. D., & Ephross, P. H. (1991). Group theory. In R. R. Greene & P. H. Ephross (Eds.), *Human behavior theory and social work practice* (pp. 177–201). New York: Aldine de Gruyter.

Garvin, C. D., & Reed, B. G. (1994). Small group theory and social work practice: Promoting diversity and social justice or recreating inequities? In R. R. Greene (Ed.), *Human behavior theory: A diversity framework* (pp. 173–201). New York: Aldine de Gruyter.

Gitterman, A., & Shulman, L. (1994). *Mutual aid groups, vulnerable populations, and the life cycle* (2nd ed.). New York: Columbia University Press.

Glassman, U., & Kates, L. (1990). *Group work: A humanistic approach.* Newbury Park, CA: Sage.

Goroff, N. N. (1979). *Concepts for group processes.* Hebron, CT: Practitioners Press.

Henry, S. (1992). *Group skills in social work: A four-dimensional approach.* Pacific Grove, CA: Brooks/Cole.

Lewin, K. (1948). *Resolving social conflicts.* New York: Harper & Row.

Middleman, R. R. (1982). *The non-verbal method in working with groups: The use of activity in teaching, counseling, and therapy* (enlarged ed.). Hebron, CT: Practitioners Press.

Middleman, R. R., & Goldberg Wood, G. (1991). *Skills for direct practice social work.* New York: Columbia University Press.

Northen, H. (1988). *Social work with groups* (2nd ed.). New York: Columbia University Press.

Roberts, R. W., & Northen, H. (Eds.). (1976). *Theories of social work with groups.* New York: Columbia University Press.

Shulman, L. (1992). *The skills of helping individuals, families and groups* (3rd ed.). Itasca, IL: Peacock.

Toseland, R. W., & Rivas, R. F. (1995). *An introduction to group work practice* (2nd ed.). Boston: Allyn & Bacon.

Weiner, H. J. (1964). Social change and social group work practice, *Social Work, 9*(3), 106–112.

I

HEALTH ISSUES

1

Group Work with Cancer Patients

Barry M. Daste

Cancer is a disease with psychological, physiological, and social consequences for the patients, as well as for their families and friends. The disease can and does strike regardless of sex, socioeconomic background, race, age, or other demographic factors. Studies by the American Cancer Society indicate that 3 million Americans are currently living with cancer and that 30% of the population will develop cancer at some point during their lives (Harmon, 1991, p. 56).

Cancer is a pervasive illness that affects three out of four families and one out of three individuals in the United States (Taylor, Falke, Shoptaw, & Lichtman, 1986). Although the treatment of cancer has become more successful in recent years, the emotional impact on individuals and their families is great (Evans, Stevens, Cushway, & Houghton, 1992, p. 229). A cancer diagnosis is considered to be one of the most feared and serious events of an individual's life. It produces significant stress on all individuals involved (Daste, 1990).

Before diagnosis, the individual normally experiences general illness that progresses to the point where malignancy is suspected. Following this period of illness, the individual is subjected to numerous physiological tests that determine whether cancer is present. Testing leads to diagnosis. The stages that follow diagnosis include surgery and/or treatment, through such means as chemotherapy or radiotherapy, evaluation of the patient's prognosis, and medical follow-up (Gilbar, 1991, p. 293). During each of the progressive stages of cancer detection, diagnosis, and treatment, cancer patients face a number of questions about their own vulnerability to the disease.

The specific issue patients face include a sense of threat to their lives, their wholeness of body, sense of self-perception, mental balance, and social functioning (Gilbar, 1991, p. 293). Patients are often concerned about the implications of the disease for their future quality of life and for relationships with family members and friends. In addition, they normally experience a wide spectrum of emotions, including anger, fear, sadness, guilt, embarrassment, and shame.

The cancer patient often expresses anger at his or her fate. Anger is also frequently directed at the medical staff, who first inform the patient of the disease or treat the patient over the course of the illness, and at family members who may attempt to protect, coddle, or treat the patient differently than before the diagnosis.

Sadness and depression are common emotions of cancer patients and may arise from many different sources. Resignation about uncompleted tasks or goals may be a cause of sadness for the patient, as well as fear and isolation often resulting from the disease itself. Physical losses associated with specific types of cancer, such as breast, colon, or laryngeal cancer, may promote a feeling of depression. Often the cancer patient is unable to discuss fears and emotions with family members, which may serve to increase the sense of isolation. A number of studies have reported that both self-help and therapy groups designed to treat cancer patients allow them to express fears, in particular the fear of death; such expression has numerous positive effects on the patient's sense of well-being and self-esteem (Ferlic, Goldman, & Kennedy, 1978; Spiegel & Yalom, 1978).

If a patient must undergo radical surgical or treatment procedures that leave visible scars or signs of the disease, he or she may be susceptible to feelings of embarrassment or shame. The appliances such as those used with colostomy patients, for example, often have side effects such as odor, which can cause the patient great embarrassment (Gilbar & Groisman, 1992). Other results of the cancer treatment, such as mastectomy or prostate removal, can cause patients to feel less sexually attractive and desirable to their spouses or lovers (Gilbar, 1991).

The changes in bodily function resulting from such procedures also require some adjustment for the patient, as well as for family members and friends. These changes may create major inconvenience in terms of planning for simple day-to-day activities, as well as limiting access to activities in which the person previously participated.

In dealing with the issues and emotions inherent in the diagnosis of cancer, family members and friends of the patient can serve as important sources of support. Studies have documented the need for social support both as a means of preventing disease and as a factor in recovery from illness (Taylor et al., 1986).

In some cases, however, family members or friends often become overwhelmed with the patient's crisis and withdraw to protect themselves and deal with their own emotional issues (Daste, 1989). In cases where the supporter and the patient may have had previous relationship difficulties, the supporter may make attempts to rectify the situation for his or her own benefit without considering the needs or wishes of the patient. For example, a spouse who may have been ready to leave a failed marriage may decide to remain in it ostensibly to protect the patient, but in reality to avoid the prospect of facing immense personal guilt. In other situations, family members may attempt to support the patient but may actually contribute to the patient's emotional distress (Daste, 1990). This occurs, for example, when supporters of the patient attempt to treat the patient in the ways they themselves would want to be treated in similar circumstances while ignoring the requests or desires of the patient to be treated as he or she wishes.

There are many issues involving family relationships when cancer develops. Both juvenile and adult cancer patients often do not express fear and sadness with family members because of their desire to protect the family system (Daste, 1990; Price, 1992). Siblings of juvenile cancer patients often experience negative emotions and are not likely to express these emotions to family members (Evans et al., 1992). Kaufman and his colleagues (1992) report that cancer diagnoses in children may exacerbate existing problems in dysfunctional families, and the resulting stress can increase the child's illness.

Support or self-help groups designed to address the specific needs of cancer patients and/or their families allow the patient to receive support and express emotions in a nonjudgmental and safe environment. These groups can provide education about the disease and about methods or techniques the patient can employ to alleviate anxiety, stress, and depression (Forester, Kornfeld, Fleiss, & Thompson, 1993; Vugia, 1991). Techniques such as visual imagery, self hypnotic therapy, deep muscle relaxation, and systematic desensitization can also help to counteract the side effects of treatment methods like chemotherapy (Forester et al., 1993; Harmon, 1991).

Researchers have concluded that groups that provide intensive group coping skills, such as those discussed above, are far more effective than traditional supportive group therapy (Telch & Telch, 1986). Liebermann (1988) has reported that although client-led self-help groups have not been proved to be an effective means of treatment because research concerning them has not been available, they do appear to have "meaningful roles in helping individuals with psychosocial problems" (p. 168).

While much information is available about different types of cancer-focused treatment groups, widespread data are not available to substantiate the effectiveness of one group treatment method over another. Telch and Telch (1986) report that supportive group therapy is the most widely used and most intensively studied form of treatment. Other researchers indicate that while a group may be designed primarily to provide education, psychological intervention is typically needed by group members.

PRACTICE PRINCIPLES

The practice principles that apply to group work with cancer patients are similar to those that apply to group work in general. The variety of issues cancer patients typically face, however, may be quite different from those of other populations and should be kept in mind when composing and facilitating groups. One issue that could have an impact on a treatment group is the treatment status of each group member. Patients who are receiving chemotherapy or radiation therapy are likely to experience such side effects as nausea, pain, or extreme fatigue. These patients may not be able to attend the group regularly during this phase of their treatment or may be disoriented and distracted if they do attend. Contracting with members of these groups requires a lot of flexibility, and contracts should always be tailored to each member. Due to the nature of cancer and the effects it can have on attendance and participation, social workers must be understanding and accepting when members cannot attend or participate. It is also important, however, for the social worker to continually encourage members to attend and participate when they are able to do so. Termination of these groups is often a flexible issue. Again, due to the nature of cancer, people cannot often predict with accuracy when they can continue to attend. Some groups formed specifically for terminally ill cancer patients are open groups and continue to function after the deaths of individual members.

Other factors that are important to group work with cancer patients include stage of the disease, type of cancer, amount of physical distress, age, level and quality of support from family and friends, religious affiliation, probability of psychiatric problems related to cancer, terminal versus non-terminal status, size of the group, and training of the leaders (Daste, 1990).

STAGE OF THE DISEASE

The stage of a patient's disease is important for a number of reasons. First, the issues faced by patients whose cancer is in remission are dramatically different from those of patients who are terminally ill. Patients whose cancer is in remission may be primarily concerned with recurrence of the disease, while patients who are terminally ill are often more concerned about their death, the process of dying, and the implications these events have for their family and friends. Understandably, patients who are dying may feel envious or may even resent those whose prognosis is more hopeful.

DIFFERENCES AMONG AFFECTED GROUPS

Cancer, while having similar implications for all patients, strikes a very heterogenous group of individuals. Particular types of cancer, such as breast or colon cancer, often have specific implications for group composition. Breast or colon cancer patients often have similar issues and can relate readily to other patients with the same concerns. Breast cancer patients may have issues relating to their sexuality and their perceived loss of femininity that they feel more comfortable discussing with other breast cancer patients. Persons who have had sarcoma of a limb may have lost an arm or a leg due to amputation or may have experienced more limited use of the limb. Issues such as limited mobility will often arise among these individuals.

Issues such as these and many other related concerns need to be kept in mind by the social worker. All such issues are often discussed with patients before they enter a group in order to offset possible problems at a later date.

DEMOGRAPHIC ISSUES

Issues such as age and religious affiliation may have significance for a treatment group. Clearly, pediatric cancer patients require a group setting that is age appropriate and allows them to discuss their own unique concerns. Also, adult patients who are at different stages in life may feel more accepted by those in a similar stage. They may be better able to deal with issues that suit their particular needs. Similarly, religious affiliation can significantly affect the cancer patient's sense of purpose and hope. The religious or spiritual orientation of the patient may influence his or her acceptance of various aspects of the disease. In addition, religion or spirituality of significant others can significantly affect how cancer patients relate to them.

LEVELS OF SUPPORT

Support from family and friends affects the cancer patient's overall sense of support and can be significant in a group setting. Some patients have far more support than others, and this can make those who have less support feel even more depressed and alone in the group. This is often the case in groups where family members and friends are allowed to attend. The social worker should be aware of situations where some patients may not have any supportive family members or friends and other patients seem to have an abundance. One way of warding off this problem is to have separate groups for patients and family members. In fact, some patients may feel more comfortable discussing sexual and other issues among fellow patients without family and friends being in attendance. Well meaning as family and friends may be, there are issues in which their attendance will inhibit discussion.

PSYCHIATRIC COMPLICATIONS

Often as a result of the disease itself, patients develop psychiatric problems. In some cases, psychiatric problems may be present before the diagnosis. These factors should be considered by the social worker who composes and facilitates the group. While there may be psychological issues that will need to be addressed, the appropriateness of including patients with significant psychiatric difficulties should be considered in terms of their ability to interact with other group members and to engage in the group process.

SIZE OF THE GROUP

Group size can have an impact on the effectiveness and level of intimacy within a group. Spiegel and Yalom (1978), in reporting on their group of patients with metastatic carcinoma, noted that the maximum effective size was seven. When the size of the group reached more than eight, the group was divided into two smaller groups (Spiegel and Yalom, 1978). Similarly, in a program designed by Cunningham and his colleagues (1991), educational groups ranged in size from 12 to 15 members, but these groups were later divided into two or more subgroups to facilitate discussion (p. 44). Smaller groups are usually more cohesive and develop closer bonds than larger groups (Daste, 1990). The concept of group size is often related to other issues, such as the presence of supportive family members and friends. As previously mentioned, the appropriateness of having family members present during discussions of subjects that the patients may want to discuss privately should also be considered.

WORKER SELF-AWARENESS

Among the most important issues in group practice with cancer patients is the social worker's own orientation to the disease. Often one of the cancer patient's most pervasive fears is of death and dying. Because of the importance of this issue, it is often necessary for the social worker to address this issue within the group setting. Consequently, the social worker may need to face his or her own feelings regarding death. This is an easy issue to trivialize, and often its full impact does not come until one is faced with it personally. This can be a very lonely time, and the issue becomes an existential one as opposed to an interpersonal one. Even in a group setting, members can feel alone and will require a lot of empathic understanding.

The social worker's interaction with the group should be clearly conceptualized and described in the planning phase of the group. In some groups, the social worker may provide education and/or psychological intervention. The literature is widely divided on what the group facilitator's role should be. In a number of groups studied, the social worker's or facilitator's role is to educate the group members. In other groups, researchers contend that the facilitator should assist the members in expressing their emotions about their disease. Cunningham et al. (1991) note that psychological interventions in cancer groups are becoming increasingly common. However, Vugia (1991) sees the role of leaders in self-help support groups as aiding members while allowing the members to maintain some authority themselves (p. 94).

OPEN VERSUS CLOSED GROUPS

Should groups be open or closed? Opinions vary among professionals in the field. The literature indicates that cancer groups frequently are open, allowing new members to enter at any time (Daste, 1989). Other research concludes that groups should be closed to new members after the first few sessions to enhance cohesion of the group and to "allow progressive work and promote good attendance" (Cunningham et al., 1991, p. 44).

In light of the information presented thus far, the social worker should keep in mind that cancer patients constitute a very heterogeneous group whose needs are vastly different and challenging. It is important to point out that work with cancer patients can be very trying (Daste, 1990). Davidson (1985) notes that the concept of *burnout* is especially applicable to those working in the field of oncology because death and the threat of death create a large emotional burden on these persons.

Persons who work with cancer patients in the group setting should be prepared to discuss such topics as death, dying, disfigurement, pain, and loss of function. Harmon (1991) discusses the experience of one group in which a member died and the leaders of the group consequently attempted to prevent the group from acknowledging or discussing it. Yalom and Greaves (1977) found that in their group, the therapists contributed to superficial group interaction because they felt that such topics might be too threatening for patients when, in reality, they were protecting themselves.

COMMON THEMES

Some of the themes that social workers should keep in mind when working with cancer patients are the following:

1. Fear of death.
2. Fear of disease recurrence.
3. Unique problems related to the long- and short-term effects of treatment.
4. Changes in personal relationships.
5. Economic issues.

There are many other common themes in conducting groups with cancer patients. These include unique problems such as changes in sexual function during treatment, partners' reactions to loss of breasts or scarring, and loss of fertility due to some types of chemotherapy. All of these present some unique difficulties, each of which has interpersonal manifestations that become significant in a group setting.

Fear of Death

The patient's fear of death is considered reasonable given the cancer mortality rates. Although cancer is a more treatable and survivable illness today than in the past, a diagnosis of cancer frequently implies the possibility of death. As noted above, often the patient's family or friends are frightened by the diagnosis and may prevent the patient from discussing the possibility of death. Some authors have reported that patients' anxiety about death was often lessened when they were able to connect on a transcendent or spiritual level (Cunningham et al., 1991, p. 52). Similarly, Spiegel (1992) found that allowing patients to discuss the possibility of death and its attendant anxieties lessened their fear of death and dying (p. 115).

Fear of Disease Recurrence

Most cancer patients experience fear of recurrence. This is especially manifested for varying periods of time following initial diagnosis and treatment. Whenever a new pain occurs, an unexplained lump appears, a cough begins, or one of many other conditions arises, the cancer patient will typically fear the worst. This is perhaps the single most difficult part of coping for those who have had one experience with cancer. It is as if a sword hangs over one's head from the time of first diagnosis until the day one dies, even though the disease may never reappear. The fear of recurrence becomes a focal point, particularly for cancer patients who have survived the initial cancer and are in remission. The fear of recurrence will continue for years.

Long- and Short-Term Effects

Other common themes with cancer patients are the effects of chemotherapy and radiation therapy, both short and long term. Various types of chemotherapy cause hair loss, as does radiation to specific body areas. Nausea and vomiting and the inability to maintain earlier eating patterns become recurrent themes. Many financial issues typically arise as well. In addition to possible loss of income during treatment, the cost of care frequently exceeds insurance benefits. Added to this is the future burden on survivors, who often have extreme difficulty obtaining or transferring insurance plans due to preexisting condition limitations. Cancer patients and survivors also report job discrimination both in hiring and in promotion. Any person who has undergone treatment for cancer is considered legally handicapped and thus has dome protection from job discrimination. This does not necessarily prevent it from occurring, however.

Interpersonal Relationships

Cancer patients often find that their interpersonal relationships alter as a result of the disease. Some become distanced from friends and family members. Some face constant questioning from others about the cancer, even when they would rather not talk about it. Some patients find that their choice of partners may become limited, frequently due to fears about the future of the patient. This problem may continue long after the person has survived cancer. Some experience either overprotectiveness or distancing from spouses or lovers. Interpersonal manifestations are multiple and often provide surprises for group members.

Economic Issues

Economic issues become a major concern with many cancer patients. Insurance may become difficult or impossible to obtain following a cancer diagnosis. Job discrimination is commonly reported in hiring, as well as in promotions and job assignments. The cost of treatment may create severe hardships. Lost wages often create further difficulty. These are some of the more common themes among group members. Each of them provides bases for discussion in the group.

RECOMMENDED WAYS OF WORKING

As there are so many variables in working with cancer patients, the social worker must be very flexible. This flexibility extends from the initial conceptualization of the group all the way to termination. Perhaps the most important thing to keep in mind is that social workers will be more effective if they structure their groups to best meet the needs of the particular cancer patients and/or cancer survivors they wish to serve. As previously mentioned, people with cancer are very heterogeneous, yet they usually have specific pressing concerns. Rather than lumping everyone with a cancer diagnosis into a large group, it seems far more beneficial to tailor each group to the specific needs of the prospective members. For example, a group for 8- to 12-year-old children who have all had chemotherapy or radiation therapy have very different concerns than a group of women dying of breast cancer. By the same token, a group of people who have been cancer free for 5 years would have a whole different set of concerns.

The agency setting and the population being served will, of course, dictate to a large extent who will be in the group. A large hospital in a major metropolitan area, for example, has far more latitude in terms of numbers and types of groups than a small rural clinic. The agency context may also define other parameters of the group, including size, space considerations, availability of coleaders, advocacy of services, and the availability of ancillary services such as meals on wheels or hospices.

The issue of open versus closed groups again depends on the population being served. Both have advantages and disadvantages. Open groups, for example, allow more utilization, while closed groups provide a more intimate atmosphere and allow for more discussion of sensitive topics.

Length of the group is also population dependent. Many social workers experienced difficulty when they specified a certain number of sessions initially, only to discover later that the members, due to treatment difficulties or other problems, found it difficult to use the preimposed format. Group length often has to be experimented with and tailored to each agency and its population. Many agencies simply offer one large long-term group for all patients and significant others. This approach avoids many selection, time, and member availability issues since the group meets on a regular basis for all who care to attend. However, it also limits the potential that smaller, more carefully planned groups may offer.

A case illustrating one of the problems of a large group open to all is as follows:

> During the weekly meeting of a large support group offered for cancer patients, friends, and families by a metropolitan radiation treatment center, several newly diagnosed persons attended for the first time. It so happened that "John," a regular member, was suffering from a brain tumor and tended to dominate conversations without allowing others to speak. For this reason, the new members, who were uncomfortable about being there and very much in need of support, were denied an opportunity to participate. Situations such as this are far easier for the social worker to control in a smaller, more carefully selected group.

A coworker pattern is usually considered to be easier on social workers and other professionals, and it has many advantages over an individual worker format, assuming that the coworkers work well together. It allows more individual attention to be given to distraught members, for example, since one worker can attend to the individual while the other attends to the group process. It also doubles the probability that the group can meet if one worker is absent. Coworkers potentially can help each other in providing both technical expertise and emotional support.

A case illustrating how a coworker format might be beneficial is as follows:

> During one of the sessions of a support group for women survivors of breast cancer, "Jackie," who had been doing fine following breast cancer 2 years previously, had just learned that her cancer had recurred. She bravely waited her turn to talk, but finally felt overwhelmed by her fear, jumped up, and ran from the room. One of the coworkers took off after her and spent a lot of time calming her down, as she felt unable to return to the group. The other coworker was able to continue without her.

One key advantage of a coworker pattern with these groups is that it allows the workers to deal with personal crises, which are often severe and require additional attention. If only one worker is present, the group as a whole must wait or must deal with the crises as a whole. In another type of therapy group this might be appropriate, but due to the nature of cancer and the potential for sudden life-or-death issues arising, the fear and panic may be so great that individual intervention is warranted.

EVALUATION MEASURES

Researchers have used many different methods to measure the effectiveness of groups in producing tangible benefits to patients. Scales that measure quality of adjustment, stress levels, affect, optimism with regard to disease treatment, and overall sensations of pain, discomfort, and anxiety, as well as other such scales would all be useful in determining the effectiveness of a cancer group intervention.

In a group organized by Speigel, Bloom, and Yalom (1981), women with metastatic breast cancer were found to have less tension, depression, fatigue, confusion, maladjusted responses, and fewer phobias than their control group counterparts.

In their study of self-perception after surgery with women who had had mastectomy, Clarke, Kramer, Lipiec, and Klein (1982) divided 40 patients into treatment and control groups. Ten weekly group psychotherapy sessions were offered. The authors used Q-sort tests and the Structured and Scaled Interview to Assess Maladjustment. While both groups showed positive change, the treatment group showed significantly greater improvement.

Other studies, such as the one conducted by Kriss and Kraemer (1986), have examined patients periodically over several time periods—for example, three times over 12 months—to determine possible changes following group treatment. Longitudinal studies covering longer time periods are also appropriate in determining changes following group treatment.

One of the difficulties in assessing evaluative research in this area is the great variety of methodology. There are many ways to conduct research in this area, and it should be noted that assessing the outcome accurately is difficult due to the number of variables involved. A lot depends on what the social worker wants to know about the group members. Both quantitative and qualitative measures may be important in assessing changes. Questionnaires and scales measuring such factors as depression, fear, and coping can be administered on a pre- and posttreatment basis. Recording group attendance, degree of participation, and demographic representation by various ethnic, racial, and socioeconomic groups will yield data that may prove useful to the social worker. Research questions should be addressed as early as possible to allow for more potential data.

CLOSING STATEMENT

Even though we are making progress in the diagnosis and treatment of cancer, this diagnosis places a great deal of emotional and physical stress on patients, as well as on their families and friends. This further mandates the need for groups designed to meet the specific needs of this population.

NATIONAL RESOURCES

American Cancer Society
1599 Clifton Road NE
Atlanta, GA 30329
(404) 320-3333 or the Cancer
   Answer Line at (800) ACS-2345
   or Cancer Information Service at
   (800) 4-CANCER

Association for Brain Tumor
   Research
3725 N. Talman Ave.
Chicago, IL 60618
(312) 286-5571

Children's Leukemia Foundation
   of Michigan
19022 W. Ten Mile Road
Southfield, MI 48075-2498
(313) 353-8222 or (800) 825-2536

Federation for Children with
   Special Needs
95 Berkeley St., Suite 104
Boston, MA 02116
(617) 482-2915

National Information Center for
   Handicapped Children and Youth
Box 1492
Washington, DC 20013
(703) 893-6061

REFERENCES

Clarke, D. L., Kramer, E., Lipiec, K., & Klein, S. (1982). Group psychotherapy with mastectomy patients. *Psychotherapy: Theory, Research, and Practice, 19*(3), 331–334.

Cunningham, A. J., Edmonds, C., Hampson, A., Hanson, H., Hovanec, M., Jenkins, G., & Tocco, E. (1991). A group psychoeducational program to help cancer patients cope with and combat their disease. *Journal of Mind-Body Health, 7*(3), 41–56.

Daste, B. (1989). Designing cancer groups for maximum effectiveness. *Groupwork, 2*(1), 58–69.

Daste, B. (1990). Important considerations in groupwork with cancer patients. *Social Work with Groups, 13*(2), 69–81.

Davidson, K. W. (1985). Social work with cancer patients: Stresses and coping patterns. *Social Work in Health Care, 10*(4), 73–82.

Evans, C. A., Stevens, M., Cushway, D., & Houghton, J. (1992). Sibling response to childhood cancer: A new approach. *Child Care, Health and Development, 18*, 229–244.

Ferlic, M., Goldman, A., & Kennedy, B. (1979). Group counseling with adult patients with advanced cancer. *Cancer, 43*, 760–766.

Forester, B. (1993). Group psychotherapy during radiotherapy: Effects on emotional and physical distress. *American Journal of Psychiatry, 150*(1), 1700–1706.

Gilbar, O. (1991). Model for crisis intervention through group therapy for women with breast cancer. *Clinical Social Work Journal, 19*(3), 293–304.

Gilbar, O., & Groisman, L. (1991). A training model of self-help group for patients with cancer of the colon. *Journal of Oncology, 9*(4), 57–69.

Harmon, M. (1991). The use of group psychotherapy with cancer patients: A review of recent literature. *Journal for Specialists in Group Work, 16*(1), 56–61.

Kaufman, K. L., Harbeck, C., Olson, R., & Nitschke, R. (1992). The availability of psychosocial interventions to children with cancer and their families. *Children's Health Care, 21*(1), 21–25.

Kriss, R. T., & Kraemer, H. C. (1986). Efficacy of group therapy for problems with postmastectomy self-perception, body image, and sexuality. *Journal of Sex Research, 22*(4), 438–451.

Liebermann, M. A. (1988). The role of self-help groups in helping patients and families cope with cancer. *Ca—A Cancer Journal for Clinicians, 38*(3), 162–168.

Price, K. (1992). Quality of life for terminally ill children. *Social Work, 34*(1), 53–54.

Smith, K., & Lesko, L. M. (1988). Psychosocial problems in cancer survivors. *Oncology, 2*(1), 33–44.

Spiegel, D. (1992). Effects of psychosocial support on patients with metastatic breast cancer. *Journal of Psychosocial Oncology, 10*(2), 113–120.

Spiegel, D., Bloom, J. R., & Yalom, I. D. (1981). Group support for patients with metastatic cancer: A randomized outcome study. *Archives of General Psychiatry, 38*(5), 527–533.

Spiegel, D., & Yalom, I. D. (1978). A support group for dying patients. *International Journal of Group Psychotherapy, 28*(2).

Taylor, S., Falke, R., Shoptaw, S., & Lichtman, R. (1986). Social support, support groups, and the cancer patient. *Journal of Consulting and Clinical Psychology, 54*(5).

Telch, E. G., & Telch, M. J. (1986). Group coping skills instruction and supportive group therapy for cancer patients: A comparison of strategies. *Journal of Consulting and Clinical Psychology, 54*(6), 802–808.

Vugia, H. D. (1991). Support groups in oncology: Building hope through the human bond. *Journal of Psychosocial Oncology, 9*(3), 89–107.

Yalom, I. D., & Greaves, C. (1977). Group therapy with the terminally ill. *American Journal of Psychiatry, 28*(2).

2

Group Work with Seriously Mentally Ill People

Charles Garvin

This chapter describes ways of providing group services to people who suffer from severe mental illness. The term sometimes used is *chronic mental illness*, although many practitioners do not use the word *chronic* because of the negative picture about recovery that it conveys. The definition of a person with this disability is "an individual who suffers from a major psychiatric disorder such as psychosis, who is so disabled as to have partial or total impairment of social functioning (such as vocational and homemaking activities), and who has had a long or a number of short stays in a mental hospital" (Garvin & Tropman, 1992, p. 284). The psychiatric diagnoses usually assigned to people who are classified as seriously mentally ill are schizophrenia, schizoaffective disorder, bipolar disorder, major depression, severe borderline personality disorder, and severe organic disorder. There are, however, many controversies regarding how to define this population related to the length of time the person is disabled and the degree of disability (Rubin, 1986, p. 10).

Many Americans suffer from severe mental illness; a recent estimate is 1.7 to 2.4 million (Garvin & Tropman, 1992, p. 284). Until the mid-1950s, many people with these diagnoses were confined in mental hospitals. At that time, however, a movement referred to as *deinstitutionalization* became a major determinant of mental health policy. This movement was propelled by the discovery of psychotropic drugs allowing for control of many of the behaviors of mentally ill people that led to their confinement. These include such manifestations of psychoses as hallucinations, delusions, and bizarre behaviors, as well as the mood swings or severe depression found in other types of clients.

Other forces that promoted the declining use of institutional care were humane concerns for the civil liberties of patients and fiscal crises related to the greater costs of institutional compared to community care. Deinstitutionalization was facilitated by the increasing number of community mental health centers designated to care for mentally disabled individuals in the community.

Recent statistics indicate that about 150,000 of the seriously mentally ill are in institutions, about 750,000 are in nursing homes (including about 400,000 who suffer from forms of senility), and between 800,000 and 1.5 million reside in the community and are likely to receive some form of care from community mental health centers (Garvin & Tropman, 1992, p. 285). Hospital stays are likely to be short, due not only to the use of medications and the provision of community-based services but also to the action of insurance providers who limit the amount of hospital care for which they will pay. Social workers are very likely to be the providers of service, and this service is often in the form of groups. Increased resources have been allocated for research and program development in this field, but much more support is required to realize the aims of the deinstitutionalization movement.

The seriously mentally ill have several common characteristics (Gerhart, 1990). These include the following:

- Many suffer from multiple problems. One study estimated that 26% of mental health clients were substance abusers (Hazel, Herman, & Mowbray, 1991); another major epidemiological study estimated that 52% of persons with alcohol abuse/dependence had had at least one other psychiatric diagnosis (Robins, Locke, & Regier, 1991).
- A severe mental illness limits the ability to cope with stress, and such persons are likely to function poorly under stressful circumstances.
- Many may have deficits in skills needed in daily living, such as preparing food, making purchases, and engaging in social activities.
- Many have difficulty keeping a job and are supported by governmental income maintenance programs.
- Many are a burden on their families because of their unpredictable ways of scheduling their lives, their emotional demands, and the problems they cause when engaging in annoying or inappropriate behavior.
- Many become homeless and live either on the street, in temporary shelters, or in facilities such as foster homes, group homes, or other supervised dwellings. It is estimated that almost 50% of the adult homeless have a chronic mental illness and/or a mood disorder (Bachrach, 1984; Kiesler & Sibulkin, 1987).
- A growing number are young adults who did not grow up in mental hospitals, as did earlier generations of mentally ill people, and are

hospitalized only when they exhibit severe symptoms. *Ma*
their families, have never been married, and have at *le*
school education. Like other members of their generation,
been exposed to street drugs and easy access to alcohol. *T*
engage in aggressive and rebellious behavior that is especial
lenging to social workers and other professionals.

Recent studies have sought to identify differences among *mer*
women and among people of different ethnic backgrounds with *res*
to serious mental illness. According to Gerhart:

> It has been suggested that men tend to develop classic schizophrenic
> conditions at a slightly higher rate than women, while the latter are
> more prone to develop schizophreniform conditions. Stressors that
> cause males to relapse seem to have some connection with their role
> performance as men, such as criticism of their physical strength or lack
> of a job, being turned down for a date, and the like. On the other hand,
> women seem more sensitive to events in their interpersonal relation-
> ships. . . . There is evidence that women are significantly more prone to
> depressive disorders than men. . . . Subsequent investigations concluded
> that it was not women's roles that caused their depression, but rather
> the uneven distribution of power between husbands and wives. (1990,
> p. 30–31)

There is no indication that the rates of severe mental illness differ
among African-Americans, Latinos/Latinas, and whites (Gerhart, 1990).
People from different cultures, however, may act differently when they
suffer from a mental illness. According to Gerhart (1990), for example,
"Blacks and Hispanics who suffer from major mood disorders tend to
exhibit more hallucinations, delusions or hostility than Whites, whereas
the latter show a higher degree of mania, depression, or guilt" (p. 32).
She concludes:

> all the research dealing with ethnic and racial differences in the appear-
> ance and treatment of mental illness is still in its infancy. Although there
> is much that we still don't know about this area, the ongoing research
> reminds us once again of the importance of being sensitive to and
> knowledgeable about our clients' racial, ethnic and cultural back-
> grounds. (p. 32)

Much is unknown about the causes of serious mental illness. Nevertheless, the current consensus is that it is a condition produced by the
interaction of biological and social circumstances with the evolving personality of the individual. Thus, it is often referred to as a *biopsychosocial*
phenomenon. The basis of the biological input is concluded from the
genetic, biochemical changes in the brain, as well as from heredity and
twin studies. The social basis is determined from studies of the family, peer
group, and other socialization circumstances of the individual. The developmental circumstances are elucidated by examining the life history of the
individual in relation to coping patterns (Gerhart, 1990, pp. 17–20).

PRACTICE PRINCIPLES

A number of practice principles are typically applied when working with the severely mentally ill in light of the characteristics of this client group. While individual (Dincin, 1985), family (Anderson, Reiss, & Hogarty, 1986), and group approaches are all utilized, the last are especially prominent. One reason is the deficits in social skills found among these clients; groups provide an excellent way to learn to relate to others by observing and practicing social behaviors. Groups can also be used to simulate a variety of social circumstances such as those found in job, recreational, and family settings. Groups also offer the client an opportunity to learn how others in similar circumstances have coped with a wide range of real-life situations. In addition, groups allow clients to participate at their current level of readiness: some may be highly active socially, while others are passive participants. This makes a group less stressful for some clients than one-on-one encounters in which they feel a strong expectation to participate actively. On the other hand, some clients may be so inappropriate in their behavior, so delusional, or so stressed by the presence of others that they would be highly disruptive if invited to a group session.

A major practice principle for group work with seriously mentally ill clients is to have a good deal of program structure, as an unstructured group may be experienced at best as a waste of time and at worst as highly stressful. Despite this, we have observed many groups led by social workers for these clients in which the only structure is the opening query "What would you like to talk about today?" Some members may prefer this experience to the loneliness and boredom of having no social interaction at all, but this unstructured approach is an invitation to not participate at all, to engage in fruitless complaints about the "system," or to talk in an unfocused manner. A more structured approach involves such things as presenting information, introducing structured exercises, identifying problems to be solved, and posing useful questions.

Another practice principle is to utilize a psychosocial rehabilitation approach more than a psychotherapeutic one. According to Sands (1991), "Programs of psychosocial rehabilitation promote effectiveness in performing activities of daily living, problem solving, interpersonal skills, employability, and employment." She goes on to state that in this approach "clients are encouraged to develop, practice, and perform psychosocial skills at the highest level possible in keeping with their individualized goals and ability to tolerate stress" (p. 242).

A traditional psychotherapeutic approach, defined as utilizing psychological interpretations and "depth"-oriented questions to enable the client to examine unconscious mechanisms, is not recommended for use with most seriously mentally ill people, either individually or in groups. As Rapp (1985) states: "Psychotherapy and psychosocial services without drugs may be harmful to the chronically mentally ill, not benign. The most prevalent hypothesis is that they overstimulate the client and lead to tension, anxiety, and exacerbation of symptoms" (p. 36). It is possible that some of these clients might benefit from this type of therapy, individually or in groups, after they have recovered sufficiently from their illness and have developed stronger coping abilities, but these will not be the majority. Some clients, however, who are defined as having borderline personality disorder might benefit from psychotherapy because of their greater ability to reflect on their circumstances.

Earlier social workers who thought of severe mental illness as a psychological manifestation produced by traumatic childhood experiences may have favored forms of psychotherapy for these clients. This, however, is not the view of most social workers today who understand the biological factors in severe mental illness. A significant consequence of this increased biological understanding is a movement away from earlier approaches that blamed mothers for acting in ways that promoted such illness or that blamed the family for engaging in communication patterns that "drove some family members crazy."

Another practice principle is to find ways to make each group session a rewarding one. This is because these clients are likely to find sessions anxiety provoking; they also have to make a considerable effort to attend, given the lethargy produced by their illness. They have to look forward with pleasure to attending, especially when they are living in the community. Even hospitalized clients may resist attending group sessions and, when pressured to do so by hospital personnel, may enter meetings with a feeling of anger.

A major way of rewarding members for attending sessions is to use program activities during at least part of each session. Such activities might include the following:

- A game, especially one designed to teach a useful skill. Some workers have invented board games, for example, that help members to formulate individual goals or identify obstacles to obtaining goals.
- A dramatic activity, such as a role play, in which members practice a social skill.
- A musical or craft activity that helps members work together, experience a sense of accomplishment, or express themselves creatively.

Another way of rewarding members for coming to meetings is to make sure that they gain a sense of having accomplished something useful at each meeting. This requires the social workers to think in terms of concrete, short-term goals for each session. Examples of such goals are learning a specific social skill, solving an immediate problem, or creating a tangible product such as through a craft activity.

Another type of practice principle is to respond to a psychotic symptom in ways that help the member to cope with it while protecting other members from some of the anxiety produced by the symptom. One way to help individuals cope with psychotic symptoms is by educating them about such symptoms and labeling symptoms as such. Thus, seriously

mentally ill members can be taught that hallucinations, for example, can be produced by their illness, and that they can use this understanding when experiencing such hallucinations to tell themselves that they are experiencing something unreal. They also can be taught that some people can be told about symptoms (e.g., the social worker), while other people should not be told because they may be upset. The worker can also empathize with the fact that hearing voices or seeing strange images can be frightening. At the same time, the worker can reassure other members that he or she understands and is able to deal with psychotic symptoms, and will help them to understand and respond helpfully when a member is experiencing such symptoms.

Groups for the seriously mentally ill are often time limited and have specific purposes and goals. The length of time varies from one or two sessions while a client is in the hospital to several months for those in the community. However, because recovery from mental illness may be slow and because there may be periods of illness for many years, some groups are self-help and support groups in which membership may continue indefinitely, such as Schizophrenics Anonymous and some Alcoholics Anonymous groups attuned to the needs of mentally ill people. Club-house-type programs for mentally ill people may sponsor ongoing social activity groups, lunch clubs, and special interest groups.

COMMON THEMES

The above discussion of services to people with serious mental illnesses should suggest to social workers that a number of themes frequently arise in such groups. The following are those that we have encountered.

Stigma

These clients are often avoided, persecuted, and denied their rights by others who become aware of their illness. Actions include being fired from jobs, denied housing, refused entry to educational programs, and other serious consequences of having the label "mentally ill." Members of groups will look for help in deciding how and when to explain their illness, how to pursue their rights in an appropriately assertive manner, and how to find advocates to help them obtain things to which they are entitled.

Coping with Symptoms

The terms *positive symptoms* and *negative symptoms* are often used. Positive symptoms are direct consequences of the illness, such as hallucinations, mania, depression, and confused thought processes. Negative symptoms are behavior deficits due to lack of adequate socialization experiences, such as lack of skill in handling social interactions. Group members will ask for help in coping with positive symptoms and in acquiring the skills to eliminate negative ones.

Housing

As indicated earlier, a lack of adequate low-cost housing severely affects this population. Housing is especially a problem to these clients because they may need support to maintain it once they find it, such as learning to care for an apartment, get along with a landlord, or locate roommates.

Employment

Many of these clients lack employment or employment for which they are adequately compensated. This may be because they have educational deficits, because they cannot tolerate the stresses of jobs for which they were trained, or because of the stigma factor. They may not be aware of vocational rehabilitation services or these may be lacking. They may also require employment in a setting that offers them some form of support or even a so-called sheltered workshop program. Thus, members may ask help from each other in identifying and utilizing employment resources.

Education

Many of these clients have had their education interrupted by episodes of illness. Despite this, they are as likely to be as capable intellectually of acquiring an education as anyone else. The group is a medium in which they can explore educational opportunities, discover how to cope with school, and learn how to utilize resources to maintain themselves in an educational program.

Medication Effects

Clients are likely to bring up issues related to the medications they are taking to control their illness. They may not be compliant with their regimen because of a fear of dependence on medication. They may also experience unpleasant side effects of the medication. The medication itself may not be helpful, and the client may be unsure of how to assess this situation and what to do about it. At times, the social workers and other group members may provide useful information. At other times, the social worker will invite medical experts to attend one or more group sessions.

Family Relations

Two family issues are often brought up in these groups. One has to do with parents and siblings with whom the members have conflicts. Some of these conflicts occur because these family members are severely stressed by the client's symptoms. The other issue has to do with the nuclear families that these clients have created and seek to create. They may, for example, have difficulty acting as a spouse and parent. For these reasons, many programs form groups for family members of persons with mental

illness and/or refer them to a major self-help organization such as the Alliance for the Mentally Ill (AMI).*

Leisure Time

Many of these clients are unemployed and are not attending an educational program; therefore, time hangs heavily on them. Their solution is often to spend a lot of time watching television or "hanging out" in a public place such as the library or park. A major service that can be provided by the group is to help such clients identify interests that can be satisfied, such as engaging in musical activities, attending sports events, or taking courses that further such interests at places such as the local "Y" or adult education programs. The group can also provide a context for engaging in recreational activities that can then be extended outside of the group.

Problems with the Treatment System

These clients are likely to complain about the way the system reacts to them. Sometimes this is because of the real inadequacies in the system and sometimes it is because of the challenges these clients provide. An additional factor is that these clients may lack the skill to make their needs known. These complaints may concern difficulty in arranging for appointments with professionals, denial of services, frequent changes in professionals, and various forms of prejudice against them. These issues contribute to low self-confidence and self-esteem. The group can help the members come to terms with situations that cannot be changed while seeking changes that are appropriate and possible. On some occasions, group members can join together to engage in social action to change the system.

RECOMMENDED WAYS OF WORKING

Several different approaches to group work with these clients have emerged in response to the needs of different agency contexts and client themes. We will briefly discuss each of these approaches in terms of these conditions.

Group Work: Mutual Aid

Social workers have utilized traditional group work methods with the seriously mentally ill and have reported successful outcomes. Poynter-Berg (1986) reports one such group whose members lived in an institution and were identified as schizophrenic. A major theme of this group

---

*We provide the address of AMI at the end of this chapter.

was coping with issues of intimacy and loss. The members approached the first session hostile to or suspicious of the group experience. The social worker was not as direct as she thought she should have been in establishing a contract with the members in which the purposes of the group and the anticipated activities were clearly enunciated. Nevertheless, the social worker sought to relate to members' feelings as they acted in hostile or disruptive ways. She also sought to introduce activities that were familiar to the women in the group, particularly craft projects. This led to a greater degree of security based on trust of the social worker and each other. A consequence of this was that as a holiday approached, the members talked with each other about painful feelings the holiday evoked, as indicated in the following record excerpt:

> The group members slowly came into the meeting room. Beverly sat with her back to the rest of the group, muttering an occasional "fuckin' mishugana." . . . The women made their instant coffee and drank it, all silently. They were much quieter and still today than usual; they appeared depressed and showed it by their slouched postures and lowered heads. I felt it might have something to do with feelings about Thanksgiving. I said everyone looked quite sad and wondered if they might want to talk about it. Rhoda furrowed her brows and moved her lips. I asked her if she wanted to say something. She shook her head. Another pause. All kept their heads lowered and Arlene, who usually talks to herself, was silent. I said they may all be having thoughts and feelings that the rest of the group might share with them. Silence. I finally said that sometimes it's hard to talk about things that are painful, like being in the hospital on holidays and maybe feeling lonely. Most of the members reacted to this by moving around in their chairs a little. I said I wondered if they did feel sad about tomorrow being a holiday. Rhoda nodded very slightly to herself, but kept her head lowered and didn't speak. Another lengthy pause, with all the ladies looking up at me briefly but not speaking.
>
> When it was time for the group to end, I commented that sometimes it's very hard to talk, like today—and especially when they might be feeling sad. I said I thought next week would be easier. They all looked up at me, and Rhoda smiled, saying, "have a nice Thanksgiving." (Poynter-Berg, 1986, p. 272)

Task-Centered Group Work

Task-centered group work, like traditional group work, models the process of helping the group to become a mutual aid system in which the members are committed to helping one another. The major difference is that in task-centered work, each member is assisted by other members in defining a personal goal, choosing activities (tasks) to reach the goal, and carrying out these tasks (Garvin, 1992). While members are helped to express and cope with feelings, this is done in the context of defining and accomplishing tasks. This is accomplished in a limited time, typically about 12 sessions.

Garvin (1992) reported excellent outcomes in utilizing this model in a community mental health setting serving the seriously mentally ill. He tested this approach with four groups composed of members who wished to enhance their use of leisure time. One group was composed of low-functioning clients, another of somewhat higher-functioning schizophrenic clients, a third of women who were trapped in highly dysfunctional family situations, and a fourth of clients who were also chemically dependent.*

The plan for the 12 sessions was as follows:

Meeting 1	Get-acquainted activities
	Orientation to task-centered work
	Clarification of group purpose
Meetings 2 and 3	Determining members' goals
	Discussion of the idea of tasks
Meetings 4 and 5	Selection of member tasks
Meetings 6–11	Working on tasks
	Learning to overcome barriers to accomplishing tasks
Last meeting	Termination and evaluation

During these meetings, the social workers used a variety of program tools to help the members maintain their interest in the group and sustain their motivation to participate. One example was a series of board games devised by the staff. Each game taught members how to accomplish some aspect of the process, such as formulating goals or tasks. In a goal game, for example, members moved their "pieces" around a board and "landed" on a problem area for which they had to formulate a goal.

Social Skills Training

A great deal of development, as well as research on effectiveness, has been devoted to creating models of social skills training for seriously mentally ill clients. Liberman, DeRisi, and Mueser (1989), who have been at the forefront of this work, define social skills as "all the behaviors that help us to communicate our emotions and needs accurately and allow us to achieve our interpersonal goals" (p. 3). Their approach involves groups, and they have prepared excellent materials the social worker can use, such as detailed manuals for practitioners, workbooks for group members, and audiovisual tapes that present models of the skills to be acquired.†

---

*This last group was not successful; the groups were formed before much was known about work with the so-called dually diagnosed, and neither of the workers had knowledge about working with that type of client.

†These materials can be obtained from Dissemination Coordinator, Camarillo-UCLA Clinical Research Center, Box A, Camarillo, CA 93011.

Liberman et al. have developed separate modules for a variety of social skills, such as recreation for leisure and medication management. Information on teaching friendship and dating skills is also contained in their text *Social Skills Training for Psychiatric Patients* (1989). These authors suggest the following steps for the group facilitator to use in planning a social skills session:

1   Give introduction to social skills training.
2. Introduce new patients.
3. Solicit orientation from experienced patients who can explain social skills training to new patients.
4. Reward patients for their contribution to the orientation.
5. Check homework assignments.
6. Help each patient pinpoint an interpersonal problem, goal, and scene for this session.
7. Target scene and interpersonal situation for dry run role play.
8. "Set up" the scene.
9. Give instructions for the scene.
10. Run the scene as a dry run.
11. Give positive feedback.
12. Assess receiving, processing, sending skills.
13. Use a model.
14. Ensure that the patient has assimilated the demonstrated skills.
15. Use another model.
16. Give instructions to patient for next rehearsal or rerun.
17. Rerun scene.
18. Give summary positive feedback.
19. Give real-life assignment.
20. Choose another patient for the training sequence and return to step 1.

The following is a brief excerpt of a social skills session reported by Liberman et al.:

(Karen, at the invitation of the therapist, has been explaining to a new member, Mark, what the members do in social skills training group. The therapist then turns to Ted, who has been in the group for a week, and asks him to add to what Karen has said.)
Therapist: Great, Karen! Ted, would you add to what Karen said?
(Ted has only been in the group for a week. He often gets angry and upset with other people. He decided to seek social skills training because he recently lost his third roommate in six months and has begun to realize that he alienates other people, including his co-workers. His boss has told him to improve his relations with work-mates or else risk being fired.)
Ted: I don't know, Karen described it.
Therapist: Well, can you think of some of the other things we can focus on?
Ted: You mean like solving our problems by looking at alternatives for communicating? And whether or not we look mad?

> *Therapist*: Right, Ted. We concentrate on facial expression and problem solving, too. When you talk to someone, they get a lot if information from seeing the kind of expression on your face. How loud we talk and our tone of voice are really important, too. Ted, how is voice tone different from voice loudness?
>
> *Ted*: Why don't you pick on someone else?
>
> *Therapist*: Because you're doing really well. You've only been here a short time, and you've learned a lot. (pp. 84–85)

Inpatient Group Psychotherapy

A major feature of contemporary hospitalization of patients with serious mental illness is that is it likely to be short—perhaps for only a week or two while the patient becomes stabilized after an acute episode. While in the hospital, patients may attend groups on a daily basis. These groups may be very unstructured, and our experience is that they are of limited usefulness. Yalom (1983) has developed and tested an approach he terms *inpatient group psychotherapy*. This approach has two variations, one for high-functioning and one for low-functioning patients. The high-functioning ones are able to make a conscious decision to enter the group, can sustain conversations with other patients that focus on interpersonal behaviors, and can remain in the group for approximately an hour. The low-functioning patients are unable to sustain that much verbal interaction. The structure of groups for the latter patients, therefore, includes more nonverbal activity such as physical exercise.

In the group for higher-functioning patients, the workers ask each member in turn to select a concern (referred to as an *agenda*) that can be worked on in a single session. Examples include telling another group member something about oneself or finding a way of coping with another member's angry response. After social workers have helped each member to chose an agenda for the session, the workers promote group interactions that will allow each member to work on her or his agenda for at least part of the session. Workers must have a good deal of skill in helping members choose a workable agenda and then pursue the agenda as part of the subsequent stage of the group's process.

After the interactional period, workers give feedback to members on how they have worked on their agendas. Yalom also often invites observers (such as interns) to attend and to comment toward the end of the session on the group's process. Members also are given a brief opportunity to react to this feedback on group processes.

EVALUATION APPROACHES

A great deal of research has been conducted to evaluate services to people with severe mental illness; this had to led to the development and testing of a variety of instruments to measure client outcomes. The following are some that can readily be used by social workers:

1. Scale for the Assessment of Negative Symptoms; Scale for the Assessment of Positive Symptoms (Schuldberg, Quinlan, Morgenstern, & Glazer, 1990). These scales are used by practitioners primarily to assess the symptomatology of schizophrenia.
2. Symptoms Checklist (Bartone, Ursano, Wright, & Ingraham, 1989). This instrument is designed to measure the frequency of such psychiatric symptoms as tenseness, depressed mood, and difficulty sleeping.
3. Cognitive Slippage Scale (Miers & Raulin, 1985). This scale is designed to measure the cognitive distortion that is a primary characteristic of schizophrenia.
4. Social Adjustment Scale–Self Report (Weissman & Bothwell, 1976). This instrument helps the social worker to assess how adequate the client is in such areas as housework; employment; dealing with salespeople, neighbors, and friends; schooling; and family relations.

CONCLUSION

Group approaches have a great deal to offer to people suffering from serious mental illnesses. These approaches provide experiences in dealing with relationships through group activities, the possibility for mutual aid as members discover the support they can give and receive, and the opportunity for members to learn vicariously when they are not ready to take a more active role. With the large number of investigations currently underway, the future is bright for the creation of even more useful ways of offering group opportunity to these clients.

NATIONAL RESOURCES

Alliance for the Mentally Ill
2101 Wilson Blvd.
Arlington, VA 22201
(800) 950 NAMI

Center for Rehabilitation Research
  and Training in Mental Health
Boston University
Sargent College of Allied Health
  Professions
1019 Commonwealth Ave.
Boston, MA 02215
(617) 353-3549

REFERENCES

Anderson, C. M., Reiss, D. J., & Hogarty, G. E. (1986). *Schizophrenia and the family.* New York: Guilford Press.

Bachrach, L. L. (1984). Interpreting research on the homeless mentally ill: Some caveats. *Hospital and Community Psychiatry, 35,* 914–917.

Bartone, P. T., Ursano, R. J., Wright, K. M., & Ingraham, L. H. (1989). The impact of a military air disaster on the health of assistance workers. *Journal of Nervous and Mental Disease, 177,* 317–328.

Dincin, J. (1985). Psychiatric rehabilitation today. In J. P. Bowker (Ed.), *Education for practice with the chronically mentally ill: What works* (pp. 18–31). Washington, DC: Council on Social Work Education.

Garvin, C. (1992). A task centered group approach to work with the chronically mentally ill. In J. A. Garland (Ed.), *Group work reaching out: People, places, and power* (pp. 67–80). New York: Haworth Press.

Garvin, C. & Tropman, J. (1992). *Social work in contemporary society.* Englewood Cliffs, NJ: Prentice-Hall.

Gerhart, U. C. (1990). *Caring for the chronic mentally ill.* Itasca, IL: Peacock.

Hazel, K. L., Herman, S. E., & Mowbray, C. T. (1991). Characteristics of seriously mentally ill adults in a public mental health system. *Hospital and Community Psychiatry, 42,* 518–525.

Kiesler, C. A., & Sibulkin, A. E. (1987). *Mental hospitalization: Myths and facts and a national crisis.* Newbury Park, CA: Sage.

Liberman, R. P., DeRisi, W. J., & Mueser, K. T. (1989). *Social skills training for psychiatric patients.* New York: Pergamon Press.

Miers, T. C., & Raulin, M. L. (1985). The development of a scale to measure cognitive slippage. Paper presented at the Eastern Psychological Association Convention, Boston, March 1985. A copy of the instrument may be found in J. Fischer & K. Corcoran (1994). *Measures for clinical practice: A sourcebook* (2nd ed.), Vol. 2: *Adults* (pp. 138–140). New York: Fress Press.

Poynter-Berg, D. (1986). Getting connected: Institutionalized schizophrenic women. In A. Gitterman & L. Shulman (Eds.), *Mutual aid groups and the life cycle* (pp. 263–282). Itasca, IL: Peacock

Rapp, C. (1985). Research on the chronically mentally ill. Curriculum implications. In J. P. Bowker (Ed.), *Education for practice with the chronically mentally ill. What works* (pp. 32–49). Washington, DC: Council on Social Work Education.

Robins, L. N., Locke, B.Z., & Regier, D. A. (1991). An overview of psychiatric disorders in America. In L. N. Robins & D. Regier (Eds.), *Psychiatric disorders in America* (pp. 328–386). New York: Free Press.

Rubin, A. (1986). Review of current research on Chronic Mental Illness. In J. P. Bowker & A. Rubin (Eds.), *Studies on chronic mental illness. New horizons for social work researchers* (pp. 5–28). Washington DC: Council on Social Work Education.

Sands, R. G. (1991). *Clinical social work practice in community mental health,* New York: Merrill.

Schuldberg, D., Quinlan, D. M., Morgenstern, D. M., & Glazer, W. (1990). Positive and negative symptoms in chronic psychiatric outpatients: Reliability, stability, and factor structure. *Psychological Assessment, 2,* 262–268.

Weissman, M. M., & Bothwell, S. (1976). Assessment of social adjustment by patient self-report. *Archives of General Psychiatry, 33,* 1111–1115.

Yalom, I. D. (1983). *Inpatient group psychotherapy.* New York: Basic Books

3

Group Work Services to People with AIDS During a Changing Pandemic

George S. Getzel

Group work and the acquired immune deficiency syndrome (AIDS) have been closely associated in the first efforts, beginning in the early 1980s, to help people with AIDS (PWAs). The model of group work for PWAs developed then reflected the desperate need to gain social support and to reduce societal isolation.

This chapter reviews the development of group work services to PWAs and suggests a reconsideration of the design and implementation of such services in light of the significant changes that have occurred in the treatment of human immunodeficiency virus (HIV)/AIDS and in the sociopolitical and cultural meanings of the disease. An overview of the biopsychosocial factors that surround HIV/AIDS is presented and is related to the core themes that emerge in a support group's interaction and content. The benefits of the group work experience for PWAs are identified.

Special attention is given to strategies for pregroup planning, the functional characteristics of groups, and the problem-solving process underlying group themes addressed by the group. Guidelines for the social worker's interventions are detailed. Finally, evaluation criteria are suggested.

OVERVIEW

In the last decade and a half, the appearance of AIDS as a major public health problem and the subsequent discovery of HIV have significantly entered the everyday lives of people in far-reaching ways (Cox, 1990); (Shilts, 1988). Although we may tend to avoid thinking about AIDS and its deathly consequences, growing numbers of people throughout the world are denied that option because their kin, friends, and neighbors infected by HIV become irreversibly ill from AIDS-related symptoms and diseases (Mann, Tarantola, & Netter, 1992).

The AIDS pandemic has produced creative and humane efforts to prevent the spread of HIV and to care for PWAs with serious illness and functional impairments. The use of groups with PWAs and with kin, friends, and volunteers caring for them has become an integral aspect of many social service and health care programs (Getzel, 1991a; Lopez & Getzel, 1984, 1987). Beginning with the discovery of the first AIDS cases in New York City, group approaches quickly were picked up by newly developing AIDS community-based organizations in other cities.

No longer can people, even in the most sophisticated developed countries, conceive of AIDS as a disease largely of gay men and intravenous drug users, as was the case when the pandemic was first recognized in the early 1980s (Cahill, 1984). The 1990s has been a period with a significant increase worldwide in the proportion of women, children, and men diagnosed with AIDS where infection is attributed directly or indirectly to heterosexual contact (Mann et al., 1992). All sexually active persons and their offspring throughout the world are at risk of developing HIV infection and the breakdown of bodily immune protection.

HIV infection and AIDS have a profound cultural and economic impact on whole societies (Bateson & Goldsby, 1988; Mann et al., 1992). The HIV disease sequence has a welter of emotional and practical effects on the lives of all involved (Christ, Weiner, & Moynihan, 1988; Getzel, 1991b). The psychosocial consequences of HIV/AIDS in many respects resemble the reactions of other categories of persons to life-threatening disease. For example, the prospect of being infected with HIV or the knowledge of being HIV positive may be met with denial, which is dangerous if a person has unprotected sex.

All major illnesses with disabling and disfiguring consequences can result in depression and agitation; it is very common for sick persons to feel shame and guilt about becoming sick, resulting in bouts of anger, isolation, and self-loathing. Sontag (1978) noted that historically, serious diseases like cancer and tuberculosis have had complex metaphorical content and values connotations; this has been strongly demonstrated in the case of AIDS. Because the first identified victims of HIV/AIDS were gay men, drug addicts, and poor persons of color in large cities, the stigma attached to persons with the disease has been insidious, resulting in incidents of withdrawal of care by professionals, violation of human rights, and violence against PWAs and their families (Altman, 1986; Bayer, 1989). The societal problems of homophobia, classism, racism, and sexism are exposed and magnified in the presence of HIV/AIDS.

As we enter the midpoint of the second decade of the AIDS pandemic, knowledge about AIDS and HIV has greatly expanded. Nonetheless, scientists have been unable to create a vaccine to prevent the spread of the virus or to find methods to eradicate it in the human body (Bartlett & Finkbeiner, 1994). A number of useful halfway medical technologies have been developed to temporarily prevent the replication of HIV in infected persons; these antiviral medications have modestly extended longevity but have not altered the nearly always fatal course of disease. Antiviral medications also present significant quality of life concerns because of side effects and the uncertain benefits for some individuals (Bartlett & Finkbeiner, 1994).

The extension of life for persons with both HIV and AIDS has increased the prevalence of complications from opportunistic infections. The longer persons live with HIV or AIDS, the more apt they are to develop chronic, persistent, disabling, disorienting, and disfiguring conditions (Bartlett & Finkbeiner, 1994).

A reconfiguration of group work services is required to respond more effectively to PWAs and the evolution of their biomedical treatment. These changes will be described below.

Review of the Literature

From the start of the first AIDS service organizations, support groups were recognized as important normalizing experiences for PWAs and for kin and friends caring for them (Lopez & Getzel, 1984) and for volunteers in these organizations (Lopez & Getzel, 1984; 1987). Support groups for professionals working with PWAs were recognized as a necessary resource somewhat later (Grossman & Silverstein, 1993). The use of groups to teach HIV prevention has been extensively reported. Peer education is widely employed to teach safer sexual techniques to gay men, women, adolescents, and other populations (Palacios-Jimenez & Shernoff, 1986; Redman, 1990; Duke & Omi, 1991; Ponton, DeClemente, & McKenna, 1991; Kelly & St. Lawrence, 1990).

The literature on group work with PWAs and caregivers, while not large, does point to the widespread use of support groups for special populations in a variety of contexts. Group work models for gay men in community-based organizations have been described in some detail (Gambe & Getzel, 1989; Getzel, 1991a, 1991b; Getzel & Mahony, 1990).

Child and Getzel (1989) describe a support group model for poor people in a urban hospital setting that is crisis oriented and capable of serving hospitalized and recently released patients with AIDS, including those with drug histories, women, and gay men of color. PWAs who are intravenous drug users can benefit from group support programs that emphasize harm reduction strategies to curtail the use of drugs while providing social support and guidance about the disease process (Bataki,

1990; O'Dowd, Natalie, Orr, & McKegney, 1991). Recently, increased attention has been given to PWAs living in rural areas who are limited in their ability to attend support groups at distant community-based organizations. Telephone support group work models have been developed for both PWAs and caregivers to break down the isolation of PWAs in rural areas also to protect their anonymity (Rounds, Galinsky, & Stevens, 1991). Telephone support groups have also been used for parents of children with AIDS (Weiner, Spencer, Davidson, & Fair, 1993) and for PWAs who are disabled in the terminal phase of the disease process (Ritter & Hammons, 1992). Group work approaches for special populations with AIDS and their caregivers are an increasing source of interest: the homeless (Mancoske & Lindhorst, 1991), family members in rural areas (Anderson & Shaw, 1994), parents of children with AIDS (Mayers & Spiegel, 1992), and gay partners of PWAs (Land & Harangody, 1990).

Gambe and Getzel (1989) emphasize that groups provide substitutes for weakened or absent social supports in PWAs' lives created by life-threatening disease, the unpredictability of the disease process, and the stigma associated with AIDS. In a similar vein, Getzel and Mahony (1990) identify the themes of loss and human finitude as causing crises in the group and forcing members to confront their personal sense of mortality. The group becomes a context in which to face painful and inchoate feelings of dread, helplessness, shame, and guilt. The social worker's acceptance of members' expressions of vulnerability and the group's constancy permit a sense of security and solidarity when members explore these themes.

PRACTICE PRINCIPLES

Work with PWAs entails a clear understanding of the functions of a support group. Critical to the use of group work with PWAs is effective pregroup planning and formation.

Pregroup Planning

The capacity of groups to meet the needs of PWAs must be clearly understood by the social worker before a group is begun. Groups have the following identified functions for PWAs:

1. Assisting members to find support from peers as a way of accepting their new status as PWAs.
2. Helping members explore ways in which family, friends, and others respond to them differently as PWAs and how to handle issues of intimacy, receiving help, and gaining acceptance.
3. Assisting members to find safe ways to express the sadness, anger, guilt, helplessness, and shame associated with the problem of living with AIDS.

4. Providing opportunities for members to find ways to counter the fright and feeling of powerlessness about death and dying.
5. Helping members examine quality-of-life options (how they want to live and die) prompted by serious illness and a likely death from complication from AIDS.
6. Assisting members with their personal belief systems about being diagnosed with AIDS and facing an uncertain future in a world that is not sympathetic to their plight.

Group Formation and the AIDS Pandemic

Early in the AIDS pandemic, support groups for PWAs consisted of members who had recently become aware of their AIDS diagnosis by becoming seriously ill with *Pneumocystis Cariniii* pneumonia (PCP), discovering a Kaposi's sarcoma (KS) lesion, or developing some other symptom associated with an opportunistic infection. Prior to the development of more effective treatments for these diseases and antiviral medication for HIV, most of the initial cohort joining a group died from complications from AIDS over 1 to 2 years (Gambe & Getzel, 1989). There was a brief early period "of quiet before the storm," soon followed by multiple hospitalizations, near-death experiences, and the appearance of other opportunistic infections such as taxoplasmosis, cytomegalovirus (CMV) infections, tuberculosis, and so forth. All of these illnesses can result in death, but not before causing extreme body wasting, incontinence, mental confusion, blindness, disfigurement, profound neurological impairments, and other dire consequences.

PWAs entering a formed group could see themselves in contrast to very sick members and could be in the group as members died in rapid succession. While this situation was intrinsically frightening and overwhelming, a basis for dropping out of the group, it also provided an opportunity to understand and prepare for the likely biopsychosocial crises to come. Other group members served as models of forbearance and coping. A member could deal with prospective and current quality-of-life issues while providing help to peers. Group members were seen to be in the same lifeboat "until death do them part."

Reconfiguring Group Work Services

While this early model of group support services is still relevant in many respects, it must be adjusted and refined in view of PWAs' increased longevity and the highly variegated cohorts of persons now affected by AIDS in many settings. What was once a single model of group work service has become a series of specialized models that reflect with more precision the disease sequence and medical treatment advances. Three general types of support groups are recommended and principles for intervention specified.

Orientation Support Group

This group's primary focus is assisting members to cope with the issue of recognizing themselves as persons with AIDS. This may also mean coming out of the closet as a gay person or a person with a history of drug abuse.

Understanding the practical and emotional consequences of the disease for the person's future orientation and management of different aspects of everyday life becomes important. Women with children have to consider custody after they die. All persons must consider how they will management their income and health care now if they become unemployed or disabled in the future. Guidance about available health and social services and how to use them is an important aspect of group activities.

Depression, guilt, shame, and powerlessness are reduced as group members gain understanding about the similarity of their reactions and their different coping strategies. The orientation support group is comprised of newly diagnosed PWAs; it is time limited (six to eight sessions) and focuses on getting on with life after an AIDS diagnosis. These groups are most effective when sponsored by community-based organizations.

Group homogeneity is an important consideration in the design of orientation support groups. Gay men, male intravenous drug users, women who are nondrug abusers infected by men, and women using intravenous drugs may benefit from homogeneous group composition that allows for more in-depth discussions of members' diagnosis, needed services, and coping strategies. Linguistic barriers and disabling conditions may necessitate special groups led in a foreign language or American Sign Language. Increased sophistication in developing specialized groups also applies to the two support group models that will now be discussed.

Relationship Support Group

This group is needed after the initial shock of the diagnosis has been handled. This model of group support focuses on the significant changes in the quantity and quality of interpersonal relationships that ensue for PWAs after they and other persons in their lives contemplate the current and prospective consequences of the disease. PWAs may see themselves as tainted or, as some PWAs have described it, as "soiled goods." The stigma attached to PWAs is reinforced when other persons, who were previously close, begin to disengage or abandon them. PWAs and others close to them may be troubled by the HIV/AIDS diagnosis and by the disclosure of homosexuality, bisexuality, drug use, or marital infidelity.

Just as PWAs become preoccupied with recurrent death anxiety, persons close to them must contemplate hospitalizations, new symptoms, and dying. Relatives and others may experience feelings of rage and emotional conflict.

Needless to say, if the PWA is presumed to have infected family members, the emotional turmoil and conflict are magnified enormously. Consider the following situation of Mr. A., a 35-year-old man, and his wife of 5 years.

Mrs. A. has been previously married. While she is pregnant with their second child, she and Mr. A. discover that Mrs. A's first husband died of AIDS (related to a hidden history of drug abuse). HIV tests are given to Mr. and Mrs. A. and their first child; the results for each of them are positive. Mrs. A. has been recently diagnosed with disseminated tuberculosis and AIDS; it will take over a year of testing to determine if the newborne is HIV infected because the mother's and the child's antibody production must be distinguished.

The need for a variety of health and social services for the A. family now and in the future is apparent. Part of a case plan for Mr. and Mrs. A. can be a relationship support group to address the welter of interpersonal problems they may face. Among the possibilities are a couples support group composed of others in a comparable situation, a women's PWA group composed of women infected by spouses, and a caregiver support group of men caring for women with AIDS.

Relationship support groups explore the current stresses in interpersonal relationships arising from being a PWA or a caregiver. These groups are time limited, with a focus on providing emotional and practical assistance in working out interpersonal conflicts and finding additional sources of support as the mounting demands of self-care and caregiving create stresses for group members. One objective of these groups is to maximize the autonomy and self-determination of the members as they make choices between the demands originating from the disease and those arising from day-to-day living. A group meeting for 8 to 12 weeks is introduced by the social workers, who state that group members will develop the understanding and skills needed to get on with their lives. Throughout this group experience, the social workers reinforce examples of members' resourcefulness in handling AIDS-related problems and making life plans. The social workers state that they believe that living with AIDS means that members get on with their lives, which includes work, friendship, intimacy, and new experiences.

Coleadership should be considered as a way of modeling roles and providing continuity when a facilitator is absent. The group members may recontract for an extension of the group as needed and as resources permit. Emphasis should be placed on enhancing group members' capacity to understand and to manage HIV/AIDS-related problems that typically arise within their kinship and friendship systems. Problems at work may also be discussed.

Relationship support groups require careful intake. The social worker helps the potential group member or couple identify possible interpersonal issues to be addressed in the group. The intake process is expedited when group candidates have first explored interpersonal concerns in an orientation support group. This model of group support can be based in AIDS community-based organizations, mental health settings, family services agencies, child care agencies, and other settings used by and accessible to PWAs, their kin, and others associated with informal caregiving.

Quality-of-Life Support Group

This group is appropriate during periods of serious illness and the end stage of the disease process. It may not address many PWAs' needs until a few years after diagnosis. Life-threatening diseases tend to occur later. PWAs frequently experience an asymptomatic period or a period of less dramatic symptomatic display when AIDs and its life-threatening potential need not occupy exclusively PWAs' cognitive and emotional lives.

A quality-of-life support group provides PWAs with a safe location to discuss their reactions to shortened life. A process of life review, more typically associated with the elderly, occurs in the group. It is occasioned by serial losses in the form of disfiguring symptoms, social isolation and abandonment, deaths of others, mental disorganization, and other disabling conditions. The group gives support and guidance as members confront humiliating, severe symptoms. For example, the group allows members to exchange opinions about undergoing experimental treatments that may cause irreversible side effects. Members can openly discuss issues like HIV dementia symptoms and even use humor to face the affront of baldness caused by chemotherapy treatments.

Particular symptoms of opportunistic diseases may warrant special efforts to develop homogeneous groups. Groups may be composed of PWAs with visual impairments resulting from the activity of a persistent, chronic cytomegaloviral infection that destroys the retina of the eye, or they may consist of members with rapidly progressing and disfiguring lesions of Kaposi's sarcoma, a form of skin cancer. In such groups, members can provide empathetic support and exchange useful information about resources: how to obtain cosmetics to disguise lesions or community resources for mobility training at home. Quality-of-life support groups are found in AIDS community-based organizations, hospitals, long-term care programs, hospices, religious organizations, and local health and social service agencies. Parallel groups of this nature for caregivers are also very useful. Coleadership is strongly recommended to provide continuity of facilitation and emotional support to leaders in these very demanding groups. This support group model is usually opened-end in time. Careful consideration and preparation must be given to the introduction of a new member (Gambe & Getzel, 1989).

COMMON THEMES

Recurrent themes emerge in group discussion and interaction that present the social worker and members with rich opportunities to work together.

An Uncertain Conditioning

Uncertainty occurs in all support groups during different phases of group development. For example, in the beginning phase of the group, members may express deep ambivalence about being in a group for PWAs because they do not understand what AIDS represents to them. Rather than confront the uncertainty of their life course, they protect themselves against death anxiety through simple denial—maybe they really do not have AIDS or perhaps they are not suited for a group of PWAs.

Approach-avoidance behaviors appear in the group. Members join subgroups that are in conflict. Some members only want to talk about cures and treatments for HIV/AIDS and castigate others who want to discuss their fear of becoming sick or the recent deaths of friends from complications of AIDS.

Recommended Ways of Working   There is a great temptation to side with one subgroup; this tendency should be avoided. The social worker should make group conflicts a problem for group members to solve. The social worker should assist group members to explore solutions that might simultaneously address the need to accept the uncertainties of disease sequence and treatment while approaching life without a morbid outlook. Group members share thoughts and problem-solve together. The social workers must walk a fine line, carefully accepting different perspectives offered by conflicting subgroups.

If the social worker is not a PWA or does not have a background similar to that of the members, he or she may become a target of group members' anger for not having to deal with the same life issues.

Case

The following incident occurs at an early meeting of gay men with AIDS after Robert returns to the group when his lover dies from an opportunistic infection:

Members are engaged in an intense discussion of the benefits of combining antiviral medications to halt HIV replication when Robert asks, in an offhanded way, if this discussion is boring to the social worker, since he does not have AIDS. Other group members stop and stare at the social worker, who begins to flush. Looking at Robert and the other group members, the social worker says, "The group seems to be reacting to Robert's important question to me."

In defense of the social worker, another member, John, says that you do not need to have AIDS to lead a group of PWAs. The social worker indicates that this might be so but wonders if Robert and some other group members might feel differently. An intense group discussion ensues in which Robert talks about his anger about the death of his lover and his distrust of anyone who does not have AIDS and has not suffered. Some group members, while defending the social worker, acknowledge their jealousy in their lives toward people who do not have AIDS. Group members, with the help of the social worker, go on to discuss their concerns about how Robert is managing after the death of his lover. The discussion slowly edges back to new treatments as the session ends.

Crisis Situations

Recurrent biopsychosocial crisis situations arise in the PWAs' interpersonal systems that necessitate in-depth attention by the group members. Previous patterns of adaptation and problem solving may no longer be available to PWAs in crisis. Acceptance of powerful emotional displays occurs in the support group. Other members can display a sense of mastery by using their learning from undergoing similar crises to help a peer in active crises.

Recommended Ways of Working The social worker must see the group members as capable of accepting crisis situations that arise among members, avoiding an overprotective stance. To the extent that the social worker encourages members to discuss how they have handled similar situations, mutual aid will be encouraged, in contrast to flight behavior, in which members give facile advice on a one-on-one basis. It is important to point out themes that reflect emotions and ideas shared by the members. The social worker may also help members reach out to each other as crisis situations arise between sessions, assuming that members agree to this type of support during the group's deliberations.

Case

A crisis situation was revealed in a women's PWA group when Mary, in a tearful, agitated manner, told the other members that she had been diagnosed with cervical cancer and would be hospitalized the next day. Mary told the group that she did not care if she lived or died but felt shame for what would happen to her two young children. Shaking convulsively, May wept, saying that she had not planned for guardianship after her husband had died 6 months ago.

Joan held Mary and the group began telling Mary that they were very worried about her. Tanya said that she used a lawyer from the social work agency when she panicked about going into the hospital. The social worker told the group that it seemed very hard to do a will and make guardian provisions. Joan said that you just don't want to think about dying but that you have to be realistic, concluding, "Better late than never." The group then began a discussion about how, after being diagnosed, they had grown more responsible in thinking about their children.

A Changed Identity

A very strong theme that emerges in groups of PWAs is participants' change of self-image linked to AIDS. For example, receiving an AIDS diagnosis can be seen as a rite of passage. Normalizing and AIDS identity is a way of coping with an otherwise unacceptable condition that others readily see as a death sentence.

Support groups simultaneously normalize the PWA status and provide guidance in understanding this status when representing oneself to outsiders. Strongly associated with a shift of self-definition is a greater capacity to look at the question of mortality and the meaning of a life threatened by AIDS.

Erikson (1964) notes that all stages of the life cycle place demands on the individual to find meaning in life in order to cope with the stresses of existence and reminders of death. Human individuality finds its ultimate challenge when a human being confronts mortality. Identity questions may become exquisitely transparent in the face of death.

Recommended Ways of Working   The group becomes a safe context to discuss concerns and express feelings about the inequity of a life ending too early, unfulfilled goals, unfinished projects, and taking leave of loved ones. With the death of a member, surviving members bear witness to the meaning of the loss and the significance of their own lives. Clearly, the social worker must be prepared to listen and not to quickly reassure. The social worker's guilt and helplessness as a survivor necessitate the presence of supervisory and peer supervision.

Case

After the group discusses the recent death of a member, Greg says to the social workers, "It is your job to remember us after we all die." The social worker, after some hesitation, replies that the deaths of group members sadden him greatly and he feels the heavy burden of loss, yet his is grateful to be part of the group, where he has met so many wonderful men. He can never forget them.

The social worker asks the group members if they have reactions to his outliving them. Some members joke, saying that he had better enjoy himself when they are gone. Paul says that he is jealous of the social worker. Gradually, the subject is adroitly changed by Paul.

EVALUATION APPROACHES

Although difficult, the evaluation of group support models for different population is very much needed. Consumer feedback about short-term support groups is a good way to begin. Measurements of consumer satisfaction, knowledge gained about resources, and the actual use of services and entitlements should be investigated. More traditional measurements of clinical outcomes can be obtained from relationship support groups.

Quality-of-life support groups present serious concerns, and ethnographic approaches should be considered because of the likelihood of physical fragility and HIV-related dementia among members. Since PWAs feel stigmatized and may have histories of stigma, respect for the integrity of their personal boundaries, confidentiality, and autonomy are critical. PWAs should be allowed to tell their stories without prejudice, coercion, or prior interpretation. Telling their stories may represent the human need to be remembered.

NATIONAL RESOURCES

American Foundation for AIDS
Research (AmFAR)
733 Third Ave.
New York, NY 10017
(212) 682-744

Gay Men's Health Crisis (GMHC)
129 West 20th St.
New York, NY 10011
GMHC Hotline: (212) 807-6655

National AIDS Hotline
(800) 342-AIDS or (800) 342-5231

PWA Coalition
31 West 26th St.
New York, NY 10010
(800) 828-3280

San Francisco AIDS Project
P.O. Box 462182
San Francisco, CA 94142-6182
(415) 863-AIDS

REFERENCES

Altman, D. (1986). *AIDS in the mind of America.* New York: Anchor Books.

Anderson, D. B., & Shaw, S. L. (1994). Starting a support group for families and partners of people with HIV/AIDS in a rural setting. *Social Work, 39,* 135–138.

Bartlett, J. G., & Finkbeiner, A. K. (1994). *The guide to living with HIV infection.* Baltimore: Johns Hopkins University Press.

Bataki, S. L. (1990). Substance abuse and AIDS: The need for mental health services. *New Directions in Mental Health Services,* no. 48, 55–67.

Bateson, M. C., & Goldsby, B. (1988). *Thinking AIDS: The social response to the biological threat.* Reading, MA: Addison-Wesley.

Bayer, R. (1989). *Private act, social consequences: AIDS and politics of public health.* New York: Free Press.

Cahill, K. M. (1984). Preface: The evolution of an epidemic. In Cahil, K. M. (ed.), *The AIDS epidemic* (pp. 2–6). New York: St. Martin's Press.

Child, R., & Getzell, G.S. (1989). Group work with inner city people with AIDS. *Social Work with Groups, 12*(4), 65–80.

Christ, G., Weiner, L., and Moynihan, R. (1988). Psychosocial issues in AIDS. *Psychiatric Annals, 16,* 173–179.

Cox, E. (1990). *Thankgiving: An AIDS journal.* New York: Harper & Row.

Duke, S. I., & Omi, J. (1991). Development of AIDS education and prevention materials for women by health department staff and community focus groups. *AIDS Education and Prevention, 3,* 90–99.

Erikson, E. H. (1964). *Insight and responsibility.* New York: Norton.

Gambe, R., & Getzel, G. S. (1989). Group work with gay men with AIDS. *Social Casework, 70,* 172–179.

Getzel, G. S. (1991a). AIDS. In A. Gitterman (Ed.), *Handbook of social work with vulnerable populations* (pp. 35–64). New York: Columbia University Press.

Getzel, G. S. (1991b). Survival modes of people with AIDS in groups. *Social Work, 36,* 7–11.

Getzel, G. S., & Mahony, K. (1990). Confronting human finitude: Group work with people with AIDS. *Journal of Gay and Lesbian Psychotherapy, 1,* 105–120.

Goldfinger, S. M. (1990). *Psychiatric aspects of AIDS and HIV infection.* New York: Jossey-Bass.

Grant, D. (1988). Support groups for youth with the AIDS virus. *International Journal of Group Psychotherapy, 38,* 237–251.

Greene, D. C., McVinney, L. D., & Addams, S. (1993). Strengths in transition: Professionally facilitate HIV support groups and the development of client symptomatology. *Social Work with Groups, 16,* 41–54.

Grossman, A. H., & Silverstein, C., (1993). Facilitating support groups for professionals working with people with AIDS. *Social Work, 38,* 144–151.

Kelly, J. A., & St. Lawrence, J. S. (1990). The impact of community-based groups to help persons reduce HIV infection risk behaviors. *AIDS-Care, 2,* 25–35.

King, M. B. (1993). *AIDS, HIV and mental health.* Cambridge: Cambridge University Press.

Land, H., & Harangody, G. (1990). A support group for partners of persons with AIDS. *Families in Society, 71,* 471–482.

Lopez, D. J., & Getzel, G.S. (1984). Helping gay patients in crisis. *Social Casework, 65,* 387–394.

Lopez, D. J., & Getzel S. (1987). Strategies for volunteers caring for persons with AIDS. *Social casework, 68,* 47–53.

Mann, J., Tarantola, D. J. M., & Netter, T. W. (1992). *A global report: AIDS in the world.* Cambridge, MA: Harvard University Press.

Mancoske, F. J., & Lindhorst, T. (1991). Mutual assistance groups in a shelter for persons with AIDS. *Social Work with Groups, 14,* 75–86.

Mayers, A., & Spiegel, L. (1992). A parental support group in a pediatric AIDS clinic: Its usefulness and limitations. *Health and Social Work, 17,* 183–193.

O'Dowd, M. A., Natalie, C., Orr, D., & McKegney, F. (1991). Characteristics of patients attending an HIV-related psychiatric outpatient clinic. *Hospital and Community Psychiatry, 42,* 615–619.

Palacios-Jimeniz, L., & Shernoff, M. (1986). *Eroticizing safer sex.* New York: Gay Men's Health Crisis.

Ponton, K. E., DeClemente, F. J., & McKenna, S. (1991). An AIDS education and prevention program for hospitalized adolescents. *Journal of the American Academy of Children and Adolescent Psychiatry, 30,* 729–734.

Redman, J. M. (1990). *Woman and AIDS: What we need to know.* A workshop manual on educating women about AIDS and safer sex. New Orleans: Planned Parenthood.

Rittner, B., & Hammons, K. (1992). Telephone group work with people with end stage AIDS. *Social Work with Groups, 15,* 59–72.

Rounds, K. A., Galinsky, M. J., & Stevens, L. S. (1991). Linking people with AIDS in rural communities: The telephone group. *Social Work, 36,* 13–18.

Shilts, R. (1988). *The band played on: Politics, people and AIDS.* New York: St. Martin's Press.

Sontag, S. (1978). *Illness as metaphor.* New York: Vintage Books.

Weiner, L. S., Spencer, E. D., Davidson, R., & Fair, C. (1993). National telephone support groups; a new avenue toward psychosocial support HIV-infected children and their families. *Social Work With Groups, 16,* 55–71.

4

Group Work with Head Injured People

Susan T. Futeral

Traumatic brain injury, as seen in head trauma patients, is defined as brain damage from an externally inflicted trauma to the head that results in significant impairment to the individual's physical, psychosocial, and/or cognitive functional abilities (Aliev, 1984). Brain injury is characterized by altered consciousness (coma and/or posttrauma amnesia) during the acute phase after injury (Bakay & Glasauer, 1980). The duration of this state varies greatly, usually depending on the severity of the injury.

A head trauma or traumatic brain injury may be an open or closed injury resulting in trauma to the brain, with neurophysiological sequelae. An open head injury may be sustained when there is intracranial penetration, such as a gunshot wound. A closed head injury is nonmissile injury in which sudden acceleration/deceleration is the primary traumatic force or a blow to the head by a blunt instrument results in an altered state or total loss of consciousness. The Glascow Coma Index Scale and the Ranchos Los Amigos Scale, with references up to 1980, are used to measure the patient's level of neuropsychological functioning after the injury. By definition, a person must lose consciousness for 20 minutes to be in a coma; and these two scales provide a means by which this can be measured.

Head trauma patients comprise a relatively new population, as many traumatically brain-injured persons were unable to survive prior to new medical advances. To plan realistically and to implement programs of rehabilitation for brain-injured clients require an understanding of what has happened to the brain and how the damage affects the total person. Traumatic brain injury differs in two ways from other types of brain damage (genetic, stroke, degenerative, drug and alcohol abuse, etc.). Head trauma happens suddenly, bringing significant change immediately, and the damage is usually diffuse and widespread throughout the brain. The effects, therefore, are multiple. Additionally, damage to the brain can be acquired in the course of what may well have been normal development (Maryland Head Injury Foundation, 1985).

The residual deficits that result from traumatic brain injury may be divided into two areas: medical (or physical) and psychological. The medical deficits may include muscle contractions, bowel and/or bladder dysfunction, and seizures. The psychological deficits may include depression, judgment loss, memory loss, impulsiveness, headaches, and lowered self-esteem.

Head injury is a significant cause of mortality and morbidity. Each year in the Untied States, 400,000 to 600,000 people suffer severe traumatic head injury. Of these, it is estimated that 100,000 deaths occur, and between 30,000 and 50,000 others are left with disabilities severe enough to preclude a return to normal life (Kraus, Black, & Hessol, 1984). Head trauma is the third most common cause of death in persons less than 38 years of age (Maryland Head Injury Foundation, 1990).

Severe head injury occurs with an overall frequency of 24 per 100,000. The peak age range is between 10 and 19 years, with an incidence of 38 per 100,000. Severe head injury occurs two to three times more often in males than in females; the largest sex difference is found in the age range of 15 to 24 years. The leading causes of injury are motor vehicle accidents in persons aged 15 to 24 and accidental falls in children under 15 years (Maryland Head Injury Foundation, 1990).

This chapter describes the effectiveness of social group work with head trauma rehabilitation patients. As head trauma patients have never survived until the past few decades, there is presently no defined therapy aimed at rehabilitating them emotionally (Maryland Head Injury Foundation, 1989). Therefore, this is an area in which social workers can explore, develop, and refine methods for their clients' mainstreaming into society (Gerring, 1986).

CHARACTERISTIC PROBLEMS

Individual and family therapies are often provided for head trauma victims; group treatment is not routinely offered in head trauma facilities. However, studies have shown group treatment to be effective in assisting troubled people reintegrate into society (Garvin, 1987).

Some of the difficulties that head trauma patients face are readjustment to social, vocational, and educational settings (Maryland Head Injury Foundation, 1989). Feelings of grief over loss of normal bodily functions and limbs may affect their self-esteem throughout the recovery and rehabilitation period (Gerring, 1986). These issues can be approached in group work.

Because of personality traits, learning styles, location, severity of the injury, and time lapse between impact and psychological reaction, the recovery rate is different for each individual. Varying degrees of physical, mental, and personality changes occur after a traumatic head injury. Although systematic comparative studies of the consequences of head trauma in adults and children have not been undertaken, evidence suggests that children experience a swifter recovery because of the greater plasticity of the immature nervous system. Determining whether a post-traumatic patient is suffering intellectual impairment as a result of the injury depends on the assessment procedures used in evaluation. A brief mental status examination may suggest normal functioning, whereas more detailed testing may uncover defects of varying degrees.

PRACTICE PRINCIPLES
Limit and Structure

For several reasons, head trauma patients often suffer from cognitive impairments that ultimately affect not only their knowledge and memory but also their decision-making ability. The group worker needs to understand that it is imperative to set limits with the members of the group. They must agree to start and end on time. The group must have structure; a beginning warm-up, a middle period of work, and a final period of sharing. Guidance is paramount, especially during periods of sharing, so that group members do not, intentionally or otherwise, react in such a way as to adversely affect the member who has shared.

The phases of the group (the beginning, middle, and final activities) must be communicated to the group members so that they, too, can follow and track their progress. Whereas in other group approaches discussed in this book these phases are not always made explicit, here, with an emphasis on structure, they are openly discussed.

Group Composition

One important feature of any group is homogeneity. Head trauma patients often experience a feeling of isolation, as if they are the only ones going throughout recuperation. Not only is it wise to provide a support group for these patients, it can also be helpful, at times, to run a multi-family group for their spouses and family members. These people can help enhance the patient's functioning and quality of life.

Worker's Role

As the emphasis is on structure, the worker's activity level needs to be high. The worker may feel that he or she is being condescending by making statements such as "You need to put your coffee down and start the group now" or "It's time to put cigarettes out and come in to start the group now." This can make a worker feel as if he or she is dealing with a grade school class and not a population of adults

When working with head trauma patients, one must be very specific. Activities must be clearly organized and defined. This clear sense of guidance makes it easier for the trauma patients to follow through and gives them a feeling of acceptance and security. Group members may feel awkward asking questions, particularly concerning the context of neurophysiological impairments such as aphasias, agnosias, work retrieval problems, and other communication disorders. The worker must be prepared to state the guidelines and goals, the intended climate of the group, and the rules for sharing, participation, and confidentiality. These rules must be adhered to strictly.

Time and Hope

The group worker must take time to process the information conveyed in the group. The events of the lives of group members may seem random, unfair, overwhelming, and confused. Helping trauma patients cope with their losses and deficits and with their families can become a severe emotional drain. Group workers cannot take all this home every night. They must find a way to leave the stress in the office and be willing to share experiences with coworkers to achieve support.

Even though Yalom (1995) says that instillation of hope is critical to head trauma patients, research shows about a 4-year recovery time. Patients need to know that they can get better and will improve with work.

A group worker should know what other services are being provided for the patient, such as occupational therapy, vocational redirection, job coaching, rehabilitation therapy, family counseling, individual counseling, skilled nursing, home visits, physical and speech therapies, and post-trauma psychological testing. Often head trauma patients have near to full IQ recovery, and this recovery needs to be pointed out to them. Hearing that "You're doing really well in your math class, and we can work together on helping you remember what period of the day you are in" can give the patient's sagging ego the boost needed to continue progress and show family members that the patient need not be totally dependent.

COMMON THEMES

A firm but gentle, focused discussion is necessary. Common group themes for discussion include a review and recapitulation of the injury; experiences while in the hospital; ongoing concurrent services; assessing what's helpful and what is not; feelings in one's body, mind, and spirit; and coping with family relationships. Financial stressors created by the injury may not be a motivating theme for change, but group members may want to discuss the realities of their new situation.

This section is divided into two shorter sections in order to gain greater understanding of group themes in practice: one focusing on youngsters and the other on adults.

Children and Adolescents

The Maryland Institute for Emergency Medicine studied 230 families of multiple trauma patients in an attempt to develop an effective treatment modality to help families confronted with the sudden or threatened death of a family member. (Epperson, 1977).

Epperson describes six phases following the catastrophic event through which the family and the patient must pass before they are able to reorganize, reintegrate, and regain a homeostatic state: (1) high anxiety, (2) denial, (3) anger, (4) remorse, (5) grief, and (6) reconciliation. These stages are viewed as the phases of recovery. The outcome of this descriptive study offers methods of family intervention for social workers in critical care settings.

Chadwick, Rutter, Brown, Chaffer, and Traub (1981) completed a longitudinal field study comparing 25 children with head injuries to an individually matched group of 25 children with orthopedic injuries, using the WISC Performance and Verbal IQ Scale. Their findings were positive to the extent that posttest measures, compared to the pretest scores obtained 1 year earlier, showed significant improvement in the head-injured group.

Gerring (1986) examined 52 children and adolescents (2 to 18 years old) who had sustained head injuries and were treated at Johns Hopkins Hospital and the Kennedy Institute. She explored the duration of coma in relation to the early and late cognitive and psychiatric sequelae. Gerring identified a spectrum of behaviors, known as the *disinhibition syndrome*, which refers to the inclusion of inappropriate words or acts, poor judgment, amotivation, apathy, carelessness in hygiene and dress, conceptual disorganization, inattention, hyperactivity, impulsiveness, aggression, hypergraphia, and pica. She also discussed preinjury psychiatric or behavioral disorders and the role of medication.

Adults

Prigatano, Fordyce, Zeiner, Roueche, Pepping, and Wood (1983) studied the cognitive and personality disturbances following closed injury in young adults. They concluded that treatment successes were manifested as less personality disturbance and better learning and memory scores after treatment than treatment failures.

Brooks and McKinlay (1983) not only explored the cognitive functioning of head trauma patients but also expanded their research to include personality and behavioral changes that occur after trauma. They found that teaching the family member or caretaker to recognize and manage personality and behavioral changes in the patient may be a crucial aspect of rehabilitation for this population.

Weddell, Oddy, and Jenkins (1990) evaluated 44 young head-injured adults over a 2-year period to monitor their social adjustment. They concluded that "In addition to developing improved retraining techniques for intellectual and personality changes, it may be important to look for better ways of helping patients and their relatives adjust to these residual mental impairments" (p. 26).

In summary, the literature supports the need for rehabilitative group work. The evidence of neurobehavioral and psychological sequelae is present in this population, even 2 years after trauma. Although it seems that children and adolescents may heal more rapidly than adults (Chadwick et al., 1981; Epperson, 1977), there are still cognitive and behavioral deficits that need to be addressed through further rehabilitation. Head trauma rehabilitation with adults is a complex issue because recovery involves the interdisciplinary treatment team at both the acute and post-trauma stages. The ongoing rehabilitation (Brooks & McKinlay, 1983; Hill, 1984; Prigatano et al., 1983) involves relatives and caretakers to promote stability in the home setting. Overall, there seems to be support for more intense outreach efforts to facilitate the emotional adaptation and social reintegration of head trauma patients.

INTERVENTIONS

Although head trauma is primarily seen in young adults, many young children and adolescents are affected by severe traumatic brain injury through sustained head trauma. In organizing a group, the agency plays a key role. The worker must conform to the rules of the agency, whether in a state-run, an inpatient, or an outpatient setting. The setting itself provides the norms for the climate of the group in terms of promoting a sharing and caring atmosphere. My preference is the closed model, in which the group worker limits the number of participants and follows guidelines for a specific structure, whether a task or behaviorally oriented recidivist model. A closed model does not allow new people to enter the group, a distracting aspect of the open model. A number of self-help groups, such as the 12-step programs, operate on the open model. However, I have found that in professionally led groups, a closed model is more successful because the social worker sets the guidelines and structure for related expectations of individuals in the group, at a given time, and for a given period. Group phases are easier to monitor, an essential consideration when working with people with severe neurological damage and other at-risk populations.

In the early stages of the group, it is essential for the group worker and coworker to facilitate and develop both short- and long-term goals. A rehabilitative approach seeks to make changes that will alleviate specific handicaps or disabilities to the individual's functioning in his or her social role (Garvin, 1987). Interventions may include therapeutic discussions, education, tutoring, arts and crafts, recreation, sports, politics, religion, sexuality, or other themes.

The goals of the group are to (1) maximize the potential of poly-injured clients within the limitations imposed by their injuries: (2) help clients readjust both psychologically and socially to their environments; (3) help clients deal with their new identities, relearn social skills, maximize communication abilities, explore new roles, and discover new vocational opportunities; and (4) emphasize the clients' functional capacities in the areas of daily living skills, communication, cognition, mobility, and psychosocial awareness and thereby reestablish their self-esteem (Garvin, 1987).

A case example of a short-term closed group is found at a metropolitan state hospital on the East Coast. The outpatient department for head trauma rehabilitation, termed The Center for Living, had a multidisciplinary focus. Its purpose was to help recovering head trauma patients adjust and reintegrate back into society. There was an equally important support system for family members and significant others. The goal of the group, because of its homogeneity, was to help the patients adjust and reenter society. Group participation was critical and the climate was relaxed, although discussions became intense. The patients in the group were reasonably familiar with one another since they were together for various activities, such as speech therapy, occupational therapy, physical therapy, and job coaching.

None of the members of this particular group was able to work, but they spoke freely about their loss of bodily control—for example, the frustration of a stuttering problem that had not existed before the injury. It was frightening for them to talk about relationships with family members. Many relatives had grieved from them and had been prepared for them to die. When they lived, their relatives were not prepared for the personality changes they experienced. Additionally, the patients did not always realize that they had undergone a personality change. Often they admitted to having a shorter temper or angrier feelings then previously, but they were truly unaware of the significance of the disinhibition syndrome that typically characterizes head trauma rehabilitation patients.

Both of the group workers in this setting were patient and focused. They assured complete safety and confidentiality to the group members. Their participation was geared to helping the members share their feelings and lives with each other. They helped patients to cope with recovery issues—the loss of body parts and bodily functions, changes in personality and attitudes—and to understand the grief of their families. By setting clear, concise goals, the members of the group were able to participate in a warm and sharing climate.

A second case example comes from the support group offered at the University of Maryland through the Maryland Institute of Emergency

Medical Systems Department. The group's members were former hospital patients who had also sustained closed head injury. This group did not receive many formal services through the university but were able to spend time sharing their experiences. The goal of this group was to understand the emotional, social, and behavioral impairments resulting from their injuries. The members were able to create a climate of safety. They considered themselves lucky to be able to maintain as healthy a lifestyle as they had. This hospital-based group met in the nurses' station, which provided a warmer atmosphere than might exist in other inpatient settings. This, too, was a closed group, but it continued for several months, in contrast to the 10-week program of the previous example.

This group set the short-term goal of helping its members obtain all of the supportive physical services they might need. Also discussed were job coaching and vocational redirection. The group's long-term goal was to help the members cope with the stress and difficulties of recovery from their injuries. These people were living independently. Although some of them received disability income, they were either employed in some capacity or completing a Department of Vocational Rehabilitation–supported training course to obtain better jobs.

They were determined to enhance the quality of their lives. Nebulous as such a group goal might seem, the members were comfortable with it and with the climate created by the group worker. They felt safe in sharing their limitations, as well as setting new personal goals as they attained better health and learned to compensate for their new deficiencies.

I found that, above all else, the ability to inspire confidence in the patients, ensure safety in the setting, and demonstrate reliability of the worker benefited the members as much as the attainment of their personal goals.

EVALUATION

To assess change in a group, the worker must evaluate both the group as a whole and the changes that occur within each group member. The worker will assess the changes in the group by offering feedback to the members as the group moves through various stages. For example, at the first meeting (the beginning/forming stage), after introductions, the group worker can ask questions such as "What brought you to the group?" "How was the injury incurred?" "How do you think the group can/will help you?" and "What goals to you have for yourself?" This will set the stage for participants to state their goals and receive feedback at subsequent meetings. The workers can monitor group participation by asking each participant to offer comments a prescribed number of times per session. Some measures of group participation plot the pattern of group communication by monitoring to whom one speaks. Another group measure involves assessing the roles each participant plays in the group, such as clown, hero, parent, rebel, peacekeeper, antagonist, and so on. As the group worker helps the participants realize their group roles, he or she can help members gain insights to share with their families, as well as their pat terns of behavior in the group.

Several methods are available to measure how individuals evolve and improve the quality of their lives, such as behavioral reports, surveys, observations, record reviews, and self-reports. In a behavioral report, someone other than the patient/client completes the instrument measuring a change in the behavior being reviewed. Behavioral reports are used in counseling, speech, and occupational therapy and may include behaviors such as communication, eye contact, body posture, and clarity clear of speech. A survey may measure attitudes, personality style, or other aspects of life by having the reporter or investigator complete a series of questions. Observational reports are often used by the social worker to determine progress at home, in the marriage/family, or at work. Items such as concentration level, ability to stay focused, and appropriate speech may be discussed. Record reviews are used most often by the professional staff, an interdisciplinary team that reads the nursing notes and progress notes in the patient's chart to see how the patient is progressing. Issued such as compliance, motivation, goal-directed behavior, and social and emotional growth are usually reviewed. Self-report measures are those that ask patients how they feel about their health, progress, relationships, self-esteem, sense of satisfaction, goals, and so on. Self-report scales allow patients to report how they view their own behaviors, thoughts, and feelings. Self-respect measures play an integral role in assessing the changes in the patient, particularly when contrasted to the other reports completed by the social worker, interdisciplinary team members, and family members.

In conclusion, it is essential for the group worker to provide a climate conducive to change. The worker must facilitate the change among the between group members and assess the change in the quality of life in the group setting, in the natural environment, and within the patients as they become increasingly rehabilitated.

NATIONAL RESOURCES

American Rehabilitation Counseling
  Association
599 Stevenson Ave.
Alexandria, VA 22304-3300
(800) 347-6647

Braintree Hospital Rehabilitation
  Network
P.O. Box 859020
Braintree, MA 02185
(617) 848-5353

Coma Recovery Association
377 Jerusalem Ave.
Hempstead, NY 11550
(516) 486-2847

Head Injury Hotline
P.O. Box 84151
(206) 329-1371

International Association for the
Study of Traumatic Brain Injury
Dr. Felix Vincenz
St. Louis State Hospital
St. Louis, MO 63139
(314) 644-8403

National Head Injury Foundation
(NHIF)
1140 Connecticut Ave. NW
Washington, DC 20036
(202) 296-6443 or
(800) 444-NHIF

Institute for Mental Health Initiatives
4545 42nd St. NW
Washington, DC 20016
(202) 364-7111

Thank You Research
818 Connecticut Ave. NW
Washington, DC 20036
(202) 872-0315

REFERENCES

Aliev, Z. M. (1984). Characteristics of the clinical course of closed head injury in children. *Soviet Neurology and Psychiatry, 17*, 65–73.

Bakay, L., & Glasauer, F. E. (1980). *Head injury.* Boston: Little, Brown.

Becker, D. P., Miller, J. D., & Ward, J. D. (1977). The outcome from severe head injury with early diagnosis and intensive management. Journal of Neurosurgery, 47, 491–502.

Brooks, D. N., & McKinlay, W. (1983). Personality and behavioral change after severe blunt head injury: A relative's view. *Journal of Neurology, Neurosurgery, and Psychiatry, 46*, 336–344.

Chadwick, O., Rutter, M., Brown, G., Chaffer, D., & Traub, M. (1981). A prospective study of children with head injuries: Part II. Cognitive sequelae. *Psychological Medicine, 11*, 49–61.

Ephross, P. H., & Vassil, T. V. (1988). *Groups that work.* New York: Columbia University Press.

Epperson, M. M. (1977). Families in sudden crisis: Process and intervention in a critical care center. *Social Work in Health Care, 2*, 265–273.

Garvin, C. D. (1987). *Contemporary group work* (2nd ed.). Rahwah, NJ: Prentice Hall.

Gerring, J. (1986). The diagnosis, treatment, and rehabilitation of severe closed head injury. Speech presented at the Johns Hopkins University School of Medicine, Baltimore, June 15.

Hartford, M. E. (1971). *Groups in social work.* New York: Columbia University Press.

Hill, J. (1984). Disorders of memory, language, and beliefs, following closed head injury. *Psychological Medicine, 14*, 193–201.

Kraus, J. F., Black, M. A., & Hessol, N. (1984). The incidence of acute brain injury and serious impairment in a defined population. *American Journal of Epidemiology, 199*, 186–201.

Maryland Head Injury Foundation. (1985). *Maryland Head Injury Foundation Newsletter*, p. 1.

Maryland Head Injury Foundation. (1989). *Maryland Head Injury Foundation Newsletter*, p. 1.

Maryland Head Injury Foundation. (1990). *Maryland Head Injury Foundation Newsletter*, p. 1.

Prigatano, G., Fordyce, D., Zeiner, H., Roveche, J., Pepping, M., & Wood, B., (1984). Neuropsychological rehabilitation after closed head injury in young adults. *Journal of Neurology, Neurosurgery, and Psychiatry, 47,* 505–513.

Weddell, R., Oddy, M., & Jenkins, D. (1980). Social adjustment after rehabilitation: A two year follow-up of patients with severe head injury. *Psychological Medicine, 10,* 257–263.

Yalom, I. (1995). *The theory and practice of group psychotherapy* (4th ed.). New York: Basic Books.

II

ADJUSTING TO CHANGE

5

Support Groups for Widows and Widowers

Carolyn Ambler Walter

REVIEW OF THE LITERATURE

The loss of a spouse is considered the most stressful life event (Holmes & Rahe, 1967). Furthermore, in many respects, American society is a death-denying culture that views death as an unnatural occurrence rather than as a universal phase of the life cycle. Our society's superficial and often sanitized reaction to death makes it very difficult for a widow or widower to give vent to genuine and, at times, intense expressions of grief. People in general are uncomfortable at the expression of unhappiness and do not want to be reminded of their own mortality (Kinderknecht & Hodges, 1990). Society can also make widowed persons "feel that their behavior is abnormal: society decides when one has grieved long enough, then lets the bereaved know that it is time to bury the dead and get on with the living" (Kinderknecht & Hodges, 1990, p. 47). A support group can combat this insensitive "society schedule" and help bereaved spouses establish their own timetable of grieving.

Many researchers have noted that "preventive intervention early in the bereavement process may lessen the morbidity and mortality associated with the death of a spouse" (Barrett, 1978; Hiltz, 1975; Jones, 1979; McCourt, Barnett, Brennan, & Becker, 1976; Rachael, 1977; Yalom & Vinogradov, 1988, p. 420). Bereavement support groups represent an excellent approach to this highly vulnerable population because the small group format can specifically address and lessen the "intense social isolation experienced by most bereaved spouses" (Yalom & Vinogradov, 1988, p. 420). Within the past 8 years, support groups for bereaved spouses have proliferated in many different settings to provide important support for working through the grief of a loss that is profound and highly stressful, changing life irrevocably (Kinderknecht & Hodges, 1990; Lewis & Berns, 1975).

PURPOSE OF SUPPORT GROUPS

Although there is some disagreement regarding the efficacy of support groups as a change agent in the lives of widows and widowers (Levy, Derby, & Martinkowski, 1993; Tudiver, Hilditch, Permaul, & McKendree, 1992), the literature in general supports the usefulness of support groups for bereaved spouses (Barrett, 1978; Folken, 1991; Kay, DeZapien, Wilson, & Yoder, 1993; Kinderknecht & Hodges, 1990; Lieberman, 1989; Lieberman & Videka-Sherman, 1986; Rognlie, 1989). Some authors state that there is a connection between the degree of social engagement and positively perceived change in the bereaved spouse's functioning (Folken, 1991; Kauffman, 1994; Lopata, 1986, p. 212). The "social linkages" within the spousal bereavement group are seen as critical factors in positive change; neither time alone nor mere contact with a self-help group is sufficient to enhance the mental health of the widowed (Lieberman, 1989; Lieberman & Videka-Sherman, 1986). In self-help groups, the widows who established new social contacts with other widows were the only ones who experienced relief from their distress (Lieberman & Videka-Sherman, 1986). Therapeutic experiences such as cognitive structuring or affective discharge alone may not be sufficient to "change the psychological balance incrementally" (Lieberman & Videka-Sherman, 1986, p. 447). These findings suggest that for certain bereaved spouses, individual psychotherapy alone may not be enough to effect change.

Support groups for bereaved spouses have several goals. One is to assist the members to cope with the pain of grief and mourning (including the "holding on" and "letting go" processes) "by creating a temporary community in which they [are] deeply understood by peers" (Yalom & Vinogradov, 1988, p. 443); a second is to help combat the social isolation that is so pervasive for this population and to provide "consensual validation" for spouses regarding their bereavement experiences (Yalom & Vinogradov, 1988); and a third is to support members as they begin to understand the changes facing them as they begin to fashion a new future for themselves.

PRACTICE PRINCIPLES

Norms

Social rules of mourning tend to encourage people to feel that it is appropriate to avoid their grief. Within support groups for bereaved spouses,

"Norms (shared agreement among group members) sanction and facilitate the experience of the pain of loss and need to be carefully cultivated and secured in the group process" (Kauffman, 1994, p. 165). The social worker must work to create a group climate that permits the expression of grief (including permission for its prolongation) while encouraging the forging of a new life (Lieberman, 1989; Yalom & Vinogradov, 1988). This is no small task, as bereaved spouses seem to experience a tension between the process of change (the letting go of one's old life and moving forward) and a sense of "devotion or love for the deceased spouse" (Lieberman, 1989, p. 439).

Kauffman (1994), Lawrence (1992), and Folken (1991) consider the critical function of "mirroring" within support groups for widows and widowers. When mirroring occurs, it sanctions grief (mutual and reciprocal recognition of one's grief) and facilitates the release and experiencing of grief. "It provides the sense that one is known by another in the intimacy of pain" (Kauffman, 1994, p. 163). Folken (1991) also discusses the importance of establishing a therapeutic bond between grieving people, which encourages a mutual acknowledgment of suffering and a recognition of differences in ways of coping with grief, and thus supports the effort at recovery. Talking or listening to others talk about their feelings reassures newly bereaved spouses that they are not losing their minds as they learn how bizarre and erratic the grief process can be. Kauffman agrees that "group members frequently discover their own feelings through recognizing the feeling in and through another" (1994, p. 163).

The mirroring function develops when group members feel comfortable with one another. Therefore, early in the group's history, a group climate must be established in which members can share openly with one another. The mirroring process lessens the sense of social isolation and the narcissistic injury associated with the loss of a spouse. The experience of normalization offered by a support group provides a feeling of acceptance that helps the individual to address the stigma associated with being a widowed adult in our society (Lieberman, 1989).

Since research (Lieberman, 1989; Lieberman & Videka-Sherman, 1986) suggests that "members who have made social linkages in the group show higher positive change . . . compared to members who attend meetings only" (Lieberman & Videka-Sherman, 1986, p. 444), norms that develop strong group cohesion through active participation and meaningful interactions among members must be encouraged to develop. Support groups with "high social exchange" characteristics develop a group climate that encourages the expression of a wide range of feelings, both unhappy and happy, and motivates group members to get together outside of the formal meetings. To encourage outside socializing, the worker can suggest that members who so choose meet after the formal group session for coffee at a local restaurant (without the leader).

Role of the Leader

Although social workers may facilitate the process by introducing topics or structured exercises, the most important task is to refrain from interfering with the natural course and currents of the group, and to be attentive to the timing of interventions so as to not inhibit important spontaneous interactions in the group (Kauffman, 1994; Kliban, Hanig, & Schnitzer-Newson, 1984; Lawrence, 1992; Lieberman, 1989; Rognlie, 1989; Yalom & Vinogradov, 1988, p. 424). The most important role of social workers seems to be to "anticipate and facilitate a natural process of self-exploration and change" by staying out of the way or by serving as "gentle midwives" to issues and concerns that emerge spontaneously (Yalom & Vinogradov, 1988, p. 445). Kauffman (1994) concurs and further suggests that leaders of bereavement groups need to be especially aware of their own reactions to the pain and the meaning of death in order to be able to create a group climate in which grieving can occur.

Structure

While the inclusion of a structured educational format may be an appropriate and helpful part of the design for a support group for bereaved spouses, a word of caution is in order: If the group is too structured, the leader may be playing into his or her own anxiety about grieving and death or allowing the group to play into theirs. "Structuring of bereavement groups often serves the purpose of suppressing the pain of loss and death" (Kauffman, 1994, p. 170). Yalom began his work with bereavement groups by using structured group exercises but soon reported that "the members welcomed a simple forum where they could talk openly and the imposition of structure was thus generally counterproductive" (Yalom & Vinogradov, 1988, p. 426).

However, educational provisions "may be informative in ways that reassure and normalize and may help focus and contain diffuse or marginally conscious grief" (Kauffman, 1994, p. 171). This author has found that a combination approach is particularly helpful. The group can begin with a "go-round" for each member to state where he or she is in the process for that particular session and then follow with some didactic material that can be discussed either in the larger group (if there are eight or fewer members) or in smaller subgroups of three members. The larger group can then reconvene for the last half hour of the session to share material and experiences of the subgroups.

Regarding the use of homework and structured exercises, Rognlie (1989) found that many participants considered remembering their spouses, by sharing photos and experiences, to be the most helpful aspect of the program, while homework was considered the least helpful. Lawrence (1992) and Yalom and Vinogradov (1988) found the use of photos was particularly helpful in facilitating the widow's ability to accept her new reality while relating to the loss she had experienced.

The literature on support groups for bereaved spouses is split on whether groups should be time-limited or open-ended. Yalom and Vinogradov (1988) advocate fairly short-term work with such groups. The advantage of short-term, time-limited groups is that a cohesive group forms more easily with a steady, unchanging membership. Within time-limited groups, the members form a stronger bond and the culture may be safer to introduce (in the later sessions) discussions about the less idealized, more problematic areas of marriage. These areas include "anger at the dead spouse and at oneself for things left unsaid in the marriage, resentment over fixed, restrictive roles, and guilt about new or future relationships" (Yalom & Vinogradov, 1988, p. 431). In addition, termination issues can be handled more directly with the group members as they relate to the grieving process. The literature surveyed indicates that time-limited groups involve 6 to 15 sessions.

However, Kauffman (1994) suggests that the "advantage of an ongoing group is that it can be available to diverse needs over time and see a person through the process, as needed" (1994, p. 171). This quality of open-ended groups mirrors the grieving process, which "flows in fits and starts" with "unanticipated outbreaks of grief and shifts in focus" (p. 171). In open-ended groups, members can choose a short-term experience and stay for 6 to 15 sessions, or they may stay for up to 1 or 2 years. Another advantage of an open-ended group is that the newer members (probably those more newly widowed) who join the group can learn a great deal from those further along in the grieving process. This experience provides hope for the newly widowed (a crucial element to recovery) and an opportunity for the experienced widows and widowers to assess their progress.

Group Composition

It is important to honor the principle of homogeneity in group composition because widowed adults wish to be with others who have had an experience like their own (Kauffman, 1994). However, the common situation of bereaved spouses is "such a powerful commonality that it [the group] is able to incorporate individual differences in background and personality" (Gitterman, 1989, p. 8) without leading to intense interpersonal conflict. Moreover, both the literature (Kauffman, 1994; Lieberman, 1989) and the author's personal/professional experiences suggest that homogeneity in group membership should be preserved for factors such as age and type of bereavement. That is, specific groups should be created for bereaved spouses under age 50, whose tasks and needs may be different from those of widows and widowers over 50. This is particularly true with regard to being a single parent and coping with children who are still living at home. Furthermore, combining men and women in support groups for bereaved spouses seems to be useful in allowing both sexes to begin to relate again to the opposite sex, something very difficult to do following the loss of a spouse.

Termination

As with all groups, termination requires two basic tasks with which social workers must provide help. The first task is to deal with the loss and say good-bye, acknowledging the ending of the group and facing other feelings evoked by termination. In a bereaved spouse group, the issue of group termination evokes powerful feelings related to the loss of the spouse allowing another opportunity to confront the grief. Time must be provided within the group for this process, as it is a most powerful one with this particular population. The second task is to deal with regret over unfinished business and work left undone by the group (Yalom & Vinogradov, 1988). This allows bereaved spouses to cope with the issue of regret over unexpressed sentiments in their marriage. The ending of the group provides an opportunity to acknowledge this reaction. One method that can be used to help this process is to have group members write a letter to their deceased spouses telling them the things that were left unsaid.

With this population, it seems helpful to encourage informal group meetings following termination of the formal group (Lieberman & Videka-Sherman, 1986; Yalom & Vinogradov, 1988). If a group is ongoing, it is important to structure the comings and goings of members and to urge members to let the group know prior to their last session, so that there is time for the group to discuss feelings about the termination.

COMMON THEMES
Loneliness and Isolation

Widowhood is considered the most isolating crisis event associated with marriage. Often the widow/widower is unprepared for the degree of isolation that experienced following the death of a spouse (Kinderknecht & Hodges, 1990; Lopata, 1986). The issue of isolation is a central one to be addressed in a support group for bereaved spouses (Folken, 1991; Kauffman, 1994; Kinderknecht & Hodges, 1990; Lieberman & Videka-Sherman, 1986; Yalom & Vinogradov, 1988).

There are two basic types of loneliness common to bereaved spouses. One involves the "loss of daily intimacies of shared routines and private moments," as well as the loss of family holidays, time spent with children and grandchildren, and sexual and romantic closeness (Yalom & Vinogradov, 1988, p. 435). The other type of loneliness is that of "no longer being the single most important person in someone's life, nor of having a single significant other with whom to share important experiences" (Yalom & Vinogradov, 1988, p. 436). One widow (aged 47 at the death of her husband) lamented, when invited by the group leader to share what members felt was most difficult for them, "I no longer feel special to anyone." The social worker can encourage possible growth for this member with a response such as "If you have felt that special to someone, you obviously made your husband feel special; you can do that again." This turns the passive grief experience of loss into a potential, active growth experience in which bereaved spouses can begin viewing themselves as active persons again. Another aspect of loneliness is the feeling that much of one's history died with one's spouse. Each member has lost the one person who has known him or her over time and who shared the same memories.

While friends and family return to their lives following this loss, widowed spouses must face the task of bereavement, for the most part, by themselves. The phase of disorientation that inevitably follows the loss of a spouse often brings with it the underlying fear that one is "going to pieces." Because of this severe degree of isolation, membership in a support group for widows and widowers can be beneficial. In one group for widows and widowers under the age of 50, a 42-year-old woman remarked, 2 months after the loss of her husband: "I can remember feeling the first break in the severe sense of loneliness and isolation I had been experiencing following the death of my husband during my drive home, after attending the second session of our support group. I knew other people felt the way I did—that I wasn't alone in the world for the first time in a long while."

Coming home to an empty house is one of the most difficult adjustments that widowed adults must make. That night following a support group session was a turning point for this widow in coming home.

Identity Change—We to I

An issue of equal importance facing widowed spouses is the task of establishing a new identity. "To lose a spouse is to lose something of one's self; many spouses experience seeing themselves as "only half a person" following the loss of their husband or wife (Kinderknecht & Hodges, 1990, p. 43). For women, one aspect of formulating a new identity is that of title because many women have been known as Mrs. Somebody. In reorganizing her life the widow must decide what her title will be.

In his research on support groups for bereaved spouses, Lieberman (1989) considers the important task of reconstituting a "coherent and consistent self-concept, including addressing feelings of grief and mourning and integrating these feelings into ongoing psychological portraits of themselves" (p. 206). Issues to be discussed in the support group surrounding this task are (1) examining the meaning and importance of the lost relationship; (2) addressing the transition necessary for bereaved spouses in negotiating a new role that is not based on a couple relationship; and (3) highlighting the problems of loosening/renegotiating old ties with friends and family and developing new social relationships.

One effective exercise is to ask group members to consider the transition from spouse to widow to single adult. Group members are invited to free-associate feelings and thoughts they have about each status, taking each one individually. The group leader writes these reactions on a blackboard or flipchart and then leads a general discussion about the group's reactions.

Another identity issue for both men and women involves their new role within the couple's old circle of friends. When the spouse who is now bereaved was part of a couple, this social network was probably comprised mostly of other couples. It can be painful to be with these friends now, and the bereaved spouse may wonder how he or she will fit in and feel comfortable as a single person in this social network.

Widows who were doing well (Lieberman, 1989; Lieberman & Borman, 1979; Vachon, 1979) displayed an ability to get on with their lives that seemed to involve a shift in identity from wife to widow to woman—a shift that allowed the past to inform the present. This movement was more evident in those who had participated in groups for bereaved spouses than in those who had not (Vachon, 1979). Lopata's (1986) review of the literature suggests that the reconstruction of the self (for widows) "requires communication with others; the women most aware of changes in the self are least isolated. The person can engage in new behavior and observe the self in change, but it is in interaction that this consciousness is crystallized" (p. 213). It seems clear that support groups can aid the widowed adult in this process of reconstruction of self.

Although there have been few documented studies of men's grief following the loss of a spouse, researchers examining gender differences have generally found more similarities than differences (Brabant, Forsyth, & Melancon, 1992, p. 35). They found that men, like women, following the death of their spouse experienced a severe loss of their sense of identity. This research seems to refute the notion that the wife is less central to the husband's life than the husband is to the wife's. One man reported: "I thought I was a real individual before she died, but afterwards I realized she was a big part of me" (Brabant et al., 1992, p. 43). In another support group for bereaved spouses, all five men in the group reported a loss of the sense of self. The men in this group experienced their wives as central to their lives and perceived that their identity as a spouse had been critical to their sense of themselves. One 45-year-old widower poignantly said: "I feel like half of me is gone now that my wife is gone—we made all of our decisions together." The restructuring of identity following the loss of a spouse may be as critical for men as for women. This is an important consideration for social workers, who may believe the popular notion that men are protected from the impact of bereavement because their wives are less central to their identities due to the strong presence of a career or work identity prior to the loss of their spouses.

Relationships

The importance of discussing relationships and intimacy is central to the issue of identity change from we to I. Following the loss of a spouse, one of the most significant areas of change is relationships—with friends, immediate and extended family, in-laws, and social networks. For bereaved spouses, particularly in the younger age group (under 60), dating is a very important, difficult, and conflicted issue, made more difficult by all of the changes in social norms and mores within the last 20 to 30 years since these adults last dated.

The issue of loyalty to one's dead spouse also plays a part in the conflict around dating experienced by many bereaved spouses. The idea of loving someone new can evoke a wide range of feelings. In a group for bereaved spouses, some members usually see this desire as a signal of healing and a readiness to move forward; others see it as a betrayal of their marriage, as if loving someone new might somehow invalidate the love they had for their spouse. It is constructive for the worker to help the group understand the fallacy of believing that only a finite amount of love is available. In one group for bereaved spouses under age 50, several new members were sharing their concern about their capacity to ever love another person again. A 32-year-old widow, whose husband had died 9 months prior to this session and who had very recently started dating, poignantly told the group that "this capacity comes in time, and what you learn to do is to keep your love for your spouse in a corner of your heart which goes untouched by any new relationship." Other group members compared this experience to the way parents often feel prior to the birth of a second child—"How will I ever love the second child as much as the first?" This comment was discussed by several members after the group session that night as being critical to their beginning to understand the possibility of loving again.

Since this issue is a very sensitive one, if the group is time limited and closed, it is better to introduce the topic of dating after some group cohesion has developed. If the group is open-ended or is an ongoing series (with sessions in the fall, winter, and spring), it is better to introduce this topic near the end, when some members who have dated can share their experiences.

Yalom and Vinogradov (1988) report that the issues of dating and relationships created a major division between the men and women in their support groups. "The men were far more driven to form new relationships," while the women were "more hesitant to become romantically involved with someone new too soon and seemed anxious about the idea of being pursued or, worse yet, being pursuers" (p. 441). In groups with which the author has been involved, this has not been the case.

Time and Ritual

Another important issue related to forging a new life from the old one while coping with the grief process is handling important marker events (such as anniversaries, birthdays, holidays, weddings, and graduations) that were once shared experiences. It is important for group members to share their experiences with regard to how they celebrated these occasions as married persons, and then to hear from "group veterans" how they handled these same marker events as single, widowed adults. At the beginning of each session, members may be encouraged to discuss important events coming up for them. A special session around family holidays on how to cope with the bereaved spouse's reactions can also be included.

Group members can be extremely helpful in sharing how they cope with the anxiety and depression surrounding holidays and may provide ways to ward off intense reactions. One young widow with five children spoke of how she handled the day of the wedding anniversary following the first year of her husband's death. Sandra described her plan of hiring a babysitter and treating herself to a day-long tour of a local arboretum with several friends. When she reported back to the group about her experience, she smiled and said that it had definitely helped her through the day.

The other major marker event is the first anniversary of the death of the spouse. One 55-year-old Protestant widow borrowed from the Jewish tradition and planned an unveiling ceremony at the graveside for close friends and family. In addition to placing the marker at the graveside, this widow shared thoughts from letters she received from many friends and family members following her husband's death. In sharing her experience with the group, she stated emphatically that this process itself helped her to let go of her husband and that life seemed easier afterward.

Another issue related to ritual and coping with marker events is confusion about the proper length of time for the grieving process. It is important to have a discussion early in the group's history about the notion of "shoulds" and how they provide an "invisible burden" for bereaved spouses (Yalom & Vinogradov, 1988, p. 427). When members are invited to share the "shoulds" they carry around, ideas like "one should grieve for a whole year" or "one should (or should not) quickly give away the spouse's clothing" quickly emerge. Discussion centering on the idea that each person establishes his or her own rhythm for grieving usually provides a liberating experience for group members.

Handling Anger and Other Negative Reactions

Handling anger and other negative reactions is often not focused on directly in support groups for bereaved spouses. In the author's experience and according to Yalom and Vinogradov (1988), dealing with negative feelings is an important part of the grieving process. However, this is a difficult issue for bereaved spouses, who are often struggling to hold on to the positive aspects of a relationship that they desperately miss. It is difficult to confront the fact that the bereaved are angry at their spouses for "leaving them" or that there are negative aspects of their marital relationship that they must let go of, as well as positive ones. This difficulty is magnified by society's tendency to "sanctify" persons who have died, putting them on a pedestal (Lopata, 1979). Yalom and Vinogradov (1988) found that group members were more able to direct anger toward physicians who had missed a diagnosis or had been insensitive to the needs of the patient and/or family. Expressing anger toward the dead spouse for abandoning the survivor, or for persistent denial while ill, was much more difficult. It is probably most effective to plan a discussion of this topic near the middle or end of a series (if closed ended) or wait until a nucleus of members has formed in an open-ended group.

One exercise that can help bereaved spouses cope with their positive and negative feelings about their marital relationship is having them work in triads, so that each member can role play and/or discuss with a partner two positive and two negative aspects of the marital relationship. After identifying each aspect, it is helpful to have the members say good-bye to that aspect of the relationship with the deceased partner.

There is also considerable anger that cannot be easily focused—"anger at life, at destiny, at the unfairness of it all" (Yalom & Vinogradov, 1988, p. 442). This can be introduced as a discussion topic, but it flows more easily from group members' comments. There is often new realization that this is an unjust world, and that neither working hard as a couple nor doing good in the world guarantees a protected life.

Taking Responsibility for and Care of Oneself

The death of a spouse confronts the remaining partner with his or her own mortality. While there are usually increased fears about being alone, feelings of abandonment, and concerns about physical safety and health, many bereaved spouses use increased awareness about death in a positive way. "The death of their spouses served . . . to teach them existential responsibility—that they, and only they, have ultimate responsibility for their life and their happiness" (Yalom & Vinogradov, 1988, p. 143). This is a profound statement, and is particularly salient for bereaved spouses who married at a young age and may have viewed their marriage and/or their marital partner as the key to their lifelong happiness. It is not easy to move from feeling abandoned by one's spouse to taking responsibility for one's life.

In the author's experience as a social worker, one of the most helpful techniques is to tell the group members from the beginning (and reinforce it in every session) how important it is to take care of oneself—to discover or rediscover what activities nourish and promote relaxation. It is also important to lead group discussions on this topic so that members can exchange ideas about the range of activities that each finds nurturing. Another method for approaching a session on taking care of oneself is to provide a more didactic review of all the areas that are subject to abuse when an individual experiences prolonged stress and/or mourning and to suggest recommendations for coping with these problems. Topics to be covered can include physical activity, exercise, sleep, nutrition, substance abuse, finances, excessive spending or frugality, social networking, and entertaining (Kliban et al., 1984).

When a review is conducted at the end of a group's sessions, members frequently state that one of the most helpful experiences within the support group was that "I learned to be good to myself" (Kliban et al., 1984, p. 14). Both men and women leave the group with this new learning for their new lives and especially appreciate the social worker's encouragement in this area.

EVALUATION APPROACHES

The literature suggests both informal and formal approaches to evaluation of support groups for bereaved adults. One informal method is to ask group members to summarize at the end of each session and to comment on its negative and positive aspects. Group leaders can complete periodic self-appraisals by using a process log to identify areas for improvement (Heiney & Wells, 1989). They can also evaluate various group processes using predetermined criteria based on the goals and important norms to be established.

A more formal evaluation approach is to use written questionnaires completed by the participants and/or the group leaders. If the group is closed-ended and meets for a defined number of sessions, these questionnaires can be distributed and completed during the final session. If the group is open-ended and ongoing, the questionnaire can be distributed to members during their last session with the group and returned by mail. In either case, questionnaires can also be mailed several months after the members' participation in the group. One questionnaire (Heiney & Wells, 1989) suggests the following questions:

1. Was it helpful to attend a bereavement support group?
2. Would you prefer an ongoing group or a series of 4, 6, 8, or 10 sessions?
3. Was the content applicable to you?
4. What areas of concern were not addressed?
5. Were books and handouts helpful?
6. What was the most helpful aspect of this group experience for you?
7. What was the least helpful aspect of this group experience for you?
8. Would you attend other meetings if it could be arranged?

Folken (1991) mailed a more formal 15-item questionnaire to 137 widowed adults who had participated in meetings within a 2-year period. This survey was conducted to determine if the leaders' perceived benefits coincided with the participants' expectations. These included "1) reaching additional widowed, 2) affording [an] opportunity to interact with a variety of other widowed in a comfortable and caring environment, 3) presenting diversity in ways of coping with grief and chances to evaluate these various methods for personal use, and 4) providing many models of progress through grief" (Folken, 1991, p. 176).

Rognlie (1989) used a more detailed instrument (see the appendix) for evaluation of the perceived short- and long-term effects of bereavement support group participation (23 of the 30 members surveyed were widowed spouses). Rognlie mailed the questionnaire and a covering letter to participants who had attended the support groups at least 1 year before completing the questionnaire. After the mailing, the subjects were interviewed by phone, and the responses to the questionnaire were collected and recorded. The questionnaire consists of questions both about the group and about personal issues. "The subjects were asked to evaluate their group experience on a rating scale from 'not helpful' to 'very helpful' as well as to answer more subjective questions in written form" (Rognlie, 1989, p. 43).

CONCLUSION

In conclusion, this chapter has provided a summary of the literature and the author's experiences related to the purposes, practice principles, common themes, and evaluation approaches in designing and leading support groups for widows and widowers. Following is a list of national sources that can be used for further information and services for widowed adults.

NATIONAL RESOURCES

Association for Deaf Education and
  Counseling
638 Prospect Ave.
Hartford, CT 06105
(203) 586-7503

Growth Opportunity Program
626 Haverford Road
Haverford, PA 19041
(215) 649-8255

Widowed Persons' Services
601 E St. NW
Washington, DC 20049
(202) 434-2260

REFERENCES

Barrett, C. (1978). Effectiveness of widows' groups in facilitating change. *Journal of Consulting Clinical Psychology, 46*, 20–31.

Brabant, S., Forsyth, C., & Melancon, C. (1992). Grieving men: Thoughts, feelings, and behaviors following deaths of wives. *Hospice Journal, 8*(4), 33–47.

Folken, M. (1991). The importance of group support for widowed persons. *Journal for Specialists in Group Work, 16*(3), 172–177.

Gitterman, A. (1989). Building mutual support in groups. *Social Work in Groups, 12*(2), 5–21.

Heiney, S., & Wells, L. (1989). Strategies for organizing and maintaining successful support groups. *Oncology Nursing Forum, 16*(6), 803–809.

Hiltz, S. (1975). Helping widows: Group discussions as a therapeutic technique. *Family Coordinator, 24*, 331–336.

Holmes, T. H. & Rahe, R. H. (1967). The social adjustment rating scale. *Journal of Psychosomatic Research, 11*, 213–218.

Jones, D. (1979). The grief therapy project: The effects of group therapy with bereaved surviving spouses on successful coping with grief. Doctoral dissertation. *Dissertation Abstracts International, 39,* 6121–6122.

Kauffman, J. (1994). Group thanatropics. In V. Schermer & M. Pines (Eds.), *Ring of fire* (pp. 149–173). London: Routledge.

Kay, M., DeZapien, J., Wilson, C., & Yoder, M. (1993). Evaluating treatment efficacy by triangulation. *Social Science Medicine, 36*(12), 1545–1552.

Kinderknecht, C., & Hodges, L. (1990). Facilitating productive bereavement of widows: An overview of the efficacy of widows. *Journal of Women and Aging, 2*(4), 39–54.

Kliban, M., Hanig, F., & Schnitzer-Newson, G. (1984, September). Bereavement counseling in groups. *Caring,* 12–18.

Lawrence, L. (1992). Till death do us part: The application of object relations theory to facilitate mourning in a young widow's group. *Social Work in Health Care, 16*(3), 67–81.

Levy, L., Derby, J., & Martinkowski, K. (1993). Effects of membership in bereavement support groups on adaptation to conjugal bereavement. *American Journal of Community Psychology, 21*(3), 361–381.

Lewis, A., & Berns, B. (1975). *Three out of four wives: Widowhood in America.* New York: Macmillan.

Lieberman, M. (1989). Group properties and outcomes: A study of group norms in self-help groups for widows and widowers. *International Journal of Group Psychotherapy, 39*(2), 191–208.

Lieberman, M., & Borman, M. (1979). *Self-help groups for coping with crisis.* San Francisco: Jossey-Bass.

Lieberman, M., & Videka-Sherman, L. (1986). The impact of self-help groups on the mental health of widows and widowers. *American Journal of Orthopsychiatry, 56*(3), 435–449.

Lopata, H. (1979). *Women as widows.* New York: Elsevier North-Holland.

Lopata, H. (1986). Becoming and being a widow: Reconstruction of the self and support systems. *Journal of Geriatric Psychiatry, 19*(2), 203–214.

McCourt, W., Barnett, R., Brennan, J., & Becker, A. (1976). We help each other: Primary prevention for the widowed. *American Journal of Psychiatry, 133,* 98–100.

Raphael, B. (1977). Preventive intervention with the recently bereaved. *Archives of General Psychiatry, 34,* 1450–1454.

Rognlie, C. (1989). Perceived short- and long-term effects of bereavement support group participation at the hospice of Petaluma. *Hospice Journal, 5*(2), 39–53.

Tudiver, F., Hilditch, J., Permaul, J., & McKendree, D. (1992). *Evaluation and the Health Professions, 15*(2), 147–162.

Vachon, M. (1979). *Identity change over the first two years of bereavement: Social relationships and social support in widowhood.* Unpublished doctoral dissertation, York University, Toronto.

Yalom, I., & Vinogradov, S. (1988). Bereavement groups: Techniques and themes. *International Journal of Group Psychotherapy, 38*(4), 419–446.

APPENDIX: BEREAVEMENT
SUPPORT GROUP EVALUATION*

Background Information

Age   Sex
Date client began support group

>   1 = Not helpful
>   2 = Uncertain
>   3 = A little helpful
>   4 = Moderately helpful
>   5 = Very helpful

1. In general, the support group was: 1 2 3 4 5
2. Learning about the grief process and the
    manifestations of grief was: 1 2 3 4 5
3. Being able to share my feelings with others who
    had gone through something similar was: 1 2 3 4 5
4. The knowledge and/or support of the group
    leaders was: 1 2 3 4 5
5. Making new friends and reaching out to other
    people in grief was: 1 2 3 4 5
6. Talking about the spouse who died was: 1 2 3 4 5
7. Hearing others talk about their feelings and
    experiences was: 1 2 3 4 5
8. Reading, writing and homework assignments
    were: 1 2 3 4 5
9. The topics covered during the groups were: 1 2 3 4 5
10. Do you feel that participation in a bereavement support group
    made a difference in the way that you dealt with your loss at the
    time? If so, how?
11. Has your past involvement in a support group affected how you
    have dealt with your loss over an extended period of time? If so,
    how? For example has it affected how you deal with stress, eating or
    sleeping patterns, or social interactions?
12. In retrospect, would you have chosen to attend a support group,
    having had the experience? Why or why not?
13. Would you recommend a bereavement support group to a bereaved
    friend or family member?
14. Have you kept in contact with, or formed friendships with, any of
    your previous group members?
15. Can you suggest how any benefits of support group interactions
    could be maintained or increased after the group is over?

---

*From Rognlie, 1989, pp. 51–52.

6

Group Work with Noncustodial Parents

Geoffrey L. Greif

Family breakup (and its correlates) looms as one of the major social problems of the 1990s. The number of one-parent families with children under 18 increased by 280% between 1970 and 1994, while the number of married-couple families fell slightly (U.S. Bureau of the Census, 1995). Even when children are not involved, divorce is often accompanied by residential and economic instability, loss of key adult relationships, destruction of one's hope of "living happily ever after," and anger, depression, and anxiety (Garvin, Kalter, & Hanswell, 1993; Pett & Vaughn-Cole, 1986). When children are present, the tasks associated with coping and the complexity of those tasks greatly increase (Portes, Howell, Brown, Eichenberger, & Mas, 1992).

After divorce, one parent often becomes a visitor in his or her child's life, a role that is not clearly defined. The parent usually loses, to varying degrees, some level of input into how that child will be raised and, in many instances, is relegated to having a minimal relationship with the child. Such a person is left in an ambiguous position both as a parent and as an adult trying to establish an identity. Sometimes isolated from friends, family, and other sources of support after the breakup, the noncustodial parent suffers.

Group experience can help reduce noncustodial parents' pain and provide a safe haven for exploring their relationship with their children.

For an earlier version of this article, see G. L. Greif & J. Kristall (1993). Common themes in a group for noncustodial parents. *Families in Society, 74,* 240–245.

This chapter describes a short-term support group for noncustodial parents, detailing common themes that emerged during the course of the group sessions.

REVIEW OF THE LITERATURE

The relationship of noncustodial fathers to their children is not clearly defined and has not been well researched (Kruk, 1994). The literature describes noncustodial fathers as struggling with and sometimes failing to maintain a relationship with their children after the breakup of their marriage. Over time, the relationship between the father and his children frequently deteriorates (Aquilino, 1994). Fathers may feel guilt about the failure of the marriage and inadequate as parents. Some fathers, smarting from the failed marital relationship, undergo intense conflict with their ex-wives that affects their ability to coparent (Dudley, 1991). When they have an acrimonious relationship with their ex-wives, it can spill over into their relationship with their children (Arditti & Kelly, 1994) and involve them in ongoing battles. Such stress may cause depression, low self-esteem, and disturbances in work performance and sleeping patterns (Coney & Mackey, 1989; Stewart, Schwebel, & Fine, 1986). Of course, not all fathers are negatively affected. Some use the single-parent experience to forge even stronger bonds with their children.

While noncustodial mothers suffer many of the same feelings and stresses as fathers (Depner, 1993; Greif, 1987), they also face additional ones. Women in our society earn less money than men. As they are socialized to be the primary caregivers of children, deviation from that norm often exposes them to disparaging comments from friends and family and creates a sense of failure. Because of the stigma associated with a mother's giving up custody, they are often reluctant to discuss their noncustodial status with others. Some choose to hide this aspect of their lives. Thus many experience guilt, shame, anxiety, and depression (Greif & Pabst, 1988; Rosenblum, 1986) and feel compelled to deal with these issues alone. Group treatment offers both of these populations the opportunity to meet with other parents in a supportive atmosphere where their reactions to being noncustodial can be approached.

PRACTICE PRINCIPLES

Meetings of the group discussed in this chapter were held at a family service agency in Baltimore. Clients were either referred from current caseloads or self-referred from advertisements describing a 4-week support group for noncustodial parents. The coleaders were the author, who was connected to the agency only during the leadership of this group, and a staff member in charge of single-parent issues who was always available to group members. Following a telephone screening interview, a core group was formed for a 4-week set of sessions. It was believed that a short-term group would have the best chance of attracting a sufficient number of members. Given the nature of this population, contracting played a large part in the establishment and initiation of the group. Contracting was important for the members because so much of their lives focused on the broken contract of marriage. In addition, many of them had been locked in legal battles concerning child support and visitation. By paying careful attention to expectations about attendance and participation, we believed we would pave the way for a successful group experience. A great deal of time was spent discussing obstacles to attendance (Shulman, 1992). Two people knew each other and were reluctant initially to share personal material; scheduling proved difficult for a few others. Contact outside of the group between members (something we did not discourage) was also discussed at the first session.

The leaders played an active role from the outset in starting and stopping the group and in guiding the discussion. We suggested topics and helped to facilitate discussion. We believed it was especially important to be central to the group, as there were only four sessions. With a longer-term group, we would have considered taking a more peripheral role in the middle stage. Interventions were kept to a minimum, though, as it was believed that the members might take suggestions as criticism or an indictment of their lifestyle. Since the group dealt with relationships in the broadest sense, we focused on this aspect of work with these parents. It became the underlying theme that we returned to continually throughout the meetings.

The group was sufficiently satisfying that the members requested two more 4-week sessions. When the group recontracted, we judged that internal leaders had emerged from the group and that we could assume a more peripheral role, except initially when a few new members joined and specific leader-related tasks had to be accomplished. In this way, our roles shifted as the group moved into later stages of its work.

With new members coming for the second set of sessions, a total of eight members attended at least one set of four group meetings. The typical number per group was five or six members. The members, who were in their mid-30s to mid-40s, were divided evenly between males and females. Their backgrounds varied. Most worked full time, though one of the men lost his job during the course of group meetings. One woman, previously unemployed, began volunteer work at the suggestion of group members. Members' children ranged in age from 5 to 22, and the number of children per parent ranged from two to four. Half of the members were remarried, and two members had children from their new marriage.

Group members varied in the amount and nature of contact they had with their children. Two mothers regularly visited their children but wanted more time because they were unhappy with the way the children were being raised. The other two mothers had little or no contact with their children. One of these mothers ended her marriage and left home; visitation was initiated while the children were living with their father.

Over time, the children became verbally and physically abusive to the mother, perhaps as an expression of their anger toward her for ending the marriage. She refused to see them until they began to treat her with respect. When she entered the group, she had not spoken with either child (both were in their teens) for 1 year. The other mother had experienced many ups and downs with her four children (12 to 22 years old); two of them refused to see her, and she refused to see the other two. Substance abuse, psychiatric hospitalizations, the suicide of a 16-year-old daughter, and a suicide attempt by another child made this mother's parenting situation extremely complicated.

The fathers also had difficult family situations. Two of them had children who lived at a great distance; although the children were allowed to visit, they did so only occasionally. Another father had regular visitation, and the fourth father had been rejected by his 22-year-old daughter and his 2-year-old son.

The different marital statuses of the members were not a critical factor in group work. Although the unmarried members seemed more lonely than those who had remarried, remarriage did not provide a buffer from the pain of separation from the children. Those who had remarried usually felt that their new spouses supported them in their anger at their children and in their battles with their ex-spouses. In some cases, the new spouses even helped escalate intrafamilial conflict. Remarriage did not seem to enhance members' ability to cope with the problems that brought them into the group.

As might be expected, relations with ex-spouses varied but tended to be acrimonious. Members showed signs of being significantly emotionally attached to their ex-spouses (Masheter, 1990), which made it difficult for some of the parents to separate their anger at their ex-spouses from their need to behave as competent coparents. This confusion emerged in the group. As members discussed their feelings toward their ex-spouses, members of the opposite sex sometimes jumped to the defense of the ex-spouses as the discussion touched on members' vulnerabilities.

COMMON THEMES

Various themes emerged during group work with these parents that could be addressed in future groups serving this population.

Children Rejecting Parents

The most painful issue for parents was their children's rejection of them. In some cases, children refused to see a parent for reasons that members often understood cognitively but found painful nonetheless. In a few instances, children chose to live with the other parent. For mothers, in particular, a child's electing to live with the father was devastating. Often, group members felt rejected when their children did not want to spend their prearranged visitation time with them if it interfered with peer activities. Group members proved particularly helpful to one of the fathers by interpreting his daughter's need to be with adolescent peers as age-appropriate behavior.

A hope frequently expressed by parents who were struggling with feelings of rejection was that their children would some day "return" to them or appreciate them more if they continued to behave in a consistent and caring manner. One mother who had not spoken with her children for a year continued to send them cards and to attend sporting events at their school so that her children would, she hoped, look back on this period in their lives and think more kindly of her. Despite this optimistic attitude, members struggled with deciding at what point their efforts to establish a relationship with rejecting children became self-defeating or too painful to continue. One parent wondered aloud how long he would continue to put himself in such an uncomfortable position.

Parents Rejecting Children

Some parents rejected their children because they felt their children had rejected them. Parents of preadolescents and adolescents in particular felt angry with their children. Rubbed raw by the divorce process and the legal wrangling that accompanied it, some parents were unable to assume an adult, parenting role. They treated their children more like peers or siblings than like children. They had difficulty seeing their children as needy because they themselves were too needy to step back and observe the parent–child dynamics. As a result, opportunities to reestablish contact with their children were often defeated by their own reactions.

Differences between Mothers and Fathers: Stigma, Money Matters, and Advice

Fathers and mothers tended to differ both in the issues they raised within the group and in their interactions with their children. Chief among these differences was the way in which they explained their noncustodial status to new acquaintances outside the group. As the literature suggests, women were much more apt to deny their noncustodial status. Two of the mothers recounted how they changed the subject or lied when they were asked if they had children. The fathers did not express such tendencies. Because fathers were generally court-ordered to pay child support, they were more likely to express anger about financial matters and having to pay lawyers.

Mothers were more likely than fathers to seek and accept advice from the group and to present themselves in a "one-down" position as the help seeker. Fathers were more likely to intellectualize problems as a defense strategy and to offer advice and assurance. This response was anticipated, given the general finding that women are socialized to seek help from and affiliation with others (Diedrick, 1991). Men, in general, are less likely to seek services and are considered a more difficult population to serve because of their typical defensive posture (Meth & Pasick, 1990).

Holidays and Special Events A great deal of group time was consumed by discussions of holidays and major life transitions for the children. Mother's Day and religious holidays are typically difficult times for divorced parents. One mother said she planned to spend Mother's Day at work so that she could be alone and avoid others who were celebrating the day. The holiday made her acutely aware of the loss of her role and status. On advice from the group, she spent time with friends instead. Fathers tended to be less affected by Father's Day and to be more adept at shutting out this holiday.

Ceremonies such as school graduation and bar and bat mitzvahs were also upsetting for the parents. Such events typically include many family members, financial expenditures, coordination of celebrations, and a public appearance of the divorced parents in the same place. Many problems surfaced at such times. Participants talked about being snubbed by in-laws, major events being canceled because parents could not make plans together, and stepparents replacing them in key roles. Fathers complained about being asked to pay for these events and then relegated to a supporting rather than a starring role. The children were frequently caught in the middle of such disputes and often withdrew to avoid further triangulation. This was interpreted as rejection by some of the parents.

Grandparent Issues

The support of grandparents, other relatives, and friends can be vitally important when a parent has little or no contact with his or her child. Some parents regressed to a childlike role in seeking reassurance from their parents. Grandparents varied in their reactions to their children and grandchildren. Some were supportive, others refused to become involved, and a small group ignored the parent in the middle (the group member) and sought contact directly with their grandchildren. This left some group members feeling undermined.

Group members who had little visitation time with their children felt caught between their wish to be alone with their children and having their children visit their grandparents. If the grandparents protested about how little time they saw their grandchildren, the parents felt a dual sense of failure. Not only could they not negotiate a relationship with their children, they were hurting their own parents' chances as well. The parents were extremely vulnerable to any criticism from their own parents and often reacted angrily, isolating themselves even more.

Emotional Triangulation

Divorced parents typically struggle to establish clear boundaries with the other parent and the children so that parenting issues can be more easily managed. When emotions are inflamed, this can prove to be a daunting task. Group members described situations in which their parenting efforts were blocked by the custodial parent, a not uncommon occurrence. Out of frustration from being unable to parent as they wished, the noncustodial parent typically exploded with anger at either the custodial parent or the child. As a result, the child often felt caught between the parents and the cause of their fighting. One child reacted by screaming at both parents when all three were on the telephone.

Triangulation also took a different form. Some parents in the group believed that the custodial parents' well-being was too closely tied to their children's affections. The custodial parents were described as having a "stranglehold" on the children's emotions and as using that overly intense connection to paint the noncustodial parent as incompetent or unworthy. At the same time, children were depicted as being unable to make decisions on their own and, conversely, as having too much power over the custodial parent's emotional well-being. In these complex symbiotic relationships, it appeared as though the children were in a lose–lose situation in which they felt they had to align themselves with and be supportive of the custodial parent. They formed the third side of a triangle but felt excluded from the other two sides.

Depending on the emotional maturity of the group member and the behavior of the custodial parent, these thorny relationships were difficult to sort out. The advantage of having a mixed-sex group was that members were able to examine their reactions and to gain insight regarding the behavior of both male and female custodial parents. When contentious relationship issues arose, members encouraged one another to behave in a way that made them feel good about themselves and did the least harm to the children. Such messages were not always acted on. For some members, revenge at any price, even at the child's expense, was the operating principle.

Children's Progress

Paradoxically, parents with the least involvement with their children were extremely interested in how the children were progressing. On the one hand, they hoped their children's lives were going smoothly. On the other hand, they took a certain amount of pleasure in learning that the custodial parent was having difficulties with the children. From the members' perspective, if the children had little contact with them but were progressing well, then they obviously were of little importance to their children and their role was diminished.

Termination Issues

Group termination was postponed twice because some of the members wanted to recontract for four more sessions. For these parents, termination of the group was closely linked with past losses that permeated their lives. A few members were also coping with the loss of jobs and the actual or impending death of a parent. Because of the multitude of losses in these group members' lives, discussion never strayed far from this topic. We tried to look at loss through a different lens and provide a new way of thinking about it. When parents talked about recontracting, we reframed it as wanting connection rather than avoiding loss.

RECOMMENDED WAYS OF WORKING

The themes discussed above unfolded within the context of the group process. Initially, members found it difficult to trust one another. Villains outside the group were easy to find. Members fed into one another's defenses by denigrating their ex-spouses and, in some cases, their children. Although trading "divorce war stories" was initially soothing and a way of normalizing their experiences, continual focus on these issues would have derailed meaningful group work.

For example, one member's stories about his children indicated a lack of willingness to be vulnerable with them, a pattern that he mirrored with other group members. Another member rarely shared her pain, "reporting" her experiences rather than expressing her feelings in a way that would make it easier for other members to connect with her.

In one extreme situation, a mother who had suffered greatly at the hands of her children considered legally divorcing her children as a way to avoid being hurt by them. She brought the group a book that offered a guide to this type of divorce. As leaders, we believed that these actions displayed the degree to which she had been hurt by her children (one of whom had committed suicide 2 years prior to her group attendance). We did not attempt to dissuade her from her plan. Rather, we listened and helped her identify her underlying feelings. We stated that this seemed a fairly serious action for her to take but one that we could certainly understand. We asked that she bring the issue back to the group in future weeks so that we could consider it further. She did reintroduce the issue at the next meeting but eventually abandoned the idea. Because she felt supported in her ruminations, she was able to explore her options.

In general, it was easier for members to give support than to ask for it. Although providing support is one of the benefits of the group process, it was especially important for these parents because it reinforced their ability to nurture (a quality that had been questioned by others). Receiving support, however, was much more difficult for them because they perceived it as an admission that they needed help and raised painful questions about whether they deserved to be supported. Admitting their need for support meant that life as a noncustodial parent was somehow deficient, which undermined their defenses.

Member–leader communication differed according to the worker. Both female and male members tended to look to the male worker for advice and approval and, in the case of male members, for camaraderie. Members looked to the female leader for emotional support. When the members were emotionally upset, the female leader's counsel was generally sought.

The group proceeded slowly at first as members sought to justify their interactions with their children. We attempted to provide a supportive atmosphere in which members could feel safe in sharing their doubts and insecurities about themselves. The group focused on members' current experiences and feelings, encouraging members to think about their interactions with their children. Some members responded better to cognitive analysis than they did to emotional content. Leaders were keenly aware of the potential for negative transference. As mentioned earlier, we were reluctant to offer advice during the first few sessions because members might interpret such advice as disapproval. Instead, we offered comments that would encourage members to reflect on their situation and behavior. As the group progressed, we helped members identify painful situations and offered more suggestions when we were confident that they would not be interpreted as criticism.

EVALUATION APPROACHES

Progress was charted through detailed note taking after each group meeting and with follow-up telephone calls 3 months after the last meeting. Positive change was noted in five of the eight members. Four members used the group to resolve difficulties with their children, and a fifth, the one with the best relationship with his children, appreciated his situation more. Another member remained passive and seemed to receive little benefit from the group experience, and one man, who was an active member, showed no change in his ability to handle his anger toward his children and ex-spouse. Another member's situation deteriorated. She had entered the group feeling the most anger toward her children, had wanted to divorce them, and continued to suffer both in her relationships with them and in her personal adjustment as a noncustodial parent.

In planning services for the growing number of single parents, social workers need to focus on noncustodial parents. Group work with this population can help ease the difficult divorce-related transitions that adults and children often have to make and can broaden the scope of services brought bring to their community.

NATIONAL RESOURCES

Parents Without Partners
401 N. Michigan Ave.
Chicago, IL 60611
(312) 644-6610

Also, contact local chapters of Mothers Without Custody (national number is (815) 455-2955) and Fathers United for Equal Rights.

REFERENCES

Aquilino, W. S. (1994). Impact of childhood family disruption on young adults' relationships with parents. *Journal of Marriage and the Family, 56*, 295–313.

Arditti, J. A., & Kelly, M. (1994). Fathers' perspectives of their co-parental relationship postdivorce. *Family Relations, 43*, 61–67.

Coney, N. S., & Mackey, W. C. (1989). Perceptions of the problems of the divorced father. *Journal of Divorce, 13*, 81–96.

Depner, C. E. (1993). Parental role reversal: Mothers as nonresidential parents. In C. E. Depner & J. H. Bray (Eds.), *Nonresidential parenting* (pp. 37–57). Newbury Park, CA: Sage.

Diedrick, P. (1991). Gender differences in divorce adjustment. *Journal of Divorce and Remarriage, 14*, 33–45.

Dudley, J. R. (1991). Increasing our understanding of divorced fathers who have infrequent contact with their children. *Family Relations, 40*, 279–285.

Garvin, V., Kalter, N., & Hansell, J. (1993). Divorced women: Individual differences in stressors, mediating factors, and adjustment outcome. *American Journal of Orthopsychiatry, 63*, 232–240.

Greif, G. L. (1987). Mothers without custody. *Social Work, 32*, 11–16.

Greif, G. L., & Pabst, M. S. (1988). *Mothers without custody*. New York: Macmillan/Lexington Books.

Kruk, E. (1994). The disengaged noncustodial father: Implications for social work practice with the divorced family. *Social Work, 39*, 15–25.

Masheter, C. (1990). Postdivorce relationships between ex-spouses: A literature review. *Journal of Divorce, 14*, 97–122.

Meth, R. L., & Pasick, R. S. (1990). *Men in therapy: The challenge of change*. New York: Guilford Press.

Pett, M. A., & Vaughn-Cole, B. (1986). The impact of income issues and social status on post-divorce adjustment of custodial parents. *Family Relations, 35*, 103–111.

Portes, P. R., Howell, S. C., Brown, J. H., Eichenberger, S., & Mas, C. A. (1992). Family functions and children's postdivorce adjustment. *American Journal of Orthopsychiatry, 62*, 613–617.

Rosenblum, K. E. (1986). Leaving as a wife, leaving a mother. *Journal of Social Issues, 7*, 197–213.

Shulman, L. (1992). *The skills of helping individuals, families and groups* (3rd ed.) Itasca, IL: F. E. Peacock.

Stewart, J. R., Schwebel, A. I., & Fine, M. A. (1986). The impact of custodial arrangement on the adjustment of recently divorced fathers. *Journal of Divorce, 9*, 55–65.

U.S. Bureau of the Census. (1995). Household and family characteristics: March 1994. P20-483. Washington, DC: Government Printing Office.

7

Group Work with Children of Divorce

Sara Bonkowski

Since 1960 the number of divorces and the divorce rate have more than doubled (Ahlburg & DeVita, 1992). Divorce is far more prevalent in the United States than elsewhere; in 1990, 1.2 million divorces occurred (Ahlburg & DeVita, 1992). Between 1970 and 1993, the number of divorced adults nearly quadrupled, while the total number of adults increased by less than half (U.S. Bureau of the Census, 1994). Divorce affects not only adults but their children as well. The odds of having parents divorce are twice as great today as they were a generation ago; over 1 million children under the age of 18 saw their parents divorce in 1990. Current estimates are that half of all children will experience the breakup of their parents' marriage (Ahlburg & DeVita, 1992).

Divorce is unlike other seemingly similar life experiences for a child, such as loss of a parent through death, in that divorce is specifically rooted in the failure of the relationship between the mother and father, who model the reliability of love and commitment (Wallerstein, 1991a). Adjustment problems in children of divorce have been documented in several realms—cognitive, behavioral, affective, and physiological (Wallerstein, 1991a)—and spill over into school performance and personal relationships (Frieman, Garon, & Mandell, 1994). Children in divorced families, compared with those in intact families, show more aggression directed toward authority figures, more difficulty with peers, more learning difficulties, and more school dropout (Furstenberg, 1990). Similar comparisons have found that children of divorce exhibit diminished coping capacity and lower self-esteem (Kurtz, 1994).

Social workers and others, concerned with both the immediate crisis and the long-term effect of parental divorce, have responded by designing interventions for children aimed at ameliorating the stress of divorce (Bonkowski, Bequette, & Boomhower, 1984; Cowen, Hightower, Pedro-Carroll, & Work, 1989; Rossiter, 1988; Stolberg & Mahler, 1989). Participation in a divorce group with other children can be fun and at the same time can promote general adjustment (Bonkowski et al., 1984; Hett & Rose, 1991). Children in divorce groups have demonstrated a decrease in problematic behaviors and an increase in school performance (Alpert-Gillis, Pedro-Carroll, & Cowen, 1989).

Thus, the ability to design and lead children's groups is an important professional skill for the social worker providing services for children of divorce. This chapter will discuss practice principles and common themes for group work with children of divorce.

PRACTICE PRINCIPLES

Designing and implementing a divorce group for children requires the social worker to consider several practice principles. Decisions made in one area may affect other decisions, so it is important to clarify the underpinnings of the group.

Who Is the Client: the Child, the Parent, or the Agency/Sponsor?

The first response may be, of course, that the child is the client. However, whenever children participate in a group, their parents must have some involvement; parental participation may include calling a community agency to enroll the child, giving permission to participate in a school-based group, providing transportation to attend the group, and occasionally bringing refreshments. In groups where children are dealing with divorce issues, some parents, especially those in conflict, may want to know what the child is saying to the group; the parent may even attempt to tell the social worker what types of issues to discuss.

The agency sponsoring the group may require some input into the group. For example, a school may decided that only children of divorce who display school problems are eligible for group participation. Some teachers and administrators expect the social worker to provide them with specific information about a group member. If so, the social worker should make it clear at the beginning of the process what can and cannot be shared.

The child and the child's needs must always be paramount. Both parents and administrators should be provided with guidelines clarifying confidentiality and participation. Clear communication regarding boundaries will prevent potential misunderstandings among administrators, parents, and the social worker.

Confidentiality

The children in the group must feel safe and free to participate fully. Confidentiality should be discussed in the first session. Children should know that it is permissible to tell their parents anything they choose, but they should be supported if they prefer not to talk with parents about the group experience. Children of divorce frequently feel powerless; helping them understand their rights gives them more control over their group experience.

All group members must be encouraged not to discuss what other members share. The social worker will guarantee the children confidentiality, explaining the one exception: when there is a danger to the child. The discussion of confidentiality may be the first time a child has been told that she or he has rights. This process will help the child apply the same principles if one parent tries to gather information about the other parent.

Children of Divorce Groups: Prevention or Treatment?

Divorce groups for children, especially in nonclinical settings such as schools, YWCA/YMCAs, and churches, are often conceptualized as prevention groups. The literature has established that children of divorce are at risk of developing many problems (Wallerstein, 1991b); thus, the goal of prevention is to provide groups for children early in the divorce process in the hope of preventing or lessening the impact of family disruption (Kaminsky, 1986).

Many children, however, enroll in groups several years after divorce. Wallerstein (1991b) states that families of divorce remain at risk for several years. Children in these families may have been struggling with such stressful life events as witnessing parental conflict, moving, changing schools, and complying with imposed visitation schedules. As a result of living with these stressors, the child may have taken on adult responsibility or is experiencing intense loyalty splits that can contribute to a range of problems, such as angry acting-out behavior, headaches, stomach problems, withdrawal from childhood activities, and so on. The goal for these children is to provide help that will improve their functioning.

In all likelihood, groups for children of divorce will have members whose parents are just beginning the divorce process and children whose parents divorced long ago. In the group, the children and social worker engage in a process that strengthens all the children. Thus, the categorization of a group as prevention or treatment serves the need of administrative planning; in reality, children's divorce groups are both.

Utilizing Paraprofessional Group Leaders

Many groups for children of divorce are led by professional leaders (e.g., Bonkowski et al., 1984; Cowen et al., 1989; Rossiter, 1988; Stolberg & Mahler, 1989). Other groups are led by volunteers who have been trained by a professional.

No evaluations have assessed the outcome of groups led by volunteers compared to groups led by social workers. Such comparison studies would provide data to make decisions about the relative importance of the professional background of group leaders. Currently, the demand for groups for children of divorce is so great that social workers may be in a position to design and lead groups or to train and supervise others.

Extent of Intervention

Most divorce groups for children are time limited, ranging from 6 weeks (Hett & Rose, 1991; Rossiter, 1988) to 14 weeks (Pedro-Carroll et al., 1992; Stolberg & Mahler, 1989). Some groups have parallel groups for parents (Rossiter, 1991; Stolberg & Mahler, 1989). When the group is completed, the intervention with both children and parents ends. For some children, there is little need for ongoing intervention; others may still have serious unresolved problems. When there is a continuing need for help, the social worker may refer children for more in-depth counseling. However, the termination of a trusting relationship with the group leader marks another loss for the child.

Given the realities of budget and time restraints, there are no easy answers to these ethical and practice concerns. However, the social worker must acknowledge the dilemma and attempt to minimize the loss for the child.

COMMON THEMES

Groups designed for children of divorce should include exercises, experiences, and information that address divorce-related issues. The divorce issues and themes discussed apply specifically to grade school children because divorce groups have been found to be an effective intervention for children between the ages of 6 to 12.

This does not imply that younger children or high school adolescents do not need help at the time of parental separation; however, the cognitive and emotional development of younger and older children have different considerations. For example, pre-school children do not have the cognitive capacity to understand the concept of divorce; they may say the word *divorce*, tell you what it means, and then ask if Daddy is coming home tonight. (See Rossiter, 1988, for a discussion of a preschool group.)

Adolescents often object to participating in a divorce group. They do not want to be labeled or pathologized by the action of their parents. Parents are able to enroll an 8-year-old in a group, but it is much more difficult to force an adolescent to do anything against his will. Teenagers may address divorce-related concerns in a general peer support group at school.

The following themes apply specifically to time-limited divorce groups for children aged 6 to 12.

Feeling Alone and "Different"

Although in any classroom 30–50% of the children may have divorced parents, many children feel they are the only one with this family situation. Typically, grade school children do not discuss intimate family concerns with their schoolmates. Instead, they interact in the immediate environment, playing ball, borrowing paper, talking about fire drills and the class bully.

The child sitting at the next desk may be in the midst of parental divorce of which her seatmate is totally unaware. Even when children know that another child's parents are getting a divorce, they seldom know how to offer support. Children need trusted adults to help them understand and master loss and stress; children also need to know that other children are coping with sad family changes.

The process and importance of peer support are often cited as an essential group ingredient: helping the child know he is not alone (Hett & Rose, 1991), fostering group support (Pedro-Carrol et al., 1992), being with others who are having similar feelings and experiences (Cantrell, 1986), and offering peer support (Bonkowski et al., 1984).

Child participants are the best spokespersons for the supportive power of the group. Eight-year-old Megan reported, "I love Tuesdays. I get to go to Wendy's group [Wendy was the school social worker]. Amy goes too. I never knew she was divorced. Her dad lives in New Jersey." Megan had felt sad because she was allowed to visit her father only every other weekend. In the group she discovered that other children were also missing their fathers, and in fact they thought she was lucky to see her father so often. Amy, her special friend in the group, was a popular, well-liked classmate; this dispelled some of Megan's fears that other children wouldn't like her if her parents were divorced.

Feeling Worried and Anxious, Not Knowing What Is Going to Happen

"I thought I would have to be on the witness stand," 10-year-old Sammy confided to the group. Sammy had been secretly worried that he would have to be part of a courtroom drama, like many he had seen on television.

Children whose parents are divorcing often know very little about what takes place in a divorce, what types of decisions will be made and by whom, when changes will occur, and, most important, what input they will have. Some children are told in advance by their parents that there is going to be a divorce and may be given an explanation of why the parents can no longer stay married; many children are told nothing.

Children need to be taught that divorce is an adult decision, not something caused by the child. They need to be prepared for the roles of attorneys and judges, and told what a court may be like and the meaning of child support, custody, and visitation. When children understand these concepts they will feel empowered, and divorce will not seem so mysterious. What is unknown to children is most frightening.

In the divorce group, children can learn about the legal process of divorce in an age-appropriate manner. Of course, cognitively, a 12-year-old will understand more than a 6-year-old.

School-age children are often fascinated with the concept of fairness; they argue at recess about fair rules and accuse teachers of not being fair. It seems logical and reassuring that there is someone, a judge, who will make fair decisions about the divorce. It is important for children to understand that their parents may not think that what the judge decides is fair, but that the judge is thinking about all members of the family, and especially about what is best for the children.

Feeling Stuck, Pressured, and Unable to Make Decisions

Children from divorced homes often face situations in which what they want to do or how they feel conflicts with one or both parents. Ginny, a shy second grader, was invited to her first birthday party. Unfortunately, the Saturday of the party was the time she had visitation with her father. Ginny desperately wanted to go to the party, but she did not know if she had any choice. Feeling stuck, she hid the invitation in her backpack.

Generating and exploring various solutions to problems is a process that can be learned. Helping children begin to understand the process of rationally thinking through different options can give them a powerful tool in facing dilemmas that arise during parental divorce.

The extent to which children can master problem-solving skills depends partially on their age. Younger grade school children need to practice very simple solutions to the problem "When you are feeling mad at your mother, what can you do?" Older grade school children can engage in more creative but realistic problem solving, such as using flow charts to trace the results of different options.

Stolberg and Mahler (1989) have developed a systematized approach to teaching problem-solving skills. To help children retain the information presented in the divorce group, they designed *Kidsbook*, a book to take home and apply the skills learned in the group to the home, classroom, and playground.

The group leader can model problem solving when issues arise in the group. Children living in emotionally labile homes may have had little experience watching adults calmly discuss options.

Not Understanding and Acknowledging Ambivalent Feelings

Adults often have difficulty accepting the ambivalence present in any intimate relationship. It is no wonder, then, that children experiencing the collapse of their parents' marriage will not understand the range of conflicting feelings they experience, especially when the feelings are emotional opposites such as anger and love.

Ralph admired his father, emulating his interest in baseball. During the time his parents were divorcing, Ralph witnessed his father physically hurting his mother; now he felt rage toward the loved, admired father. Ralph shut down emotionally because he could not allow himself to feel both love and hate for his father. After the group leader helped him express how much he missed and loved his father, and how he hated him for hurting his mother, Ralph's previous outgoing personality gradually returned. Encouraged by Ralph's understanding that he could have both of these feelings, other group members began to share their feelings.

The expression of feelings may temporarily make the child feel sad, angry, and so on. However, in the long run, it is healthier for the child to express and acknowledge the pain and ambivalence of parental divorce than to freeze emotional responses.

Needing Encouragement and Modeling to Promote Communication with Important Others

Promoting clear communication is the goal of many social work interventions, and it is important for children of divorce to be able to communicate with others about their needs, feelings, and wishes related to parental divorce. The most important people the child communicates with are her parents, but under some circumstances the child may need to communicate with attorneys or judges.

Elaine was a valuable member of her sixth-grade volleyball team. The volleyball games were played on Saturday mornings, but every other Saturday she was with her father, who elected not to take her to the games. Afraid that she would hurt his feelings, Elaine had been unable to tell her father that she wanted to go to the games.

In the divorce group, she practiced telling her father exactly how she felt and asking him to take her to the volleyball games. Much to Elaine's relief, her father responded by telling her how much he appreciated her letting him know about the games and stating that he had been unaware of their importance. He began taking her to volleyball on the Saturdays she was with him.

Communication is not only talking. Children can communicate through writing letters, drawing pictures, making a tape, or writing a story. After identifying their feelings, children can decide how to communicate those feelings to their parents. (This process links the identification of feelings, problem solving, and communication.)

An important caveat needs to be included in a discussion of communication. In some instances, it may be dangerous for a child to communicate feelings and wishes to a parent. The parent may react with anger or disbelief, use the child's feelings in the divorce battle, or ignore expressed wishes. The social worker should help the child realistically assess the possible outcomes of communication.

Children should be aware that communicating clearly does not guarantee an outcome. For example, a child may tell his father that he does not want to visit. The father may respond that he understands his wishes but that the child will still have to visit.

Children from intact families do not get all of their wishes either. They too must do things they do not want to do. It is never desirable for a child to be in charge of his parents, but it is important for parents to listen and consider the child's feelings. The lack of power children have in divorcing families is often frustrating for both the children and the social worker; all parties can be empowered by communicating this frustration.

Experiencing Low Self-Esteem

Parental divorce and the accompanying stress often weaken the child's ability to maintain a good self-image. "If my family is having these awful problems, we must not be a very good family and I must not be a very likable person" is the child's reasoning.

The social worker may want to include group exercises that specifically identify the child's strengths and interests (Bonkowski et al., 1984). During divorce and in a divorce group, there will be a focus on divorce. But children are much more than part of their parents' divorce; it is important to value and acknowledge the whole child—soccer player, dog lover, potential veterinarian, comedian, and so on.

Needing Fun

Divorce is not fun for anyone. But children need to have fun, to laugh, to be silly. Children and their social worker can have fun at the group meetings. This does not mean that difficult topics or unpleasant feelings are ignored; in fact, the group gives children a safe place to face these topics and feelings.

However, every group meeting must include some fun time, such as telling jokes, playing a guessing game, or discussing Halloween costumes. Social workers dealing with children need to be able to play, to value nonverbal experiences, and to tolerate being touched, hugged, and kissed.

RECOMMENDED WAYS OF WORKING

Group activities, the length and number of sessions, and the number of adult leaders will vary depending on the ages and number of children in the group, available resources, specific population characteristics, and the leader's interests and strengths. However, there are general guidelines that will aid in planning the group.

First, in the writer's opinion, having more than one adult leader will benefit both the children and the leaders. Children are energetic and often demand individual attention. When two adults are available, there is always one to keep the group focused and the other to respond to the unexpected. If it is not feasible to have two social workers, then college students or adult volunteers can be utilized.

Each session should have specific objectives, with activities designed to help achieve these objectives. Art projects, role plays, puppetry, film strips, letter writing, games, making a video, singing, story telling, and relaxation exercises are examples of techniques that can be used to meet specific group objectives.

For example, if the group objective is to help the children understand divorce, the children can take turns playing the role of a mother or father telling their children (played by the other group members) what divorce is and why the parent is getting a divorce. Another method of addressing the same objective is to have the children paint a picture of divorce. After completing the pictures, the group can discuss their artwork, highlighting different ideas and feelings.

Tried-and-true program activities can be used in subsequent groups. But when the composition of the group varies, the social work leader should be flexible and free to change exercises, using activities that will be most effective with a specific group.

If time and resources allow, providing a snack—an apple, a fruit drink, cookies—is nurturing and can build cohesion. Feeding the children helps them feel cared for and important. For some, this may be the only time in the week they feel special.

The most emotionally laden divorce content should be discussed in the middle third of the sessions. For example, if the group is to meet for 8 weeks, weeks 4, 5, and 6 are the best times to deal with potentially charged issues. In the first few sessions, getting acquainted, building trust, and introducing problem solving are safe objectives. The final sessions, designed to help the children leave the group feeling whole and hopeful, can examine self-esteem and termination.

Termination is a sensitive issue for children of divorce, as they are facing many changes and losses in their lives. Making memory books, exchanging phone numbers, and taking a group picture are concrete ways of helping the child take some of the group with him.

EVALUATION APPROACHES

Evaluation of interventions provides social workers with needed knowledge of what works and with whom. Several methods have been utilized to evaluate the effectiveness of groups for children of divorce.

When the group is in progress, the group leader can evaluate each session and the overall group experience (Bonkowski, et al., 1984). These evaluations are usually qualitative, providing clinical and descriptive data (e.g., Were the children engaged in the session? Did the planned activity result in meeting the group's objective?)

Data assessing the child's behavior and adjustment before and after the group meetings can be gathered from the children (Pedro-Carrol et al., 1992), parents (Alpert-Gillis et al., 1989; Bonkowski et al., 1984), and teachers (Alpert-Gillis et al., 1989; Cowen et al., 1989). Drawing on information from several sources provides the social worker with multidimensional measures that help answer the question "Did participation in the group facilitate adjustment to parental divorce?"

Brown, Portes, and Christensen (1989) stress the need to tie specific interventions to known risk factors and then to assess the effectiveness of such interventions with controlled studies. Grych and Fincham (1992) challenge the social work practitioner to strengthen the link between theory and research. For example, critical areas that still require research are the following: What process promotes positive change and adjustment? What interventions can ameliorate the effect of divorce for children known to be most at risk (boys, early elementary school children, and children exposed to parental violence)?

Although empirical evaluation is crucial, the evaluation often most meaningful to the practitioner comes spontaneously from the children Ten-year-old Jeff, at first a reluctant group member, said, "I don't want these meetings to be over. I really like coming."

NATIONAL RESOURCE

Parents Without Partners
401 N. Michigan Ave.
Chicago, IL 60611
(312) 644-6610

REFERENCES

Ahlburg, D., & DeVita, C. (1992). New realities of the American family. *Population Bulletin, 47*(2), 1–44.

Alpert-Gillis, L. J., Pedro-Carroll, J. L., & Cowen, E. L. (1989). The Children of Divorce Intervention Program: Development, implementation, and evaluation of a program for young urban children. *Journal of Consulting and Clinical Psychology, 57,* 583–589.

Bonkowski, S. E., Bequette, S. Q., & Boomhower, S. (1984). A group design to help children adjust to parental divorce. *Social Casework, 6,* 131–137.

Brown, J. H., Portes, R. P., & Christensen, D. N. (1989). Understanding divorce stress on children: Implications for research and practice. *American Journal of Family Therapy, 17,* 315–325.

Cantrell, R. G. (1986). Adjustment to divorce: Three components to assist children. *Elementary School Guidance and Counseling, 15,* 163–173.

Cowen, E. L., Hightower, A. D., Pedro-Carroll, J. L., & Work, W. C. (1989). School-based models for primary prevention programming with children. *Prevention in Human Services, 7,* 133–159.

Frieman, B. B., Garon, R., & Mandell, B. (1994). Parenting seminars for divorcing parents. *Social Work, 39,* 609–613.

Furstenberg, F. F., Jr. (1990). Divorce and the American family. *Annual Review of Sociology, 16,* 379–403.

Grych, J. H., & Fincham, F. D. (1992). Interventions for children of divorce: Toward greater integration of research and action. *Psychological Bulletin, 111,* 434–446.

Hett, G. G., & Rose, C. D. (1991). Counselling children of divorce: A divorce lifeline program. *Canadian Journal of Counselling, 25,* 38–49.

Kaminsky, H. (1986). The divorce adjustment education and support group for children. *Conciliation Courts Review, 24,* 45–49.

Kurtz, L. (1994). Psychosocial coping resources in elementary school-age children of divorce. *American Journal of Orthopsychiatry, 64,* 554–563.

Pedro-Carrol, J. L., Alpert-Gillis, L. J., & Cowen, E. L. (1992). An evaluation of the efficacy of a preventive intervention for 4th–6th grade urban children of divorce. *Journal of Primary Prevention, 13,* 115–129.

Rossiter, A. B. (1988). A model for group intervention with preschool children experiencing separation and divorce. *American Journal of Orthopsychiatry, 58,* 387–396.

Stolberg, A. L., & Mahler, J. L. (1989). Protecting children from the consequences of divorce. *Prevention in Human Services, 7,* 161–176.

U.S. Department of Commerce, Bureau of the Census. (1994). *Marital status and living arrangements: March 1993,* Series P20-478. Washington, DC: Government Printing Office.

Wallerstein, J. S. (1991a). The long-term effects of divorce on children: A review. *Journal of the American Academy of Child and Adolescent Psychiatry, 30,* 349–360.

Wallerstein, J. S. (1991b). Tailoring the intervention to the child in the separating and divorced family. *Family and Conciliation Courts Review, 29,* 448–459.

8

Group Work with Elderly Persons

Susan Rice

WHO ARE THE ELDERLY?

The purpose of this chapter is to provide the beginning group worker with an understanding of doing social group work with elderly clients. The demographics of the elderly population in this country and others dramatically demonstrate that the aging population is growing. In the United States, the older population, as a proportion of the total population, has tripled in this century (*Aging America*, 1991). Between 1989 and 2030, the population that is 65+ is expected to more than double. Additionally, the population that is 85+ is expected to more than triple. In other countries, similar compelling statistics make the examination of group work services for the elderly an important topic for study. In most developing countries, the elderly account for at least 1/10th of the citizenry. (Sokolovsky, 1990). For these reasons, there is a compelling need to provide effective, user-friendly group work services to the elderly in order to enhance both the quality and the span of their lives.

There is a second compelling need for a social worker to provide effective groups for the elderly: One of the primary problems of elderly clients is isolation. What better method is there than working with people in groups to combat this daily dilemma?

REVIEW OF THE LITERATURE

The elderly population is made up of two groups. The term *oldest old* (denoting people who are 85+ years old) was coined as a refinement of the term *old old* (Neugarten, 1975) and with the recognition that issues, themes, and practice principles need to be modified, depending on the health, morale, economic circumstances, and other situational factors affecting older clients. There has been a tendency for the literature and research to focus on social group work with the *young old*, ignoring the special needs of the very frail elderly. This chapter will attempt to address the distinction between the two groups in the discussions of practice principles and themes.

Why do people age? The aging process apparently involves failure of the surveillance, repair, and replacement process typical of a young body (Christiansen & Grzybowski, 1993). The body loses the ability to replace cells that compose most of its tissues. The immune system loses the ability to eliminate cancerous cells. Tissues that are damaged in daily life can no longer be repaired. When all of these processes occur, senescence appears, causing the organism to deteriorate and eventually die. This accounts for the physical and mental deterioration that occurs in old age, although for many people it does not happen fast enough to cause severe functional problems before some dramatic disease or occurrence causes immediate death.

Just as significant as the real changes that take place in an older person are the perceived changes, those largely due to the ageism that permeates our society. Ageism "can be seen as a systematic stereotyping of and discrimination against people because they are old. . . . Old people are characterized as senile, rigid in thought and manner, old-fashioned in morality and skills. . . . Ageism allows the younger generation to see older people as different from themselves; thus they subtly cease to identify with their elders as human beings" Butler, 1994, (p. 3). And just as society treats older people as different and less human, older people treat themselves that way. When an older person has a physical complaint, he or she will often say, "So, what can a doctor do about it? I'm getting old." When that message is reinforced by the medical profession, the individual starts to believe it, and no longer thinks of the body as something that he controls. When a person forgets the house keys and says "I must be getting senile," and the reply is "It happens to everyone over 60," the individual believes that her memory is failing and that there is nothing she can do about it. It is apparent how easily people, and the support systems around them, slip into a mindset that allows deterioration to occur without being concerned about the changes that are atypical and are causing that individual great trouble in functioning.

One method of assisting the elderly is to provide social support, often correlated with reducing health and mental health problems (Maguire, 1983). Social support groups are an effective way of providing this support. Senior citizen centers, in which older people find a network of peers with whom they can share common ground, are one common source of these groups. The elderly find companionship, use time productively and satisfactorily, make contributions, discover new interests and skills, and rediscover and maximize old ones (Gitterman & Shulman, 1994). This chapter uses the mutual aid model to explore the practice principles, themes, and ways of working with older people.

PRACTICE PRINCIPLES

Group work practice has been defined in a number of ways. In working with the elderly, the large majority of groups function most effectively using the mutual aid model of practice, developed and elaborated on by Gitterman and Shulman (1994) and first described by Schwartz (1977). The mutual aid model states that clients have difficulties that arise from three interrelated problems of living: life transitions, environmental pressures, and maladaptive interpersonal processes. Using the mutual aid process to address these problems gives each member of a group the ability to help every other member. The purpose of the leader in such a group is to be a mediator, facilitating the engagement of individual members with the group as a whole. The mutual aid model allows older people to function in a way that draws on their strengths and allows them maximum freedom in determining the scope and course of the group.

How do these general practice principles fit group work with elderly clients? Most social work practitioners envision a model of social work practice (individual or group) that includes a focus on assessment, planning, contracting, building rapport, direct action, indirect action, evaluation, and termination (Johnson, 1995). Each phase needs to be modified to fit the needs of groups composed of elderly clients. In all phases of practice, the level of the social worker's activity is high, perhaps higher than in working with younger clients. The reasons for this are numerous. Many elderly clients have had minimal exposure to the world of social work. They have more or less adequately resolved their own problems throughout their lives, counting on informal support systems to help them through hard times. As people reach their 80s and 90s, those informal systems disappear. The individual is left to flounder and often seeks social work services for the first time, not really knowing what to expect. The worker's job is then to model what a social group worker does by being active in the group from the very beginning. For example, in assessment, the social worker is often trying to understand the degree to which group members are willing to provide mutual aid and to share their solutions to a problem. The worker needs to demonstrate actively how the mutual aid process takes place. The worker does this by drawing on his or her knowledge of each member's experience and encouraging that member to share that experience with the rest of the group. The worker also encourages all members to see the similarities among them and tries to help each client understand the source of his or her discomfort.

Contracting is often done on an informal basis in support groups for the elderly because the themes of groups are so amorphous. In general, when a younger client or a client with a concrete need contracts for services (or a worker offers services), there is a fairly clear understanding of what the agency is prepared to offer and what the client wants to receive. Groups with clear contracts include those where clients want to learn to be better parents or where older people are learning to deal with insulin-dependent diabetes in order to manage their illness effectively. However, social support groups are often seen as a forum for clients to adjust to losses or changing life situations. That rubric could fit almost everyone, and so, in practice, the contract becomes a statement of allowing members to decide, as they participate in the group, what the benefits might be and what they might want to focus on.

Such informality also provides a safety net that allows fearful, timid clients to "try out" the group without being committed to one specific goal for change in their lives. Informality does not necessarily mean lack of clarity. Shulman (1991) describes contracting as "clarifying the worker's purpose and role, and reaching for client feedback of purpose" (p. 48). He stresses the importance of eliminating jargon in contracting and urges workers to state clearly what they can offer. For example, in a group that has been formed to help frail elderly clients to continue living independently in the community, a leader might say, "This group will be a place where you can explore the feelings you have about living alone or feeling isolated some of the time." Each client is then free to pick up on that theme in whatever way seems appropriate.

There is a general belief (Corey & Corey, 1992) that older people need support and encouragement more than they need confrontation. The goal of group work with the elderly is less oriented toward radical personality change than it is toward making life in the present more meaningful and enjoyable. The social worker, for example, is more likely to be an advocate for the group that needs help with transportation (indirect intervention) than he or she is to empower the members to either work out the transportation problem as a way of building strength or to empower them to advocate for themselves (direct intervention). This is a fine distinction because sometimes one does want older people to see the extent to which they can remain powerful (Browne, 1995). Often, however, workers try to make it easier to attending the group as part of the goal of offering a service that will enhance the quality of members' lives.

The general theme of learning to resolve conflict is related to this goal. Many theorists (Garland, Jones & Kolodny, 1976; Levine, 1991) agree that conflict is an integral part of group development and allows members to become intimate and work together more beneficially. For older people, conflict is often seen as threatening to the relationships they are taking significant risks to build. Learning skills of conflict resolution can allow true intimacy to develop in groups, facilitating the mutual aid process.

Termination is an area that needs to be planned carefully in groups with older people. Termination is important both in the here and now and also because of the memories the experience evokes for clients in relation to past terminations in their lives (Levine, 1991; Shulman, 1991). For people who are seeing friends, family members, and acquaintances die on a regular basis, all endings take on an especially poignant meaning. In fact, many elderly clients will bluntly say that they do not want to become close to other group members "because they're only going to die anyway." Nevertheless, those who run groups and those who attend them believe that the benefits of being close to people, and feeling supported in one's efforts to improve one's quality of life, outweigh the pain involved in separations and endings.

Social workers need to make group endings (and endings of individuals who leave a group) positive and honest, allowing the expression of a wide range of feelings. For example, when a person drops out of a group because he or she becomes too ill to attend, it is useful to encourage the rest of the group to write to the member or pay a visit to the member's home or the hospital to provide closure. This is not only helpful to the individual but also provides a reassuring message to the rest of the group: My absence is important, and people care about what happens to me. Similarly, when a group ends, the members need to be helped to express the importance that it has had in their lives, as well as frustrations about what was not accomplished in the group. Social workers also need to be aware of their own feelings about endings in order not to ignore what group members need to express and explore.

COMMON THEMES

The most common themes encountered in groups for the elderly are loneliness, social isolation, loss, poverty, the feeling of rejection, the struggle to find meaning in life, dependency, feelings of uselessness, hopelessness, and despair, fears of death and dying, grief over others' deaths, sadness over physical and mental deterioration, depression, and regrets over past events (Corey & Corey, 1992).

If this seems like a list of negative, depressing concerns, one can turn to an emphasis on the wellness model of aging (George & Clipp, 1991), which says that the norm is very different from that of people who are struggling. However, as discussed above, it is difficult to age without struggling. One of the themes mentioned is a pervasive sadness related to physical and mental deterioration. When I first began writing about aging, I coauthored a very up-beat article related to love and sexual intimacy among the elderly (Rice & Kelley, 1987). When my own parents (who were in their late 70s at the time) read it, their reaction was, "What garbage! When you physically ache when you wake up in the morning, it's hard to believe this stuff." At the time, I shrugged off that sentiment, and said to myself, well, they never were very romantic. Now they are in their late 80s, and I have seen the ravages of physical change and understand that sentiment much better.

We need to keep the wellness model of aging in mind so that we do not stereotype all older people as invalids. But we also need to appreciate the degree to which physical changes affect mental status and emotional involvement in different situations. A balance needs to be achieved between focusing on positive and negative themes. Some groups promote activities that emphasize the positive, and others plan activities that allow safe expression of negative feelings (Morrin, 1998; Samberg, 1988). The fact is that the efficiency of the human body does decline gradually with age (Markson, 1992). Ironically, what people are most aware of first are the cosmetic changes associated with aging, such as gray hair, wrinkles, and a widening pelvis. These are the changes that make people feel that they are getting old, although they do not relate to physical functioning at all.

Mental functioning is perhaps the essence of who we are, and when one sees one's own functioning deteriorating, or sees it in others, the effects are devastating. Alzheimer's disease causes cruel changes in a person's personality and cognitive abilities that effectively isolate the person from everyone. Group work services to such clients can have a number of beneficial effects (Toner, 1993), including a chance to foster peer experiences and emotional support, stimulating and encouraging the functioning of all remaining intellectual and social capacities, affirming a sense of individual identity, eliminating frustrating expectations, and replacing them with supportive social and group controls. While this chapter focuses on the elderly as clients, it is important to note that groups for caregivers can also help relieve the tension and strain that tear families apart as they watch a loved one, previously capable, competent, and intelligent, deteriorate.

Loneliness and Social Isolation

Close to one-third of all elderly people live alone (8.9 million Americans aged 65 and over in 1989). Among people who are over 85 years old, almost half live alone, a trend that is expected to continue into the next century (*Aging America*, 1991). The themes discussed in this section are all related, as people who live alone also have lower incomes than other older people and have more chronic health problems that make it harder for them to remain independent. Framing these statistics is gender; in 1989 women accounted for almost four-fifths of all elderly people living alone (*Aging America*, 1991, p. 210). Ethnic differences also exist. Hispanic elderly live alone much less frequently than white and African–American elderly. However, since the minority elderly population is increasing more rapidly than the white elderly population, those numbers will change too. By the year 2020, the number of Hispanics aged 65 and over who live alone is expected to quadruple.

Of those who live alone, 24% have incomes that are below the poverty level, compared to only 14% of those who live with others. In general, the economic situation of the elderly population is expected to improve, but the exception will be elderly people living alone. African-American and Hispanic women may be particularly at risk (Ozawa, 1995). The percentage of people who are poor or nearly poor increases as people get older (18% of those who are 65–74 compared with 28% of those who are over 85) (*Aging America*, 1991, p. 215).

Therefore, it is no surprise that loneliness, social isolation, and poverty are common themes in groups composed of elderly clients. Feelings of uselessness, hopelessness, despair, and regrets over past events are also the foci of many discussions in social support groups. Retirement represents a significant milestone for older people. Particularly for men in our society, there can be a loss of meaningful job roles, productivity, and relationships that have been central throughout adult life (Carter & McGoldrick, 1989). (Again, there is a link with poverty because retirement usually is associated with a reduction of family and/or individual income.)

One way to conceptualize these feelings is through the work of Erik Erikson. Erikson (1963) describes the last two developmental stages of life—generativity versus stagnation and ego integrity versus despair—as two sides of a coin. *Generativity* refers to the concern about establishing and guiding the next generation. When one feels that one has not been instrumental in this process, either through one's own children, or by giving to society in a larger way, a pervasive sense of stagnation occurs. *Ego integrity* is the sense that one has accepted "one's one and only life cycle as something that had to be and that, by necessity, permitted of no substitutions" (Erikson, 1963, p. 268). If one cannot feel that way about one's life, despair is the result. If one looks back at one's life and blames oneself for the paths not taken, the overall feeling is one of making wrong choices. The elderly often struggle with these issues in groups.

Fears About Death and Dying and Grief Over Others' Deaths:

Death and dying remain a taboo subject in our society. Many people cannot (or will not) openly discuss these significant issues, although they secretly harbor strong feelings about them. Death remains a hidden secret, as eroticized as it is feared (Nuland, 1994). We focus instead on concrete issues such as relieving specific ailments. Meanwhile, the controversy rages about how death should occur and how much control we should have over it. When Daniel Callahan wrote *Setting Limits: Medical Goals in an Aging Society* (1987), some critics were afraid it would be used to support "killing off" old people by refusing them medical care (Abels & Rice, 1990; Hentoff, 1987). When Derek Humphry published *Final Exit* (1991), a suicide manual of sorts geared people with terminal illnesses, it became an immediate best-seller and made people fear that suicide would become acceptable. What does this do to the older person who is seeing people die constantly? This theme recurs in groups, although it is rarely brought up unless the group worker is willing to facilitate the sharing of painful and risky feelings related to the topic.

RECOMMENDED WAYS OF WORKING

First, in order to work with clients, we need to reach them. A sobering fact is that for most types of social work services, including group work, minorities are served less often—not because there are fewer potential clients for a given service but because of perceived and actual barriers to receiving that service (Cunningham, 1991). Successful attempts to increase minority representation in client groups include efforts to have minority staff (speaking one's own language or coming from one's own culture provides familiarity that makes accepting help much easier), as well as training workers to be sensitive to cultural differences. Since in our country minority status is often tied to lower income, accessibility issues need to be addressed too, including transportation, cost of services, and flexibility of hours.

In developing groups of clients, it is important to pay attention to issues of homogeneity and heterogeneity (Rice & Goodman, 1992). In general, groups need to have maximum homogeneity in terms of degree of vulnerability and capacity to tolerate anxiety. In other words, the ego strength of all members needs to be at similar levels. On the other hand, maximum heterogeneity in participants' conflict areas and patterns of coping allows input of new ideas and perspectives on the situations that clients face. Regardless of the themes discussed, this balancing rule between difference and similarity will allow participants to use the mutual aid model to share with each other.

These themes can be incorporated in most groups that allow clients to determine the focus of the discussion. For 5 years, this author directed a weekly support group for members of a retirement community. Pairs of undergraduate students facilitated weekly support groups that lasted for a full academic year, and combined small-group discussions and programs with occasional large-group workshops and potluck dinners (Black, Kelly, & Rice, 1994). These groups were ongoing, in the sense that many members stayed with the groups from year to year, but the student workers changed every September. As people grew older and frailer, there was a fairly high degree of turnover among the group members, and ways of working with them needed to change while maintaining the initial purposes of the group.

For example, the potluck dinners were initially a wonderful opportunity for members to demonstrate their culinary skills and to "give," in a concrete way, to their friends and to the student workers. Over time, the participants' cooking abilities faltered as their vision, hearing, and health deteriorated. It was decided to cater the main dish for the potluck dinners, and the members brought desserts to share. Even with dessert, however, we saw a gradual change from the "famous homemade recipe for brownies" to boxes of cookies that were store bought. This change saddened those staff who had been with the group from the beginning. However, it was a wonderful example of changing the parameters of the situation so that the members could still enjoy the essence of the program. Most recently, the potluck dinners were changed to potluck luncheons because more members were having trouble getting out at night even within their gated community.

Workers must be sensitive to the environmental changes that need to be made to allow the substantive work of the group to continue. The purpose of the potluck dinners has remained constant: They combat the social isolation and loneliness of the members (about 70% of whom live alone) and allows them to feel part of a community and a family.

In addition, workshops held twice each semester gave members specific skills to improve their ability to function within the group. For example, this author held a 3-hour workshop on conflict resolution skills, including teaching "I-messages," discussing innate styles of conflict (turtles or sharks), and demonstrating skills of negotiation and mediation. A presentation of these skills coupled with an opportunity to discuss the feelings attached to them primed members to use them outside of the group.

In addition to retirement communities, groups for the elderly can be located in institutions. In contrast to retirement communities, where residents live independently in whatever manner they choose, institutions provide the assistance needed for their residents to perform the tasks of daily living at the cost of lessened freedom. In an examination of institutions, Schmidt (1990) begins by describing people's feelings about them. "Most elderly persons entering a home for the aged view this move as their last one. But, whatever sense of loss they may feel, they are concerned also with the life they can make there. Thus, homes for the aged become laboratories of human behavior as residents deal with change on a scale for which their previous lives have not prepared them" (p. 1).

Reminiscing groups can be utilized in both community and institutional settings to assist clients to "relive, re-experience, or savor events of the past that are personally significant" (Burnside & Schmidt, 1994, p. 164). Reminiscence can increase morale, self-esteem, and life satisfaction, as well as help clients feel an increased sense of control over their environment. For younger social workers, it can be a way to learn about the past and gain a deeper understanding of their clients as they hear about the experiences that brought their clients to the present. Group members feel an increased sense of understanding and support for other members as they realize the depth of the commonality of their experiences.

Programming (using an activity to further a major goal for the group) can also be used in beneficial ways. In one group session, the worker brought in the game "Trivial Pursuit" (immensely popular at the time). The game consists of a board, dice, and cards with questions on them, asking for answers about different topics including science, nature, history, entertainment, arts and leisure, and sports. The usual game is played by competing against each other (individually or in teams), and trying to win by being the first to answer questions correctly in each category. The rules were modified for this group by abandoning the board, the dice, and the competitive aspect of the game. Instead, the worker read a question and all group members tried to answer it, often asking each other questions about their personal circumstances during the event in question. For example, to the question of when a baseball player broke the world record, the answer came via a path that included deciding if it was before or after World War II, where each group member had been during those years, and what they were doing. There was no score keeping, and no winner or loser. The group spent as much time as they wanted on one question, and it ended when the right answer was given or the group as a whole gave up. The entire session utilized only four or five cards from the game, but the group emerged with a sense of closeness and cohesiveness that had not been present before.

EVALUATION MEASURES

How does one know when a group is successful? Much has been written about single-subject design and about the importance of every practitioner's evaluation of his or her own practice (Hepworth & Larson, 1993; Woods & Hollis, 1990). This emphasis exists because we need to know if the money spent on a resource is effective and if the interventions we are using are helpful. To evaluate social support groups for older people, one of the most effective ways is to go to the source—the consumer.

In most groups, sessions end with a 1-minute evaluation. This evaluation consists of three questions: What was the most helpful thing that happened for you here today? What was the least helpful thing that happened for you here today? What would you suggest that we do differently next time? If the clients are able to write, this can be done on a sheet that is handed to each member. If writing is too burdensome, the clients can answer these questions quickly in a round-robin format.

More formal evaluations can be done at the quarter point, midpoint, and/or endpoint of a time-limited group. Clients can be asked about their overall satisfaction, about the effectiveness of specific techniques or sessions, and about how the enjoyment of their group is related to the goals they wanted to reach.

With all evaluation, the introduction is crucial to its success. If the worker asks for feedback in a way that implies that only positive feedback is welcome, that may be what he or she will get. If the members think that the continuation of the program is riding on their feedback, it will be greatly distorted. Allowing time for critique and change sends a welcome message to participants. It puts them in control of their group and enables them to make it the best it can be. With groups of elderly persons as with other groups, evaluation can be an ongoing part of group work that contributes to the group's overall effectiveness.

NATIONAL RESOURCES

American Association for Retired
  Persons
1909 K Street NW
Washington, DC 20049
(202) 434-2277

Alzheimer's Disease and
  Related Disorders Association
70 East Lake
Chicago, IL 60601
(800) 621-0379 (in Illinois)
(800) 572-6037

American Association of Homes
  for the Aging
Department 5119
Washington, DC 20061-5119
(800) 508-9442

Foundation for Hospice and
  Homecare
519 C St. NE Stanton Park
Washington, DC 20002
(202) 547-6586

National Association of Area
  Agencies on Aging (N4A)
600 Maryland Ave., SW
Washington, DC 20024
(202) 296-8130

National Institute on Aging
9000 Rockville Pike
Bethesda, MD 20892
(301) 496-1752

Widowed Persons Service
1909 K St. NW
Washington, DC 20049
(202) 728-4370

REFERENCES

Abels, P., & Rice, S. (1990). Stop the World, I want to get off: Rationing health care for the elderly. *Social Thought, 16*, 41–47.

Aging America; Trends and projections. (1991). DHHS Publication 91-28001. Washington, DC: U.S. Senate Special Committee on Aging.

Black, J., Kelly, J., & Rice, S. (1994). A model of group work in retirement communities. In I. Burnside & M. Schmidt (Eds.), *Working with older adults: Group processes and techniques* (3rd ed., pp. 240–249). Boston: Jones and Bartlett.

Browne, C. (1995). Empowerment in social work practice with older women. *Social Work, 40*, 358–364.

Burnside, I., & Schmidt, M. (Eds.). (1994). *Working with older adults: Group processes and techniques* (3rd ed.). Boston: Jones and Bartlett.

Butler, R. (1994). Dispelling ageism: The cross-cutting intervention. In R. Enright (Ed.), *Perspectives in social gerontology* (pp. 3–10). Boston: Allyn & Bacon

Callahan, D. (1987). *Setting limits: Medical goals in an aging society.* New York: Simon & Schuster.

Carter, B., & McGoldrick, M. (Eds.). (1989). *The changing family life cycle: A framework for family therapy* (2nd ed.). Boston: Allyn & Bacon.

Christiansen, J., & Grzybowski, J. (1992). *Biology of aging.* St. Louis: Mosby.

Corey, G., & Corey, M. (1992). *Groups: Process and practice* (4th ed.). Monterey, CA: Brooks/Cole.

Cunningham, C. V. (1991). Reaching minority communities: Factors impacting on success. *Journal of Gerontological Social Work, 17,* 125–135.

Erikson, E. (1963). *Childhood and society.* New York: W. W. Norton.

Garland, J., Jones, H., & Kolodny, R. (1976). A model of stages of group development in social work groups. In S. Bernstein (Ed.), *Explorations in group work* (pp. 17–71). Boston: Charles River Books.

George, L. K., & Clipp, E. (1991). Introduction. *Generations: Journal of the American Society on Aging, 15,* 5–6.

Gitterman, A., & Shulman, L. (Eds.) (1994). *Mutual aid groups and the life cycle* (2nd ed.). New York: Columbia University Press.

Hentoff, N. (1987, September 8). The death doctors. *Village Voice,* pp. 25–27.

Hepworth, D., & Larsen, J. (1993). *Direct social work practice: Theory and skills* (4th ed.) Belmont, CA: Wadsworth.

Humphry, D. (1991). *Final exit: The practicalities of self-deliverance and assisted suicide for the dying.* Eugene, OR: Hemlock Society.

Johnson, L. (1995). *Social work practice: A generalist approach* (5th ed.). Boston: Allyn & Bacon.

Levine, B. (1991). *Group psychotherapy: Practice and development.* Prospect Heights, IL: Waveland Press.

Maguire, L. (1983). *Understanding social networks.* Beverly Hills, CA: Sage.

Markson, E. (1992). Physiological changes, illness, and health care use in later life. In B. Hess & E. Markson (Eds.), *Growing old in America* (4th ed., pp. 173–186). New Brunswick: Transaction.

Morrin, J. (1988). Art therapy groups in a geriatric institutional setting. In B. W. Maclennan, S. Saul, & M. B. Weinder (Eds.), *Group psychotherapies for the elderly* (pp. 245–256). Madison, CT: International Universities Press.

Neugarten, B. (1975). The future and the young-old. *The Gerontologist, 15,* 4–9.

Nuland, S. (1994). *How we die: Reflections on life's final chapter.* New York, Alfred A. Knopf.

Ozawa, M. (1995). The economic status of vulnerable older women. *Social Work, 40,* 323–333.

Rice, S., & Goodman, C. (1992). Support groups for older people: Is homogeneity or heterogeneity the answer? *Groupwork, 5,* 65–75.

Rice, S., & Kelly, J. (1987). Love and intimacy needs of the elderly: Some philosophical and intervention issues. *Journal of Social Work and Human Sexuality, 5,* 89–96.

Samburg, S. (1988). Dance therapy groups for the elderly. In B. W. MacLennan, S. Saul, & M. B. Weinder (Eds.), *Group psychotherapies for the elderly* (pp. 233–243). Madison, CT: International Universities Press.

Schmidt, M. G. (1990). *Negotiating a good old age: Challenges of residential living in late life.* San Francisco: Jossey-Bass.

Schwartz, W. (1977). Social group work: The interactionist approach. In J. E. Turner (Ed.), *Encyclopedia of social work,* Vol. 2 (pp. 1328–1337). New York: National Association of Social Workers.

Shulman, L. (1991). *Interactional social work practice.* Itasca, IL: FE Peacock.

Sokolovsky, J. (Ed.). (1990). *The cultural context of aging: Worldwide perspectives.* New York: Bergin and Garvey.

Suzman, R., Willis, D., & Manton, K. (1992). *The oldest old.* New York: Oxford University Press.

Toner, J. (1993). Concepts of respite care: A gerontologist's perspective. In L. Tepper & J. Toner (Eds.), *Respite care: Programs, problems and solutions* (pp. 123–131). Philadelphia: Charles Press.

Woods, M., & Hollis, F. (1990). *Casework: A psychosocial therapy* (4th ed.). New York: McGraw-Hill.

III

VIOLENCE: VICTIMS
AND PERPETRATORS

9

Working with Victims of Ethnoviolence

Joan C. Weiss

Incidents of harassment, intimidation, assault, or vandalism can be particularly traumatic and have long-lasting effects when directed against people because of their race, ethnicity, religion, or sexual orientation. The terms *hate crime*, *bias crime*, and *ethnoviolence* are used interchangeably to describe such incidents. This chapter will provide social workers with an understanding of the nature of such incidents and their effects on victims.

Knowledge of ethnoviolence is critical for all group work because any group may contain members whose experiences of ethnoviolence may affect their reactions to and behaviors regarding a wide range of issues and actions, as well as to other people both in and out of the group. In communities dealing with intergroup tensions and incidents, there may be a clear need for a group of victims of ethnoviolence. Ethnoviolence can occur in neighborhoods or workplaces, such as when an individual or a family is the first of a minority group to appear on the block or in the office; in public places; or when someone is attacked while walking down a street.

A group format is particularly well suited to this population for several reasons. All members of a family are affected when one member has been victimized, so group work with one or more families may be indicated. Also, when one person in a community has been targeted, such as for racial reasons, there are frequently others who have had similar experiences. Further, seldom is there only one isolated incident; victims often have experienced numerous incidents over time. Perhaps most important, being a victim of violence stigmatizes and isolates individuals. Sharing the experiences and ways of coping with them in a group can be cathartic and healing and can provide a support network for the future.

REVIEW OF THE LITERATURE

Although victimization based on race, ethnicity, religion, or sexual orientation is not new, it is only during the last 10–15 years that social workers have worked with groups whose primary characteristic is their members' experiences of ethnoviolence. Prior to that time, people who were victimized because of their group identity, rather than for any act they committed, turned to institutions representing their groups for support. African-Americans could count on support from the NAACP or local churches; Jews turned to the Anti-Defamation League or the American Jewish Committee; and so on. Informal support often came from family members and neighbors.

In 1979, police departments began keeping records of bias crimes. The Boston and New York City police departments were two of the first in the country to do so and had units designated to handle such crimes; other cities soon followed. In Maryland, Montgomery and Baltimore counties were two jurisdictions whose police departments began keeping such records early. Each assigned community relations specialists to deal with the problems of investigating hate crimes and their impact both on the victims and on the communities involved.

Local and state human rights agencies began working with victims of hate crimes and began formal efforts to provide support to victims. Programs that agencies developed included those designed to train citizens to respond to victims in their communities. The "Network of Neighbors" and "Network of Teens," created by the Commission on Human Relations in Montgomery County, Maryland, to provide support to adult and youthful victims, are examples of programs that have been replicated in other jurisdictions. Training on issues of victimization and in basic skills of support is available to people who join the groups (Montgomery County Commission on Human Relations, 1984).

National organizations that have tracked racially and religiously motivated incidents, as well as neo-Nazi, Ku Klux Klan, and other hate group activities, include the Southern Poverty Law Center and its affiliate, Klanwatch, in Alabama and the Anti-Defamation League in New York City. In 1985, the first national organization devoted exclusively to research, education, and training on the problem of ethnoviolence was established in Baltimore. The National Institute Against Prejudice and Violence (now operating as The Prejudice Institute) conducted the first nationwide study of ethnoviolence and its effects on victims.

National attention to the problem of hate crimes, and the efforts of a coalition of organizations representing a wide range of minority populations and civil rights groups, led to the passage of the Hate Crime Statistics Act of 1990. The law requires the Attorney General of the

United States to compile data and publish a summary of crimes that "manifest evidence of prejudice based on race, religion, sexual orientation or ethnicity" for 5 years beginning in 1990.

While there are no accurate nationwide data on the prevalence of hate crimes, the data that do exist reveal a widespread problem that warrants serious attention. The Uniform Crime Reporting Section of the FBI is responsible for maintaining the data collected under the Hate Crime Statistics Act. In its report *Hate Crime Statistics 1993*, the FBI indicated that 6,865 law enforcement agencies (of the 16,000 that report to the FBI), representing 46 states and the District of Columbia and covering 58% of the U.S. population, had reported 7,587 bias-motivated criminal incidents.* These incidents involved 9,372 victims and 8,987 offenses. Seventy percent of the offenses were crimes against persons. Sixty-two percent of the incidents were motivated by race and 17% by religion. Sexual orientation was the motivation in 11% of the incidents. The rest, 9%, were motivated by the ethnicity of the victims, primarily Hispanic. Fifty-nine percent of the racial incidents were antiblack; 31% were antiwhite. The rest were directed largely against Asians, Native Americans, or multiracial groups. Eighty-eight percent of the incidents motivated by religious bias were directed against Jews. There were 16 murders, 15 rapes, 1,452 aggravated assaults, 1,754 simple assaults, and 3,056 acts of intimidation, as well as 2,666 property crimes (FBI, 1995).

Official statistics understate the problem of hate crimes because many victims of hate crimes do not report them to the police. Reasons for not reporting vary. For immigrant groups, there is often a language barrier and, for some, fear of the police. In some communities, victims do not trust the police. For other victims, the level of frustration with the inability of police to apprehend perpetrators convinces them that reporting an incident will not accomplish anything. In cases of assault where the perpetrator is known, there is frequently fear of retaliation. In addition to nonreporting by victims, official statistics are low because police do not always accurately identify or record the motivation in a bias incident.

Information from organizations that represent victimized populations further illuminates the problem. The Anti Defamation League, which documents anti-Semitism, publishes an annual audit of incidents reported to its offices around the country. In 1993, they recorded 1,867 incidents against Jews in 44 states and the District of Columbia. The incidents represented an 8% increase over 1992, primarily in incidents directed against persons rather than property (Anti-Defamation League, 1994).

The National Gay and Lesbian Task Force Policy Institute publishes an annual report of anti-gay incidents. Victim service agencies in six cities— Boston, Chicago, Denver, Minneapolis/St. Paul, New York City, and San

---

*The four states for which there were no reports are Hawaii, Nebraska, West Virginia, and Minnesota.

Francisco—documented 1,813 incidents in 1993, a decrease of 14% from 1992 (National Gay and Lesbian Task Force Policy Institute, 1994).

In April 1994, the National Asian Pacific American Legal Consortium published their first annual report, *Audit of Violence Against Asian Pacific Americans, 1993*. The Consortium documented 335 reported anti-Asian incidents in 1993, including 30 homicides in which racial animus was suspected or proven.

Little is known about victims of ethnoviolence, their responses to incidents, and the impact of victimization on their lives. There are anecdotal reports that have been collected over the years and some studies. The reactions to being a target of ethnoviolence are both similar to and different from those of victims of random acts of violence. On the one hand, the feelings of victims of ethnoviolence are common to victims of crime in general: anger, fear, vulnerability. Many crime victims experience psychosocial adjustment problems including disorientation, fear, helplessness, anger, and depression (Davis, 1987; Office for Victims of Crime, 1994; Resick, 1987). Further, being victimized by crime sparks fear of further victimization, often resulting in changes in behavior (Skogan, 1987).

As with other crime victims, the seriousness of the crime does not necessarily determine the extent of reactions of a victim of ethnoviolence (Ehrlich, Larcom, & Purvis, 1994). That is, the victim of repeated harassment who suffers no physical injury may take longer to recover emotionally and return to a normal pattern of activities than the victim of a serious assault. The duration of reactions and the level of life disruption depend on a host of factors, including the social context of the incident, the meaning of the incident to the victim, availability of a network of support, and individual coping mechanism.

On the other hand, being targeted for who one is rather than for something one has done creates fears and feelings that separate victims of ethnoviolence from victims of random violence. Research findings indicate that victims of ethnoviolence suffer more in response to incidents of comparable violence than do victims of random crimes (Ehrlich et al., 1994). If one is convinced that being a victim was a matter of time and place, one can try to avoid those circumstances. But correctly believing that one is being attacked for how one looks, or for one's identity, can create an ongoing level of fear that one is forever at risk.

In 1986, the National Institute Against Prejudice and Violence conducted a pilot study of the effects of hate crimes on minority group members. Ten focus groups were convened around the country and victims, identified through police departments, human rights organizations, and community leaders, were interviewed using open-ended questions. Crimes the victims had experienced included physical assault; harassment and threats by mail, telephone, and in person; vandalism to their homes; and symbols or slogans of hate on their property. The costs to victims can be emotional, physical, and financial, and the effects can be long-lasting. The most prevalent reaction was anger toward the perpetrator (68%), followed by fear for the safety of their families (51%). Over one third indicated a feeling of sadness. Behavioral changes were also reported by one-third of the victims. Actions taken by victims included moving, reducing social interactions, taking security measures, and purchasing guns, both for increased safety and in preparation for retaliation if attacked again. Almost one-third of the victims never reported their experiences to the police (Barnes & Ephross, 1994; Ephross, Barnes, Ehrlich, Sandnes, & Weiss, 1986; Weiss, 1990).

The first national study designed to assess the prevalence and impact of ethnoviolence and other forms of victimization was also conducted by the National Institute Against Prejudice and Violence in 1989. Telephone interviews, using a stratified random sample, were completed with 2,078 respondents. To determine how the experience of being victimized in general compared with being victimized because of prejudice, interviewers asked subjects about symptoms they experienced that are associated with stress. A comparison of four groups of respondents—nonvictims, victims of group defamation, victims of random crimes, and victims of hate crimes—revealed that victims of ethnoviolence experienced the greater number of negative psychophysiological symptoms, as well as the greatest number of social and behavioral changes of any group. (Examples of psychological and psychophysiological symptoms included feeling depressed or sad, feeling more nervous than usual, having trouble sleeping, and feeling very angry. Social and behavioral changes included moving to another neighborhood, trying to be less visible, buying or carrying a gun, and taking a self-defense class.) The study concluded that victims of ethnoviolence exhibited more symptoms with greater frequency than did victims of random violence (Ehrlich et al., 1994).

PRACTICE PRINCIPLES
Maintain Objectivity and Balance

In working with victims of ethnoviolence in groups, it is critical that social workers be in touch with (1) their own experiences with ethnoviolence that might affect the way they view others' experiences and (2) prejudices that might interfere with working with such victims. While this principle applies under all circumstances, work with victims of ethnoviolence calls for a particular combination of skills.

> A worker must be empathic and sensitive to the pain, yet maintain sufficient detachment to be effective. . . . Maintaining this delicate balance can cause a worker considerable stress. Additional strain often derives from the inherent limits of the situation: legal remedies are often infeasible or unenforceable. The perpetrator is nameless and faceless, official response sometimes denigrates the experience, and the ultimate enemy—the conditions and institutions that breed the isms in society—seem undefeatable. (Weiss & Ephross, 1986, p. 134)

Understand Intergroup Relations

It is critical for the social worker not only to have a general understanding of the history of minority groups and their interactions with each other, but also to have clear sense of the intergroup factors that exist in the community in which one is working. For example, the stereotypes minority groups have about each other, and the possibility of competition between victim groups, can interfere with the goals of the group. The social worker must understand the history and current state of black–Jewish relations, for example, or the feelings of other minority groups regarding the apparent success of Asian-American immigrants. The interplay of race/ethnicity and social class influences reactions such as resentment and lack of empathy and must be understood.

Focus on the Present and on the Individual

The issues surrounding intergroup relations and the historical factors affecting victims' feelings demand that the social worker acknowledge the impact of the past. Racial/ethnic group histories can become a major force to be contended with in victim groups and can be used by group members to avoid dealing with current victimization issues. Victims may want to talk about historical events that affected their families and are recalled by the current incidents. Without minimizing the impact of history, the social worker must help the individual and the group stay focused on recent events and how they affected the victim. It is important to help group members see the costs and benefits of identifying themselves as victims and the positive results that could result from their gaining a feeling of empowerment.

COMMON THEMES

Fear

The fear connected with ethnoviolence often affects not only the individual victim, but the family and community as well. An underestimated aspect of ethnoviolence is the ripple effect on the community. One case the author dealt with involved a black family who had a cross burned on their lawn. They had a young daughter and, after the incident, were very fearful about the possibility that the unknown perpetrator would attack again. Overly cautious behavior began to govern their lives. They no longer allowed their daughter to walk to her friends' houses on the same block alone. Worse, families in the neighborhood—well-meaning and supportive on the surface—did not let their children visit the home of the victim family for fear that their children might be in danger if another, more serious incident occurred while they were visiting.

Fear associated with having been targeted for attack can affect the entire group. Individuals may be highly suspicious of others and reluctant to trust the social worker or, if it was a racial incident, any members of another race, for example.

Anger

Many victims of ethnoviolence are angry. The anger is directed not just toward the perpetrator, whether known or unknown. Frequently, there is a great deal of anger toward the police. The rate of arrests for crime is low to begin with and extremely low in cases of property crime where the perpetrator acted under cover of darkness, without witnesses. Victims often feel frustrated by the lack of resolution and afraid of the nameless, faceless enemy, about whom they can do nothing. That frustration is often directed at the police and other aspects of the criminal justice system. Anger and frustration may also be directed at the social worker and other members of the group.

Members must be given an opportunity to vent their feelings, and have them validated by others in the group, lest they turn the anger toward themselves. A major goal of the group is to help victims move beyond their anger so that they can deal with the aftermath of incidents constructively and return their daily routines to normal.

Physical and Psychological Symptoms and Behaviors

Like other types of victimization, ethnoviolence can result in a wide range of physical and psychological symptoms. Examples of physical symptoms are changes in sleep patterns (difficulty falling asleep, waking frequently during the night), weight loss or gain, and development of nervous tics. Psychological symptoms include fear of all strangers who look like the perpetrator (or imagined perpetrator), being particularly jumpy in response to unexpected noise, or being suspicious of everyone, including friends and acquaintances if the act was committed by a stranger ("How do I know who I can trust?"). Changes in behavior include resuming or increasing smoking or drinking, changing routes walked or driven to work, changing jobs, moving, staying home, or becoming particularly protective of children. Some symptoms may manifest themselves in ways of which victims may be unaware. Conversely, victims can blame their victimization for things that occur in their lives that may or may not be connected to the victimization. A critical role for the social worker in working with groups of victims of hate crimes is to facilitate discussions of symptoms and behaviors that are problematic for the group members, and help them separate the ones related to the victimization from those that need other types of attention.

Dealing with Legal Issues and the Criminal Justice System

It is important that the social worker serve as an advocate for the victims, and make appropriate referrals to legal resources, while maintaining clear boundaries. Acts of ethnoviolence may or may not be crimes by legal definition. Some victims, for example, may be suffering because of repeated verbal harassment that allows no legal recourse because the incidents did not qualify as crimes. In some cases, the victim may be working with the police to identify perpetrators; in others, there may be no leads to the perpetrators. In still other cases, the victims may be loath to report the victimization to police, either because of fear (as in the case of illegal aliens who are victims) or because of past experience leading to the conviction that the police cannot do anything (Doerner & Lab, 1995). Issues and concerns frequently arise that are related to working with the criminal justice system. Victims worry, Will I be in danger if I identify the perpetrator or testify at a trial? Will my family? Can the police protect me? What will happen during the trial? Who will pay for the damage to my property?

As with all groups, members can benefit greatly from each other's experiences. Social workers should be knowledgeable about the laws that apply both statewide and locally, and be able to answer basic questions. While it is appropriate for social workers to be advocates, and to identify appropriate resources and information within the criminal justice system that might be helpful to clients, they should not give advice on whether to press charges or take particular actions that the police might recommend; instead, they should facilitate group members' own decision-making processes.

Continued Interaction with the Offender/Perpetrator

When the incidents have occurred in the workplace or when the perpetrator is someone with whom the victim comes in contact regularly, such as a next-door neighbor, victims need guidance on how to handle unavoidable interactions and how to avoid confrontations. Discussion of these realities often forms a significant part of groups' content and consciousness.

RECOMMENDED WAYS OF WORKING

Agency Context

One type of agency particularly well suited to groups of victims of hate crimes is a local human rights (or human relations) agency that deals with discrimination in housing, employment, and public accommodations. Since 1980, human relations commissions have added a community relations unit that specializes in intergroup conflict in the community. School systems, also used to dealing with intergroup tension, can also provide the official context for such groups, particularly when juveniles are involved, either as victims or as perpetrators.

Time Frame

Groups of victims of ethnoviolence need immediate crisis counseling and help in dealing with the immediate aftermath of the incident. It is important to provide assistance within a few days so that the immediate fear of danger can be addressed. Although there is no reason why groups of victims should not meet for a long period (12 months or more), and although group members could certainly provide support for each other through the often grueling period of arrest and trial, if they occur, the most critical time is the first few weeks following an incident. A short-term group (4 to 6 weeks) can frequently address the most critical issues.

Open versus Closed Groups

While either type can be used, there are several advantages to an open group when working with victims. One never knows when support for victims will be needed, and it is better for a victim to have immediate access to an ongoing group, and deal with problems of acceptance and entry, than to wait until a new group starts. Incidents, with or without physical harm, should be treated as crises initially. Also, victims at different stages can help each other, not only with emotional support but also with practical advice (such as dealing with the police and other parts of the justice system).

Coleadership Involving a Team with Different Races, Ethnicities, or Orientations

Victims of ethnoviolence are often more wary of other groups after an incident. While a coleadership team can represent only a few categories, it is frequently advantageous for such a team to work with a victim group. Coleaders can defuse the fear and distrust that might exist toward a particular person who may look like the perpetrator. Also, coleaders can model openness about racial or other sensitive issues. Because white social workers feel less successful when working with minority group members than do minority social workers (Davis & Gelsomino, 1994), and because groups of hate crime victims may be composed entirely or primarily of members of minority groups, a coleadership team may contribute to the success of the group.

Working with the Entire Family When the Victim Is a Child

Sometimes the group consists simply of the family. An important issue when a child is attacked, either in the neighborhood or in school, is that of parents becoming overprotective. In some cases, the children want to return to normal routines, which may make parents uneasy. Parents sometimes want the child to change schools or stop walking to school when the child is worried more about the stigma attached to those behaviors than to any danger. In order cases, a child who has been harassed or intimidated is too ashamed to tell parents and is worried about their reaction, particularly if the parents have told stories of their own experiences. The social worker can help family members separate the realities from the fears, and can help the parents and child sort out what is relevant from the past and what needs to be addressed now.

Dealing with Language Barriers

An inadequate command of the English language coupled with cultural differences may prevent some victims of ethnoviolence from reporting incidents or participating in programs of support. Studies by service providers have pointed to the language barrier as one factor that makes access to services difficult for some minority groups (Browne & Broderick, 1994). There are several ways to address this problem. One is for materials providing helpful information and resources to be printed in as many languages as possible for a given community. Another is to limit some groups to a particular victim population and arrange for an interpreter to work with the social worker if a social worker who speaks the language of the victims is not available or trained to work with groups. In addition, social workers can train bilingual members of the victim community to serve as facilitators in self-help groups. Of course, attempts by the worker to gain even minimal command of other languages are helpful and appreciated by group members.

Mediation Between the Victim and the Offender

Ad hoc short-term groups can be an important tool of social workers dealing with ethnoviolence. Mediating the conflict between the victim and the offender can be the purpose of such a group, particularly when there is continued interaction between the victim and the offender through work, school, or neighborhood contact. Critical group work skills are required for effective mediation. Following is a case study of a successful use of mediation:

> A 16-year-old white youth assaulted a black youth of the same age on a basketball court during an informal after-school game, calling him names such as "dirty nigger," The fight was stopped by a school official. Police were not called because there were no serious injuries and no weapon was involved. Because a racial epithet had been used, however, and because school officials learned that the white youth had been harassing the black youth for some time, they contacted the local human relations commission and asked for assistance. They were afraid that the tension between the youths would spill over to other students and become more violent. The community relations specialist, a white female social worker, had the school arrange a meeting with both youths at the school one evening. Each student was required to bring one parent. The social worker brought a black male police officer experienced in community relations work. No school official was permitted to participate. Over the

course of two sessions of 2 hours each, the black student talked about his feelings about being called racist names and being attacked. The white student expressed no remorse at first, only anger toward the black student, who had teased him for months because he was very short. When the black student realized how painful the white youth's stature was for him, and had been for years, he was able to forgive the assault. The mediation was followed up by periodic contacts for the rest of the school year; the intervention was successful in averting what could have been an explosive situation.

EVALUATION APPROACHES

There have been no rigorous evaluations of work with groups of ethnoviolence victims. However, it is not difficult to evaluate their impact. The primary purpose of such groups is to help victims express and work through the psychological and psychophysiological symptoms they experience and empower them to make critical decisions about the criminal justice system, if that is relevant, and about choices they need to make (such as whether to move, change jobs, etc.).

One way to evaluate the effectiveness of the group experience is to have members fill out questionnaires at the inception regarding the nature of the incident, symptoms they are experiencing, concerns they have, and decisions they would like to make. They could then complete another questionnaire when they leave the group to determine how much they felt they had accomplished.

With juveniles, both they and their parents could fill out relevant questionnaires. Follow-up could be done with them, as well as with their teachers, if the victimization was affecting classroom performance and/or behavior.

CONCLUSION

Groups offer particular advantages for work with victims of ethnoviolence. Working with such groups calls for sophisticated knowledge both of the issues involved and of group work skills. Social workers must have a clear understanding of the manifestations of victimization based on race, religion, ethnicity, or sexual 'orientation in order to determine whether crises in the group are related to the group process, the stage of development, or individuals' experiences of trauma.

Knowledge about ethnoviolence is also valuable for social workers called on to work with other types of groups. Interorganizational task groups or committees created to address violence in schools, workplaces, or communities would benefit from social workers' knowledge of ethnoviolence and the ways in which it affects both individuals and the groups to which they belong.

NATIONAL RESOURCES

Anti-Defamation League
823 United Nations Plaza
New York, NY 10017
(212) 490-2525

National Asian Pacific American
  Legal Consortium
1629 K St., NW
Washington, DC 20006
(202) 296-2300

National Association for the
  Advancement of Colored People
  (NAACP)
4805 Mt. Hope Drive
Baltimore, MD 21215
(410) 358-8900

National Gay and Lesbian Task
  Force Policy Institute
1734 14th St., NW
Washington, DC 20009-4309
(202) 332-6483

The Prejudice Institute
Center for the Applied Study
  of Ethnoviolence
Stephens Hall Annex
Towson State University
Towson, MD 21204
(410) 830-2435

Southern Poverty Law Center
400 Washington Ave.
Montgomery, AL 36104
(334) 264-0286

U.S. Department of Justice
Community Relations Service
5550 Friendship Boulevard
Chevy Chase, MD 20815
(301) 492-5929

REFERENCES

Anti-Defamation League. (1994). 1993 *audit of anti-Semitic incidents.* New York: Author.

Barnes, A. J., & Ephross, P. H. (1994). The impact of hate violence on victims: Emotional and behavioral responses to attacks. *Social Work, 39*(3), 247–251.

Browne, C., & Broderick, A. (1994). Asian and Pacific Island elders: Issues for social work practice and education. *Social Work, 39*(3), 252–259.

Davis, L. E., & Gelsomino, J. (1994). An assessment of practitioner cross-racial treatment experiences. *Social Work, 39*(1), 116–123.

Davis, R. C. (1987). Studying the effects of services for victims in crisis. *Crime and Delinquency, 33*(4), 520–531.

Doerner, W. G., & Lab, S. P. (1995). *Victimology.* Cincinnati: Anderson Publishing Co.

Ehrlich, H. J. (1990). *Campus ethnoviolence and the policy options* (Report No. 4). Baltimore: National Institute Against Prejudice and Violence.

Ehrlich, H. J. (1992). Campus ethnoviolence: A research review (Report No. 5). Baltimore: National Institute Against Prejudice and Violence.

Ehrlich, H. J., Larcom, B. E. K., & Purvis, R. D. (1994). *The traumatic effects of ethnoviolence.* Baltimore: The Prejudice Institute, Center for the Applied Study of Ethnoviolence.

Ephross, P. H., Barnes, A. J., Ehrlich, H. J., Sandnes, K. R., & Weiss, J. C. (1986). *The ethnoviolence project pilot study.* Baltimore: National Institute Against Prejudice and Violence.

Federal Bureau of Investigation, U.S. Department of Justice. (1991). *Training guide for hate crime data collection.* Washington, DC: Author

Federal Bureau of Investigation, U.S. Department of Justice. (1995). *Hate crime statistics, 1993.* Washington, DC: Author.

Herek, G. M. & Berrill, K. T. (eds.). (1992). *Hate crimes: Confronting violence against lesbians and gay men.* Newberry Park, CA: Sage.

Levin, J., & McDevitt, J. (1993). *Hate crimes: The rising tide of bigotry and bloodshed.* New York Plenum Press.

Montgomery County Commission on Human Relations. (1984). *People helping people: Training in support and communication skills.* Rockville, MD: Author.

National Asian Pacific American Legal Consortium. (1994). *Audit of Violence Against Asian Pacific Americans, 1993.* Washington, DC: Author.

National Gay and Lesbian Task Force Policy Institute. (1994). *Anti-gay/lesbian violence, victimization and defamation in 1993.* Washington, DC: Author.

Office for Victims of Crime, U.S. Department of Justice. (1994). *Report to Congress.* Washington, DC: Author.

Pincus, F. L., & Ehrlich, H. J. (1994). *Race and ethnic conflict: Contending views on prejudice, discrimination and ethnoviolence.* Boulder, CO: Westview Press.

Resick, P. A. (1987). Psychological effects of victimization: Implications for the criminal justice system. *Crime and Delinquency, 33*(4), 468–478.

Skogan, W. G. (1987). The impact of victimization on fear. *Crime and Delinquency, 33*(1), 135–154.

Weiss, J. C. (1990) Violence motivated by bigotry: "Ethnoviolence." *Encyclopedia of Social Work* (18th ed., 1990 supplement, 307–319). Silver Spring, MD: NASW Press.

Weiss, J. C., Ehrlich, H. J., & Larcom, B. E. K. (1991–1992). Ethnoviolence at work. *Journal of Intergroup Relations, 18*(4), 21–33.

Weiss, J. C., & Ephross, P. H. (1986). Group work approaches to hate/violence incidents. *Social Work, 31*(2), 132–136.

10

Group Work with Women Who Have Experienced Abuse

Margot Breton and Anna Nosko

This chapter discusses specific aspects of group practice with women who have experienced abuse in their relationships with male partners. This practice is based on a recognition of the women's strengths and of their competence to identify what they want and what they need, as well as the competence of practitioners to activate the mutual aid dynamics of groups. One mutual aid group is used to illustrate various points: it is sponsored by the Family Services Association of Toronto (which has sponsored such groups for over a decade) and will be referred to as the *FSA group*. It meets in a multiservice center that has a full health clinic, a full legal clinic, and a counseling unit; the coleaders of the group are in the counseling unit. Working out of a multiservice center helps the group leaders maintain a broad perspective on the context of the group and on the members' issues and needs. It also allows them to keep in mind that, when dealing with a social problem such as violence against women, interdisciplinary cooperation is essential to providing effective services, as research findings indicate (see, e.g., Horton & Johnson, 1993).

The female coleaders of the FSA group have worked for 10 years with women who have experienced abuse. They have learned that it is best if the decision on whether the group should remain open or closed is not predetermined before the group begins to meet but rather is made by the coleaders and the group members together. Although the FSA group has a limit of 12 members, the group may be closed when, after several weeks, there is a core of 7 or 8 members, and both the workers and the members agree that the size is right for a productive group. If the membership drops off, then the members can be asked how they feel about allowing more women into the group. Their answer has always been that they want more women in their position to benefit from the group experience. Whether the group is short- or long-term is negotiated between the women and the agency—the number of women awaiting entry into the group being one of the most important determining factors for reopening the group.

Even though the cost of having two workers exceeds that of having only one, experience has shown that the increment in benefits of having a coleader is greater than the increment in costs because coleadership (1) provides the women with a model of a relationship based on equality, respect, and caring; (2) demonstrates to the women that two people can be different and yet can accept their differences, work together, accommodate, and adapt to each other; (3) offers the workers the opportunity to debrief after the sessions, which lessens the probability of burnout, always high in work with this population, as studies have shown (see, e.g., Horton & Johnson, 1993); and (4) becomes a support system for the workers (Chataway & Nosko, 1989).

The major reasons for working with the women *in a group* are that (1) groups offer a warm, accepting, and caring milieu in which the women can feel secure and appreciated—the tendency of professionals in responding to the plight of women who have experienced abuse is to consider them *deviant* for staying with the abusers (Saunders, 1993): other women "in the same boat" do not have that tendency; (2) groups provide the ideal structure for consciousness raising, that is, for dispelling a number of false perceptions (including that of being alone with the particular problem and/or that of being somehow responsible for the violence they experience), as well as for instilling new perceptions (such as that of connecting their personal situations with the structural/political conditions that affect them collectively); and (3) groups are the most efficient venue for accessing information on how other women handle their situations and on what they have done or are doing to change these situations. Sharing such information is one of the aspects of mutual aid groups most highly valued by the women. As Killilea (1976, p. 72) noted: "what constitutes 'help' is often a new definition of the problem and specific information about practicalities learned through experience and shared with others because it 'works'."

REVIEW OF THE LITERATURE

Knowledge of wife assault is evolving, and perhaps because this is a relatively new field of study, many myths still abound (Saunders, 1993). Compounding the problem, the etiology of female battering is difficult to explore, for the privacy of the family, traditionally paramount in most societies, is respected both legally and socially. This hampers the work of researchers who wish to conduct empirical studies of spouse abuse (Horton

& Johnson, 1993). Furthermore, some of the earlier work in the field is being challenged, if not discredited. For example:

> Clinical lore of a decade ago presented similar profiles of the offender and victim. They were both said to be from violent homes, to be isolated, to be deficient in communication skills, and to have low self-esteem. Recent reviews of empirical studies make it clear that it is the offender who differs most from the norm. Hotaling and Sugarman (1986) reviewed controlled studies of husband-to-wife violence. Out of 15 risk factors reviewed, the men had nine, including nonassertiveness, alcohol abuse, and a propensity to abuse their children. The women, on the other hand, had only one risk factor: a greater likelihood of having witnessed violence between their parents. (Saunders, 1993, pp. 209–210)

The early literature on female spouse abuse presents issues from a psychological/victim perspective, viewing the women as pathological; for example, the concept of masochism assumes that women enjoy suffering (see Gelles, 1979, on this point). The literature then moves from pathology to social and structural issues; for example, social learning theories postulate that one learns to be a victim first through intergenerational transmission of violence and then through rigid sex role definitions (MacLeod, 1987). This theory of learned helplessness assumes that women do not learn the skills necessary to leave abusive situations (Walker, 1983). Social interaction theory views men as attempting to gain control over their spouses through various means, including the use of violence; this is deemed particularly relevant where there is a threat from female competence (Saunders & Hanusa, 1986). Resource theories connect abuse to economic issues, surmising that a woman's greater status and resources undermine the man's traditional role as breadwinner, with violence seen as a way to regain control (Brown, 1980). Sociocultural theories view violence as endemic to society and therefore as normal (Straus, 1980). The structural/political approach (Dobash & Dobash, 1979; Pahl, 1985), adopting a historic overview, examines how social institutions, over the millennia and in all societies, condone a husband's authority over his wife and support laws such as the "rule of thumb" in England, whereby a husband could hit his wife with a stick no wider than his thumb. (For an excellent and comprehensive review of the above literature, see Health and Welfare Canada, 1989.)

More recent studies focus on women who cope with abusive situations (Nurius, Furrey, & Berliner, 1992) or have successfully ended them. For example, Horton and Johnson (1993) document the tremendous investments women make to end the abuse in their lives. This new research recognizes women's strengths and resourcefulness. Building on this research, it is important to look for new solution. Until recently, one of the most common approaches to the problem of spouse abuse was to enjoin women to leave their spouses. Yet research indicates that the majority of women return to their partners (Horton & Johnson, 1993). This information challenges the field to find out from the women themselves what it is they want changed. It also indicates that it is time to develop practice principles that build on the strengths and resourcefulness of women who have experienced abuse.

Before discussing these principles, we want to make a point about the use of theories in the kind of group practice we advocate. Practitioners should not focus on theories that purport to explain wife assault or women battering but should listen to the women themselves as *they* explain their reality. In other words, it is essential to stop looking at the women through the lenses of theories. A change of theoretical lenses does not suffice, for these lenses always distort. It is not a question of adopting a particular clinical or political stance or theoretical perspective, whether it represents the latest research or the latest fad, because the women and their experiences (recognized as diverse; see, e.g., Nurius et al., 1992) simply do not fit neatly within any one theory. The leaders of the FSA group, instead of teaching the women, as they used to do, about the theory of learned helplessness for example, now ask them if that theory applies to them. Some say yes and others no, and the leaders, willing to learn from the women, treat the answers as information that becomes a learning tool for everyone in the group. This in no way implies that practitioners do not have a very important leadership role to play in a group, nor that they can ignore the latest research and theories. It simply emphasizes that they need to subordinate the theories to what the women identify as their reality.

PRACTICE PRINCIPLES

The practice principles that should guide social workers beginning with a group of women who have experienced abuse are essentially the same as those principles guiding all practice that is focused on strengths and competence and is empowerment oriented (see, e.g., Breton, 1994; Cowger, 1994; Saleebey, 1992). Such practice demands that from the outset the workers *demonstrate respect for the women*. This first principle is operationalized through the following actions and attitudes: (1) *let each woman tell her story* and encourage her to use her new-found voice to "name [her] world" (Freire, 1993, p. 159); (2) *believe the women*, their stories, and what they understand as the facts. In other words, accept their representation of their situation as "legitimate knowledge" (Weick, 1992, p. 23), and do not assume that the women have low self-esteem (Saunders, 1993). A rather telling and funny dialogue took place in the group one day:

Woman: I have no self-esteem.
Worker: What does self-esteem mean to you?
Woman: I don't know, really.
Worker: Well then, maybe you have some.
Woman: Well, yeah . . .

This interchange emphasizes the need for workers to have a sense of humor, which, as Malekoff (1994, p. 7) points out, refers to "the ability to see the humor in a situation or exchange and the capacity not to take oneself too seriously." This "in no way refers to making light of deadly subjects as an end in itself. What it implies is a flexibility of mind and spirit and the faith and trust that the group can and will, with a little assistance, move through the humor in a growth inducing way" (p. 8); (3) *facilitate the process of consciousness raising:* (a) affirm the actual and potential competence and strengths of the women, emphasizing "how they have survived thus far" (Goldstein, 1992, p. 32) and using their stories and their "own knowledge of their lives . . . as a natural resource" (Weick, 1992, p. 24); (b) confront the oppressor within (Freire, 1993) and challenge negative self-images and self-evaluations; (c) help the women to identify, as they become aware of the patterns in their stories, the common social, political, economic, and cultural contexts of their situations. This last guideline should not be construed as a license to proselytize and to impose the workers' belief system or values on the members. On the contrary, it is up to the women themselves to choose what to do with the awareness they develop of the interconnection of issues. The workers should inform them of various alternatives, including some form of social action, but the choice remains the women's.

Thus the second principle, which flows from the first, is that workers *base all interventions on member self-determination.* To make this operational requires that the workers *trust the members.* In a group, one major manifestation of the workers' trust is the emergence of a mutual aid system, for this happens when workers trust the members to help one another. From the very beginning of the group, as the women tell their stories, each woman realizes that hearing the stories of others makes her feel less alone and better about herself. When the workers acknowledge that the women are indeed the experts at helping each other, the process of mobilizing and supporting their competence and strengths can begin.

Self-determination also requires that workers *identify what the women want.* As Rapp (1992, p. 48) states unequivocally: "if client self-determination is to be taken seriously, the client's desires must be given absolute primacy." This may cause problems for workers when a group member chooses to stay with an abusive partner, but it is *not* the workers' prerogative to dictate what another person should want. Challenging, discussing, confronting—those behaviors are in the workers' rightful domain; pretending to know what is best for other people is not. It is important to signal here that the notion of contracting, as a formal mechanism to ensure self-determination and to establish the specific conditions under which the group will operate, may not always be relevant to work with a group of women who have experienced abuse; it may have to be abandoned if the women interpret it as a constraint that locks them into a situation and once again makes them feel controlled. What is essential is to be accountable to the women; how this accountability plays itself out will vary, depending on a number of factors, including the cultural background of the women and their individual motivations, including their distrust of would-be helpers, their fear of failure, and their aversion to risk taking (Breton, 1985).

To be accountable and to base interventions on self-determination means that workers are guided by a third principle, that of *individualization*. Pray (1991) makes a strong case that this principle is given lip service more than genuinely honored in traditional problem-focused and pathology-centered social work approaches. A renewed and vigorous interpretation of the principle, one that is congruent with a focus on strengths, competence, and empowerment, demands that workers (1) *eschew preconceived plans and solutions*, generic goals, and all other forms of "homogenization of clients" (Rapp, 1992, pp. 51–52)—*and of groups*, we hasten to add. This suggests a flexible approach to group structure. As indicated above, choosing an open or closed format, for example, will depend on the needs of the group at various points in its evolution. Individualization also suggests that the process of termination be left to the women to determine and be individually tailored; each member's termination should occur when she has achieved the goals she has set for herself and does not believe the group can be of further help

Individualization further requires that workers (2) *reject labels*, such as "abused women" and "abused women's group"; this implies seeing the women as whole persons, not just as victims. The idea is to reject the connotation of passivity that pervades the label of "victim" without rejecting the fact of victimization/oppression. The intention is to always put the accent on the women as active subjects, not as passive objects. Thus the reference to the members of the FSA group as "women who have experienced abuse" provides them an opportunity to take back some control over their lives by identifying the abuse as something *they* experienced, and not primarily as something *others* perpetrated against them. Workers who forget that women who have been victimized "above all are whole human beings with the same potential and aspirations as anyone else . . . further victimize them" (Breton, 1990, p. 26).

Seeing the women as whole persons demands that workers (3) *promote a group context and encourage group programs in which the women can demonstrate and share their specific strengths*, showcase their talents, and acknowledge their abilities, including their ability to empathize, nurture, and comfort each other, and practice and develop their skills. The group should enable the women to translate into action their changing ways of thinking and feeling about themselves.

However, like all human beings, the women need ongoing support networks, not only to sustain their present strengths and to maintain changes already achieved, but also to develop potential strengths and continue to make changes, a condition of survival and growth in this world. Although women who have experienced abuse usually need the support of a professionally led mutual aid group for a relatively long period of time, their relationship with the group and the workers eventually ends. The workers, knowing that the group's support is time limited, have the responsibility to ensure postgroup support that will endure over time.

Therefore, the last principle is that workers *make maximum use of natural supports in the community*. This entails that workers (1) *perceive the community as a resource* (Sullivan, 1992), identifying natural helpers and natural resources such as recreation centers, libraries, and Ys, informing women about these people and resources, and connecting them to each other if the women so wish. The principle also demands that workers (2) *maximize the potential support in the women's environment*, modifying existing structures or creating new ones to meet the members' needs (Wood & Middleman, 1989). Where personal natural support networks are nonexistent, workers encourage group members to see themselves as the first links in a new natural support system, one that exists outside of the group and will continue to exist once they leave the group (Breton, 1985). Finally, workers will be required to (3) *create partnerships in the community* (Breton, 1994). By acknowledging community strengths, and by accepting collaboration as partners with natural helpers and with normal community services and institutions, workers facilitate the women's perception of being not only members of a group but also members of a community, and thus facilitate their integration into that community.

COMMON THEMES AND HOW TO DEAL WITH THEM

Workers need to be prepared (tuned in) to pick up on themes that regularly come up in groups of women who have experienced abuse. An important one to emphasize from the very beginning is that of *power*. For example, assuming that the members cope with their situations, and expecting that they will share how they cope, harnesses the positive interactional energy of the group. The workers presume that each woman has some power and that together the women have greater power. Starting from a proactive position (namely, a position that postulates that the women already have strengths) lays a foundation for them to acknowledge the choices they make and to move toward different choices. This proactive stance is illustrated when workers ask "What are you doing to keep yourself safe?" instead of "Are you keeping yourself safe?"

Assuming that the women have *choices* creates an atmosphere of respect and encourages the women to see themselves as capable and open to yet other choices:

> *Barbara:* You know, I really don't want to leave my husband because I love him. I've invested too much for too many years to go—
>
> *Tina:* Me too. For thirty years I looked after him and raised my children so they would have a mother and father, but my job is done and I don't need to take it anymore.
>
> *Karen:* I have left many men, and I still haven't learned how to find a good man; do they exist?
>
> *Heddy:* If they abuse you, get rid of them, find someone else.

Many significant themes emerge from each interchange among the members. The workers keep a list of these individual "strands" and rethread them through the discussions. The women themselves then weave these strands into a coherent and resilient tapestry in which they are highlighted and from which radiates the support they get from and give each other.

One of these other significant themes is *safety*. It needs to be kept in the foreground of the group. The workers approach it from the perspective that each woman is responsible for her safety and that of her children, which again presumes that each woman is capable and competent. The concern for their children often motivates the women to do something about the violence they experience:

Jan: I won't let my child suffer like I did.

Heddy: It's not fair to the children. They shouldn't have to suffer from seeing all this abuse. I worry about how it is affecting them.

This concern is well founded; a Canadian national survey indicates that children witnessed violence against their mothers in almost 40% of marriages with violence (Rodgers, 1994; see also Hotaling & Sugarman, 1986). The theme of safety thus expands into the theme of *love for their children*, and the women move from considering their own experiences to reflecting on the different experiences they want their children to have. Workers who trust that it is the members who know best what will help them to reach their goals support the transformations or evolutions of themes.

The theme of safety also involves a consideration of *violence* per se and an examination of its possible sources. This often leads to exploring the *resources available* to do something about violence. These resources include knowledge of the legal system and of various social agencies, the role of the police and of one's physician, and so on. At this point, the women have an opportunity to share their experiences about resources and to pursue the themes of their *right to protection under the law* and their *right to access community resources*, the themes of the *adequacy of services* offered and of the *cultural and societal biases* influencing the reactions of police and physicians, as well as other related themes. As research indicates (Horton & Johnson, 1993, p. 490), "Clinicians' advocacy and educational roles are important factors in stopping the cycle of abuse."

It can be argued that *mutual aid* with its "strength in us" dynamic, constitutes the leitmotif or dominant theme that recurs throughout the duration of the group. For example, Miller (1991, p. 199) believes that one of the strengths women possess is being relational, that is, being adept at "using one's power to help another . . . increasing the other's resources, capabilities, effectiveness and ability to act." The mutual aid system of the group encourages and buttresses this relational strength or competence. As members explore themes important to them, they experience positive human relations:

> *Susan:*   I feel so comfortable talking about how I feel. If I'm dis-
> appointed with myself, I don't fear being judged or put down here,
> like I do by my husband.

The sense of acceptance and of respect is also achieved through another
mutual aid dynamic; the dialectical process that recognizes diversity and
differences along with the common ground:

> *Tina:*   You young women should save yourselves, don't wait till you
> are old like me.
> *Susan:*   Tina, you give me hope that it is never too late to change.
> *Worker:*   Each one of you has much to share; you can help each
> other in different ways.

Themes provide a "mirror" in which each woman sees part of herself
or her issue (Alonso & Rutan, 1988). For example, as Mary tells Jane to
stand up for herself (the theme of *assertiveness*), she also sees this advice
reflected back to her. In this way, many topics that are perceived as threatening or painful to broach are made safe because they are accessed indirectly. When the theme of abuse is activated and women *choose* to talk
about their experience, or even when only one woman, at a particular
point, chooses to talk, all the women become part of the disclosure; each
woman need not directly disclose all the specific details of her situation
because it is captured in the stories of others—hence the group mirror.

Any time the group discusses one of the themes, new knowledge is
gained. The group workers' role is to monitor these themes, label them,
reintroduce them when appropriate, add information that may be helpful,
expand, and connect them. For example, when the women talk about
how they have been trying hard to get their husbands to change, the
workers raise the point that they are presently focusing on changing the
other, yet earlier they had agreed that one can only change oneself. This
comment connects the discussion to earlier themes (those of *responsibility*
and *change*) and challenges the women to look in a direction in *which they
have more control and choice.*

EVALUATION APPROACHES

Evaluating the progress made by the abused women in the group would
enhance the process through which they acquire a voice, as suggested by
all empowerment research (Tolan, Keys, Chertak, & Jason, 1990). This
demands that the women participate in planning the evaluation, that is, in
deciding what will be evaluated and how. Indeed, if the purpose of
research is to provide useful information, "not just for professionals, but
for their clients" (Holmes, 1992, p. 159), then the participation of the
women as partners in the evaluation is imperative. In a collaborative
approach to the evaluation process, the members become research participants whose stake in the research is fully recognized (see, e.g., Lee, 1991).

As early as possible, therefore, and with the encouragement and help of the workers, the members should consider how the evaluation could "authenticate the resources and transformation capacities" that they have as individuals and as a group (Saleebey, 1992, p. 178) and how it could help them "to redefine their experience of the world, [and] to act within it from a position of greater human potential and power" (Holmes, 1992, p. 164). Empowerment research challenges the traditional assumption that what is important in the evaluation process is how the *professional* judges if there is change. In their study of women who have ended abuse, Horton and Johnson (1993, p. 491) recognize the inherent limitations of self-reporting but conclude that "Nevertheless, the women . . . were 'experts' on wife abuse. Researchers' tasks are to summarize the data victims provide, explore their strategies for ending abuse, and report what works and does not work."

In the FSA group, the workers no longer use formal evaluation measures to assess the women's progress. The women do this themselves in an ongoing way, every time they meet and throughout their meetings. For example, as she arrived one day, Lisa told the workers that her ex-boyfriend had been phoning her frequently during the past week, and she didn't know if she should let him come back. Her dilemma was brought up in the group, and as she discussed with other women what she should do, she evaluated the changes she had made thus far. She then admitted that to maintain the progress she had made, she would have to be very careful about not being enticed back into the relationship by her ex-partner's sweet words. To help her chart her progress, she employed an unorthodox but effective measure of progress used repeatedly in the group: "the garbage collection day" metaphor. The women had decided that each week, in the group, they have the opportunity to throw out old, useless ideas and behaviors to make room for new ones. As they help each other to discard their "garbage," they are conscious of making choices, making progress, and moving forward. This is, for them, a meaningful and valuable evaluation process. The more garbage they throw out, the more progress they make.

Evaluation of progress is essential in groups of women who have experienced abuse, but it is more significant *for the women* and more supportive of the changes *they* want when it is incorporated in the group's life and becomes a natural feature of the work that goes on in the group. An ongoing parallel process of evaluation must take place between the workers, not only for them to fully understand what is happening in the group, but so that the group never suffers from unresolved issues arising within the coleaders subgroup (Nosko & Wallace, 1992).

CONCLUSION

The group practice presented in this chapter is driven not by the preferred ideologies and theories of professionals, but rather by what the group members say they need and want. The principles discussed above should help practitioners who work with women who have experienced abuse to listen to what the women say and pay heed to their voices. This, as pointed out earlier, does not mean that workers cannot challenge the women, or cannot plan or prepare for the group, but simply that they should not pre-determine what the work of the group will be or what changes the women will seek in the way they conduct their lives and/or in the way social systems limit their lives. When practitioners believe in, and take into account, the strengths that individuals bring to groups and further develop in and through groups, the possibilities for all kinds of changes are as vast as the human spirit that characterizes women who have experienced abuse and are willing to work together in a group to overcome these experiences.

NATIONAL RESOURCES

Sources of information for social workers who wish to begin a group of women who have experienced abuse exist at the national, provincial/state, regional, and local levels. A good place to start is the local Family Services Association, where a list of other relevant resources may be available. Municipal libraries are also a good source of information, though in some rural areas, women's shelters may be the best resource.

Canada

National Clearinghouse on Family
  Violence
Family Violence Prevention Division
Health and Welfare Canada
Government of Canada
Ottawa, Ontario, K1A 1B5
(613) 957-2938 or
  (800) 267-1291

Telephone Devices for the Deaf
(613) 952-6396 or (800) 561-5643

United States

National Coalition Against Domestic
  Violence
P.O. Box 18749
Denver, CO 80218
(303) 839-1852

National Resource Center on
  Domestic Violence
Pennsylvania Coalition Against
  Domestic Violence
6400 Flank Drive
Harrisburg, PA 17112
(800) 537-2238

REFERENCES

Alonso, A., & Rutan, S. (1988). The experience of shame and restoration of self-respect in group therapy. *International Journal of Group Psychotherapy, 38*(1), 3–14.

Breton, M. (1985). Reaching and engaging people: Issues and practice principles. *Social Work with Groups, 8*(3), 7–21.

Breton, M. (1990). Learning from social group work traditions. *Social Work with Groups 13*(3), 21–34.

Breton, M. (1994). Relating competence-promotion and empowerment. *Journal of Progressive Human Services, 5*(1), 27–44.

Brown, B. W. (1980). Wife employment, marital equality and husband–wife violence. In M.A. Strauss & G. T. Hotaling (Eds.), *The social causes of husband–wife violence* (pp. 176–187) Minneapolis: University of Minnesota Press.

Chataway, C., & Nosko, A. (1989). *Group work with abused women*. Paper presented at the 11th Annual Symposium of the Association for the Advancement of Social Work with Groups, Montreal, October.

Cowger, C. D. (1994). Assessing client strengths: Clinical assessment for client empowerment. *Social Work, 39*(3), 262–268.

Dobash, R. E., & Dobash, R. P. (1979). *Violence against wives: A case against the patriarchy*. New York: Macmillan.

Freire, P. (1993). *Pedagogy of the oppressed* (20th anniversary ed.). New York: Continuum.

Gelles, R. J. (1979). *Family violence*. Beverly Hills, CA: Sage.

Goldstein, H. (1992). Victors or victims: Contrasting views of clients in social work practice. In D. Saleebey (Ed.), *The strengths perspective in social work practice* (pp. 27–38). New York: Longman.

Health and Welfare Canada (1989). *Family violence: A review of theoretical and clinical literature*. Catalogue No.: H21-103/1989E, ISBN: 0-662-16951-4.

Holmes, G. E. (1992). Social work research and the empowerment paradigm. In D. Saleebey (Ed.), *The strengths perspective in social work practice*. (pp. 158–168). New York: Longman.

Horton, A. L., & Johnson, B. L. (1993). Profile and strategies of women who have ended abuse. *Families in Society: The Journal of Contemporary Human Services, 74,* 481–492.

Hotaling, G. T., & Sugarman, D. B. (1986). An analysis of risk markers in husband to wife violence: The current state of knowledge. *Violence and Victims, 1,* 101–124.

Killilea, M. (1976). Mutual help organizations: Interpretations in the literature. In G. Caplan & M. Killilea (Eds.), *Support systems and mutual help: Multi-disciplinary explorations*. New York: Grune & Stratton.

Lee, J. A. B. (1991). Empowerment through mutual aid groups: A practice grounded conceptual framework. *Groupwork, 4*(1), 5–21.

MacLeod, L. (1987). *Battered but not Beaten . . . Preventing wife battering in Canada*. Ottawa: Canadian Advisory Council on the Status of Women.

Malekoff, A. (1994). A guideline for group work with adolescents. *Social Work with Groups, 17*(1/2), 5–19.

Miller, J. B. (1991). The development of women's sense of self. In J. V. Jordan, A. C. Kaplan, J. Baker Miller, J. P. Stiver, & J. L. Surfey (Eds.), *Women's growth in connection: Writings from the Stone Center* (pp. 11–26). New York: Guilford Press.

Nosko, A. & Wallace, R. (1992). *Female and male coleadership*. Paper presented at the 14th Annual Symposium of the Association for the Advancement of Social Work with Groups, Atlanta.

Nurius, P. S., Furrey, J., & Berliner, L. (1992). Coping capacity among women with abusive partners. *Violence and Victims, 7*(3), 229–243.

Pahl, J. (Ed.) (1985). *Private violence and public policy*. London: Routledge & Kegan Paul.

Pray, J. E. (1991). Respecting the uniqueness of the individual: Social work practice within a reflexive model. *Social Work, 36,* 80–85.

Rapp, C. A. (1992). The strengths perspective of case management with persons suffering from severe mental illness. In D. Saleebey (Ed.), *The strengths perspective in social work practice* (pp. 45–48). New York: Longman.

Rodgers, K. (1994). Wife assault: The findings of a national survey. *Juristat: Service Bulletin, 14*(9). Ottawa: Statistics Canada. Catalogue 85-002 ISSN 0715-271X.

Saleebey, D. (Ed.) (1992). *The strengths perspective in social work practice*. New York: Longman.

Saunders, D. G. (1993). Woman battering. In R. T. Ammerman & M. Hersen (Eds.), *Assessment of family violence. A clinical and legal sourcebook* (pp. 208–234). New York: Wiley.

Saunders, D. G., & Hanusa, D. R. (1986). Cognitive-behavioral treatment of men who batter: The short-term effects of group therapy. *Journal of Family Violence, 1,* 357–372.

Straus, M. A. & Hotaling, G. T. (Eds.) (1980). *The social causes of husband–wife violence*. Minneapolis, University of Minnesota Press.

Sullivan, W. P. (1992). Reconsidering the environment as a helping resource. In D. Saleebey (Ed.), *The strengths perspective in social work practice* (pp. 148–157). New York: Longman.

Tolan, P., Keys, C., Chertak, F., & Jason, L. (Eds.) (1990). *Researching community psychology*. Washington, DC: American Psychological Association.

Walker, L. E. (1984). *The battered woman syndrome*. New York: Springer.

Weick, A. (1992). Building a strengths perspective for social work. In D. Saleebey (Ed.), *The strengths perspective in social work practice* (pp. 18–26). New York: Longman.

Weick, A., Rapp, C., Sullivan, W. P., & Kisthardt, W. (1989). A strengths perspective for social work practice. *Social Work, 34,* 350–354.

Wood, G, & Middleman, R. (1989). *The structural approach to direct practice in social work*. New York: Columbia University Press.

11

Group Treatment of Spouse Abusers

Steven Stosny

Wife abusers, who every year injure well over 2 million women (Novello, 1992), constitute one of the most difficult populations served by social workers in terms of cooperative participation in treatment (Faulkner, Cogan, Nolder, & Shooter, 1991; Stosny, 1994; Tolman & Bennett, 1990). Although predominantly court ordered into counseling, their attendance is inconsistent, with 40–60% dropping out long before completion. Even more disheartening, over one-half of the completers of the most often used group treatment model are likely to reabuse within a year (Harrell, 1991; Stosny, 1995). The factors contributing to this formidable resistance have much to do with why spouse abusers offend in the first place. Primary among these are deficits in affect regulation that produce an inability to process guilt, shame, and abandonment anxiety. In treatment sessions abusers tend to convert these vulnerable feelings into anger, just as they do at home. The difference lies in the behavioral enactment of the anger. In the group room it looks like resentful (and superficial) compliance or numb, seemingly indifferent, withdrawal. But at home it generates patterns of abusive control of loved ones, enforced by periodic episodes of violence (Dutton & Painter, 1993).

EMPIRICAL AND CLINICAL FINDINGS

The link between violence in childhood and violence against one's spouse in adulthood has been well established in the empirical literature (Stith & Farley, 1993; Tolman & Bennett, 1990). This connection has been most often explained from a perspective of social learning theory, that is, behaviors reinforcing violence as an acceptable means of prevailing in a dispute are modeled at vital learning stages in the early lives of abusers. Unfortunately, social learning theory offers little help to clinicians treating spouse abusers, who will be hard put to find one who does not abhor and condemn the violence of his childhood, much less find it acceptable. From a clinical standpoint, violence in childhood is less significant for what it teaches the male child about interpersonal conflict resolution than for what it prevents him from learning about himself, that is, that he is valuable, acceptable, powerful, and lovable. In other words, violence in childhood inhibits development of a tolerable sense of self.

Attributions and Locus of Control

Abusive men tend to see themselves as powerless victims forced into abusive behavior. Afflicted with an external locus of control and a tendency to make external causal attributions, they tirelessly blame their behavior on family members, on the broad social context, or on the specific situations in which the abuse occurred (Bograd, 1988; Dutton, 1986; Eisikovits, Edleson, Guttmann, & Sela-Amit, 1991; Flournoy & Wilson, 1991; Rouse, 1984; Sapiente, 1988). Obviously, this has grave consequences for the acceptance of personal responsibility for abusive behavior and for motivation to change (or even participate) in treatment.

Sense of Self and Self-Esteem

Virtually every published study of abusers notes their low self-esteem. Many have related spouse abuse to a poor sense of self (Dutton, 1994; Neidig, Friedman, & Collins, 1986; Rosen, 1991; Stosny, 1995), some concluding that abusers often feel inadequate and dissatisfied with themselves (Flournoy & Wilson, 1991; Murphy, 1991). Although no consistent personality profile of spouse abusers has emerged in the research and clinical literature (Geffner & Rosenbaum, 1990; Gondolf, 1988; Saunders, 1987), one group of deficits seems virtually universal, not only in male heterosexual abusers but in gay and lesbian partner abusers as well. These can be understood as *attachment deficits.*

The term *attachment deficits* refers to the inability to form and maintain viable attachment bonds. It includes doubts about one's capacity to love and be loved, to trust and be trusted, to feel compassion and be worthy of compassion, to maintain interest in a significant other as an autonomous person, and to hold the interest of another autonomous person. The evidence seems overwhelming that spouse abusers, regardless of sexual orientation, exhibit great difficulties in intimacy, trust, mutuality, compassion, jealousy, fear of abandonment, and fear of engulfment, that is, fear that the self will diminish or disintegrate in sustained proximity to another (Barnett & Hamberger, 1992; Crawford & Gartner, 1992; Dutton, 1994; Dutton, Saunders, Starzomski, & Bartholomew, 1994;

Flournoy & Wilson, 1991; Island & Letelier, 1992; Murphy, 1991; Murphy, Scott, Meyer, & O'Leary, 1992; Renzetti, 1992; Stosny, 1995).

Doubts about one's status as an attachment figure tend to flood the self with the disorganizing experience of guilt, shame, and fear of abandonment. With little internal regulatory skill (the result of a diminished sense of self and an external locus of control), abusers blame these feelings on their spouses, which allows them temporary pain relief and empowerment through anger arousal (Dutton, 1994; Dutton et al., 1994; Stosny, 1995). Of course, the more they blame their internal experience on their spouses, the more powerless over their own feelings they become. This pervasive sense of powerlessness exacerbates the external locus of control and explains the high level of anger widely observed in spouse abusers (Barnett & Hamberger, 1992; Dutton, 1994; Dutton et al., 1994; Maiuro, Cahn, Vitaliano, Wagner, & Zegree, 1988; Stosny, 1995). [See the following for empirical support for anger as an attribution of blame (Averill, 1982; Epstein, 1979); a cry of powerlessness (Novaco, 1975; Tavris, 1987); mobilization of the organism for the exertion of power and control (Izard & Schwartz, 1986; Novaco, 1975); and protection from shame (Retzinger, 1991; Scheff, 1990).]

THE ETHICS OF TREATING COURT-ORDERED CLIENTS
Empowerment or Brainwashing?

The treatment of court-ordered clients raises important ethical considerations for clinicians. The urgent need to protect victims of abuse creates the risk of misusing power and authority to impose the majority's familial values on a minority. Abusers are ordered into treatment to help keep them from breaking the law, not to become spouses who conform to the values and preferences of therapists or their agencies, no matter how humanitarian and nobly egalitarian these may seem. For this compelling ethical reason, treatment should avoid the temptation to espouse particular familial values and should strive instead to nurture moral agency, that is, to help clients build the self-regulatory skills necessary to make moral judgments and act on them with integrity. Fortunately, the nurturance of moral agency is not only an ethical pursuit for clinicians, it has tremendous therapeutic value for clients. Moral agency is the product of a powerful—that is, compassionate—sense of self. The topic of morality becomes therapeutic when used overtly in treatment to enhance rather than impugn the self (Gilbert, 1994; Stosny, 1995). In simple behavioral terms, this constitutes an operant conditioning model, emphasizing that as a function of the internal reward of the survival-based need to form attachment and social bonds (Bowlby, 1969, 1973, 1980), people like themselves more when they experience compassion than when they don't; genuine self-esteem depends on our capacity for compassionate morality, at least toward loved ones. In this context, clients experience moral reasoning as therapeutically empowering rather than as a source of guilt and shame. They realize the hope of transcending a powerless abusive past by growing into the genuinely powerful condition of moral agency.

PRACTICE PRINCIPLES AND SPECIAL CONSIDERATIONS IN TREATING SPOUSE ABUSERS

There is widespread agreement that structured groups constitute the treatment of choice for spouse abusers (e.g., Edleson & Tolman, 1992; Pence & Paymar, 1993; Tolman & Bennett, 1990). *Structured* simply means that the content and time agenda of the group are developed in advance rather than emerging from the dynamics of the group itself. Most clinicians agree that lack of structure, particularly in the beginning phases of the group, risks allowing the anger and deviant morality of many group members to establish group norms. The male bonding noted by several authors (Edleson & Tolman, 1992; Harrell, 1991; Stosny, 1995) tends to form around the lowest common denominator, which, in the case of spouse abuser groups in the beginning phases of treatment, is perceived victimization by wives (and women in general) and by a court system unfairly biased in favor of women. For that reason, it may be advisable to forbid early discussion of the court system or of individual court cases. I find it more efficient, and safer for victims, to remove the need for such distorted thinking through therapeutic enhancement of the self than to spend time and effort confronting these highly defended but relatively superficial outposts of the client's meaning system.

Virtually every form of group treatment has currency in the clinical literature. Closed groups offer stability to clients who have suffered lifelong difficulties in forming and terminating bonds, which would only be exacerbated by members constantly joining and leaving the groups. Edelson and Syers (1990, 1991) found no difference in outcome between short- and long-term groups but did find that clients were more likely to complete the former. Coleaders of mixed gender model a healthy balance of power and authority between the sexes. It is especially useful to model disagreement-resolution techniques between the coleaders, at least one of whom should, if possible, match the social class or ethnicity of the group. By the way, social class and ethnicity will be determined almost entirely by the location of the agency, as spouse abuse occurs frequently in every socioeconomic and ethnic class (U.S. Health and Human Services, 1985).

The safety of clients and victims is a crucial consideration for this vulnerable population, with the following points of paramount importance: (1) give clients and their spouses a written emergency plan with hot line numbers; (2) avoid interventions that stimulate guilt, shame, and abandonment anxiety before affect regulation techniques are learned (this may take discipline on the worker's part, but victims will pay for any unregulated guilt, shame, and abandonment anxiety that unskilled clients take home from the sessions); (3) don't let any client go home upset without making every attempt to help him resolve his distress; call him at home to be sure he stayed calm during the drive; (4) secure a contract in which clients agree to avoid discussing hot issues until they have learned emotional regulation techniques; (5) follow up with dropouts; (6) administer the Conflict Tactics Scale (see the Evaluation section of this chapter) to spouses quarterly for the first year following treatment.

Inevitably, countertransference lurks in the shadows when treating abusive populations. If you cannot "hate the sin and love the sinner," this is not the area of social work in which you can be of help. These men have difficulty distinguishing behaviors from the self, which makes the possibility of behavioral change seem obscure to them. They need therapists to help them make this crucial distinction. Treatment that reinforces their self-concept as "bad boys" will make it more likely that they will do bad things. Rather, workers should try to come up with at least one characteristic to admire in each client at the beginning of treatment. That one element of admiration will likely be at the heart of the client's capacity to change abusive behavior. Clients need us to ally with that part of their consciousness that does not want to abuse loved ones.

While it is important that clients remain ever cognizant of external motivations to desist from abuse (legal sanctions and group disapproval), they need ultimately to develop the internal motivation of prosocial behavior: the feeling of well-being stimulated by the experience of compassion. To fully understand how this works, ask yourself why you do not beat up people you love. Is it because you fear going to jail or worry about what others might think of you? Your desisting from violence probably runs much deeper. At bottom, you know that you will not like, value, and respect yourself if you injure people you love, and that you will like, value, and respect yourself if you experience compassion for them. This self-destructive element of attachment violence and contrasting self-building nature of compassion for loved ones must be internalized by clients if they are to remain abuse free.

MIXING VICTIMS WITH PERPETRATORS IN GROUP

Whether to include spouses in abuser groups is an issue of controversy in the clinical literature. Some argue that it places the woman in jeopardy should she say something in group to embarrass her abuser (Edleson & Tolman, 1992). This is certainly true in couples counseling and in unstructured couples group treatment (Stosny, 1995). But this particular risk disappears in highly structured groups in which clients' verbal participation is minimal before emotional regulation techniques are learned. More important, when the victim is part of the group, the entire membership is invested in her well-being, which serves as a potent deterrent to abuse. Best of all, an incomparable mechanism of change occurs frequently in mixed groups when an abuser finds himself experiencing compassion for another man's wife who bears, he realizes, the same scars from subtle and overt abuse as he has caused his own spouse.

Some feminist writers loathe the inclusion of women in abuser treatment groups because it seems to blame the victim (e.g., Bograd, 1984). This view must be taken seriously. Whether in mixed or segregated groups, abusers and victims alike must be reminded often that *nothing* a partner does justifies abuse; victims can do nothing to cause their abuse or be worthy of blame for it. Even abusive behavior in retaliation for perceived abuse is unjustified and only does greater damage to the attachment bond. Receiving this empathic message on the level of a group theme, with spouses present, has more symbolic and literal power than hearing it in segregated abuser and offender groups.

Blaming the victim constitutes a serious argument against ordering victims into treatment. But as long as their participation is completely voluntary, it becomes a cruel kind of revictimization to deny them the same treatment as their abusers. Before we opened the Compassion Workshop to the spouses who wanted it, I had countless complaints about the unfairness of excluding victims from what seemed to them to be obviously beneficial to their husbands. As one woman expressed it, "I get beat up and he gets all this great stuff!" Actually, on the deepest level, the treatment needs of perpetrators and victims are quite similar, insofar as both need help in the area of toxic blame. The abuser blames his internal state on the victim, rendering himself powerless over his own experience, while the victim internalizes blame for the internal state of the abuser, rendering herself powerless to heal her own wounds. Treating them jointly has the advantage of helping them internalize responsibility for their own experience and for no one else's. The therapist helps clients establish boundaries by pointing out the liberating power that responsibility for one's own thoughts, feelings, and behavior gives to each individual, while blame creates nothing but a painful void of powerlessness waiting to be filled with anger and self-contempt.

KEY ISSUES AND COMMON THEMES

The primary theme of abuser groups must be the safety of everyone in the family, as described above. Crucial to the issue of safety is client skill in affect regulation. Spouse abusers require training in affect regulation before they are given any opportunity to ventilate anger in group. (Ventilation of anger has been shown in numerous studies to increase anger; see, e.g., Biaggio, 1987; Lewis & Bucher, 1992.) Once safety issues are thoroughly discussed and affect regulation techniques mastered (after 4 weeks or so of practice), *power* emerges as the most common group theme. Many abusers have been socialized to confuse destructiveness with power, resulting in endless power struggles created by their attempts to exert power over others. Discussion must bring out the fact that internal power (over one's own thoughts, values, feelings, and behavior) entails the ability to resist destructive impulses; *genuine power* is *constructive*. Now interpersonal power can be reframed as empowerment, that is, helping loved ones to find mutually beneficial solutions rather than coercing them to accept one's own solutions. This no-lose notion of empowerment departs drastically from the no-win nature of power struggles, in which the seeming winner of the dispute inevitably pays with future displays of resentment and hostility from the loser.

Other key themes for group discussion include personal responsibility, masculinity, intimacy, communication skills, resentment, forgiveness, and relapse prevention. Responsibility for one's behavior must be framed as a form of personal power; in contrast, blame renders one completely powerless (if my bad feelings are my wife's fault, I'm utterly powerless over them). Many abusers are insecure about aspects of their masculinity. Anger and anxiety regulation are keys to the success of expanding this theme to include related issues of intimacy and communication skills. When feeling more in control of emotions, clients tend to be far less rigid about their masculinity. Resentment is another theme that requires special attention. Fear of their own anger forces many abusers to drag long chains of resentment of loved ones into treatment. A good way to approach the theme is through its opposite: forgiveness. Once again, with emergent skill in emotional regulation, clients are better able to appreciate that there is far more power in forgiveness than in resentment.

In the final phase of the group, relapse prevention is the major theme. Clients should be given a checklist of early warning signs of relapse, such as returning to pretreatment levels of social isolation and feeling an urge to control their spouses or to spy on them. The return of jealous or envious feelings can presage relapse, as can a series of stressful life events, increased irritability, anger in traffic, and trouble sleeping. The relapse package should include prevention strategies and support numbers to call if the clients' risk of relapse begins to increase.

THE COMPASSION WORKSHOP

This highly structured group treatment has been developed over 4 years of work with more than 600 abusers (Stosny, 1995). Because abusers have trouble regulating the internal penalties of threatened attachment bonds, namely, guilt, shame, and abandonment anxiety, the treatment emphasizes the great reward for enhancement of attachment bonds: well-being and increased self-esteem. In fact, compassion serves a dual function: as an incompatible response strategy for the dissipation of anger arousal (Baron, 1984) and as a self-enhancing mechanism; clients simply like themselves better when they experience compassion for loved ones. The treatment is based on the assumption that human beings attempt to exert power and control over others when they feel powerless themselves.

In other words, the rush of arousal in exerting power over others fills in gaps in the sense of self, providing a temporary illusion of wholeness and personal power. The Compassion Workshop eliminates the exertion of power and control over loved ones by reducing the need for it through enhancement of the self, particularly the sense of power over one's internal experience. The mechanism of enhancement is the development of self-regulatory skills that lead to moral agency.

The skill-building centerpiece of the Compassion Workshop is the five-step emotional regulation technique HEALS, an acronym for the letters of the word *H*EALING: *E*xplain to yourself which is the deepest of the core hurts you're feeling (unimportant, disregarded, accused-guilty-mistrusted, devalued, rejected, powerless, unlovable); *A*pply self-compassion to heal the core hurt; *L*ove yourself by feeling compassion for loved ones; *S*olve the problem.

HEALS uses self-compassion to reduce the guilt, shame, and rejection anxiety that tend to encapsulate abusers in a narcissistic shell. While locked within narcissistic shells, abusers remain insulated from accurate processing of the social cues that normally mediate aggressive impulses. This allows the abusive impulse to gain temporary empowerment qualities through emotional arousal as internal controls, under the painful assault of shame, weaken, permitting full objectification of the victim as nothing more than a source of negative affect. The application of HEALS to the arousal itself breaks the narcissistic shell, allowing the abuser to take the perspective of the potential victim, which stimulates pain-relieving, prosocial compassion.

Through rigorous practice, the development of self-regulatory skills internalizes the sense of personal power, usually within 3 or 4 weeks. Now clients are able to learn interpersonal empowerment techniques to avoid power struggles at home. By this time, they understand the interrelated well-being of attachment figures: that we cannot hurt or diminish those we love without hurting or diminishing ourselves. Thus the goal of conflict resolution is not to "win the dispute" (for that means creating resentment and hostility), but rather to have everyone in the dispute come out feeling important, valuable, acceptable, and lovable. In role play, clients experience the greater power of self-enhancement available through empowerment of loved ones.

The last of 38 required homework assignments (for abusers, not victims), the Healing Letter of Apology, provide abusers with a way of making a clear demarcation between the self-destructive styles of thinking, feeling, and behaving of the past and the self-building styles they've learned in the present. Completion of the assignment promises to close the door on the past and open the door to the future. The letter should serve as a kind of blueprint for reversing periods of relapse. The content must recount the steps of the client's recovery, including what needs to be done to advance recovery. One objective of the assignment is to create a document that can be read during vulnerable periods in the future, to tell clients what to do for renewed progress and inspire them to fulfill their emerging identity as compassionate persons. Clients tend to hate this exercise when it is first assigned, but the vast majority find it a wonderfully healing process in the doing. On the final day of treatment, clients read their letters aloud. It's a powerfully moving session, especially if the wives are present. Other group members are asked to give feedback on how well the letter meets the requirements and objectives of the assignment.

Case

Gary was court ordered into treatment following the most acute of a long series of violent abuses of his wife Sharon. Gary's violence typically occurred as a result of his jealousy. Virtually every time they went to a party Gary accused Sharon of "coming on" to any man with whom she casually spoke. Gary's interpretation that his wife caused his painful feelings rendered him powerless over them; he was like a robot responding to whatever button Sharon might inadvertently push. He continually exerted power over his wife to control her behavior, lest she make him feel emotions that he could not handle. When she inevitably rebelled against his pervasive distrust and his stranglehold on her autonomy, Gary enforced his desperate control with violence.

Through treatment, Gary understood that his jealousy came from his own deep belief that he was defective as an attachment figure and, at least some of the time, unlovable. (If we believe ourselves unworthy of love, we cannot fully believe those who say they love us; they *must* want someone else.) Of course, the more Gary hurt the person he loved, the more unworthy of love he felt. In learning to use compassion for himself and his wife as an incompatible response to anger and aggression, he began to heal the wounds that made him feel unlovable.

To stress once again the critical importance of teaching affect regulation techniques before any discussion of anger and jealousy, by the end of treatment Gary was certain that, had we asked him to talk about jealous before he learned HEALS, he would have fallen into the trap of trying to force his wife to regulate his vulnerable feelings. Her inability to do so would have resulted in more violence. In the 3 years following treatment, Gary and Sharon have lived completely free of violence.

EVALUATION

An ethical imperative for workers who treat abusers requires careful and continuous evaluation of outcome effectiveness. The Conflict Tactics Scale (Straus, 1979) is an accessible, easy to administer, widely used instrument to measure verbal and physical aggression in intimate relationships. In the Compassion Workshop, we give these scales to victims every 4 months for a year following treatment. We ask them to keep logs of any verbal abuse and urge them to call us between scheduled contacts if physical abuse threatens to recur. In stark contrast to the predominant treatments that focus exclusively on stopping abusive behavior, the Compassion Workshop boasts a 75% completion rate, with completers remaining 88% violence free and 75% emotional abuse free at 1 year of follow-up, based on reports of victims. It's unwise to rely on the report of abusers for evaluation purposes. They have great interest in lying, particularly after treatment, when reabuse likely means jail time. Because many victims decide to stay with their spouses in the often illusory hope that treatment will be effective, the historical success rate of the treatment should be made available to them from the beginning. In addition, victims should know of the posttreatment assessment of their abuser's risk factors. These should include a standardized measurement of self-esteem, the depth and breadth of the client's written or verbal accounting of strategies to avoid abuse, and the therapists' assessment of the abuser's improvement in perspective taking, compassion for self and loved ones, validation of the emotional experience of self and loved ones, and the development of an emotional vocabulary adequate for the regulation of complex emotional experience.

CONCLUSION

Spouse abusers constitute one of the most difficult treatment populations. They suffer grave difficulties in regulating guilt, shame, and abandonment anxiety, in which they abound, as a result of their inability to form viable attachments with others. Afflicted with an external locus of control and external causal attributions, they see themselves as powerless victims. Structured groups that provide self-enhancement through basic emotional regulation and interpersonal skills for attachment relationships seem the optimal treatment. But clinicians must resist the temptation to impose their own family values on court-ordered abusers and should instead help them to achieve moral agency. Rigorous evaluation of treatment efforts is an ethical imperative in this vulnerable population, as are protocols for relapse prevention.

NATIONAL RESOURCES

A Compassionate Approach to
 Spouse and Child Abuse
Community Outreach Service and
 Associated Catholic Charities
2109 Derby Ridge Lane
Silver Spring, MD 20910
(301) 588-2297

Ending Men's Violence National
 Referral Directory
RAVEN
P.O. Box 24159
St. Louis, MO 63130
(314) 725-6137

REFERENCES

Averill, J. R. (1982). *Anger and aggression: An essay on emotion.* New York: Springer.

Barnett, O. W., & Hamberger, L. K. (1992). The assessment of maritally violent men on the California psychological inventory. *Violence and Victims, 7*(1), 15–28.

Baron, R. A. (1984). Reducing organizational conflict: An incompatible response approach. *Journal of Applied Psychology, 69,* 272–279.

Biaggio, M. K. (1987). Clinical dimensions of anger management. *American Journal of Psychotherapy, 16,* 417–427.

Bograd, M. (1984). Family systems approaches to wife battering: A feminist critique. *American Journal of Orthopsychiatry, 54,* 558–568.

Bograd, M. (1988). Feminist perspectives on wife abuse: An introduction. In K. Yllo & M. Bograd (Eds.), *Feminist perspectives on wife abuse* (pp. 11–26). Newbury Park, CA: Sage.

Bowlby, J (1969). *Attachment and loss:* Vol. I. *Attachment.* New York: Basic Books.

Bowlby, J. (1973). *Attachment and loss:* Vol. II. *Separation: Anxiety and anger.* New York: Basic Books.

Bowlby, J. (1980). *Attachment and loss:* Vol. III. *Loss, depression and sadness.* New York: Basic Books.

Crawford, M., & Gartner, R. (1992). *Women killing: Intimate femicide in Ontario, 1974–1990.* Toronto: Women's Directorate, Ministry of Social Services.

Dutton, D. G. (1986). The outcome of court-mandated treatment for wife-assault: A quasi-experimental evaluation. *Violence and Victims, 1,* 163–175.

Dutton, D. G. (1994). Behavioral and affective correlates of borderline personality organization in wife assaulters. *International Journal of Criminal Justice and Behavior, 17*(3), 26–38.

Dutton, D. G., & Painter, S. (1993). The battered woman syndrome: Effects of severity and intermittency of abuse. *American Journal of Orthopsychiatry, 63,* 614–622.

Dutton, D. G., Saunders, K., Starzomski, A., & Bartholomew, K. (1994). Intimacy-anger and insecure attachment as precursors of abuse in intimate relationships. *Journal of Applied Social Psychology, 24,* 1367–1368.

Edleson, J. L., & Syers, M. (1990). *The relative long-term effects of group treatment for men who batter* Minneapolis: Domestic Abuse Project.

Edleson, J. L., & Syers, M. (1991). The effects of group treatment for men who batter: An 18-month follow-up study. *Research on Social Work Practice, 1,* 227–243.

Edleson, J. L., & Tolman, R. M. (1992). *Intervention for men who batter: An ecological approach.* Newbury Park, CA: Sage.

Eisikovits, Z. C., Edleson, J. L., Guttmann, E., & Sela-Amit, M. (1991). Cognitive styles and socialized attitudes of men who batter: Where should we intervene? *Family Relations, 40,* 72–77.

Epstein, S. (1979). The ecological study of emotions in humans. In P. Pliner, K. R. Blankstein, & I. M. Spigel (Eds.), *Perceptions of emotion in self and others* (pp. 265–298). New York: Plenum Press.

Faulkner, K. K., Cogan, R., Nolder, M., & Shooter, G. (1991). Characteristics of men and women completing cognitive/behavioral spouse abuse treatment. *Journal of Family Violence, 6,* 243–253.

Flournoy, P. S., & Wilson, G. L. (1991). Brief research report: Assessment of MMPI profiles of male batterers. *Violence and Victims, 6,* 309–320.

Geffner, R. A., & Rosenbaum, A. (1990). Characteristics and treatment of batterers. *Behavioral Sciences and the Law, 8,* 131–140.

Gelles, R. J. (1974). *The violent home: A study of physical aggression between husbands and wives.* Newbury Park, CA: Sage.

Gilbert, P. (1994). Male violence: Toward an integration. In J. Archer (Ed.), *Male violence* (pp. 352–389). London: Routledge.

Gondolf, E. W. (1988). Who are those guys? Toward a behavioral typology of batterers. *Violence and Victims, 3,* 187–203.

Harrell, A. (1991). *Evaluation of court-ordered treatment for domestic violence offenders.* Washington, DC: The Urban Institute.

Island, D., & Letelier, P. (1991). *Men who beat the men who love them: Battered gay men and domestic violence.* Binghamton, NY: Haworth Press.

Izard, C. E., & Schwartz, G. M. (1986). Patterns of emotion in depression. In M. Rutter, C. Izard, & P. Read (Eds.), *Depression in young people: Developmental and clinical perspectives* (pp. 33–70). New York: Guilford Press.

Lewis, W. A., & Bucher, A. M. (1992). Anger, catharsis, the reformulated frustration-aggression hypothesis, and health consequences. *Psychotherapy, 29,* 385–392.

Maiuro, R. D., Cahn, T. S., Vitaliano, P. P., Wagner, B. C., & Zegree, J. B. (1988). Anger, hostility, and depression in domestically violent versus generally assaultive men and nonviolent control subjects. *Journal of Consulting and Clinical Psychology, 56*(1), 17–23.

Murphy, C. (1991). *Sex role strain, emotional vulnerability, and wife abuse.* Ann Arbor, MI: UMI Dissertation Information Service.

Murphy, C., Scott, E., Meyer, S., & O'Leary, K. D. (1992). *Emotional vulnerability patterns in partner assaultive men.* Paper presented at a symposium for the 1992 American Association of Behavioral Therapy convention, Boston.

Neidig, P. H., Friedman, D. H., & Collins, B. S. (1986). Attitudinal characteristics of males engaged in spouse abuse. *Journal of Family Violence, 1,* 223–233.

Novaco, R. W. (1975). *Anger control: The development and evaluation of an experimental treatment.* Lexington, MA: Heath.

Novello, A. C. (1992). From the Surgeon General, U.S. Public Health Service. *Journal of the American Medical Association, 267,* 3132.

Pence, E., & Paymar, M. (1993). *Education groups for men who batter: The Duluth model.* New York: Springer.

Renzetti, C. M. (1992). *Violent betrayal: Partner abuse in lesbian relationships.* Philadelphia: St. Joseph's University Press.

Retzinger, S. M. (1991). *Violent emotions: Shame and rage in marital quarrels.* Newbury Park, CA: Sage.

Rosen, I. (1991). Self-esteem as a factor in social and domestic violence. *British Journal of Psychiatry, 158,* 18–23.

Rouse, L. P. (1984). Models, self-esteem, and locus of control as factors contributing to spouse abuse. *Victimology, 9*(1), 130–141.

Sapiente, A. A. (1988). *Locus of control and causal attributions of maritally violent men*. Unpublished doctoral dissertation, California School of Professional Psychology, Los Angeles.

Saunders, D. G. (1987, July). *Are there different types of men who batter? An empirical study with possible implications for treatment*. Paper presented at the meeting of the Third National Family Violence Research Conference, University of New Hampshire, Durham.

Scheff, T. J. (1990). *Microsociology: Discourse, emotion, and social structure*. Chicago: University of Chicago Press.

Stith, S. M., & Farley, S. C. (1993). A predictive model of male spousal violence. *Journal of Family Violence, 8,* 183–201.

Stosny, S. (1994). "Shadows of the heart": A dramatic video for the treatment resistance of spouse abusers. *Social Work, 39,* 686–694.

Stosny, S. (1995). *Compassion: The extinction of attachment abuse*. New York: Springer.

Straus, M. A. (1979). Measuring intrafamily conflict and violence: The Conflict Tactic Scales. *Journal of Marriage and the Family, 41,* 75–88.

Tavris, C. (1987). *Anger: The misunderstood emotion*. New York: Simon & Schuster.

Tolman, R. M., & Bennett, L. W. (1990). A review of quantitative research on men who batter. *Journal of Interpersonal Violence, 5,* 87–118.

U.S. Health and Human Services. (1985). *Domestic violence*. Rockville, MD: Author.

12

Group Work with African-American Youth in the Criminal Justice System: A Culturally Competent Model

Aminifu R. Harvey

There is no wealth where there are no children.

African proverb

There is national concern about the plight of African-American males in the United States. Gibbs (1989) is so alarmed that she discusses the possibility of this population's extinction. Central to this concern is the large number of African-American boys who endanger their lives or their prospects for a physically, mentally, spiritually, and economically healthy life by their involvement in criminal activities (Wilson, 1990).

African-American boys between 14 and 18 years of age are a significant percentage of the youths involved in the juvenile justice system (Wilson, 1994). Their offenses include selling drugs, rape, armed robbery, auto theft, burglary, and a host of other crimes. These crimes are destructive to the boys, their families, and their communities. The youths are either sentenced to serve time in institutions or are put on probation. A disproportionate number of African-American youths are sentenced to institutions (Wilson, 1994). Because of this discriminatory practice, the juvenile justice system is exploring alternative methods of intervention and supervision.

The purpose of this chapter is to address issues of working with groups of African-American boys involved in the juvenile justice system. One effective program based on small groups of African-American boys 14 to 18 years of age who are on probation will be described.

REVIEW OF THE LITERATURE

There is almost no social work literature on group work with African-American youth. Only two recent articles were located (Franklin, 1989; Lee, 1989). Although neither one deals specifically with males or with the issues of probation, they both affirm the importance of small groups working with African-American youths. Franklin points out that the issue of respect is significant in the lives of African-American youths and must be addressed in the context of the group. He also states that the group can serve as an "alternative peer reference group" (p. 330) to counteract negative peer influences and provide support in the face of adversity. Lee (1989) presents a group work model that is school based but has applicability to other settings. This model reinforces the approach for working with African-American males presented later in this chapter. Lee's model is not gender specific; it can be generalized to males or females. He contends that a concentrated effort is needed to develop comprehensive interventions that reflect the needs and contemporary realities of black youths. He further states that it is important to create methods of incorporating African-American culture into the helping process because culture-specific approaches have the potential to transform basic aspects of African-American life generally ignored or perceived as negative into positive psychoeducational experiences. Lee contends that "in order to maximize the effectiveness of cultural specificity in the helping process, emphasis should be placed on group approaches to guidance and counseling with Black youth" (p. 294).

Non–social work publications contain material on risk factors, resiliency factors, and concepts for interventions pertaining to African-American male youths. Kunjufu (1985) identifies the following factors that enable African American youths to overcome the negative influences of inner-city life: strong family background, positive peer pressure, social survival skills, participation on athletic teams, high teacher expectations, low student-teacher ratio, and religious participation. Similarly, Lewis and Lewis (1984) identify effective mental health prevention programs for African-American families and children as those that help them in developing satisfying relationships, acquiring effective cognitive problem-solving skills, managing personal stress, and maintaining positive self-concepts. Hill (1972), in his seminal work on the strengths of African-American families, identifies the following resiliency factors: strong achievement orientation, strong work orientation, flexible family roles, strong kinship bonds, and strong religious participation.

It is recognized that high-risk behaviors are significantly interrelated, especially among youths (Penkower et al., 1991). According to Dryfoos (1990), one in four young people in America "do it all" and are in jeopardy of not growing into responsible adults unless immediate interventions occur. This is more likely to happen among those with low self-esteem, low educational aspiration, low social skills, and low social approval (Botvin & McAlister, 1981; Millman & Botvin, 1983).

Through a complex system of formal and informal networks rooted in family life and ongoing socialization processes, families, adult relatives, and communities traditionally maintained effective social control and instilled common values in their members (Kornhauser, 1978; Sampson, 1987). Marital and family disruption, predominance of streetcorner peer groups, and decline of formal and informal social controls have all contributed to the demise of traditional constraints on the behavior of adolescents (Krohn, 1986). By the 1980s, as children approached adolescence, there appeared to be a progressive decline in the influence of parents and adults and a corresponding increase in the impact of peer networks (Glynn, 1981; Hare & Hare, 1985).

While parents and adult networks tend to hold values, norms, and attitudes that discourage criminal behavior (Wills & Vaughan, 1984), street peer groups that are prone to antisocial behavior may encourage criminal behavior (Skogan, 1986). Due to what has been characterized as "adolescent egocentrism" (Elkind, 1978), adolescents tend to have a heightened sense of self-consciousness concerning their appearance, personal qualities, and abilities. The combination of adolescent egocentrism and the increased influence of street gangs tends to promote substance abuse and other criminal behaviors among many inner-city youths. This is particularly true among inner-city African-American boys, for whom the "street culture" is a major institution comparable to the family, the school, and the church (Perkins, 1986). The more such traditional institutions in the African-American community abdicate their responsibility for socialization of their children, the greater the influence of the street gangs (Harvey, 1988).

Research reveals that several problem behaviors appear to be caused by the same underlying factors (Jessor, 1982). For this reason, it is suggested that prevention programs be developed that target the underlying determinants of several theoretically and empirically related problem behaviors (Botvin, 1982; Swisher, 1979). This assumes that an effective treatment program should aim at promoting youths' general personal and social competence, vocational aspirations, and self-esteem, thereby affecting the factors that underlie many types of delinquent behaviors.

Perkins (1986) states that an Afrocentric cultural approach is needed to deal effectively with the antisocial behavior of high-risk African-American youth and to outline a youth rites-of-passage program. Warfield-Coppock and Harvey (1989) describe various rites-of-passage programs across the nation targeted at African-American boys and girls. According to them, the rites-of-passage approach is based on African and African-American cultures, which seek to restore traditional social constraints on the behaviors of African-American youths, help them to develop their emotional and cognitive abilities in a constructive fashion, and prepare them to become responsible members of society.

An Afrocentric Approach

An Afrocentric approach to the delivery of psychosocial educational treatment services is based on a humanistic and naturalistic orientation. An

Afrocentric view recognizes that African-American culture is a nexus between Western culture and traditional African culture. It is within the African culture—a holistic and naturalistic orientation to the world—that the value system and behavioral patterns of African-Americans have their roots. The philosophical concepts work in conjunction with the natural order, working toward such principles as balance in one's environment; family/personal life, and a multifunctional, discretionary, harmonious approach to life rather than a one-dimensional, predetermined, conflictual approach. The Afrocentric approach incorporates the individual, the family, and the community as an interconnected unit, so that any intervention must include interactions with all three entities. This approach recognizes the presence of spirituality (Pinkett, 1993) and interconnectedness (Richards, 1989) in the African-American community and that these characteristics are key in understanding the psychosocial dynamics of the African-American community, family, and individual in order to develop and implement appropriate, effective interventions.

The goal of the Afrocentric approach is to facilitate the development of persons who are aware and who can operationalize their sense of unity or collective, extended selves (Nobles, 1976). The desired outcome is to influence families and persons to cooperate; to understand and respect the sameness of self and of other persons; and to have a strong sense of responsibility for the well-being and harmonious interconnection between self and others (Nobles, 1976).

The Nguzo Saba ("Seven Principles" in Kiswahili) are employed as a value system to foster and evaluate these outcomes. The Nguzo Saba created by Karenga (1965) are as follows:

Umoja/Unity. To strive and maintain unity in the family, community, nation, and race.

Kujichagulia/Self-Determination. To define ourselves, name ourselves, and speak for ourselves instead of being defined and spoken for by others.

Ujima/Collective Work and Responsibility. To build and maintain our community together, and to make our brothers' and sisters' problems our problems and to solve them together.

Ujamaa/Cooperative Economics. To build and own stores, shops, and other businesses and to profit from them.

Nia/Purpose. To make our collective vocation the building and developing of our community in order to restore our people to their traditional greatness.

Kuumba/Creativity. To do always as much as we can, in the way we can, to restore our people to their traditional greatness.

Imani/Faith. To believe in our parents, our teachers, our leaders, our people, and ourselves, and in the righteousness and victory of our struggle.

Another goal of an Afrocentric psychosocial program is to provide principles (Harvey, 1988) (and to assist in their internalization) by which youths and families can become constructive contributors to their community through appreciation of themselves and their culture.

Principles of Afrocentricism

The principles of Afrocentricism (called RIPSO) are the seven Rs: responsibility, reciprocity, respect, realness, restraint, reason, and reconciliation; three Is: interconnectedness, interdependence, and inclusivity; three Ps: participatory, patience, and perseverance; three Ss: sharing, sacrifice, and spirituality; and three Others: cooperation, discipline, and unconditional love.

PRACTICE PRINCIPLES

The philosophical orientation of the social worker is critical. The social worker should view the youths as being misdirected and victims of a system that discriminates and has intentionally denied African-Americans access to their cultural identity (Akbar, 1991; McRoy, 1990). It is important for the social worker to hold the belief that the youths are capable of change when involved in a program designed to reduce the factors that place them at risk. These programs should be formulated from a group work perspective since African-American youths move through adolescence in peer groups. For these youths, group intervention must provide a positive perspective on African and African-American culture, assist them in developing their own African-American group identity, and provide them with tools to deal with the oppressiveness of white supremacy (Welsing, 1991; Wilson, 1990; Wright, 1984).

To establish rapport and connectedness, it is important for the youths to believe that the social worker is truly interested in them and is not working with them only because required to do so. The youths will usually state the latter belief directly or indirectly. It has been effective to employ the analogy of Michael Jordan, who enjoys playing basketball but at the same time is paid to do so. We explain that this is similar to why we choose this work: that we work with them both out of a concern for their well-being and because we enjoy it.

With African-American youth, it is necessary to place the group within the program rather than label the program a "group." Many youths have been placed in psychotherapeutic groups in institutions and believe that being involved in a group implies that something is innately wrong with them or that they are crazy.

If the service is being provided by an agency contracted with the court system, it is important to establish a referral process that connects the youth, the group leaders, the youth's parents (guardian or another family member), and the probation officer. This process enables the youth to experience connectedness between the agencies and to know from the very beginning that the probation officer and the social worker will be in contact with each other and are working together as a team. Connecting with the family early in the referral process demonstrates respect for the rights of the family and establishes a cooperative relationship. Many families have control and influence over the behavior of their children and want to work with the social worker to promote the well-being of their children.

There are issues that African-Americans will not raise but will discuss if the group leaders introduce them. These include issues of skin color (Harvey, 1995), body type, sexual identity, and inter/intraracial identification. The latter include the negative perceptions that white supremacy promulgates about African-American youths.

In working with African-American youths, it is critical for the social worker to respect their opinions and their right to voice their opinions, even when these differ from the opinions of the social worker. This does not mean agreeing with their opinions but rather giving them the opportunity to develop and express their ideas. It also means that it is the worker's responsibility to challenge their opinions but not to use the authority of the worker's position to impose views.

The worker gains respect by skillfully handling differences that arise. The youths will assess whether the social worker remains "cool" (Majors & Billson, 1992) or is easily intimidated. The youths give respect based on the social worker's ability to handle situations, not because of the social worker's professional degree or authority provided by the job title.

Structure is important, and each session needs to be planned. Nevertheless, the social worker must be flexible enough to focus on the concerns the youths might have during each session, such as a friend's being shot either by another youth or by the police.

These youths want the group leaders to be "real." Thus, it is critical that the group leaders self-disclose appropriately (Yalom, 1995) in a manner that demonstrates familiarity with the African-American culture and community.

The transformational process is greatly enhanced when the group leaders are African American, as they act as positive same-race role models. The lack of positive African-American role models is one factor in African-American youths being at risk. This lack of same-race role models has been critical in fostering a sense of hopelessness in African-American boys.

COMMON THEMES

The following questions and themes are consistently raised by African-American youths:

- "Why should I change my behavior when I see adults involved in illegal activities?" Youths state that the only thing wrong with their behavior is that they were caught. The task is to help them respect moral and upright behavior.

- "What are the alternatives to violence?" Youths state, "If I don't fight back, my peers will think I am a punk and abuse me on a regular basis." Also, people respect you on the street only if you "kick their ass." People think you are a punk if you try to work out conflicts verbally.

- "How do I maintain my self-respect and moral upbringing without being a social isolate and without being perceived as vulnerable to the violence of other youths?" This is important, as many of the youths' parents stress morality, a characteristic of African-American culture. There is a tension between the morality and materialism of American society that creates conflicts in family values.

- A reputation for being "cool" is important (Majors & Billson, 1992) for self-protection. If you do not display any affect or emotion, people cannot read you and thus hesitate to challenge you physically or mentally. Being cool also attracts females to you because it implies that you are street smart and not a nerd.

- Issues pertaining to male–female relationships: sex and respect for females and nonviolent behavior toward females. Many youths perceive male–female relationships from a superior–inferior paradigm rather than a harmonizing, diunital paradigm (T'Shaka, 1995).

- Issues of respect from police officers whom youths perceive as harassing them, being dishonest, and violating the law. Police are perceived as the enemy. A dilemma for these youths is how to interact with police, who at times do harass them, so that they do not become victims of police brutality.

- Critical to this population are issues of racism: how to deal with the reactions of white people to them in stores and on public transportation, as well as the racism of teachers and school administrators.

- Lack of cultural identification and racial appreciation, and lack of knowledge of the African and African-American heritage. Central to this issue is how to be successful, yet remain connected to the African-American community (Hines, Gracia-Preto, McGoldrick, Almeida, & Weltman, 1993) and not "become white." Sometimes being white erroneously means being a good student, speaking proper English, or pursuing activities such as tennis.

RECOMMENDED WAYS OF WORKING
The MAATIAN Youth Group Model

Given a social environment where children are physically violent to other children (Wilson, 1991) and are seduced or forced into selling and taking drugs, it is essential for children to be involved with a group that operates out of a positive frame of reference, with guidance from well-trained social workers. The goal of the group is to assist youth in developing the emotional strength to become self and community advocates guided by the MAATIAN principles of truth, justice and righteousness (Obenga, 1995). This is accomplished by providing youth with higher values to employ as life guidelines (Nguzo Saba) and a support group of peers who can assist each other in self-evaluation and provide emotional and physical support to do the right thing.

The group helps youth develop interpersonal skills, fostering new relationships and building a positive self-concept. The emphasis is on youths interacting with youths to develop constructive lifestyles and positive solutions to life problems, as well as to recognize their personal and cultural strengths and abilities. The small-group model employed is a youth rites-of-passage model, a group model many African-American practitioners advocate (Hare & Hare, 1985; Long, 1993; Perkins, 1986; Warfield-Coppock, 1990; Warfield-Coppock & Harvey, 1989).

When a referral for the rites-of-passage Program is received from the court, the probation officer and the group leaders coordinate a meeting with the youth and a parent/guardian. At this meeting the program is explained, including the parent's/guardian's participation in a parenting skills group.

The youths participate in an orientation entitled "Brotherhood Training," which lasts for 8 weeks. This prepares them for the sacredness of the transformation of the rites of passage. During this phase the youths are oriented to the group process, the Nguzo Saba, and the Afrocentric principles; at this time, the group is accepting new members while others are dropping out. At the end of this 8-week period the youths, who are called *preinitiates*, participate in a weekend retreat focusing on cultural and personal survival and enhancement of the community. At the end of the weekend, 15 youth are selected to become initiates based on an evaluation conducted by the coleaders and a group of older male adults called *Elders*. Youths who pass the evaluation are called *Initiates*. *Initiates* are required to take an Initiates' Code of Conduct Oath and to participate in a sacred initiation ritual in which they pledge to uphold the Nguzo Saba, receive an African name based on the day of the week on which they were born (Assem & Dodson, 1994), and are given a special identifying symbol to be worn at all group sessions. At this point in the group process, membership is closed. The group develops a sense of we-ness; its members are integrated into the group, trust each other, and are ready to work.

The group meets once a week for 90 minutes. Each participant is expected to participate in a unity circle as part of the opening group ritual. All members hold each other's hands, and one member reads a spiritually oriented text followed by the pouring of a libation (respect for the community of ancestors). Water, a symbol of life, is poured into a group-owned plant, a symbol of growth and transformation, as names of ancestors are called out loud by the members.

Each group is co-led. The leaders have included social workers, as well as a person with a master's degree in African-American studies, an artist, and a person with expertise in music and the theater. Group meetings are supplemented by follow-up home visits with the family, focusing on the impact of the program on the youths' overall development. The group incorporates creative intervention techniques such as music (use of rap songs to analyze life or create songs as a project), films, videos, and audiotapes. African-American guest presenters are invited to conduct meetings on specific topics, called *modules*. All aspects of the group are structured to develop an appreciation for African and African-American culture. The following is a list of possible modules: Principles and Guides for Living, Win-Win Relationships, Entrepreneurial Development, Personal Development and Self-Control, Mental Health Issues (Skin Color, Negative Names, Body Type), Meditation for Self-Development and Self-Control, African-American Culture and Heritage, African Culture and Heritage, Male–Female Relations, Fatherhood, Motherhood and Marriage, Male and Female Health Issues, Teenage Pregnancy, HIV/AIDS and Sexually Transmitted Diseases, Oppression and Racism, Alcohol Abuse, Tobacco and Other Drug Use, Date Rape and Incest, and Family Violence.

Each module consists of four to six sessions. The first session includes a presentation by a person of African descent who is knowledgeable concerning the topic area. The second session consists of a discussion of the information contained in the topic and how it relates to the youth's life. In the remaining sessions, the youths develop a project related to the topic to demonstrate transformation on the cognitive, emotional, spiritual, and behavioral planes. The variation in sessions allows flexibility in creating the project. Adolescents receive a certificate for the completion of the module at a small ceremony. A youth who misses a session has a follow-up meeting with the probation officer, a home visit, and a letter mailed to the parent/guardian. If an Initiate is consistently disruptive or noncooperative, he is presented to his peers, who recommend how he should reconcile with the group.

At the completion of all the modules, each youth conducts a self-evaluation and is evaluated by his peers, the group leaders, and the elders in order to pass into the final phase: a transformational weekend. During this experience, the Initiates are expected to demonstrate all they have learned and prepare for their rites ceremony.

On successful completion of the transformational weekend, Initiates participate in a final transformation ceremony. It is at this ceremony, to be witnessed by family, friends, court personnel, agency staff, its board of directors, and the general community, that the youths demonstrate specific knowledge, attitudes, and skills indicative of maturation. They announce their sacred name (based on their personality) received at the transformational weekend, to the public, and receive a symbol and a certificate of sacred transformation. Each family who participates in the program will also receive a certificate of transformation. The Initiates, in conjunction with the group leaders, plan and implement the ceremony, allowing the adolescents to experience kuumba (creativity), ujima (collective work and responsibility), and other principles of the Nguzo Saba.

CASE STUDIES: APPROACHES TO DEALING WITH COMMON THEMES

Case 1

The issue of respect for females is critical in the development of African-American males, especially since there has been an influx of antifemale rap videos and T-shirts targeted to the African-American community. In this particular session, an African-American transit policewoman was invited as a guest. The youths discussed how they handled relationships with their female peers. One youth stated that if a woman doesn't do as you say or dates someone else, you should "kick her ass." The officer asked how the group members would feel if someone "kicked their sister's or their mother's ass." The youths reacted angrily, stating they probably would retaliate. Then the worker asked if they should not respect every woman as their mother or sister. Some youths agreed and others tried to explain the difference, but it was evident that they were now beginning to question their value system.

The session continued, with the group leaders raising the issue of spirituality. Emphasizing that each person is unique, has a special reason to be here, and is a reflection of the Creative Force, the leaders asked how one could justify oppression against a woman. This helped the youths to consider alternative methods of dealing with confrontational situations. It also allowed the group leaders to pursue the emotions the youths were experiencing. They reported being angry because they had been treated with disrespect. When probed, they acknowledged that they were hurt emotionally. They also stated that if they did not respond physically, their friends would think they were punks. At that point, the group leaders had them participate in a role play to experience alternative behaviors, thoughts, and emotions.

Case 2

White (1984) contends that the issue of racial identity in African-American youth is crucial to the development of a positive self-concept that includes appreciation of and identification with African-American culture. A number of Afrocentric techniques are employed to facilitate this development. For example, youths are provided with biographies of African-American personalities and are asked to select a person they admire. Each youth is presented with a challenging situation and is asked to think, feel, and behave like the African-American personality he admires in order to resolve the problem. The purpose of this exercise is to enhance the Initiate's ability to employ high-level principles in his thought process, to feel the emotions of a constructive African-American, and to behave in a positive manner in challenging situations.

Some youths react to the infusion of African and African-American culture by stating that they are not African. The group leaders take this opportunity to explain the importance of the rituals, their history, and the role Africa has played with its well developed cultures, such as the Mali and Songhai (deGraft-Johnson, 1986), in world development. The group leaders show videos and films concerning the culture. Many African-American youth use the word *nigger* as both an affective and a derogatory term when addressing their peers. Harvey (1995) explains this as the "paradox of blackness": The oppressor's definition is employed to define one's culture in both positive and negative terms simultaneously because the oppressed culture has not defined itself based on its own world view. In this situation, the history of the term is provided and the paradox is explained. Then the youths are guided through a relaxation exercise to allow them to "feel" their physiological reaction to the world. The youths almost always state that the word creates funny feelings in their stomachs. Then they ask them to use the term *brother* affectionately. They respond that the new term "feels good."

Outcomes

Following group participation, it is anticipated the youths will experience:

- Increased appreciation of the African and African-American heritage and culture.
- Reduction in repeated criminal activity.
- Enhanced positive engagement with their family and community.
- Increased school attendance.
- Improvement in school grades.
- Increase in employment for youth of appropriate age.
- Increased sense of self-worth.
- Increased sense of respect for self, family, and community.

EVALUATION

The participants are evaluated through a process evaluation and a final evaluation. Their degree of participation and transformation while in the program are evaluated. The seven principles of African life (Nguzo Saba) Assessment Scale is employed by the Council of Elders in evaluating the development of the youths. Each youth must score at least a 3 out of 5 points on each dimension of the Likert-type scale in order to graduate from the program.

Preliminary results indicate that over 80% of the youths who complete the orientation phase of the program complete the entire program.

Family members report an increase in school attendance, in obeying curfews, in performing household chores, and in showing respect. When the youths are asked what they learned from the program, all of them report that they learned to respect themselves and appreciate their heritage.

NATIONAL RESOURCES

African Rites of Passage
United Kollective
P.O. Box 10586
Atlanta, GA 30310
(404) 755-8283

Black Family Institute
175 Filbert Street
Oakland, CA 94607
(510) 836-3245

MAAT Center for Human and
Organizational Enhancement, Inc.
5113 Georgia Ave. NW
Washington, DC 20011
(202) 882-9744

Office of Juvenile Justice and
Delinquency Prevention
633 Indiana Ave. NW
Washington, DC 20531
(202) 307-0751

The National Consortium for
African American Children
University of the District of
Columbia
4250 Connecticut Ave. NW
Washington, DC 20008
(202) 274-5609

The Urban Institute
2100 M St. NW
Washington, DC 20037
(202) 857 8627

U.S. Department of Health and
Human Services
Public Health Services
Substance Abuse and Mental
Health Services Administration
Center for Substance Abuse
Prevention
5600 Fishers Lane, Rockwall II
Rockville, MD 20857
(301) 443-0353

REFERENCES

Akbar, N. (1991). *Visions for black men*. Tallahassee, FL: Mind Productions and Associates.

Assem, K., & Dodson, J. (1994). Strengthening the African-American family: The birth to re-birth life cycle. In G. R. Preudhomme & K. Assem (Eds.), *National public policy institute* (pp. 6–15). Detroit: National Association of Black Social Workers.

Botvin, G. J. (1982). Broadening the focus of smoking prevention strategies. In T. Cotes, A. C. Petersen, & C. Perry (Eds.), *Promoting adolescent health: A dialog on research and practice* (pp. 137–148). New York: Academic Press.

Botvin, G. J., & McAlister, A. (1981). Cigarette smoking among children and adolescents: Causes and prevention. In C. B. Arnold (Ed.), *Annual review of disease prevention* (pp. 222–249). New York: Springer.

deGraft-Johnson, J. C. (1986). *African glory*. Baltimore: Black Classic Press.

Dryfoos, J. (1990). *Adolescents at risk: Prevalence and prevention*. New York: Oxford University Press.

Elkind, D. (1978). Understanding the young adolescent. *Adolescence, 49,* 127–134.

Franklin, A. J. (1989). Therapeutic interventions with black adolescents. In R. L. Jones (Ed.), *Black adolescents* (pp. 309–337). Berkeley, CA: Cobb & Henry.

Gibbs, J. T. (1989). Black adolescents and youth: An update on an endangered species. In *Black adolescents* (pp. 3–27). Berkeley, CA: Cobb & Henry.

Glynn, T. J. (1981). From family to peer: Transitions of influence among drug-using youth. In D. Lettieri & J. Ludford (Eds.), *Drug abuse and the American adolescent* (pp. 57–81). DHHS Pub. No. (ADM) 81–1166. Washington, DC: National Institute on Drug Abuse.

Hare, H., & Hare, J. (1985). *Bringing the black boy to manhood: The passage*. San Francisco: Black Think Tank.

Harvey, A. R. (1988). Extended family: A universal and naturalistic salvation for African Americans (pp. 11–19). In *Proceedings of The Black Task Force on Child Abuse and Neglect*. New York: Black Task Force on Child Abuse and Neglect.

Harvey, A. R. (1995). The issue of skin color in psychotherapy with African Americans. *Families in Society: The Journal of Contemporary Human Services, 76*, 3–10.

Hill, R. B. (1972). *The strength of black families*. New York: Emerson Hall.

Hines, P. M., Gracia-Preto, N., McGoldrick, M., Almeida, R., & Weltman, S. (1993). Intergenerational relationships across cultures. In J. B. Rauch (Ed.), *Assessment: A sourcebook for social work practice* (pp. 371–394). Milwaukee: Families International.

Jessor, R. (1982). Critical issues in research on adolescent health promotion. In T. Coates, A. C. Petersen, & C. Perry (Eds.), *Promotion of adolescent health: A dialog on research and practice* (pp. 447–465). New York: Academic Press.

Karenga, M. (1965). *Kwanzaa: Origin, concepts and practice*. Los Angeles: Kawaida Publications.

Kornhauser, R. (1978). *Social sources of delinquency*. Chicago: University of Chicago Press.

Krohn, M. (1986). The web of conformity: A network approach to the explanation of delinquent behavior. *Social Problems, 33*, 81–93.

Kunjufu, J. (1985). *Countering the conspiracy to destroy black boys*, Vol. II. Chicago: African American Images.

Lee, C. C. (1989). Counseling black adolescents: Critical roles and functions for counseling professionals. In R. L. Jones (Ed.), *Black adolescents* (pp. 293–308). Berkeley, CA: Cobb & Henry.

Lewis, J. & Lewis, F. (1984). Prevention programs in action. *Personnel and Guidance Journal, 62*, 550–553.

Long, L. C. (1993). An Afrocentric intervention strategy. In L. L. Goddard (Ed.), *An African-centered model of prevention for African-American youth at high risk* (pp. 87–92). CSAP Technical Report No. 6. Rockville MD: U.S. Department of Health and Human Services.

Majors, R., & Billson, J. M. (1992). *Cool pose: The dilemma of black manhood in America*. New York: Lexington Books.

McRoy, R. G. (1990). A historical overview of black families. In S. M. L. Logan, E. M. Freeman, & R. G. McRoy (Eds.), *Social work practice with black families: A culturally specific perspective* (pp. 3–17). New York: Longman.

Millman, R. B., & Botvin, G. J. (1983). Substance use, abuse, and dependence. In M. D. Levine, W. B. Carey, & A. C. Crocker (Eds.), *Developmental-behavioral pediatrics* (pp. 683–708). Philadelphia: W. B. Saunders.

Nobles, W. W. (1976). African consciousness and black research: The consciousness of self. In L. M. King, V. Dixon, & W. Nobles (Eds.), *African philosophy: Assumption and paradigms for research on black persons* (pp. 163–174). Los Angeles: Fanon Center.

Obenga, T. (1995). *A lost tradition: African philosophy in world history*. Philadelphia: Source Editions.

Penkower, L., Dew, M. A., Kingsley, L., Becker, J. T., Satz, P., Scherf, F. W., & Sheridan, K. (1991). Behavioral, health, and psychosocial factors and risk for HIV infection among sexually active homosexual men: The multi-center AIDS cohort study. *American Journal of Public Health, 81,* 194–196.

Perkins, U. E. (1986). *Harvesting new generations: The positive development of black youth*. Chicago: Third World Press.

Pinkett, J. (1993). Spirituality in the African-American community. In L. L. Goddard (Ed.), *An African-centered model of prevention for African-American youth at high risk* (pp. 79–86). CSAP Technical Report No. 6. Rockville, MD: U.S. Department of Health and Human Services.

Richards, D. M. (1989). *Let the circle be unbroken*. Trenton, NJ: Red Sea Press.

Sampson, R. J. (1987). Urban black violence: The effect of male joblessness and family disruption. *American Journal of Sociology, 93,* 348–382.

Skogan, W. (1986). Fear of crime and neighborhood change. In A. J. Reiss & M. Tonry (Eds.), *Communities and crime* (pp. 203–229). Chicago: University of Chicago Press.

Swisher, J. D. (1979). Prevention issues. In R. L. Dupont, A. Goldstein, & J. A. O'Donnell (Eds.), *Handbook on drug abuse* (pp. 423–435). Washington, DC: National Institute of Drug Abuse.

T'Shaka, O. (1995). *Return to the African mother principle of male and female equality,* Vol. 1. Oakland, CA: Pan African Publishers and Distributors.

Warfield-Coppock, N. (1990). *Afrocentric theory and applications: Adolescence rites of passage,* Vol. I. Washington, DC: Baobob Associates.

Warfield-Coppock, N., & Harvey, A. R. (1989). *Teenage pregnancy prevention: A rites of passage resource manual*. Washington, DC: MAAT Institute for Human and Organizational Enhancement.

Welsing, F. C. (1991). *The Isis papers: The keys to the colors*. Chicago: Third World Press.

White, J. L. (1984). *The psychology of blacks: An Afro-American perspective*. Englewood Cliffs, NJ: Prentice-Hall.

Wills, T. A., & Vaughan, R. (1984). *Social support and smoking in middle adolescence*. New York: Academic Press.

Wilson, A. N. (1990). *Black-on-black violence: The psychodynamics of black self-annihilation in service of white domination*. Bronx, NY: Afrikan World Infosystems.

Wilson, A. N. (1991). *Understanding black adolescent male violence: Its remediation and prevention*. Bronx, NY: Afrikan World Infosystems.

Wilson, A. N. (1992). *Awakening natural genius of black children*. Bronx, NY: Afrikan World Infosystems.

Wilson, J. J. (1994). Disproportionate minority representation. *Juvenile Justice*, *2*(1), 21–23.

Wright, B. E. (1984). *The psychopathic racial personality and other essays*. Chicago: Third World Press.

Yalom, I. D. (1995). *The theory and practice of group psychotherapy* (4th ed.). New York: Basic Books.

13

Group Work with Sex Offenders

Paul H. Ephross

Social workers are frequently called on to provide group treatment to change the behavior of sex offenders. One can acquire the label of sex offender in a variety of ways: most commonly, one is found guilty in court of violating a law against a particular sexual behavior. These prohibitions are of several types. One, often viewed as archaic by social workers but still on the books in many jurisdictions, prohibits a particular form of sexual expression, without regard for the consenting nature of the act or the relationship between the adult partners. The fact that laws banning normative behaviors—oral sex, in private, between adult partners married to each other, for example—are still on the books makes for rueful comments on late-night television programs and produces cartoons of the "believe it or not" genre. Less amusing is the fact that selective prosecution, or the threat of it, is sometimes used to discredit persons who express and promulgate views seen as undesirable by people in politically or socially powerful positions.

In this chapter, however, the term *sex offender* refers to two other types of persons: (1) those who have coerced others into participating in sexual activities through either force or the threat of force and (2) those who have engaged in sexual activities with partners who are incapable of giving informed consent. Children and adolescents under the legal age of consent and persons of diminished capacity, regardless of age—such as mentally retarded people and mentally ill people—illustrate categories of forbidden partners, while perpetrators of child sex abuse form part of the coercive cohort. In recent years, there has been a growing awareness of adolescents as sexual abusers of younger children and as perpetrators of sexual coercion on other adolescents.

While technically one must be adjudicated as such in order to be known as a sex offender, in fact there may be as many persons unknown as known who have carried out or perpetrated the same destructive and illegal behaviors. Judging from studies of the prevalence of rape and the behaviors of rape victims, for example, even today only about one-half— in the past, even fewer—of rapes committed in this country are reported to the police or to any other official agency (Bureau of Justice Statistics, 1993, 1995). The true prevalence rates of sexual coercion and abuse are unknown, in part because of the peculiar and confusing mixture of attitudes towards (1) sex and sexuality in general and (2) deviant, coercive, and illegal sexual activities, that characterize American culture and its various subcultures at the end of the twentieth century. It is important to try to understand these attitudes and perceptions before we can analyze in any depth the issues involved in group treatment of sex offenders.

"THAT SUBJECT"

One of the world's most distinguished, if often controversial, scholars of human sexuality, writing in 1994, bluntly characterized contemporary American culture as "taboo-ridden [and] antisexual." In the same discussion, he characterized sexual identities that differ in any way from society's prescriptive norms as "unspeakable monsters." He notes, "Being literally unspeakable, an unspeakable monster is not spoken of" (Money, 1994, p. ix). Many writers have commented on how difficult it is for Americans to talk about sex in general and their own sexuality in particular. Although some may think that men find it easier to talk about sex than women, a noted authority on male sexuality states, "men have been, and to a large extent still are, extremely secretive about their sexuality . . . other than . . . bits of bravado, most men simply don't talk about sex to anyone" (Zilbergeld, 1978, p. 4). Allgeier and Allgeier point out that "Our cultural norm of segregating the 'sexual' from the rest of our experience begins to be taught in infancy" (1988, p. 393). Some observers find the roots of widespread inability to communicate about sex even with a partner in common childhood experiences:

> As children, most of us were discouraged from saying much about sex and many never learned the terminology to describe their sexual anatomy. . . . So, part of the hesitancy people have in talking about sex . . . is actually a carryover from these childhood taboos (Masters, Johnson, & Kolodny, 1986, p. 259)

One can relate the difficulties of talking about sex to the ambivalence about sexual experience that is reflected in the culture of our society. Carole Vance has noted, with regard to women's experiences:

The tension between sexual danger and sexual pleasure is a powerful one in women's lives. Sexuality is simultaneously a domain of restriction, repression and danger as well as a domain of exploration, pleasure, and agency (1984, p. 1).

Small wonder, then, that discussions about sex, especially about feelings, experiences, fears, perceptions, doubts, and joys, are viewed as potentially dangerous. In addition, to the extent that they are pleasurable, that very pleasure may be experienced as illicit.

Sex is difficult to talk about even for people whose sexual behavior and identities have been labeled as normal. How much more difficult, then, is it for people whose sexual behavior has been labeled as actually or potentially criminal? The stigmas associated with being labeled abnormal, criminal, evil, and, if the victim is a child, unnatural as a man or woman (Scaveo, 1989) combine for a convicted sex offender. Few identities are as universally despised as that of a sexual abuser of children. In prison, the known abuser of children is often at risk of being physically attacked, or worse, by other inmates. Neither murder nor treason, robbery nor criminal conspiracy carry the perceived loathesomeness that attaches to sexual abuse of children and certain other sexual offenses. The sex offender, then, faces a difficult task while carrying multiple stigmas: to admit to oneself and others the nature of the offense and to participate in discussion of feelings, alternatives, reasons, cognitive and emotional triggers, related to sex—a subject difficult and dangerous to discuss at best.

Difficulty communicating about sex is not restricted to people of lower educational or social classes. The title of this section, "That Subject," was the term used by a senior, highly regarded educator to characterize the topic of a graduate student's thesis research in a school of social work. The student, a gifted researcher, was studying women's experiences of orgasm: "that subject," as the professor described it. The student produced a study that made a genuine contribution to the research literature on an important topic. In general, and with apologies to a few exceptional people within the profession, one cannot describe social work as having distinguished itself in the front rank of the sexual revolution, nor even in promoting healthy and open discourse on sexual subjects. At times, social workers have been willing to discuss sexual pathology but not sexual normality—sexual harassment, for example, rather than the sexuality of organizational life. For the most part, one looks in vain for positive, affirmative discussions of sexual expression in the literature of our profession.

While the dominant culture of the United States is ambivalent about sexuality at best and antisexual at worst, there is great variation among various American subcultures, whether defined by religion, national origin, or race. It is a curious fact, remarked on by behavioral scientists for many decades, that there is generally a sexual aspect to racism (Bettelheim & Janowitz, 1964, pp. 287–88). Sexual superiority is attributed to the oppressed group, and this attribution plays a part in the ideology of the dominant group. It is partly for this illogical reason, perhaps, that minorities of color and certain immigrants have at times been viewed as sexual athletes, and thus simultaneously as both desirable and fearsome. Sexuality is one of the topics about which it is often difficult to communicate across ethnic/racial/cultural barriers of difference.

One of the factors that make communicating about sex difficult both in groups and in other interpersonal settings, is the choice of vocabulary. There is an uncommonly wide range of terms available for English speakers to use about sex, virtually all of it unacceptable for some people for various reasons. Professionals often escape to the use of multisyllabic medical terms of ancient Latin or Greek heritage. Besides communicating a vague sense of disapproval, such words are often unknown to ordinary people. For example, the word *coitus,* a more or less standard medicolegal term, is hardly ever heard in spoken English and is therefore unknown to many people. The word *fuck,* which is known to everyone, is unacceptable-to-offensive to virtually everyone. Social workers are often concerned about "lowering" themselves by using street language to describe sexual activities. This is a legitimate concern, as is the fear that clients simply do not understand the language that social workers feel is more appropriate. Given this question of words and its importance in relation to communication, I suggest here three guiding principles:

1. Ask group members which terms they use and feel comfortable with. Either use their terms or explain why you prefer to use other terms. Let them practice using the new ones together with you. The object is effective communication; there are no *good* or *bad* terms.
2. Be sure that you (and group members) understand the meaning of terms. There is probably no subject on which more deliberate obfuscation is employed in the choice of words. Be sure, to the point of being boring, if necessary, that you understand the behaviors to which words refer. "We . . . you know . . . did it . . . we had relations" sounds behaviorally specific. Sometimes it is not. Ask questions. Men who have sex with other men may or may not identify themselves as homosexual, depending on the specific roles taken during particular sexual activities and on ethnocultural definitions (Doll et al., 1992; see also Chapter 3, this volume).
3. Watch out for your own assumptions that may get in the way of your understanding the words that others are using. This is especially true when (a) group members' age- or sex-specific expectations are different from the social worker's or (b) when the abusive, coercive, or paraphilic behaviors are so distasteful to the worker that a sensation of horror replaces a desire for effective listening. This aspect of working with sex offenders in groups will be discussed below under "Practice Principles."

Sexual fantasies, sometimes bizarre, often accompany racist perceptions and attitudes, as has been noted. These aside, several subcultures and cultural groups in American society are less sex negative, or erotophobic, than is the culture as a whole. Among these are communities defined by race, by culture and language, by being foreign born or native born of foreign parents, and by ethnic identity. There is also abundant evidence that views on the nature of male and female sexuality, and on the nature and origins of heterosexuality and homosexuality, vary by social class and have varied over time, reflecting and responding to other societal changes (D'Emilio & Freedman, 1988). To take just one example, living quarters and standards of past generations and past centuries allowed for, or required, much less privacy for most Americans than is thought necessary by contemporary middle- or working-class standards. Not only birth and death, but also many other behaviors, including sexual behavior, were more visible to others in the household simply because people lived closer together.

At present, communicating about sex has been made more difficult by the imposition in some professional settings of political limits to discourse focusing on the "discomfort" of anyone present. Certain words and concepts, in this view, are so offensive that they should be banned from civilized discourse. Since sexual topics, almost by definition, can be guaranteed to make someone uncomfortable in a social context that is ambivalent about sex, these topics become doubly taboo because of the possibility that whoever introduces them will be viewed as a harasser by those who experience discomfort. Certainly whatever discomfort is introduced into a treatment group for sex offenders by a discussion of sexual subjects and specific sexual behaviors should be recognized, but this should hardly serve as a justification for avoiding such charged and super-charged topics.

We have been discussing difficulties in communicating about sex, especially about deviant sexual behaviors. By now, the reader may wish to protest that contemporary American society is obsessed with sex—that sexuality, sometimes of the most primitive and evident sort, is displayed daily and nightly on television and in other mass media, on advertising billboards, and in the lyrics of popular songs. This obsession should not be viewed as a sign of growing openness and greater comfort with communicating about sex, but rather as the opposite. It is precisely the potential titillation and inherent discomfort accompanying sexual display and images that give TV images and billboard illustrations dramatic power. Sex as tenderness, as communication, as love, as communication and closeness between two people is rarely portrayed. Nor are the concomitants of sexual activity, such as pregnancy, sexually transmitted diseases, occasional sexual dysfunction, or various other aspects of human sexual behavior, visible. In their own way, the mass media of our society treat sex as an "unspeakable monster," as Money has observed.

COMMON GROUP THEMES

What makes these observations relevant to the task of treating sex offenders in groups? First, not only the group but also the worker(s) is doing something that is relatively deviant in our society, namely, legitimating group members' talking about their own sexual behaviors, sometimes in an explicit and detailed way. The worker needs to anticipate and develop comfort with the fact that *resistance in such groups takes many forms,* often including intense fantasizing about the worker. The worker's own sexual experience, motivation for working with a group of sex offenders, and feelings toward the group members may become, for a time, common topics of conversation both inside the group and in the group's interstices—before and after meetings, for example. Some of these issues may be projections of group members' discomfort, guilt, shame, and fears elicited by being in an offenders' group and the process that brought them there. Other comments and discussions may be part of the process of *testing the worker,* a process that is universal in such groups, in this writer's experience.

There are various theories about the origins of destructive sexual behaviors that violate laws and the rights and needs of other people. Regardless of their theoretical orientation, however, a wide range of researchers and practitioners, from a variety of professional backgrounds, agree on the importance of group experience and group treatment for sex offenders (Haugaard & Reppucci, 1988; Ingersoll & Patton, 1990; Maletzky & McGovern, 1990; O'Donahue & Letourneau, 1993). Writers differ as to *whether group treatment should be the primary treatment of choice,* long-term, supplemented by individual therapy on a diminishing frequency basis, which would be the first choice of this writer. Some treatment programs employ two forms of group treatment: one for offenders only and one for couples or, in some cases, entire families formed into groups.

There are biases built into most social workers' education, and perhaps into our culture in a broader way, that tend to prejudice therapists and, through them, clients in favor of individual therapy as being deeper and more effective—in short, better. Such an assumption, often unexamined, characterizes many treatment programs. Assertions are blithely made about readiness for group treatment, who can and who cannot be treated in groups, the issue of confidentiality, the unbearable strains supposedly placed not only on group members but also on group therapists, and other reasons why group treatment can work as a supplement to individual therapy but not as the primary modality for service delivery. The suggestion here is that if a reader is faced with some of the projective rationalizations cited, an appropriate response is to smile and ask calmly for the research findings that support such anti-group treatment views. None will be cited, for there are none that support such views. A good follow-up for social workers of the individualistic heresy is to prescribe a careful reading of Falck (1988).

Most sex offenders have violated both the legal codes and the civilized norms of sexual interaction. They have also demonstrated an inability to understand the concepts of individual boundaries and rights. *These represent failures of learning, either from socialization in general or from interpersonal and group experiences in particular. Group experience is the primary setting in which such failures can be remedied through new learnings.* As one participates as a social worker in treatment groups with sex offenders, one is frequently struck by the lack of empathic ability, in the literal sense of being unable to take or understand others' roles, that many group members display. One may also observe a woodenness and lack of skill in understanding any aspect of others' communications beyond the literal.

As mentioned above, there are two routes to membership in sex offenders' groups. The first is adjudication. In effect, those found guilty of sexual offenses are given the "choice" of attending a treatment program or going to prison. For such group members, and for groups composed entirely of such (actually) involuntary members, the *fact that membership is involuntary is a major issue with which the group must deal if it is to form in any genuine sense.* Confidentiality, at least within the group, is less of an issue since the facts of the members' deviant sexual activity are known, at least to the court and, often, the correctional system. With regard to the outside world, *confidentiality is a major issue, especially if reports of group attendance and/or participation need to be made to a court, a parole officer, or another official.*

Nor are issues of authority resolved by one discussion, even an extensive one. Issues of authority, the involuntary nature of the group, and the power that the court or social agency has over members in terms of compelling attendance tend to resurface repeatedly. If the group is having the desired effect, each resurfacing of this concern will be a bit less intense and the group members themselves will be able to reassert the group's purpose and the group's contract progressively more easily as time goes on.

The second route to membership is a voluntary one, undertaken by the group member without the coercion of the court, even though fear of being arrested and prosecuted is often a strong motivating factor for seeking treatment. For such members, confidentiality is an overwhelming concern. The sexual behaviors involved may have been hidden —may still be, for that matter—from significant others in the group member's life. Often, such *group members express such an intense terror of exposure* that one cannot help wondering whether this "coming out" is something that some people both fear and want, even though the latter desire may well be unconscious.

There is no lack of evidence that victims of sex offenders can suffer serious, long-term harm. Lives can be blighted and sexual activity turned from the natural route to connectedness with a loving partner and expression of one's deepest impulses, as it should be, to an area of life poisoned by fear and degradation (see, e.g., Allgeier & Allgeier, 1988, pp. 569–635; Donaldson and Cordes-Green, 1994; Haugaard & Reppucci, 1988; Mandell & Damon, 1989, pp. 1–4; Roth, 1993). Nonetheless, *denial*

remains a prominent theme for many sessions of many sex offenders' groups.
This denial takes several forms. One is that the person has been wrongly
accused and wrongly charged. Either the act of which the member
is accused did not take place or it did not take place in the manner
described. The group member is, according to this pattern, the real
victim: being set up by a vengeful spouse, being persecuted by the police,
wrongly accused in an atmosphere of hysteria.

Another variation is that the offender hasn't done anything that others
do not do. The main difference is that the offender got caught. Group
members will sometimes seek to get confirmation by going around the
group and interrogating others—sometimes including the worker—about
their sexual activities. Again, often there is said to be a villain in the piece:
the spouse, a relative of the victim, a misunderstanding and unsympa-
thetic bystander, a nosy neighbor, or some other person who butted in.

*One of the most disturbing versions of denial places the major blame on
the victim.* The rape victim was seductively clothed and "was just asking
for it." The stepdaughter was flirtatious: "The kid just came over and sat
right down on my lap." Without in any way questioning the fact that children, especially adolescents, can be seductive, and that some victims of
sexual assault wear short skirts, it is very important that these behaviors be
reinterpreted in the group as *not* being invitations to coercive, illegal, and
destructive sexual activity. "I couldn't help myself" is an avoidance of
responsibility and a copout. It is often a false, post facto rationalization.

*Substance abuse and dependence and their role in the offending behav-
iors are often the "uninvited guests" in offenders' treatment groups.* Patterns
of dealing with this content vary widely. The substance use may be part of
what is denied. Alternatively, it may be used as a justification and explanation for the behavior. "I was really stoned out of my mind and barely
remember what happened" is a characteristic presentation from this
stance. The message of the group needs to emphasize the issue of responsibility with regard to the substance use as well as the sexual behavior.
Experience has taught this writer of the truth of the position generally
taken by experts in substance abuse: Unless the abuse/addiction is being
treated effectively, by whatever means, treatment for other pathologies is
usually wasted. Gains dissolve into the pattern of abuse or addiction.

*"I/a man/someone like me/a person of my background/she gotta have
it"* is another characteristic theme. Often this is combined with accusing
the worker—or other members—of not being able to understand because
they are so different from the group member talking. The essence of
the group's message, and the worker's, should be that sexual drives,
urges, and appetites are strong, real, and natural, but need to be and can
be under the conscious control of their owners. A great deal is yet to be
learned about what Money (1986) has called *lovemaps,* the patterns of
sexual attraction that each person develops. The *DSM-IV,* the *Diagnostic
and Statistical Manual* of the American Psychiatric Association clearly
identifies various paraphilias as disorders. The culture of victimhood how-

ever, is not helpful for sex offenders, whether individually or in groups, since it relieves one of responsibility for one's actions. In the short run, such a stance is countertherapeutic. In the long run, it holds out only the "hopes" of death or incarceration for life, since it denies the possibility of change that is, at least partly, under the individual's control.

Several of these themes are alternative forms of a presentation for self as *helpless* in the face of internal and external sexual cues. Altering and reversing this view of one's own sexuality and sexual appetites is the major task of these treatment groups. Support, skill teaching, learning alternative ways of structuring time, and, strangely enough, legitimating a healthy frequency and intensity of sexual activities with an appropriate and consenting partner are other positive outputs of treatment groups. Why is legitimating sexual activity needed? Although one should always be aware of the dangers of stereotyping, a surprising proportion of sex offenders view sexual activity as illicit, as needing to be imposed on others by force or other coercive means. The concept of their being viewed as sexually desirable is mind boggling.

Case

Neal was attending the group as part of a plan worked out with the state's attorney's office after having admitted to an incestuous relationship with his daughter, who had been in his custody, from ages 11 to 14. (The daughter had been removed to another state by her grandparents, with whom she now was living.) Neal told the group that something unexpected had happened to him this past week. He had been advertising a room in his house since he needed the money and had three extra bedrooms. About 2 months ago, a woman named Sybil had rented the room. She seemed a pleasant enough person who paid her rent on time, but conversation between the two of them had been limited to brief inquiries about using the washing machine and where to get one's shoes fixed. The other night, Sybil, who is 28, knocked on his bedroom door and asked whether he would like some company. This led, the following night, to the two of them going out to dinner and then "'making love,' as she likes to call it." In the group discussion, Neal revealed that he had never before had a sexual experience with a woman older than 18, the age his wife had been when she left him. Group members interrogated Neal thoroughly to make sure that the activity had been voluntary, and combined congratulating him with sympathy and warnings about how he needed to learn to treat Sybil.

PRACTICE PRINCIPLES

In working with sex offenders, it is particularly important to avoid going to extremes: being seduced into accepting the group members' views of the world or viewing the group members as loathesome and less than human. Either set of perceptions and attitudes on the part of the worker is both unhelpful to the group and poses a serious danger of burnout for the worker. One worker said that working with groups of offenders had the danger of turning her into a " prohibitionist," an antisex erotophobe.

Worker boundaries need to be kept. Testing of the worker may include inquiries about the worker's own sexual past and present. One needs to be both transparent as to one's feelings and responses in the group and reserved with regard to a sphere of privacy in one's own life. Perhaps most difficult, one needs to feel legitimated in both spheres as a worker.

It is useful to provide some structure for group meetings. For long-term, open-ended groups, one fruitful technique is to "bridge" from one meeting to another. This involves using some time—say, the last 5 or 10 minutes of a meeting—to summarize learnings from this meeting and to plan together the content, or at least the starting points, of the next meeting.

Shorter-term groups and groups with fixed life spans—say, 12 meetings over 12 weeks—can be problematic in treating sex offenders. These groups often move slowly for quite a while. Members need to get involved in looking at attitudes and behaviors they may have learned over a long period of time or even an entire lifetime. Genuine change is rarely dramatic but needs to be processed over time. Sometimes membership is not under the worker's control.

In a group that meets within a correctional facility, for example, a person may have completed the term of a sentence, or may have been released on parole, and may leave the group as a result. Generally, however, it is good practice to contract with members for participation in the group as a relatively long-term commitment that will pay long-term rewards to the member and to the group as a whole.

As a worker/therapist, one should mistrust sudden conversions, protestations of "seeing the light," and protestations of virtue. There is what may be called a *culture of conning* that surrounds many inpatient and outpatient correctional processes, and those noted here are among the classic signs that this culture is at work.

Violence is absolutely antithetical to group work and group process. As a worker, you should share with the group what your response will be should any violence be threatened or undertaken. You should make the necessary administrative and logistical arrangements to act on your statements and should do so at the first hint that interpersonal violence is even being seriously contemplated.

Cotherapy is sometimes very productive, as with a mixed-sex coleadership team with sexually assaultive men. However, coworking takes careful thought, attention, and follow-through. Unless you have a positive reason for coworking (see Chapter 1, this volume), a solo worker format is recommended.

Do not, under any circumstances, make "deals" with group members, no matter how innocent they may appear. Subgroups or entire groups may participate in a "splitting" process in which an attempt is made to split the worker from the sponsoring organization. Don't be seduced into doing this. If you have tensions or problems with the organization, find productive means for dealing with them but leave them outside of the group.

Do be creative with program techniques, discussion starters, and ways of posing problems for the group to consider. Often newspaper articles, television stories, or readily available video clips do well and introduce a productive note. As noted above, sex is often hard to talk about, and deviant and criminal sex harder yet.

EVALUATION

Groups for the treatment of sex offenders have objectives that are unique to groups of this type, objectives shared with some other types of groups, and objectives shared with groups in general. The evaluation plan should be discussed and requisite permissions obtained at the time a member joins the group, if it is an open-ended group, or at the time the group begins, if it is a closed-ended group.

The unique objective is the prevention of repeat offenses, and every treatment group should be evaluated in terms of success in achieving this objective. It will generally be necessary to obtain information from other sources in addition to group members' reports. Permission to get this information from, for example, police records will need to be obtained from voluntary group members; those adjudicated are generally viewed as having waived their right to privacy with regard to criminal conduct or have signed such a waiver as a condition of having been released on parole or placed on probation. Family members, those sharing living quarters, and friends may also serve as sources of information, although discretion must be used and permission obtained, in most cases, to use these sources.

As with other types of treatment groups, pre-during-post measurements may be sought in an attempt to accomplish two purposes. The first is evaluation of the effectiveness of the group. The second is the stimulus it provides to members to reflect on their experiences in the group and on their meaning.

This writer is committed to the value of feedback *during* the sessions because it can be useful to the worker and the group members in modifying the content, process, or time allocations of the group. All too often, the post measurements provide feedback that, were there time to act on it, would have made the group more meaningful, effective, or satisfying to its members. When these data are available in an organized way only when the group has finished or is about to finish its life span, the most one can do is seek to apply the knowledge gained to future group experiences.

Experience with both structured and precoded questionnaires, on the one hand, and with less structured one-page questionnaires with four to five questions and space for comments, on the other, have demonstrated both that each kind can furnish valuable information and that each kind can be sabotaged. Clearly there are situations—when one is taking part in a study involving many groups, for example—in which structured instruments, tested for validity and reliability, are preferred. What is most important, however, is the willingness of the worker—and, where appropriate, the group—to *listen to and hear* the data and the feedback they provide.

REFERENCES

Allgeier, A. R., & Allgeier, E. R. (1988). *Sexual interactions* (2nd ed.). Lexington, MA: D. C. Heath.

Barnard, G. W., Fuller, A. K., Robbins, L., & Shaw, T. (1989). *The child molester: An integrated approach to evaluation and treatment.* New York: Brunner/Mazel.

Bettelheim, B., & Janowitz, M. (1964). *Social change and prejudice, including dynamics of prejudice.* New York: Free Press.

Bureau of Justice Statistics, U.S. Department of Justice. (1993). *Criminal victimization in the United States, 1991.* Washington, DC: Government Printing Office.

Bureau of Justice Statistics, U.S. Department of Justice. (1995). *Criminal victimization, 1993.* Washington, DC: Government Printing Office.

Conrad, P., & Schneider, J. W. (1992). *Deviance and medicalization: From badness to sickness* (expanded ed.). Philadelphia: Temple University Press.

D'Emiio, J., & Freedman, E. G. (1988). *Intimate matters: A history of sexuality in America.* New York: Harper & Row.

Diagnostic and statistical manual of mental disorders. (4th ed.) (DSM-IV). (1995). Washington, DC: American Psychiatric Press.

Doll, L. S., Petersen, L. R., White, C. R., Johnson, E. S., Ward, E. W., & the Blood Donor Study Group. (1992). Homosexually and nonhomosexually identified men who have sex with men: A behavioral comparison. *Journal of Sex Research, 29,* 1–14.

Donaldson, M. A., & Cordes-Green, S. (1994). *Group treatment of adult incest survivors.* Thousand Oaks, CA: Sage.

Falck, H. S. (1988). *Social work practice: The membership approach.* New York: Springer.

Haugaard, J. J., & Reppucci, N. D. (1988). *The sexual abuse of children.* San Francisco: Jossey-Bass.

Horton, A. L., Johnson, B. L., Roundy, L. M., & Williams, D. (Eds.). (1990). *The incest perpetrator: A family member no one wants to treat.* Newbury Park, CA: Sage.

Ingersoll, S. L., & Patton, S. O. (1990). *Treating perpetrators of sexual abuse.* Lexington, MA: D. C. Heath.

Maletzky, B., & McGovern, K. B. (1990). *Treating the sexual offender.* Newbury Park, CA: Sage.

Mandell, J. G., & Damon, L. (1989). *Group treatment for sexually abused children.* New York: Guilford Press.

Masters, W. H., Johnson V. E., & Kolodny, R. C. (1986). *Sex and human loving.* Boston: Little, Brown.

Money, J. (1986). *Lovemaps: Clinical concepts of sexual/erotic health and pathology, paraphilia, and gender transposition in childhood, adolescence and maturity.* New York: Irvington.

Money, J. (1994). *Reinterpreting the unspeakable: Human sexuality 2000.* New York: Continuum.

O'Donohue, W., & Letourneau, E. (1993). A brief group treatment for the modification of denial in child sexual abuses: Outcome and follow-up. *Child Abuse and Neglect, 17,* 299–304.

Pithers, W. D., Kashima, K. M., Cumming, G. F., & Beal, L. S. (1988). Relapse prevention: A method of enhancing maintenance of change in sex offenders. In A. Salter (Ed.), *Treating child sex offenders and victims: A practical guide.* Newbury Park, CA: Sage.

Roth, N. (1993). *Integrating the shattered self: Psychotherapy with adult incest survivors.* Northvale, NJ: Jason Aronson.

Rutan, J. S., & Stone, W. N. (1993). *Psychodynamic group psychotherapy* (2nd ed.). New York: Guilford Press.

Salter, A. C. (Ed.). (1988). *Treating child sex offenders and victims: A practical guide.* Newbury Park, CA: Sage.

Scaveo, R. R. (1989). Female adolescent sex offenders: A neglected treatment group. *Social Casework, 70,* 114–117.

Shaffer, J., & Galinsky, M. D. (1989). *Models of group therapy* (2nd ed.). Englewood Cliffs, NJ: Prentice-Hall.

Vance, C. S. (Ed.). (1984). *Pleasure and danger: Exploring female sexuality.* Boston: Routledge & Kegan Paul.

Whitaker, D. L., & Wodarski, J. S. (1988). Treatment of sexual offenders in a community mental health center: An evaluation. *Journal of Social Work and Human Sexuality, 7,* 49–68.

Zilbergeld, B. (1978). *Male sexuality.* New York: Bantam Books.

14

Group Work with Sexually Abused Children

Sharon England

Although not all sexually abused children and adults who were molested as children will experience emotional, physical, and sexual problems, those who do require professional intervention and treatment. Group work has become the most common form of treatment, if not the treatment of choice, with this population, especially with child victims (Faller, 1988, p. 377; Mandell & Damon, 1989, p. 2; Sturkie, 1992, p. 332).

REVIEW OF THE LITERATURE

The impact of child sexual abuse has been the subject of much study and research. Accordingly, there now is an abundant literature available to beginning social workers that explores the causes, characteristics, and treatment of this complex social problem. Finkelhor (1986) reports that the evidence "conveys a clear suggestion that sexual abuse is a serious mental health problem, consistently associated with very disturbing subsequent problems in a significant portion of its victims" (p. 152).

Despite the enormous needs of this population, Friedrich (1990) reports that much of the treatment of child sexual abuse "is frequently relegated to a continually changing group of novice therapists" (p. 277). Therefore, it behooves beginning group leaders to prepare and to obtain as much guidance as possible before attempting to conduct groups or any other type of treatment with sexually abused children.

Sources that discuss the history, dynamics, characteristics, impact, cultural variations, and treatment of child sexual abuse include Finkelhor

(1986, 1995), Friedrich (1990), Kilpatrick (1992), O'Donahue and Geer (1992), and Renvoize (1993). Resources that address group work with sexually abused children include Faller (1988), Friedrich (1990), Mandell and Damon (1989), Sgroi (1982), Sturkie (1992), and Hack, Osachuk, and DeLuca (1994). Beginning group leaders will find that child sexual abuse prevention curricula, including those of Harms and James (1983) and Schonfield (1984), also are good sources for assistance in leading groups of sexually abused children.

Conducting groups with sexually abused children is very demanding and challenging. Social workers planning to conduct such groups must possess great creativity, initiative, and persistence. Since group work with children requires interaction with child participants, their caretakers (parents, guardians, or foster parents), and other professionals, social workers also must become skilled in working with several different client populations and with colleagues.

PRACTICE PRINCIPLES

Several social work practice principles are particularly relevant when conducting groups with sexually abused children. They include self-awareness, contracting, use of authority, dealing with issues of confidentiality, and handling termination.

Self-Awareness

In all social work practice, social workers must constantly strive to maintain objectivity and to identify any personal biases that could have a negative impact on their clients. This is especially true when working with sexually abused children.

Social workers treating this population must recognize their attitudes regarding sexual abuse of children and their own sexuality (Einbender, 1991, p. 115; Faller, 1988, p. 5; Friedrich, 1990, p. 278). Unresolved issues or possible past sexual victimization can interfere with social workers' ability to evaluate objectively their capacity to conduct groups with sexually abused children. Social workers should consult with a supervisor or colleague for help in determining whether they should practice with this population.

Sexual acting out and the use of childish, sexually explicit, or vulgar language by sexually abused children are common. Often social workers experience discomfort when listening to children discuss their sexual victimization in graphic detail. They must control their inadvertent responses of shock, amusement, and/or disapproval that can inhibit group discussion.

Conducting groups of culturally diverse children requires group workers to be sensitive and respectful of different cultures. Man Keung Ho (1992) reports that "Minority clients . . . initially experience difficulty in talking about personal and family problems in a group setting and in front of a stranger who is the group therapist. However, group inter-action and group therapy, if properly provided, may have advantages that individual and family therapy do not" (p. 178).

Social workers should not assume that all children will share informa-tion that they perceive as unique to their circumstances, as the following example, brought to my attention, illustrates:

> One African-American child told her new African-American therapist that she believed her abuse stemmed from the fact she was darker-skinned than her sister. This revelation led to a discussion of the child's body image and racism. When asked why she had not said this before, the child said she didn't believe her previous white social workers would understand.

Resources that provide social workers with help in treating diverse populations include Devore and Schlesinger (1987), Ho (1992); Lynch and Hanson (1992), and Vacc, Wittmer, and Devaney (1988).

Finally, social workers must avoid re-creating their child clients' fam-ily dynamics. Often children in sexually abusive families have been social-ized to consent to or forced to accept conduct that was contrary to their best interest. Therefore, social workers should consider the ramifications of asking children to participate in unusual activities, such as interviews with the media or confronting perpetrators. Children's assent may reflect their eagerness to please their social workers rather than comfort or will-ingness to participate in such activities.

Contracting

Contracting with child clients, their caretakers, and other service providers is invaluable in group work. Contracts provide everyone with clear expectations regarding the purpose of the group, meeting schedule, attendance, transportation, and group rules. Written contracts created and signed by each party facilitate compliance.

Prior to the first group meeting, group workers should interview each child and caretaker if possible. To establish a basis on which to build trust and rapport with children, group workers should use this initial meeting to clarify the purpose and goals of the group. In the author's experience, children often are given vague or no reasons for attending groups. Some-times referring social workers may not have had time to explain the group's purpose adequately, or the explanation may have been given long before the group began. Caretakers, wishing to avoid a child's discomfort or refusal to attend, may be uncomfortable or reluctant to discuss the reason for the child's referral to the group.

As the group will become an important source of support to children, consistent attendance is critical. Group leaders should discuss the chil-dren's transportation at this introductory meeting. Various methods should be considered, including coordinating a car pool with other social workers, asking an outside funding source to finance a bus service, providing bus tokens for older children, and arranging for caretakers to transport their own children. The last method is generally used when parents' groups are held simultaneously with the children's.

Group leaders should help groups establish rules at the first group meeting. To facilitate adherence to rules, children should be encouraged to participate in this process. Generally, children will make many suggestions. The rules can then be written down and posted in the group room.

Use of Authority

Social workers must consider their use of authority with this population and take the time necessary to help children overcome their natural resistance in groups rather than force them into uncomfortable situations. To promote group cohesion and trust, all children should be informed and willing participants.

Sexually abused children may have maladaptive control issues that cause them to challenge social workers' exercise of authority. Often, offenders have used and abused their position of authority to gain control over and sexually assault these children (Groth, 1982, p. 224). In the author's experience, children will generalize this misuse of authority to their social workers and expect them, too, abuse their authority.

This testing of authority provides an opportunity for constructive learning for the group members. Social workers should anticipate these challenges to their authority and respond so that children can experience authority in a more appropriate manner. First, group leaders must make the limits of their authority clear. At a minimum, children should be told that they will not be permitted to hurt themselves or another group member, nor will they permitted to break or destroy any of the toys or equipment in the play room.

Second, group leaders should identify and tolerate healthy challenges to their authority even if these challenges frustrate clinical intervention. These concessions may include allowing children to change a group topic, avoid a group activity, skip a meeting, or even leave the group. Often children who are beginning to experience empowerment through the treatment process will test both their ability to exert control over their own lives and their social workers' promise of support by withdrawing from the group or other forms of treatment. Invariably, these children can be dissuaded more effectively from leaving treatment with sensitive guidance and patience than by an overt refusal. In the author's experience, children who are permitted to exercise control in these areas do not withdraw permanently from the group or treatment.

Finally, social workers should consider these dynamics before recommending that a child be court ordered to attend a group. Group members require a high degree of trust and comfort to discuss their sexual abuse experiences. Such discussions do not occur easily. When children are coerced into attending groups, they can become resistant. As a result, other members may become inhibited, fearing that the resistant member will not respect their revelations and keep them confidential.

Dealing with Confidentiality

It is unrealistic and erroneous to tell children that everything they say is confidential. However, it is important for children to know which information will be shared with their caretakers and other professionals. Group leaders should tell all children that if they say anything indicating that they may be or have been abused or hurt again, either by themselves or by others, their group leaders will take action to protect them. This statement should be made in the initial interview and reiterated throughout the life of the group. If a child's statement must be revealed, group leaders should inform the child of the decision and the reasons.

In the author's experience, this message does not inhibit children's discussion or revelations. Children will continue to reveal important information, counting on social workers to act responsibly and to take protective action on their behalf. When social workers give unrealistic assurances of confidentiality or fail to take protective action, children can be harmed and their trust irrevocably broken.

Depending on the caretakers' status as parents, guardians, or foster parents, they and the children should be informed regarding what they can expect to learn from their child's group participation. Group workers should discourage caretakers from questioning children about group discussions and activities. Group workers also should tell children how to handle unwanted questions from caretakers and other children. They should reiterate the importance of the group as a safe haven from parental intrusion and emphasize other group participants' need for confidentiality with members and caretakers.

Handling Termination

Termination issues in groups should be handled with the utmost concern and attention. Sexually abused children often have experienced many abrupt and traumatic endings in their lives. They may have been removed from their homes on disclosure of the sexual abuse. Parents or other family members accused of the abuse may have been incarcerated or forced to leave the home. There may have been little or no opportunity to say goodbye to family members or neighborhood friends.

The reality of these traumatic, abrupt endings in these children's lives should be considered in determining guidelines for group termination. Failing to do so can hinder children's social adjustment and progress in treatment.

In one group consisting of latency-aged sexually abused girls, the group leaders failed to address termination issues. The group was open-ended, with no planned termination. As members grew too old for the group they left, sometimes abruptly. The group leaders failed to address the needs of both the girls departing and those left behind. Members perceived the departures as a rejection. When asked to draw pictures of their group, girls included former group members who had left months earlier while omitting new members. These girls leaving the group felt no sense of completion. Recognizing that the group was exacerbating the girls' chaotic lives, the group leaders attempted to redefine these endings. However, the poorly handled departures proved to have a more lasting impact than the subsequent intervention. Finally, the group leaders closed entry into the group and began to work on termination issues with the remaining members. Eventually, the group was disbanded.

Social workers conducting groups with sexually abused children should provide a well-defined termination process. Short-term or time-limited structured groups, with or without closed membership, can facilitate this process. By making group termination an expected and positive outcome, social workers can help children plan more thoroughly for endings. They can encourage children to explore their feelings about the group's conclusion and their past unhealthy departures.

COMMON THEMES

Several common themes have been observed in treating sexually abused children. The seven discussed below are not an exhaustive list. In addition, social workers should not assume that all children will experience any or all of them.

Fear

Fear has been identified in both empirical and clinical literature as the most common effect of child sexual abuse (Berliner, 1991, p. 99; Finkelhor, 1986, p. 149; Porter, Blick, & Sgroi, 1982, p. 117). Typically, children fear repeated abuse, the consequences of sexual activity, and retaliation and separation from their families (Johnson, 1991, p. 279; Porter et al., 1982, p. 117; Sturkie, 1992, p. 333).

It is important to help children distinguish between realistic and unrealistic fears. Children's fears are reasonable when the perpetrator has continued access to the child, the child is not believed or supported by a caretaker, or the child is exposed to unsafe situations. If these conditions exist, social workers must advocate for changes in children's environment and/or for caretakers' participation in treatment. Otherwise, progress in group or any other treatment is unlikely.

Diane, Mary, and George participated in a child sexual abuse treatment program, along with their mother. Their father, who had molested and seriously beaten the children several times, had been convicted and incarcerated. The children revealed that their mother punished them by sending them to the "ghost room," the room where the abuse frequently had taken place. The group leaders alerted the mother's social workers to persuade her to use another means of discipline.

Anger

Anger is another common reaction to child sexual abuse (Finkelhor, 1986, p. 149). Often children express anger toward the caretaker who had not protected them from the abuse or who had not responded protectively after the abuse was revealed. "Many victims say little initially because they are afraid to confront their own anger and unsure of their ability to handle their feelings. They compensate by being unassertive and by saying as little as possible" (Porter et al., 1982, p. 121).

It is critical to give children permission and opportunities to identify and work through this anger in order to make progress in other areas of treatment. Groups can provide a safe forum to express and explore these angry feelings. "This process can be facilitated by the use of exercises that make the feelings concrete and direct them at an appropriate target, after they are identified" (Porter, 1986, p. 56). Techniques such as role plays, punching bags, letter writing, and art therapy are particularly helpful in assisting children to ventilate and examine their feelings.

Guilt

Guilt and shame are frequent reactions to child sexual abuse (Finkelhor, 1986, p. 149; Porter et al., 1982, p. 115). Children may perceive themselves to be responsible for the sexual abuse, its disclosure, and the resulting family disruption.

> Mary, age 13, was blamed for her grandfather's incarceration and subsequent fatal heart attack. Eight-year-old Vicki believed herself to be an unfit "parent" who caused her five siblings to be placed in three different foster homes. Vicki's father forced her to adopt her deceased mother's parental and marital role. Disclosure occurred when neighborhood children saw Vicki's father raping her through the bedroom window. Cindy, age 10, felt shame for experiencing pleasure during oral sex with her aunt.

Unfortunately, children's guilty feelings often are aggravated by their family's, community's, and professionals' attitudes and responses. "Amazingly, the perpetrator's assertion that a seductive child is responsible for the sexual behavior is often given credence by judges, attorneys, police officers, physicians, social workers, and the like" (Porter et al., 1982, p. 115). However, some children will need help to identify "appropriate guilt feelings" when they have used their "favored position" to manipulate and behave inappropriately toward others (Porter et al., p. 117).

In the author's experience, the belief that sexually abused children are irrevocably damaged and without innocence is a prevalent attitude. The mere statement that "it's not your fault" does little to extinguish these children's guilty feelings. Addressing this normalization of children's guilt is most appropriate for a group setting, where children can receive constant and consistent reassurance from their peers through group discussion and structured activities.

Depression

Depression, suicide, and self-mutilation have been observed in both sexually abused children and adults (Beitchman, Zucker, Hood, Da Costa, Akman, & Cassavia, 1992; Pisaruk, Shawchuck, & Hoier, 1992; Young, 1992). Young (1992) reports that self-abuse may occur when survivors believe they cannot trust their own bodies because they feel vulnerable or shame or because they felt some pleasure while the abuse was occurring. Social workers should evaluate all children in treatment for child sexual abuse for possible depression and suicidal ideation.

> Sarah, 11, who was forced to perform oral sex on her mother, slashed at her wrist with a pen knife, put broken glass in her mouth, threatened to swallow the pieces, and kept several doctors, nurses, and social workers at bay before she was finally hospitalized. Eight-year-old Michah, who was sexually abused by her mother's three boyfriends, reported to her group that she planned to jump out of her second-story window onto the concrete pavement below. Terry, 6 years old, lay down in the middle of a busy street in an attempt to kill herself.

Inability to Trust

Sexually abused children's impaired ability to trust themselves, adults, and other children has been reported in the clinical literature (Einbender, 1991, p. 115; Mandell & Damon, 1989, p. 1; Porter et al., 1982, p. 121). Social workers often are viewed with suspicion rather than seen as a source of protection and support.

Often this impairment of trust is manifested by children's frequent testing of social workers' trustworthiness, which may be confused with challenges to social workers' authority. Group leaders' cancellation of group sessions, broken promises, and alliances with other children or authority figures can be viewed as rejections and evidence of group leaders' untrustworthiness.

Einbender (1991) reports that "sexually abused children often take longer to form a trusting relationship with the therapist that is secure enough to allow them to begin to explore the actual abuse" (p. 115).

Anxiety Regarding Legal and Court Intervention

It is important that social workers dealing with sexually abused children understand both the criminal and civil legal systems. Often children will require assistance in understanding both the purpose and the outcome of legal intervention. Children may experience fear or anxiety regarding testifying in court, retaliation by the perpetrator, not being believed, being on trial themselves, or embarrassing question on the witness stand (O'Donohue & Geer, 1992, Vol. 2, p. 298).

By contrast, some children demand to have "their day in court" and become angry if they are not allowed to testify at trial or at sentencing. Green (1992) reports that testifying in court has potential advantages, including giving children an active role in mastering the trauma, offering children a chance to be believed and to see justice work, and providing children a constructive outlet for their anger (p. 298).

Children also may feel dejected after completion of the court process, despite the outcome. Sometimes, at the conclusion of court intervention, social workers, investigators, police, and prosecutors may discontinue or curtail their services to children, thus leaving the children to cope with the aftermath of court intervention alone.

Delayed Development and Socialization Skills

Finally, many sexually abused children experience significant delays in their development and socialization skills (Friedrich, 1990, p. 25; Mandel & Damon, 1989, p. 1). As a result, children's communication, negotiation, and play skills can be hampered. These delays can thwart the development of rapport, cohesion, and trust among the members and, consequently, the promotion of group goals.

Therefore, "intervention must also be geared to the enhancement of age-appropriate skills" (Mandel & Damon, 1989, p. 2). However, social workers' premature intervention into group members' interactions and conflicts may deny children critical learning experiences. Group workers must strike a delicate balance between doing too much or too little when helping children overcome these developmental delays and acquire appropriate socialization skills. Intervention must be constructive without denying group members opportunities to work out conflicts and to learn cooperative play and negotiation skills on their own.

RECOMMENDED WAYS OF WORKING

Establishing a Group Within an Agency

Group work can occur in almost any agency setting. However, conducting groups within agencies typically is fraught with difficulties. Besides having to convince sometimes skeptical administrators about the value and effectiveness of group treatment, social workers must struggle to ensure that adequate space and supplies are available. These efforts to establish or fortify an existing group within an agency can be just as important as the clinical techniques used during each group session.

The availability of a regular group room to promote privacy, consistency, and access to art and play supplies to encourage group interaction and communications is important in promoting rapport and trust among the members. Unfortunately, such resources and supplies are often difficult to obtain in agencies with budget and space limitations. Social workers' initiative and ingenuity are essential to overcome these obstacles.

> In one urban agency, group leaders effectively advocated the conversion of a staff room to a child's play room. They negotiated for the exclusive use of the room for evening group sessions, while agency social workers were given daily access to conduct child interviews. Another group leader got several donations from community toy and art stores. The result: an exceptionally well-stocked play room well beyond the agency's limited budget.

Group Structure

The developmental age of the members and the purpose of the group are critical in determining the structure of the group. Younger children require less autonomy and are generally more comfortable with a structure similar to a school setting that provides order and consistency. Agendas that include a time for free play, organized group play, a snack, and group discussion can be used. Adolescents require more autonomy and should be encouraged to participate in determining the group's structure and activities.

Groups designed to provide children intensive therapy or long-term support usually are longer and open, allowing old members to leave and new ones to enter. As previously discussed, group leaders should take special care to address children's termination and separation issues. Also, new members should be added in pairs or threes to reduce possible discomfort and the feeling of not belonging.

Educational groups and groups formed for child abuse prevention, parenting, teenage sexuality, socialization and play skills, and so on can be shorter term, with closed membership. These groups are usually more structured, with specific information to be conveyed and discussed at each meeting.

The size of the group also is determined by such factors as the developmental age of its members. Younger groups should be smaller, with six to eight children. Adolescent groups can be larger, with 10 members being the upper limit. These numbers can be increased if there are coleaders.

Group leaders also must consider the composition of their groups. They must be careful to distinguish between children's chronological age and developmental age.

Yvonne, a physically mature 12-year-old, had been sexually abused by her mother's boyfriend and sexually active with neighborhood boys for over a year. Her placement in a latency-aged group was fraught with difficulties. Yvonne wanted to discuss her sexual experiences with her boyfriend, while the other members could not comprehend why anyone would engage in sex willingly. Group leader suggested an early graduation for Yvonne and transferred her to the older adolescent group.

Group leaders can successfully combine latency-aged boys and girls in a group setting. Such a mixture provides many positive experiences for both sexes. Boys, who generally are more reticent about discussing their sexual victimization, often become less reluctant on listening to girls describe their experiences. Girls, whose most significant contact with older boys and men has been abusive, are provided an opportunity to experience males in more positive ways.

Rose, 8 years old, was sexually assaulted by a neighborhood boy. She declared that she did not trust boys and was afraid to even touch them. This announcement led Tom, also 8 and a typically disruptive and inattentive group member, to offer to shake Rose's hand. Although Rose initially refused, Tom continued thoughtfully to offer his hand throughout the meeting. Eventually, Rose accepted his gesture. This interchange led to a discussion of Rose's diminished aversion to boys and recognition of Tom's persistent efforts to comfort and nurture another group member.

In the author's experience, the combination of boys and girls in one group makes it important to have both a male and a female coleader. However, group leaders should be prepared for the children's tendency to sexualize the relationship between the leaders.

When setting the table for a snack, the group members consistently seated the two group leaders together. When asked why, the children said they thought the leaders would want to be together since they were married or boyfriend and girlfriend. In other groups, children frequently asked if the group leaders were dating or married.

The decision on whether the group should be co-led is important. There are both advantages and disadvantages. Coleaders can give each other support and encouragement and an opportunity to talk over the group process with another colleague. Continuity problems are reduced when one leader is absent. Also, two observers reduce the likelihood of missing important interchanges among the members.

However, when groups are co-led, leaders can dominate the group process and the service is more costly. Social workers should carefully analyze their ability to conduct a group with each other. Dissension or personality conflicts between group leaders will be readily apparent to members and can dramatically impair group effectiveness. However, if the group leaders are aware of possible conflicts and willing to examine them constructively, they can provide excellent opportunities to model conflict resolution behavior for the group members.

Group Techniques

Once group leaders establish the group and an agenda has been set, the first task is to help group members develop rapport, trust, and cohesion. Activities designed to address children's impaired communication and negotiation skills are particularly helpful.

Ice-breaking games are great for a first group. Young children especially enjoy name games that make the chore of learning new names fun. One favorite is a circle game in which the children and social workers sit in a circle and introduce themselves. The first child says his name; the next says her name and the one before her's; then the next child says his own name and the two before his; and so on. the game can be varied by the child's adding an adjective or animal name with the first letter of the child's name. Names such as Tiger Tim, Shining Sheryl, and Lovable Larry create both a sense of fun and camaraderie among the members as they try to help each other remember the names.

Older children respond well to activities designed to ease their anxiety about the group in more sophisticated and direct ways. Children anonymously write notes that answer the following questions: How do you feel about being in this group? What is one thing you like about this group? What is one thing you do not like about this group? Invariably, the children find that their concerns and fears are quite similar, thus universalizing their experience and building cohesion among them.

Art activities provide excellent opportunities to encourage group cohesion and beginning socialization skills. Group leaders can use art activities inexpensively. If resources are limited, paper and crayons can suffice. The author made frequent use of art activities to facilitate cohesion and discussion in younger children's groups. Initial activities should be simple and require minimal verbal interaction. Subsequent activities should become progressively more involved, requiring more demanding interaction.

Group finger painting is an excellent technique to encourage cohesion and communication at a nonverbal level. The children stand around a table where one large sheet of paper with finger paints is placed. They are told not to talk. As the children design the finger painting, they have fun and experience closeness in a nonthreatening manner. The final product, signed by each member, can be hung in the group room. When group ends, portions are given to each member as a keepsake.

At the next session, a variation on the finger painting, a group collage—a common school activity that requires more verbal interaction, planning, and cooperation—can be used. Children can cut pictures from magazines and past them on poster board paper. To complete the activity, children must negotiate how the space will be used and what media to include in the collage. Invariably, the pictures and captions chosen by the children express volumes about the children's personal issued. The collage can be used to facilitate difficult discussions through the life of the group or can be combined with other techniques, such as Richard Gardner's *The Mutual Story-Telling Technique* (1975, p. 101).

Body tracings, in which the group leader traces the children's bodies as they lay down on long pieces of paper, also can facilitate difficult discussions about sexuality and body image. After children color their tracings, their observations often provoke discussions of many topics, such as virginity, puberty, diseases, medical exams, homosexuality, and pregnancy. Children also use the body tracings to depict their interests in sports, dance, and careers. One boy's body tracing led him to reveal that he had been sexually abused by a woman, not a man, as had been suspected.

Rose, identified earlier, colored her body entirely in white crayon with a bright red heart that presented a strikingly vulnerable appearance and caused many comments. This tracing prompted Rose to identify her fear of boys that inspired Tom to offer to shake her hand.

Art activities also can be helpful in encouraging children to discuss their relationships with each other and assisting social workers in assessing the group's development progress. Members can be asked to draw a picture of the group or a picture of the group doing something.

Nine-year-old Lea was drawn with two mouths in one member's group picture, with an extra large mouth in another's and with no mouth in a third's. When the children were asked why this was so, they readily pointed out that Lea talked too much. A constructive discussion then followed on how Lea's monopolizing of the meeting prevented the other members from talking. The discussion concluded with Lea asking the other girls to tell her when she starts talking too much.

A common attribute of a beginning group is one-upmanship. Often the children describe their sexual abuse experience in a storylike manner, followed by a presentation of the next child's ordeal. This pattern results in superficial discussions. In response, group leaders and children have developed the *stop-name-card game.*

Children are each given a card that they can throw in the center of the table when they want to raise an issue. Before another member can raise a similar or new topic, the current speaker must have finished his or her turn and received appropriate responses from the other members. If a child throws in a card prematurely, the group leaders throw out a red stop card, showing that it is not time to move on to a new person or topic. Eventually, the children ask to have their own stop cards so that they can identify when other members are interrupted prematurely. The result is more meaningful and insightful discussions regarding each child's issue and group process.

A common technique used in groups with older sexually abused children is *letter writing*. This technique is best presented spontaneously as a solution for children who have trouble talking about their sexual abuse. Members write letters to their perpetrators or nonsupportive caretakers and express their feeling about their abuse. The children can then read their letters aloud, have another member read it silently or aloud, send it to their perpetrators, and/or destroy it.

Role play is an excellent technique to help children of all ages to express their anger, practice interaction with parents, or cope with anxiety regarding testifying in court. In one latency-aged girls' group, the leaders attempted to use an "alter-ego" role play in which a leader planned to whisper responses to a group member while she role-played a conversation with her "mother." As the group leader was awkwardly describing the role play to the children, Sally jumped up and exclaimed, "I know what you mean." Sally went on to show the technique the social worker was attempting to describe and then chose the most reticent group participant for the role play.

> Eleven-year-old Lorraine was an extremely quiet, timid group member who rarely spoke. Although Lorraine's mother had kicked her boyfriend, the abuser, out the house, Lorraine was angry with her for allowing another boyfriend to move in. As Sally whispered into Lorraine's ear, Lorraine became stronger and more assertive. Within minutes Lorraine was pounding her hand on the table, expressing for the first time, in a raised voice, her anger toward her mother. Following this meeting, Lorraine, with her social worker, confronted her mother. Lorraine, also became a less shy and more vocal group member.

Videotaping group members for clinical purposes also can be valuable. The author videotaped a group session to facilitate a discussion of group interaction. This activity led to the identification of a group scapegoat and a productive exchange about how group members can use other members as scapegoats to avoid painful discussions.

> Sally, the helpful child in the previous example, was frequently disruptive. She would often leave the group circle, wander throughout the room, or go to the blackboard and draw. The other children frequently complained about Sally, thus interrupting a valuable discussion of another's child's experiences. Sally behaved in her usual manner in the video. On viewing the video, the children recognized how they actually encouraged Sally to behave badly while complaining about her to avoid painful emotions and discussions. Sally, embarrassed by her behavior, asked the other group members to help her change.

Bibliotherapy, in which children read books or short stories on child sexual abuse or other problems, can be very helpful. Books that focus on child sexual abuse prevention also are beneficial, especially since many of these children have a high risk of future abuse. (A bibliography is provided at the end of this chapter.)

EVALUATION APPROACHES

Several methods can be used to assess the effectiveness of group intervention. The author used art, group activity, and group observation to determine the children's progress in treatment.

In each short-term closed group, the children were asked to paint their self-portraits at the beginning of the group and again at the end. Each time this was done, both the group leaders and the children noted the marked difference between the portraits.

> Eight-year-old Danny compared his obviously distorted and depressed first portrait with his happier and smiling second portrait and said, "Oh, that one [the first self-portrait] was because of what happened to me [sexual abuse] and how sad I was; the other [second self-portrait] was because I was happier, 'cause I was in group and I got to talk about everything." Another child had painted bars over his first self-portrait as a symbol of protecting himself from his incarcerated father. His second, more healthy portrait had no bars and showed him smiling.

Another technique used to evaluate change and progress in short-term, closed groups was *the group members' session*. To encourage the development of children's communication and cooperative play skills, members are asked to plan the last group session. The only condition was that the session should reflect what the children had learned in the group. Group leaders set aside 10 minutes of several preceding groups so that the children could plan this session without their participation. Generally, this activity was a huge success. Each time the children planned a well-organized group session that accurately reflected the objectives of the group.

Invariably, the children chose to give a performance, such as a play or puppet show that demonstrated what they had learned in the group. The children's caretakers were invited to this session, which included a graduation ceremony, a display of art work and projects, and refreshments provided by the group leaders and the children.

Many of the techniques and activities discussed above also provide opportunities to assess the children's progress and group development. Children's spontaneous gestures to help one another are the most significant and positive behaviors social workers can observe in the group. Midway through the group, the children started bringing in special snacks or birthday cakes for each other. Children made extra puppets or projects for times when they thought others would not have one.

Children also would comfort and encourage members during difficult discussion or in anticipation of court hearings. Such conduct shows that group members have attained a healthy degree of trust and cohesion. It also shows an improvement in the children's self-esteem, confidence, and ability to nurture and be nurtured.

CONCLUSION

The author has found conducting groups with sexually abused children to be a professionally rewarding experience. Group work is one of the most effective treatment modalities for addressing the needs of this vulnerable population. Children who refuse to speak of their abuse and consequently thwart clinical intervention disclose their victimization more readily within groups and experience relief on meeting and hearing from other children with similar experiences. The discovery that they are not alone combined with the opportunity to help other children provides group members the most significant curative experience of all.

NATIONAL RESOURCE

National Resource Center on Child
  Sexual Abuse of the National
  Center on Child Abuse and
  Neglect
2204 Whitesburg Drive
Huntsville, AL 35801
(205) 534-6868 or
(800) 543-7006

REFERENCES

Beitchman, J. H., Zucker, K. J., Hood, J. E., DaCosta, G. A., Akman, D., & Cassavia, E. (1992). A review of the long-term effects of child sexual abuse. *Child Abuse and Neglect, 16,* 106–107.

Berliner, L. (1991). Cognitive therapy with a young victim of sexual assault. In W.N. Friedrich (Ed.), *Casebook of sexual abuse treatment* (pp. 93–111). New York: W. W. Norton.

Devore, W., & Schlesinger, E. G. (1987). *Ethnic-sensitive social work practice.* Columbus, OH: Merrill.

Einbender, A. J. (1991). Treatment in the absence of maternal support. In W. N. Friedrich (Ed.), *Casebook of sexual abuse treatment* (pp. 112–136). New York: W. W. Norton.

Faller, K. C. (1988). *Child sexual abuse: An interdisciplinary manual for diagnosis, case management, and treatment.* New York: Columbia University Press.

Finkelhor, D. (1984). *Child sexual abuse: New theory and research.* New York: Free Press.

Finkelhor, D. (1986). *A sourcebook on child sexual abuse.* Thousand Oaks, CA: Sage.

Finkelhor, D. (1995). The victimization of children: A developmental perspective. *American Journal of Orthopsychiatry, 65,* 177–193.

Friedrich, W. N. (1990) *Psychotherapy of sexually abused children and their families.* New York: W. W. Norton.

Friedrich, W. N. (Ed.). (1991). *Casebook of sexual abuse treatment.* New York: W. W. Norton.

Gardner, R. A. (1975). *Psychotherapeutic approaches to the resistant child.* New York: Jason Aronson.

Green, A. H. (1992). Application of psychoanalytic theory in the treatment of the victim and the family. In W. O'Donahue & J. H. Geer (Eds.), *The sexual abuse of children: Clinical issues* (Vol. 2, pp. 285–300). Hillsdale, NJ: Erlbaum.

Groth, N.A. (1982). The incest offender. In S. Sgroi (Ed.), *Handbook of clinical intervention in child sexual abuse* (pp. 215–239). Lexington, MA: Lexington Books.

Hack, T. F., Osachuk, T. A. G., & DeLuca, R. V. (1994). Group treatment for sexually abused preadolescent boys. *Families in Society, 75,* 217–228.

Harms, R., & James, D. (1983). *Talking about touching.* Seattle: Seattle Institute for Child Advocacy, Committee for Children.

Ho, M. K. (1992). *Minority children and adolescents in therapy.* Thousand Oaks, CA: Sage.

Johnson, T. C. (1991). Treatment of a sexually reactive girl. In W. N. Friedrich (Ed.), *Casebook of sexual abuse treatment* (pp. 270–290). New York: W. W. Norton.

Kilpatrick, A. C. (1992). *Long-range effects of child and adolescent sexual experiences: Myths, mores, and menaces.* Hillsdale, NJ: Erlbaum.

Lynch, E. W., & Hanson, M. J. (Eds.). (1992). *Developing cross-cultural competence: A guide for working with young children and their families.* Baltimore: P. H. Brookes.

Mandell, J. G., & Damon, L. (1989). *Group treatment for sexually abused children.* New York: Guilford Press.

O'Donohue, W., & Geer, J. H. (Eds.). (1992). *The sexual abuse of children: Clinical issues,* Vols. 1 and 2. Hillsdale, NJ: Erlbaum.

Pisaruk, H. I., Shawchuck, C. R., & Hoier, T. S. (1992). Behavioral characteristics of child victims of sexual abuse: A comparison study. *Journal of Clinical Child Psychology, 21,* 16–17.

Porter, E. (1986). *Treating the young male victim of sexual assault: Issues and intervention strategies.* Syracuse, NY: Safer Society Press.

Porter, F. A., Blick, L. C., & Sgroi, S. M. (1982). Treatment of the sexually abused child. In S. G. Sgroi (Ed.), *Handbook of clinical intervention in child sexual abuse* (pp. 109–145). Lexington, MA: Lexington Books.

Renvoize, J. (1993). *Innocence destroyed: A study of child sexual abuse.* New York: Routledge.

Schonfield, M. (1984). *Talking about touching with preschoolers: A personal safety curriculum.* Seattle: Seattle Institute for Child Advocacy, Committee for Children.

Sgroi, S. M. (Ed.). (1982). *Handbook of clinical intervention in child sexual abuse.* Lexington, MA: Lexington Books.

Sturkie, K. (1992). Group treatment of child sexual abuse victims: A review. In W. O'Donohue & J. H. Geer (Eds.), *The sexual abuse of children: Clinical issues* (Vol. 2., pp. 331–364). Hillsdale, NJ: Erlbaum.

Vacc, N.A., Wittmer, J., & Devaney, S. (1988). *Experiencing and counseling multicultural and diverse populations.* Indianapolis: Accelerated Development.

Young, L. (1992). Sexual abuse and the problem of embodiment. *Child Abuse and Neglect, 15,* 98–99.

SELECTED BIBLIOGRAPHY ON
SEXUALLY ABUSED CHILDREN

Aho, J. S., & Petras, J. W. (1985). *Learning about sexual abuse.* Hillsdale, NJ: Enslow.

Dayee, F. (1982). *Private zones.* New York: Warner Brothers.

Gordon, S. (1985). *When living hurts.* New York: Union of American Hebrew Congregations.

Gordon, S. (1992). *A better safe than sorry book.* Buffalo, NY: Prometheus Books.

Krause, E. (1983a). *For Pete's sake, tell.* Oregon City, OR: Krause House.

Krause, E. (1983b). *Speak up, say no.* Oregon City, OR: Krause House

Loontjens, L. (1984). *Talking to children/talking to parents about sexual assault.* Santa Cruz, CA: Network Publications.

MacLean, J. (1987). *Mac.* Cambridge, MA: Houghton Mifflin.

Mazer, N. F. (1988). *Silver.* New York. Morrow Junior Books.

15

Group Work with Offenders

Margaret M. Wright

Social work with offender populations is a challenge to the beginning worker. One of the first hurdles that the worker must face is the "lock them up and throw away the key" attitude of some of the most vocal members of the public and the tendency of politicians to take on this theme as their electoral rallying cry and an easy way of garnering votes. This hostile attitude is sometimes present in the institution among staff and administrators. Social workers are often viewed as being naive and easy prey for manipulative inmates who are looking for ways to increase their privileges and speed up their release. The challenge for the social worker is to demonstrate clearly to all segments of the institution, both staff and inmates, that he or she has a valuable service to provide that does not minimize the inmates' responsibility for their behavior. Some research indicates that prison wardens in the United States are receptive to the rehabilitative ideal within a controlled environment (Cullen, Latessa, Burton, & Lombardo, 1993). This reflects research into attitudes of the public:

> It is often said that Americans are a punitive people, but it also seems that we are a people who see the wisdom of providing even those who have victimized others with the opportunity and help to pursue productive lives. (Cullen, Skovron, Scott, & Burton, 1989)

I would like to thank members of the social work department of the Ontario Correctional Institute for their suggestions about what should be included in this chapter.

The social work service can be seen as credible when presented as a concrete effort to help inmates confront the issues, over which they have control, that resulted in their imprisonment.

The population of offenders in prisons is very difficult to categorize. It is generally accepted that most offenders come from disadvantaged backgrounds and tend to be the poorest citizens of the area in which they reside (U.S. Department of Justice, 1988). The ethnic or racial composition of offenders reflects the degree of representation of the ethnic and racial groups among the poor in the community from which the offenders originate. Specific population groups, then, differ depending on the area from which the prison derives its catchment. Most inmates are poorly educated, and may have not had a stable employment pattern (Adler, Mueller, & Laufer, 1994).* One clear characteristic of most prison inmates is that most of them are male (Griffiths & Verdun-Jones, 1994). The management of men and women in prisons differs considerably because of the clearly different issues presented by the gender of the offender.

Male offenders' issues are usually depicted as relating to substance abuse (alcohol and/or drug abuse), aggression and assaultive behavior, impulsivity and poor frustration tolerance, poor education and work skills, and employment record. Problems in relationships with family members or social isolation resulting in the absence of any significant attachment to another person also exist.

Female offenders frequently have issues related to substance abuse as well as poor education and work skills, but one of the primary concerns for many female offenders is the problems related to their role as mothers (Baunach, 1992). A Canadian study of women inmates serving sentences of more than 2 years shows that two-thirds of them are mothers and that, of these, two-thirds have been single parents for at least part, if not all, of their children's lives (Shaw, 1992). They are trying to cope with maintaining contact and relationships with children who are in the care of relatives or social agencies and who do not understand why their mothers have left them.

The prison environment has been described by many writers (e.g., Goffman, 1973; Sykes, 1958). It is consistent with Goffman's descriptions of asylums and is similar to other total institutional environments. It is potentially a more oppressive environment for both inmates and staff then some other total institutions because of the traditional focus on the prison as a paramilitary structure in which inmates are kept against their will by the superior physical force of their keepers. This involuntary environment has not traditionally had any component of helping in the way that other total institutions, like hospitals for the mentally ill, have had.

---

*This good basic text is useful to the beginning worker in this field. Also useful are R. E. McCormick, and L. A. Visano (1992), *Canadian Penology: Advanced Perspectives and Research* (Toronto: Canadian Scholars Press) and C. T. Griffiths, S. N. Verdun-Jones (1994), *Canadian Criminal Justice* (Toronto: Harcourt Brace).

While the effect on keeping people against their will may be the same, the message sent to the inmates is different and much more obviously oppressive in the prison context.

One of the major issues/problems in prisons is the violence or the threat of violence that is part of the fabric of prison life. In most judicial jurisdictions, the population of inmates assigned to or choosing to live in protective custody (apart from other inmates and usually alone for up to 23 hours a day) has become a significant management problem because of their increasingly large numbers. Those inmates who do not choose to enter protective custody usually have to accept a lifestyle that involves violence in the conduct of everyday life, an "attack or be attacked" mentality (McCorkle, 1992). Not all prison environments have the same level of inmate subculture and violence or staff control. There is a wide variety of possible prison environments, ranging from relatively open, community-focused, minimum security, or halfway house environments to maximum security, closed institutions in which the presence of mechanisms for physical restraint like mace, batons, or other weapons is obvious. Each level of security presents its own challenges and opportunities to the social worker. Work in the most secure institutions presents the greatest number of limitations to the social worker in terms of group programs because mobility and potential interaction among the inmates are severely limited. According to Griffiths and Verdun-Jones (1994, p. 500), these limitations may be due to the level of acting out of the inmates. This conclusion is questionable because of the custom of putting protective custody offenders who may otherwise present the lowest risk for acting out in maximum security. The inmates' need may be great, but support for social work intervention, particularly in groups, is likely to be low on the list of institutional priorities. Social workers are more likely to work in medium and minimum security institutions simply because the emphasis on physical security is reduced and the opportunities for inmates to interact are greater.

PRACTICE PRINCIPLES

The social worker who hopes to provide a group work service to inmates has to take the environment into account in constructing and operating the group. The environment is the immediate context in which the inmate lives. The staff who work in the prison are also part of the inmate's social context. The social worker cannot work in isolation from other staff in the institution and must attempt to develop positive relationships with custodial/correctional staff, as well as with nurses, teachers, administrators, and as many staff as possible in order to have the greatest possible impact on the environment, which consists of much more than the physical structure of the facility.* Social group work (in fact, all social work) should be an authentic experience (Lang, 1978; Papell & Rothman,

---

*Middleman and Goldberg-Wood's (1991) quadrant model is useful in thinking about working with clients within this context.

1980), and any attempt to ignore the reality of the social context will, at best, result in an artificial attempt to intervene with people for whom the environment is very important.

The inmates in correctional institutions usually attempt to construct their own reality in opposition to the one imposed on them by the official institution. As noted earlier, this subculture has a hierarchical form in which the physically strong and the most antisocial are at the top and the physically weak and most intellectually and emotionally vulnerable are at the bottom. The values of this subculture are not compatible with prosocial functioning, but are strongly held and often supported within the prison by the staff, who believe that allowing this system to exist will keep the prison under control. When these values are shared by the inmates and the staff, the result is an understanding that the victims or potential victims of violence will be isolated and the belligerents will have the highest level of privilege. This contradicts the stated purpose of prisons, which is to sanction and/or rehabilitate the aggressor in order to protect the victim and possible future victims. The social worker cannot operate groups or any other programs that support these subcultural values but must recognize and confront their existence on a daily basis. The strength of the subculture in any given institution will affect the social worker's ability to form and guide authentic empowering group experiences for inmates. These prison realities make the contracting process an indispensable part of the social worker's intervention. Inmates must have a clear understanding of what is involved in the group and an awareness of how the group will fit into the institutional milieu. Will membership in the group enhance their lives in the institution or will it put them at risk?

At the point of contracting, it is important to recognize that the members of the group may be quite skeptical about the group's usefulness to them. They may be even more skeptical about the usefulness and trustworthiness of the worker. The worker will have to recognize and address these doubts.* What in some settings may be signs of lack of motivation to change in a prison environment may simply be a reflection of the inmate's response to the involuntary nature of the setting and the implications that has for involvement with a social worker (Behroozi, 1992).† In beginning a group within a correctional environment, the worker must acknowledge that the activity of the group is taking place in an authority-focused setting and that there are limits to what the group can do based on the limits of members as inmates in an institution. The worker must help the members identify the limits imposed by the setting and articulate them explicitly. The worker must also make it clear that although the limits are significant, there is a lot that the group can do.

---

*For a thorough discussion of the issue of gaining the trust of clients, see J. A. Jones and A. Alcabes (1993), *Client Socialization: The Achilles Heel of the Helping Professions* (Westport, CT: Auburn House).

†See Behroozi (1992) for a schema of pregroup and group behaviors suggested for social workers dealing with involuntary clients.

For example, although women inmates cannot be with their children in the community, they can discuss the problems they share as mothers in prison. They can help each other to explore new ways of dealing with the questions their children ask during visits and discuss how to prepare themselves and their children for their return to the community. The focus of the social workers is on what can be done in the present context of the prison to prepare the inmates for the future context of their home community. Part of the purpose of contracting is to let group members know what skills and strengths of the worker will enable the members to explore issues that they need to work on. The members need to decide as a group what their focus will be.

Confidentiality

In order to create a sense of safety, the group worker must state that personal disclosures will not be shared inappropriately with inmates and staff who are not part of the group. Providing this assurance is not easy for the worker in a prison because of the emphasis on security and the inmate's environment. The worker must emphasize to the members of the group, both in pregroup interviews and in the first session, the importance of keeping confidences within the group and the damage that can be done to individuals and to the group as a whole if confidences are violated. The worker's own ability to maintain confidentiality must also be made clear. The worker must make a commitment not to talk about the group to other staff without the inmates' permission but must also admit the responsibility to inform other staff members about disclosures that may signal a potential for suicide in a member, a potential for one member to possibly assault another inmate or a staff member, or to inform other authorities about confessions of child abuse. New workers may be concerned that an admission of limits to the ability of the worker to maintain confidentiality may damage the worker's relationship with the group. In fact, honest acknowledgment of the reality that many inmates are already aware of usually enhances the worker's credibility. In keeping with concerns about confidentiality, the worker should caution group members against sharing areas of vulnerability without thinking and should help them to make careful, informed, and deliberate decisions about sharing this information. The worker should encourage group members to take their time in developing their comfort with and their position in the group. The worker should not tell the members *not* to use or invest in the group but should tell them to go slowly and to develop their relationships as group members gradually, rather than expecting to make disclosures and develop closeness immediately.

Composing the Group

Given the power of the environment discussed above, it is important for the social worker to think carefully about the composition of the group.

Klein (1972, chapter 2) discusses some key considerations in the selection of members for a group. The emphasis is on balance and compatibility. The group members may not have many things in common, but they must at least have a common goal and some complementary characteristics in terms of similar life experiences or behavioral attributes (Bertcher & Maple, 1985). In a correctional institution, one of the main things that people have in common is their status as inmates. For this reason, it is useful to think about forming the group from the living unit on which the inmates are held. Because of the size of some living units, this may mean that the group would be a subset of the living unit composed of people who have a similar identified need. Groups based on living units ensure that offenders in the group have the same security status and, generally speaking, the same behavioral capacity in terms of their overall relationship to the institution. When the group is composed on this basis, the potential for rivalries based on differing levels of privilege or risk is minimized. In addition, their presence on the same living unit allows the inmates to develop their relationships outside of the group more completely if they choose to. They have the opportunity to discuss issues raised in the group outside of meetings without concern about violating the confidentiality of the group. The group is thereby a more real or authentic experience because it is relevant to their lives, rather than existing for 1 or 2 hours a week apart from their other realities.

Even though the residents of the same living unit share similar security issues, they may not share the same desire to make changes in their lives. For this reason, the social worker should screen potential group members closely for their motivation to make use of a group. As mentioned earlier, the issue of motivation to change is complex in the prison environment. The worker must not confuse motivation with level of difficulty; that is the worker must not assume that the inmates with the best social skills who can easily articulate reasons for being in the group are necessarily more motivated than inmates who experience more difficulty in presenting themselves succinctly and who express more concern about their ability to change. Many inmates who genuinely want to make changes find it difficult to do so without the guidance of a group and may appear at first to be resistant or hesitant because they are unsure about what is possible. The more articulate inmates can sometimes be those who are not interested in change but rather in using the group to improve their chances for parole or to increase their privileges within the institution. The social worker should attempt to determine the level of need of the inmate for the group and should attempt to group inmates accordingly.

Open or Closed Group

Both open- and closed-ended groups are possible and desirable in correctional settings. The group structure will vary depending on the purpose of the group. Some purposes can be met without developing a high level of cohesion among the members and therefore can be carried out in an open-ended format. These tend to be groups in which the social worker is attempting to provide an educational service that also gives the members a chance to become comfortable enough to ask questions and to solicit advice from both the social worker and other group members. In constructing a group on these lines, the social worker should be clear as to what he or she wants to accomplish and should not expect a high level of cohesion or intimacy to develop among the members (Lang, 1987; Schopler & Galinsky, 1984; Sulman, 1987).

If the social worker wants to create a group atmosphere in which the members can safely discuss deeply felt personal struggles and challenges, the worker must recognize that an open-ended group is generally not capable of providing that opportunity. This is particularly true in the correctional institution. The worker needs to develop a climate of safety in order to facilitate successful work at this level. There are some notable exceptions to this general observation, which usually characterize groups that consist of a small number of inmates sharing a common residence (unit or halfway house) where the turnover of inmates is usually low and where the social worker uses the principles of the mainstream model mentioned earlier (Wright, 1993). The worker must determine to what extent a closed-ended group is possible in his or her setting. Can a group of 10 or 12 inmates meet together regularly for a significant period of time without fear of losing much of the membership to parole, discharge, or transfer to another institution? The worker will need to be familiar enough with the setting, and with the policies and practices concerning the transfer of inmates, to be able to ensure stability of membership.

COMMON GROUP WORK THEMES
Substance Abuse

Many studies of prisoners indicate that substance abuse is reported by 75–80% of them. This may include alcoholism, drug abuse, or both. Some offenders are incarcerated because of drug abuse but many have been convicted of robberies committed to obtain money to buy drugs. Group work with substance abusers can take the form of structured group interaction with education about the risks of drug abuse. However, most prisoners are already experiencing the consequences of drug abuse, and want and need an opportunity to explore alternatives, share their fears, and talk about the lifestyle they have developed around their addiction. While it is not necessary to structure a closed group experience in order to provide education, it may be necessary to ensure a closed-group opportunity for the exploration and integration of the information and in which the difficult concept of changing the drug or alcohol lifestyles can be addressed. Peat and Winfree (1992) studied the progress of drug-addicted inmates and found that they performed better and reported more success in a therapeutic prison community, that is, on a unit devoted to the treatment of such addicts, rather than when worked with in open-ended groups. They maintain that the closed unit was the only way in which the effects of the subculture could be counteracted or negated. When a therapeutic milieu and even a closed group are not possible, it is important, as noted above, to attempt to control the intake and exits from the group so that the opportunity exists to develop a level of trust and openness.

Relationship Issues

Some offenders have families that they have left behind when they entered prison. Many other offenders have burned their bridges in terms of family and other relationships and are searching for reasons for their failure in this area. Groups dealing with relationship issues should be conducted separately for these two populations. Inmates who are experiencing family and/or marital separations will not have much in common with those who are having problems finding positive relationships nor will they have much tolerance for them. Men, and especially women, who have spouses and children who visit them, frequently experience a great deal of guilt about being incarcerated and fear that they will lose their families as a result. These people need a group to share their experience of this difficult life situation and to gain mutual support.

Those inmates, usually young men, who have difficulty forming and maintaining relationships often exhibit a wider range of difficulties. They are usually more unsocialized and antisocial in a variety of ways, and may require life and social skills training before they can begin to deal with more complex relationship issues. For these men, the worker will need to provide a higher degree of structure than might otherwise be required in group work with inmates. Some individual work may be necessary before group membership is possible. A clear educational format in which a certain degree of didactic instruction and dyadic practice/role play are provided will be necessary. This is a group in which coleadership is advisable because of the demanding nature of the inmate client whose unsocialized behavior is demonstrated in an inability to sustain focus in a group. Such groups often resemble groups of latency-age children who require activities as well as opportunities for talk and sharing.

Aggression Management

Some inmates identify themselves as having problems with their tempers and/or are described as being assaultive or explosive by people in the community or in prison. Unfortunately, these offenders have often used their aggression as a method of coping both inside and outside prison. Some of them may be the same inmates who identify themselves as having problems in developing close relationships with others. They will need to explore their use of violence as a means of coping with perceived

threats or getting what they want. They need to explore the effects of violence on their own lives and on the lives of those with whom they attempt
to become close. Structured anger management techniques are important
to incorporate into this group, but they will not be sufficient. These
inmates need opportunities to share their histories of powerlessness and
their own feelings of vulnerability and threat so that they can experience
openness without threat and have opportunities to practice anger management and conflict resolution techniques outside of a structured group.
As noted above, they may need some individual work prior to being
referred to group. This individual work could focus on reducing their
anxiety about joining a group by using systematic desensitization techniques through which they can learn to improve their listening skills
before becoming group members.

Abuse

Issues of abuse are evident in inmate populations, both perpetrators and
victims. Although there is some debate about the long-term effects of
abuse on eventual criminality, Widom (1989a, 1989b, 1989c, 1989d), in
a series of studies on the methodological weaknesses in research into the
possible link between child abuse and the development of adult pathology, found a higher rate of delinquency and adult criminality in a study of
individuals who were abused as children than in a nonabused control
group. Scudder, Blount, Heide, and Silverman's (1993) work supports
Widom's conclusions. Dutton and Hart (1992) found that in inmates
who reported having been abused as children, there was a significant correlation between the type of crime they committed and the kind of abuse
they had experienced. Dutton and Hart recommend that consideration
be given to providing treatment for the posttraumatic stress disorder
symptoms that these inmates may exhibit. Those who have been abused
and have not become abusers should not be put into groups with abusers.
Female survivors of abuse should not be put into cocorrectional or coed-
ucational situations with men with whom they may feel at risk. It may be
most efficacious to put men who have been abused and are abusers in
groups separate from others in order to explore how both of these complex areas interact in their particular circumstances.

     Men who are abusive need to discuss their experiences of abuse as
children, but the primary focus of any group with this population must be
on their responsibility for the abuse and their plans for ensuring that they
will not be abusive in the future. Goldberg-Wood and Middleman (1992)
have described a process for working with men who batter that incorporates challenges to the men's view of women as chattel and that allows the
men to make changes in their perceptual and value systems. Their model
is also valuable, with some modifications, for work with men who sexually
abuse both women and children. Social workers who are attempting to
provide service to male abusers should always have information from

sources other than the offender about the nature of the abusive behavior and, if possible, the degree of harm done by him. These men will usually minimize both their responsibility for the abuse and the harm done. Good assessment increases the worker's effectiveness (Becker & Quinsey, 1993; Mair, 1993). Several helpful texts focus on relapse prevention (e.g., Laws, 1989; Wilson, 1992). However, many of these groups do not allow the group to develop in the way the mainstream model of social work with groups suggests is possible and necessary. These approaches can be useful if the worker incorporates a social group work approach. Some education is necessary with abusive men, especially input that challenges their notions of patriarchy and examines concepts of male socialization. The idea of biology as destiny, and the resultant excuses and sense of entitlement that these ideas foster, must be challenged. But these men must also have the opportunity to develop as a group and to explore the meaning of their behavior to themselves and to others.

Women who have been incarcerated for offenses involving child abuse and neglect need to be approached differently in groups than men who commit similar or other acts of abuse (Breton, 1979; Butler & Vintram, 1991; Home, 1991; Lewis, 1992; Lovell, Reid, & Richey, 1992). They have had different socialization and life experiences and react differently to being convicted of child abuse. Breton (1979) describes the ways in which these women need to be "nurtured" in order to be helped to change abusive patterns.

Coping with Stigma

Most inmates raise issues at some point related to the label that they carry as identified criminals. They present this label as an impediment to any change in behavior that they may wish to make regarding both personal relationships and job opportunities. They need group experiences in which they can share their fears and needs in terms of strategies to deal with the label they have earned through deviant behavior in the past. The group experience gives them the chance to talk about common concerns while attempting to achieve a common solution to a problem that inmates have always shared.

Discharge Planning

The issue of stigma may be addressed on its own in a specifically formed group or it may be discussed in groups on discharge planning, one of the most frequently identified needs of prison inmates. Although inmates should be encouraged to think about planning for their discharge from the time of their admission, a group dealing with this issue should be composed of inmates who are reasonably close to discharge. In this way, the focus of the group can be real and immediate. As well, group members can be encouraged to think about community services or groups that may be helpful in their reintegration. Members can also be supported in efforts to arrange appointments with these resource services prior to their discharge, or supported for temporary absences from the institution close to the time of discharge, or encouraged to arrange appointments soon after their release.

As noted earlier, this group could be either open- or closed-ended. If it is open-ended, the turnover of members should not be so great at any one time that the group repeatedly has to spend a great deal of time dealing with issues of trust.

Identity

Depending on the demographics of the prisoners in the group, the social workers may deal with issues of race and culture in all group interactions. In some institutions, the prisoners may belong to different racial groups and may benefit from specialized services. Usually the racial groups present will consist of several cultural subgroups, so the group should not be considered homogeneous. There will probably be a common ground on which to meet, however, since the experience of oppression and the history of the group may be unifying themes. For example, native inmates in many Canadian prisons come from a range of tribal groups but they have as shared themes the history of native spirituality and practices that have a common core, although they may vary. These are self-help groups in terms of their organizational style. Institutional social workers are directly involved in these group programs. The groups are guided by members of Native Sons organizations from the community. The role of the social worker is to develop and maintain links with these community organizations so that they come into the prison to provide the service.

AIDS

In the past few years, one of the biggest new issues in dealing with prison populations was that because of the significant number of inmates with a history of intravenous drug use, they are at high risk of contracting and/or passing on the human immunodeficiency virus (HIV). This makes social work intervention important in a number of ways. First, social workers should work with health care professionals and community AIDS organizations to develop and deliver educational programs that help inmates and correctional staff understand how AIDS is transmitted and what precautions they should take with respect to drug use and sexual practices. Second, social workers should work with inmates who are HIV positive to provide both education and support. Groups are useful in both of these situations. Education about AIDS presented in groups allows the group members to discuss their fears and misconceptions and to have them addressed. Group work with inmates who are HIV positive can provide them with mutual support in what is a difficult life circumstance in any environment, but one that is further complicated by the fact that the prison environment is even more afraid of and hostile to them than many communities would be. As well, these individuals do not have ready access to AIDS support groups and to supportive family and friends.

Working with Female Offenders

As noted at the beginning of this chapter and as alluded to above, female offenders as a group may have some problems in common with male offenders, but generally the approach to meeting their needs has to be different (Adelberg & Currie, 1993; Axon, 1989; Gelsthorpe & Morris, 1990). Women are frequently attempting to cope with issues related to their children. They are concerned about what is happening to their children while they are incarcerated and about how their children perceive them as inmates or as bad mothers who have deserted them. They are also worried about the staff of the social agencies concerned with their children. They feel powerless and without sufficient resources to cope with the day-to-day reality of prison and the pressures created by their children and other family members. These women need to explore their feelings, to provide support for each other, and to discuss how to cope with and reduce their feeling of powerlessness.* Some women who have been abused will display self-mutilating behavior while incarcerated. Both the women and the institutional staff will need considerable help in dealing with this issue positively.†

Women who have been prostitutes may need to come together in groups to identify and work on the issues that this occupation has created for them. A feminist perspective should be used in work with all women but is imperative in this type of group (Moyer, 1992). Women need to enter groups without feeling that they will be judged as "bad women." They may be especially sensitive to male workers because of their experience with the sexuality of some males. Social workers should take this into account in planning any intervention.

RECOMMENDED WAYS OF WORKING

As noted above, the social worker must always consider the correctional environment as part of the client "package."

Case

Male offenders of a correctional center asked for a group to talk about issues concerning relationships with women. In the third group session, one member brought up concerns about his perfor-

---

*Judith Lee's 1994 book *The Empowerment Approach to Social Work Practice* (New York: Columbia University Press) is particularly useful in work with women in these circumstances.

†Any social worker dealing with incarcerated women should read the 1991 biography of Marlene Moore by Anne Kershaw and Mary Lasovitch, *Rock-a-Bye Baby: A Death Behind Bars* (Toronto: McClelland & Stewart). This work is particularly helpful in educating workers about self-mutilation behaviors.

mance in sexual relationships with women. Another member, a leader on the living unit, expressed disapproval about discussing this material in front of the female social worker. The disgruntled member refused to participate and sat in stony silence, nonverbally disapproving of the group members' attempts at discussion. All efforts on the part of group members to address his silent control of the process failed. Finally, he announced that he would not be returning. The social worker met with the inmate alone after the group session. She indicated that there was no possibility of a male worker replacing her and that the group was important to the members. She was careful to discuss the fact that any influence that he brought to bear on the remaining members of the group living on the unit might seriously damage the usefulness of the group. He agreed to come back for the next session, explain his position, and attempt to reassure the group members that he would not make fun of them or otherwise harass them about their continuing membership. After he did so, the members appeared to be reassured both by the fact that he was no longer there and by his stated intention to respect their group. In the next two sessions, group members dealt directly and indirectly with issues of trust. The worker recognized the need for the group to deal with these basic forming issues and did not push the group. In the third session after the crisis, the members once again began to discuss concerns about sexuality. The remaining sessions were characterized by increasing openness and comfort in dealing with sensitive relationship issues.

The success of the group was determined by the worker's handling of the threat posed by the disgruntled inmate and by her understanding of the importance of the feeling of safety to the members. Safety and competence are primary issues for inmates in groups. Workers must always keep them in mind.

Lee (1994) has developed a useful framework for assessing the client that is particularly appropriate for the correctional setting, which she titles "Assessment for Empowerment" (pp. 143–145). The social work role in correctional facilities is to help the client group to become socialized to the possibility of positive, satisfying nonexploitive, relationships. As noted above, to do this, the worker must overcome the skepticism of both inmates and correctional officers. To be genuinely helpful, the social worker must help clients develop skills that will help them reach their fullest potential. This will involve the use of currently popular empowerment approaches summarized as follows:

> social work practice with groups encompasses both intervention within the group and intervention outside the group, i.e., that the group is both a context and an instrument of change involving actions by the group and its members inside group meetings as well as actions by

the group and its members in situations outside the group. (Moore & Starkes, 1992, p. 183)

However, the worker must use considerable judgment and careful planning in deciding what form that empowerment takes. Advocacy for and empowerment approaches with inmates should not set up the inmates or allow them to set themselves up for failure or punishment. On the other hand, approaches that do not include empowerment treat inmates as incapable of positive and reasonable social action.

Case

Women in a local jail were concerned because the director did not allow many community leaves. They discussed their anger about the difficulty of achieving these privileges, and one particularly angry inmate advocated a hunger strike as a way of "getting back at" the director. Other women jumped on the bandwagon and began to plan the protest. The social worker leading the group asked the members to pause and think about the possible negative consequences to them of this course of action. After they listed several, she guided them into a discussion of what other courses of action might be more effective. They concluded with a general discussion about how to get what they wanted in prison in ways that did not make them more vulnerable.

Training is necessary to help inmates overcome their sense that lawful or traditional ways of trying to solve problems do not work for them. They will need to practice empowerment strategies within institutions, but they must be helped to choose and plan strategies that have a very high probability of success. The social worker must have a very good working knowledge of the particular correctional environment in order to know what these opportunities might be.

Group workers like Lee (1982, 1989, 1991, and in Schwartz, 1978), Breton (1979, 1985, 1989), Jacobs (1964), and Brooks (1978) give graphic examples of the effectiveness of the social group work method in helping people to take an active part in decisions that affect them. Giving inmates the opportunity to experience relationship building and decision-making successes while they are in the institution helps them to feel better about their chances for achieving similar success in the community when they are released and lifts some of the depression that is a constant reality for them as prisoners. Middleman and Goldberg-Wood's structural model of social work, originally described in 1974 and further developed in subsequent publications (Goldberg-Wood & Middleman, 1989, 1991, 1992; Middleman & Goldberg-Wood, 1991), helps the worker to keep his or her focus on the clients as whole persons who are capable of self-determination while still keeping the reality of their limitations in view.

EVALUATION APPROACHES

Social workers in correctional institutions are always faced with the problem of determining success or failure in their work with clients in almost life-or-death terms. The traditional test of success with offenders is whether or not they offend again. This information may tell the social workers something about the offender's experience of incarceration in general, but the absence of a return to jail does not necessarily entitle the social workers to claim that his or her group was a success. Nor is a return to jail an indication of a group's failure. Research into correctional treatment indicates that many factors have to be taken into consideration (Gendreau & Andrews, 1990). The worker must then decide how to judge the utility of the intervention for the members of the group. One way of doing this is through a qualitative* study of the life of the group. An analysis of the group's progress may tell the worker whether or not the group was able to do the work for which it contracted. Did the members use the group in a meaningful way? Did they discuss the issues that they agreed to at the outset of the group? Did all members make use of the group? Was there a high dropout rate? Did the group end prematurely? Did the members express satisfaction with the group while it was meeting? In addition to a qualitative analysis of the group's ongoing functioning, the social worker can conduct exit interviews with the participants to learn about their experience with the group. The worker can also give the group members a written questionnaire before the group begins, asking for their expectations of the group, and another questionnaire at the end asking whether the original expectations were met. The questionnaires may be anonymous so that the fear of consequences can be minimized if members have negative feedback about the group experience. As well, the social worker should ask front-line correctional staff for their impressions of the usefulness of the group, either at the end or while it is still ongoing. Some front-line workers may not support the notion of rehabilitation of inmates and may feel that groups are useless in general, but many correctional officers will provide concrete feedback on whether or not the inmate's behavior has been influenced by the group experience.

CONCLUSION

When all is said and done, prison inmates are people who have come from a variety of communities and who may have been engaged in social work interventions in other settings. The primary challenge of the social worker in a prison environment is to come to grips with the fact that this environment is a "shadow client" that must be worked with concurrently as the social worker works with the person. There can be no success without a clear acknowledgment of this reality.

---

*For those workers who feel pressure to use only quantitative models of evaluation, Ann Hartman's editorial "Many Ways of Knowing" in *Social Work* (1990) will be useful.

NATIONAL RESOURCES

Social workers should use as many local organizations as are available to them. For example, most communities now have AIDS organizations that will provide support to inmates who are HIV positive and education to others. The following national organizations may be helpful in providing workers with local city or province/state groups that could be helpful.

Elizabeth Fry Society
195A Bank St.
Ottawa, Ontario, Canada K2P 1W7
(613) 238-1171

John Howard Society
404-383 Parkdale Ave.
Ottawa, Ontario, Canada K1Y 4R4
(613) 761-7678

National Institute on Drug Abuse
5600 Fishers Lane
Rockville, MD 20857
(301) 443-4577

National Prison Project
American Civil Liberties Union
1616 P St. NW
Washington, DC
(202) 234-4830

REFERENCES

Adelberg, E., & Currie, C. (Eds.) (1993). *In conflict with the law: Women and the Canadian justice system.* Vancouver: Press Gang.

Adler, F., Mueller, G. O. W. & Laufer, W. S. (1994). *Criminal justice.* New York: McGraw-Hill.

Axon L. (1989). *Model and exemplary programs for female inmates: An international review.* Ottawa: Solicitor General of Canada.

Baunach, P. J. (1992). Critical problems of women in prison. In I. Moyer (Ed.), *The changing role of women in the criminal justice system. Offenders, victims and professionals* (pp. 99–112). Prospect Heights, IL: Waveland Press.

Becker, J. V., & Quinsey, V. L. (1993). Assessing suspected child molesters. *Child Abuse and Neglect, 17,* 169–174.

Behroozi, C. S. (1992). A model for social work with involuntary applicants in groups. *Social Work with Groups, 15,* 223–238.

Bertcher, H. J. (1994). *Group participation: Techniques for leaders and members.* Thousand Oaks, CA: Sage.

Bertcher, H. J. & Maple, F. (1985). Elements and issues in group composition. In M. Sundel, P. Glasser, R. Sarri, & R. Vinter (Eds.), *Individual change in small groups* (pp. 186–208). New York: Free Press.

Breton, M. (1979). Nurturing abused and abusive mothers: The hairdressing group. *Social Work with Groups, 2*(2), 161–174.

Breton, M. (1985). Reaching and engaging people: Issues and practice principles. *Social Work with Groups, 8*(3), 7–21.

Breton, M. (1989). The need for mutual aid groups in a drop-in for homeless women: The sistering case. In J. A. B. Lee (Ed.), *Group work with the poor and oppressed* (pp. 47–59). New York: Haworth.

Breton, M. (1991). Toward a model of social groupwork practice with marginalized populations. *Groupwork, 4*(1), 31–47.

Brooks, A. (1978). Group work in the Bowery. *Social Work with Groups, 1*(1), 53–63.

Butler, S., & Wintram, C. (1991). *Feminist groupwork*. Newbury Park, CA: Sage.

Cullen, F. T., Latessa, E. J., Burton, V. S., Jr., & Lombardo, L. X. (1993). The correctional orientation of prison wardens: Is the rehabilitative ideal supported? *Criminology, 31*(1), 69–92.

Cullen F. T., Skovron, S. E., Scott, J. E., & Burton, V. S., Jr. (1989). Public support for correctional treatment: The tenacity of rehabilitation ideology. *Criminal Justice and Behavior, 17*, 6–18.

Dutton, D. G., & Hart, S. D. (1992). Evidence of long-term, specific effects of childhood abuse and neglect on criminal behaviour in men. *International Journal of Offender Therapy and Comparative Criminology, 36*(2), 129–137.

Gelsthorpe, L., & Morris, A. (Eds.). (1990). *Feminist perspectives in criminology*. Philadelphia: Open University Press.

Gendreau, P., & Andrews, D. A. (1990). Tertiary prevention: What the meta-analyses of the offender treatment literature tell us about "what works." *Canadian Journal of Criminology, 32*, 173–184.

Goffman, E. (1963). *Asylums: Essays on the social situations of mental patients and other inmates*. New York: Doubleday.

Goldberg-Wood, G. & Middleman, R. R. (1989). *The structural approach to direct practice in social work*. New York: Columbia University Press.

Goldberg-Wood, G., & Middleman, R. R. (1991). Advocacy and social action: Key elements in the structural approach to direct practice in social work. *Social Work with Groups, 14*, 53–63.

Goldberg-Wood, G., & Middleman, R. R. (1992). Recasting the die: A small group approach to giving batterers a chance to change. *Social Work with Groups, 15*, 5–18.

Griffiths, C. T., & Verdun-Jones, S. N. (1994). *Canadian criminal justice*. Toronto: Harcourt Brace.

Hartman, A. (1990). Many ways of knowing. *Social Work, 35*(1), 3–4.

Home, A. M. (1991). Mobilizing women's strengths of social change: The group connection. *Social Work with Groups, 14*, 153–154.

Jacobs, J. (1964). Social action as therapy in a mental hospital. *Social Work, 9*(1), 54–61.

Jones, J. A., & Alcabes, A. (1993). *Client socialization: The Achilles' heel of the helping professions*. Westport, CT: Auburn House.

Kershaw, A., & Lasovitch, M. (1991). *Rock-a-bye baby: A death behind bars*. Toronto: McClelland & Stewart.

Klein A. F. (1972). *Effective groupwork: An introduction to principle and method*. Bloomfield, CT: Practitioners Press.

Lang, N. (1988). Social work practice in small social forms: Identifying collectivity. *Social Work with Groups, 9*(4), 7–32.

Laws, D. R. (1989). *Relapse prevention with sex offenders*. New York: Guilford Press.

Lee, J. A. B. (1982). The group: A chance at human connection for the mentally impaired older person. *Social Work with Groups, 5*(2), 43–55.

Lee, J. A. B. (1994). *The empowerment approach to social work practice.* New York: Columbia University Press.

Lee, J. A. B. (Ed.) (1989). *Group work with the poor and oppressed.* New York: Haworth Press.

Lewis, E. (1992). Regaining promise: Feminist perspectives for social group work practice. *Social Work with Groups, 15,* 271–284.

Lovell, M. L., Reid, K., & Richey, C. A. (1992). Social support training for abusive mothers. *Social Work with Groups, 15,* 95–108.

Mair, K. J. (1993). The nature of the act: A neglected dimension in the classification of sex offenders. *British Journal of Criminology, 33,* 267–275.

McCorkle, R. C. (1992). Personal precautions to violence in prison. *Criminal Justice and Behavior, 19*(2), 160–173.

McCormick, R. E., & Visano, L. A. (1992). *Canadian penology: Advanced perspectives and research.* Toronto: Canadian Scholars Press.

Middleman, R. R., & Goldberg-Wood, G. (1991). *Skills for direct practice social work.* New York: Columbia University Press.

Moore, E. E., & Starkes, A. J. (1992). The group in institution as the unit of attention: Recapturing and refining a social work tradition. *Social Work with Groups, 15,* 171–192.

Moyer, I. L. (1992). *The changing roles of women in the criminal justice system.* Prospect Heights, IL: Waveland Press.

Papell, C. P., & Rothman, B. (1980). Social group work models: Possession and heritage. In A. Alissi (Ed.), *Perspectives in social groupwork practice* (pp. 66–77). New York: Free Press.

Peat, B. J., & Winfree, L. T. (1992). Reducing the intra-institutional effects of "prisonization": A study of a therapeutic community for drug-using inmates. *Criminal Justice and Behavior, 19*(2), 206–225.

Scudder, R. G., Blount, W. R., Heide, K. M., & Silverman, I. J. (1993). Important links between child abuse, neglect and delinquency. *International Journal of Offender Therapy and Comparative Criminology, 37*(4), 315–323.

Schopler, J. H., & Galinsky, M. J. (1984). Meeting practice needs: Conceptualizing the open-ended group. *Social Work with Groups, 7*(2), 3–21.

Schwartz, W. (1978). Rosalie. *Social Work with Groups, 1*(3), 265–278.

Shaw, M. (1992). Issues of power and control: Women in prison and their defenders. *British Journal of Criminology, 32*(4), 438–452.

Sulman, J. (1987). The worker's role in collectivity. *Social Work with Groups, 9*(4), 59–67.

Sykes, G. (1958). *The society of captives: A study of a maximum security prison.* Princeton, NJ: Princeton University Press.

U.S. Department of Justice. (1988). *Report to the nation on crime and justice.* Washington, DC: U.S. Government Printing Office.

Widom, C. S. (1989a). Child abuse, neglect and violent criminal behavior. *Criminology, 27*(2), 251–271.

Widom, C. S. (1989b). Child abuse, neglect and adult behavior: Research design and findings on criminality, violence and child abuse. *American Journal of Orthopsychiatry, 59*(3), 355–366.

Widom, C. S. (1989c). Does violence beget violence? A critical examination of the literature. *Psychological Bulletin, 106*(1), 3–28.

Widom, C. S. (1989d). The cycle of violence. *Science, 244,* 160–165.

Wilson, P. (Ed.). (1992). *Principles and practice of relapse prevention.* New York: Guilford Press

Wright, M. M. (1993). Family-like group in a correctional setting. *Social Work with Groups, 16*(4), 125–135.

IV

SUBSTANCE ABUSE

16

Group Work in the Prevention of Adolescent Alcohol and Other Drug Abuse

Andrew Malekoff

The problematic use of alcohol, drugs, and tobacco is unquestionably the nation's number one health problem. While all segments of society are affected, the future of young people is most severely compromised by this epidemic. A recent study by Brandeis University's Institute for Health Policy (1993) revealed the following use rates for eighth graders: alcohol (70%), tobacco (44%), marijuana (10%), and cocaine (2%). For 12th graders, use rates were alcohol (88%), tobacco (63%), marijuana (37%), and cocaine (8%).

Beyond use rates for youth are the staggering findings of the National Institute on Alcohol Abuse and Alcoholism (1990; Hosang, 1995). There are 28 million children of alcohol- and drug-abusing parents, or one in every four children. They have estimated that 50% of children who grow up in these homes are likely to become alcohol or drug abusers themselves without intervention.

The pervasiveness of the problem extends well beyond the individual. Alcohol and drug abuse play a major role in "destroying families, crippling U.S. businesses, terrorizing entire neighborhoods, and choking the educational criminal justice and social service systems" (Brandeis University, 1993, summary p. 1). As social workers committed to youth, and to the families and communities in which they live, we cannot escape the need to address the problems of alcohol and drug abuse, regardless of the setting of our work. Where there are people, there is alcohol and drug abuse. Where there are youth, there are youth at risk. The purpose of this chapter is to highlight group work as a protective factor, a powerful preventive tool for youth who show early signs of alcohol and other drug abuse and who are at risk for alcoholism and drug addiction.

REVIEW OF THE LITERATURE

What differentiates people with negative outcomes from those who grow up in similar circumstances and bounce back from great adversity? This question has stimulated much speculation and a dramatic growth of the literature on vulnerability, resiliency and risk, and protective factors (Garmezy, 1991, Garmezy & Rutter, 1983; Goleman, 1987; Rutter, 1979; Sameroff, 1988; Schorr, 1989; Werner, 1989, 1990). What differentiates youth who become alcohol and drug abusers from their contemporaries from similar backgrounds who do not? This questions illustrates the special concern of those interested in understanding the relationship between risk reduction strategies and substance abuse prevention (Bernard, 1991; Hawkins, Catalano, 1992a; Hawkins, Catalano, & Miller, 1992b; Vega, Zimmerman, Warheit, Apospori, & Gil, 1993; Werner, 1986).

Risk factors include constitutional (i.e., physiological) deficits and contextual realities (i.e., the physical, cultural, social, political, and economic environments). Examples of risk factors for youth include a history of alcohol and drug abuse/addiction in the family; neighborhood disorganization; being a victim of child abuse; becoming pregnant; having a chronic history of school failure; being economically disadvantaged; having attempted suicide; and associating with alcohol- and drug-abusing peers.

Protective factors are the individual's constitutional assets (i.e., intelligence, temperament) and family and environmental supports (i.e., a close, lifelong bond with an adult relative or mentor) that have the potential to reduce risk. Hawkins, Catalano, and Associates (1992) emphasize the importance of bonding as a key protective factor:

> Antidrug attitudes are strengthened by promoting adolescents' bonds, including relationships with non-drug users, commitment to the various social groups in which they are involved (families, schools, community, prosocial peer groups), and values and beliefs regarding what is healthy and ethical behavior. (p. 27)

Some of the settings in which group approaches have been used to address and study the preventive needs of youth at risk include the school (Bilides, 1992: Brown, 1993; Hanson, 1992: Kantor, Candill, & Ungerleider, 1992; Shields, 1986), the public housing development (Schinke, Orlandi, & Cole, 1992), the community mental health center (Malekoff, 1994a; Walthrust, 1992), and the criminal justice system (Freidman & Utada, 1992; Smith, 1985). Comprehensive approaches have been described by Hawkins et al. (1992) and by Felner, Silverman, and Adix (1991).

Beyond the physical setting of the service are the cultural context of substance abuse (Vega et al., 1993); Wallace, 1993; De La Rosa & Andrados, 1993; Catalano et al. 1992; Bachman, Wallace, Kurth, Johnston, & O'Malley, 1991; Bilides, 1990) and the family context (Gross & McCane, 1992; Knight, Vail-Smith & Barnes, 1992; Treadway, 1989; Emshoff, 1989; Efron, 1987; Deckman & Downs, 1982; Black, 1979).

A protective network of supports has the potential to increase the individual's resistance to risk, placing him or her in a better position to avoid alcohol and other drug problems. Group work can be an important part of constructing such a network.

PRACTICE PRINCIPLES

Beginning group work with at-risk adolescents requires careful planning, thoughtful programming, and attention to helping the group members to become a system of mutual aid. When combined, these principles set the tone for an experience that provides a sense of order and an opportunity for role flexibility, something often missing in the lives of youth at risk.

Planning

The planning model, as formulated by Kurland (1980, 1982) and further explicated by Northen (1988), identifies seven variables necessary for the formation of successful groups. Careful preparation can make the difference between groups that thrive and groups that fail. The seven variables are:

Needs: What are the needs of prospective members?

Purpose: What are the tentative goals and objectives of the group?

Composition: Who are the potential members?

Structure: What concrete arrangements are necessary to proceed?

Content: What means will be used to enable the group to achieve its purpose?

Pregroup Contact: How will prospective members be recruited?

Agency and social context: What obstacles exist and how might they be overcome?

Good planning is invaluable when working with youth who live in disorganized families and or communities. Consistency, predictability, and structure elude them in their day-to-day lives. *A well planned group experience serves as a counterforce to living in a capricious environment.* What begins as a counterforce can become a protective factor, mitigating against risk and stimulating healthy development.

Programming

Redl and Wineman (1952) describe programming as "activities which require a certain amount of definite planning, on the part of the children themselves, of the adults, or both" (p. 76). Breton (1990) asserts that "the way we structure groups is all-important, for a group can be structured so that the whole person in each member is invited to participate, or it can be structured so that only the troubled, or broken, or hurt parts of the person [are] invited to participate" (p. 27).

Programming is the activity that the group does to achieve its purpose. How programming is determined and implemented can make the difference between a group in which members' strengths are supported and one in which deficits (i.e., pathology) are highlighted. In the case of adolescents at risk, it is important for the social worker to structure the group to invite the whole person, to blend discussion and activity with an eye toward promoting competency (Malekoff, 1994b).

Mutual Aid

A critical question for all social workers working with groups is "Am I the central helping person here or do I enable others to help one another?" The latter stance, "the valuation of members as helper" (Middleman & Wood, 1990, p. 11) distinguishes social work with groups from other group treatments (with the notable exception of self-help groups, such as Alcoholics Anonymous and Alanon, which are leaderless mutual aid groups). The practice of promoting mutual aid implies faith in the group and its potential to function autonomously. Furthermore, it suggests the social worker's commitment to "learn not only *about* but *from* group members" (Breton, 1990, p. 23). Attention to planning, programming, and mutual aid can lead to the creation of a healthy group environment in which trust is established, various roles are practiced in safety, and reliance on self is broadened to include reliance on others. To structure the group "to invite the whole person," the social worker must have a good understanding of normal adolescent development, the adolescent in the group, the social worker in the group, and the group in context. The following practice principles will address these issues.

1. *Alliance formation with parents and other involved persons and systems is a prerequisite to establishing an engaged group membership* (Malekoff, 1991).

   Adolescents cannot be seen in a vacuum. Sanction from parents and cooperation with related systems (e.g., school) are necessary for ongoing work with the group. By establishing working alliances with these significant others, the social worker models collaboration and establishes the groundwork for mediating with the various systems. Working relationships with parents help to reduce the guilt that children often feel about betraying the family. Working relationships with all involved persons and systems help to reduce the possibility that dysfunctional interactions will be extended to the helping system.

In the Youth of Culture Drug Free Club, an after-school program for youth at risk located in Long Island, New York (Malekoff, 1994a; and Walthrust, 1992), a well-planned and organized dance for local youth was marred by a post-dance fight in which a youngster was slashed with a razor. The staff team worked closely with parents in the aftermath of the incident. This collaboration, in light of a chaotic and potentially tragic situation, enabled the group members to work through the crisis in a thoughtful manner despite their fear that the club might be terminated.

2. *An appreciation for paradox and an ability to differentiate the words from the music is essential to working with adolescents in groups* (Malekoff, 1994b).

Just below the surface of the strident facade or apathetic veneer that many adolescents project are the deeper meanings that not many adults are privileged to discover. Often the familiar refrain "Leave me alone!" carefully conceals the cry for help. It's not always easy to hang around to hear the music underneath the static of the words. Yet to work with adolescents, one must hang in there. Too many adults have already bailed out.

3. *Cultural awareness and sensitivity are essential for practicing social work with groups in a society of ever-increasing diversity.*

Social workers must be aware of racism, sexism, and homophobia, as well as other cultural issues and values, as well as how they impact on group members and how they have affected their own lives. Bilides (1990) suggests some guidelines for putting one's multi-cultural awareness into practice with groups. These include the following: "discuss stereotypes at all levels (personal, familial and societal) . . . point out commonalities . . . explore the meanings of words and language . . . recognize and acknowledge your own discomfort about race, color, ethnicity, and class issues" (pp. 51–56).

The Youth of Culture Drug Free Club reflects some of the values suggested above in their choice of club name. A predominantly African-American group, they planned and presented a communitywide "inter national cultural day" in which they modeled traditional clothing from various cultures. This was a step in the direction of opening the club to members of other groups, including growing immigrant populations from Central America and Haiti.

4. *Use the self and access childhood memories.*

Awareness of what the group experience evokes in oneself is invaluable, especially with a population in motion. This includes conscious memories of the social worker's earlier years and struggles during adolescence (e.g., personal and/or familial experiences with alcohol and drugs). The feelings that inevitably bubble up in the lively context of the adolescent group must not be ignored. Feelings and experiences can be disclosed at times, using good judgment. For example, the purpose of disclosure should never be to gain the acceptance of the group or to tacitly encourage acting-out behavior for a vicarious thrill. This is where good supervision enters the picture.

5.   *Don't go it alone.*

Social workers working with at-risk adolescents in groups need support from colleagues. Too many adults (professional or otherwise) disapprove of the group modality when adolescents are involved. They question the efficacy of the work when confronted with the noise, action, and attitudes that seem absent in the adult group. Colleagues with a track record and an inclination to work with youth can be invaluable partners. This includes good supervision from peers or adults and opportunities for teamwork. Coleadership of groups is an approach that requires adequate time for planning and reflection. Too many human services workers without adequate group training operate under the false assumption that coleadership is better, easier, or less stressful than one-person leadership. Maybe it is, but this depends entirely on the match and on the commitment and honesty that develop in the partnership. Simply throwing workers together to run groups is to be avoided at all costs.

COMMON THEMES

Groups may be formed specifically for children living in families with a present or past history of alcohol or drug abuse. Other groups may be composed of youth who evidence a variety of related risk factors. Substance abuse prevalence rates (and practice experience) suggest that in either case the social workers must have knowledge of the impact of alcohol and drug abuse (including alcoholism and addiction) on the individual in the family.

What are the implications of growing up in a dysfunctional family? How might these issues influence the individual in the group? How might they affect the group as a whole? (Although the attention there is to substance abuse, these questions may also apply to families in which there is child abuse, domestic violence, or severe mental illness.) The following six themes will address these questions.

1.   *Children who grow up in families with alcohol and drug abuse/ addiction learn to distrust to survive.*

Attention to the beginning phase of group developmet is critical in building trust. By exercising anticipatory empathy, the social worker tunes into the experience of the group members, taking an important step in helping to build a safe environment for mutual exchange. At the beginning the social worker allows and supports distance, searches for common ground, invites trust gently, establishes group purpose, facilitates exploration, begins to set norms, and provides program structure (Garland, Jones, & Kolodny, 1965; Malekoff, 1984).

2. *Children growing up in alcohol- or drug-abusing/addicted families become uncomfortably accustomed to living with chaos, uncertainty, unpredictability, and inconsistency.*

It has been said that children growing up under these conditions have to "guess at what normal is." The group experience must provide a clear structure with norms and reasonable limits. Issues of membership (Is it an open or closed group? If it is open, how do new members enter? How do members exit?), space (Is there a consistent meeting place?), and time (Does the group meet at a regular time for a prescribed period?) are all important considerations. Group rituals might be considered to reinforce a sense of order and to establish value-based traditions. For example, in the Youth of Culture Drug Free Club referred to earlier, the members all recite a drug-free pledge at the beginning and end of each meeting.

3. *Denial, secrecy, embarrassment, and shame are common experiences of children who live in alcoholic or addicted families.*

Joining a group of outsiders might in itself be felt as an act of betrayal, a step toward revealing the "family secret." Awareness at this juncture allows the social worker to invite trust gently while paying careful attention to questions of trust and confidentiality throughout the life of the group.

4. *Growing up with the ever-present threat of violence (verbal and physical) contributes to a pervasive sense of fearfulness, hypervigilance, and despair.*

The group can become a place where differences can be safely expressed and where conflicts need not be a matter of life and death. Conflicts can be resolved and differences respected in a thoughtful and increasingly mature manner in the group. The group is a place where members can practice putting a reflective pause between impulse and action and where despair can be transformed into hope.

In response to another violent incident, an interracial murder in the community, the Youth of Culture Drug Free Club organized the largest youth contingent in a March for Unity. Again they acted to replace despair with hope, and an anticipated riot was averted.

5. *Children, who grow up in alcohol- and drug-abusing/addicted families become rigidly attached to roles.*

Many of those growing up in alcohol- and drug-abusing/addicted systems construct a wall of defenses and repressed feelings by adopting rigid family roles (Wegscheider, 1981, pp. 86–149). Accompanying these roles are stultifying family rules, unspoken mandates, such as *don't talk, don't trust, don't feel.* A group experience can provide members accustomed to assuming rigid roles with an opportunity to practice role flexibility, broaden their intra- and interpersonal repertoires, and gain competence in coping with the environment.

In the Youth of Culture Drug Free Club, the members planned a holiday party for themselves and organized a trip to a local nursing home, offering gifts and spending time with an isolated population of AIDS patients. Both activities, the party and the visit, required careful preparation, enabling the members to assume diverse roles and to work in partnership to accomplish the group's goals.

6.   *Growing up in an alcoholic or addicted family system leaves youths with little hope that things will ever change.*

The group is a social system that develops a life of its own, marked by a developing history of events and relationships. As in any system, there are decisions to be made, problems to solve, and crises to surmount. If a dysfunctional family system is the primary frame of reference for a young person, he or she may have little experience in successfully resolving conflicts or overcoming obstacles. The group can provide members with a growing sense of confidence that difficult and frustrating circumstances can be overcome. The group worker must be turned in to the sense of hopelessness that such members bring to the group so as not to become easily discouraged. It cannot be emphasized strongly enough that group work with this population requires hanging in for the long haul and modeling a sense of hope.

One of the activities of the Youth of Culture Drug Free Club is wilderness outings (hiking, canoeing, camping), providing members with multiple obstacles (frustration, fatigue, fear) to confront and overcome. The members learn quickly that surviving in the wilderness requires more than self-sufficiency. They must come to trust and rely on one another to navigate a current or climb a mountain, powerful metaphors for what they face daily. With each trip they experience change as they stretch their limits together, and with each successful journey they increase their appreciation of themselves and their fellow group members. In time the group itself becomes a valuable frame of reference.

RECOMMENDED WAYS OF WORKING

The agency context of the service being offered is a key determinant of the success or failure of the endeavor. In other words, do the values of the agency lead to policies and practices that allow the group to work toward its purpose in a hospitable environment? The answer to this question becomes obvious when arrangements for staffing, space, time, and materials are negotiated. To work effectively with at-risk adolescents, the host agency must sanction the activity in word and deed. The social worker's responsibility is to see to it that the work of the group reflects the stake that the agency and group members have in one another. It is not enough to be available to run a group. Good planning and sound social work practice often require mediation and advocacy.

The Place of North Shore Child and Family Guidance Center is an alcohol and drug treatment and prevention program for youth and their families. Located in a low-income minority community in Nassau County, New York, The Place's clientele and staff represent a multicultural mix that reflects a growing number of suburban communities. The services of The Place include an intensive after-school program that is a comprehensive blend of group, family, and individually oriented activities. The group program includes services for adults, children, and adolescents; alcoholics and drug addicts; nonaddicted substance abusers; and at-risk, non-substance-abusing significant others (youths and adults).

Some adolescents are seen as referred clients who are admitted to the program following a formal evaluation and case disposition. Others are seen in a variety of after-school programs that do not require a formal clinical evaluation. The Youth of Culture Drug Free Club is an example of the latter. Many adolescents participate in both programs as clients and as community members.

In her landmark work on "breaking the cycle of disadvantage," Schorr (1989) asserts that "most successful programs find that interventions cannot be routinized or applied uniformly. Staff members and program structures are fundamentally *flexible* and *see the child in the context of family and the family in the context of its surroundings*" (p. 257).

Groups at The Place vary in composition, length, and purpose. Content includes psychoeducation, socialization, discussion, counseling, therapy, outings, arts and crafts, cultural awareness activities, and community service. Staff members work in teams. This enables program participants to become engaged with the agency as well as with an individual social worker or counselor. Regularly scheduled team meetings are held for the purposes of case assignment and management, program development, supervision, and skill development.

Family involvement is an important value at The Place. All incoming families with adolescents are assigned to an 8-week multiple-family group program. There are generally four to seven families per group, ranging from 8 to 20+ people. The group's purposes include helping families with drug and alcohol problems to learn from one another, to decrease isolation, and to address the shame that children carry as a secret. These issues are addressed in the service of prevention. The content includes a combination of alcohol and drug education, discussion, role play, and psychodrama. The first two sessions are structured to allow time for the adults and youth to meet briefly in separate groups to identify needs and make connections. The groups are co-led by two or three social workers. The number of workers is determined by group size and by the presence of younger (school-age) children. When the group divides, one of the three workers meets with the children. The different age groups tend to ally, early on, with different workers, who are tuned in to the importance of modeling collaboration as differences arise. The cultural diversity of the staff enriches this process as group members see people of different racial and ethnic backgrounds working together with mutual respect.

The fifth session of one multiple-family group series began with a staff presentation of normal development in the latency and adolescent periods and its relationship to the family life cycle. (Psychoeducation on normal development is of great value for families in which the members have grown accustomed to uncertainty and consequently must guess at what normal is. In the group this process serves to provide support, encourage dialogue, and reduce isolation. When the theme of separation was presented, one of the group members, a Hispanic mother who understands and speaks English but prefers Spanish, addressed the bi-lingual worker:

If I may I want to respond to something that the other workers said about separation. In my country [Colombia], it is different. The kids are expected to stay with their families until they marry. If they go to college they stay home. This [discussion] is a problem for us [motioning to her husband, a practicing alcoholic] and upsetting that the children are encouraged to leave.

Once this statement was translated, a lively discussion ensued as the group, consisting of four families of various cultural origins (Columbian, African, Yugoslavian, and Italian), exchanged their feelings about separation. At one point the Hispanic mother's 17-year-old son, who was referred to The Place following a single incident of binge drinking, spoke:

"I didn't know this." He spoke in short, choppy sentences and was encouraged to elaborate. "Well, now that I know [what she thinks], I'll think about looking into colleges close to home, but I'm not staying there until I got married." Everyone laughed, including the boy's parents. One of the social workers summed up, turning to the boy. "It sounds like you're willing to negotiate with your parents." He acknowledged her comment with a smile.

In this interchange the group was warming up to the meeting, testing the waters, and reestablishing trust. (Remember that distrust is more often than not the norm in these families.) An emotionally charged issue surfaced. Differences along cultural and generational lines were drawn. Respect for differences was modeled by the social worker, who encouraged discussion. Four different cultural groups (one bilingual), four sets of parents (and one grandparent), and four sets of adolescents produced no dire consequences.

All of the adolescents had abused alcohol and/or had tried other drugs on at least one occasion. In all four families the fathers, only one of whom was present, were alcoholic or drug addicted. As is often the case, the adolescents and their presenting problems were the key to getting help. As the session proceeded, separation issues gave way to issues of limits, boundaries, and private space. The adolescents and parents began to draw battle lines as parents revealed their suspicions.

The group was now heated as the adolescents referred to their parents as "nuts," "stupid," "crazy," and "ridiculous." A 14-year-old girl who had verbally assaulted her mother last week took the offensive again. When one of the social workers reminded her of the rule of not attacking and allowing others to finish speaking, she smiled and said, "Okay, okay." The social workers then asked what a parent should do if she suspects that her child is using drugs? The parents discussed various issues, including the circumstances under which they would search their children's rooms. The mother of the 14-year-old girl then said, somewhat defensively, "People don't know what they would do until it really affects them. I never thought I'd be going through my daughter's room, but I had a feeling and it was right. It was a good thing I followed my instinct because now I can get help." Then for the first time in five meetings, the Hispanic mother spoke in English and directly to the other mother. She exclaimed, "You did right! You did the right thing and I would too, to help my child." This was a moving moment in which a mother who was struggling with an aggressive 14-year-old who abused her in the group setting was supported by others in the presence of her daughter. Returning to Spanish, the Hispanic mother made an impassioned request of the worker: "Please tell her [the girl] if she didn't love her she wouldn't have done this. It is an act of caring, and her daughter is so aggressive. "When this was translated, the 14-year-old girl asked: "What's 'aggressive' mean?" It was described as "hostile." By this time, the group was becoming very intense as the adolescents were beginning to bond in anger against the parents. As angry glances were exchanged across the generational dividing line, one social worker acknowledged the feeling and suggested an activity to promote empathy. Addressing the 14-year-old but speaking to the group, she explained what a role reversal is and said, "I find it helpful to try this when parents and children are in conflict." She then asked the 14-year-old to "put yourself in your mother's shoes. If you thought your child was in danger, that she might have weapons or drugs in her room, would you search it?" The girl became pensive and clearly thought deeply about this, as did the others, judging from their facial expressions and body language. She finally responded, "Yes, I think I would." It was with this reflection, as the other soaked in her response, that the group moved to an ending. One social worker concluded with a brief restatement of the rules regarding confidentially and repeated that there would be no consequences for what was shared in the group. The 14-year-old girl seemed more relieved than offended by the definition of her behaviour as aggressive and hostile. A limit was being set that perhaps she had been seeking all along.

The illustration of the multiple-family group can be considered in light of the specific group process described or from a metaphorical perspective. In the latter case, the reader might consider the ways in which the family can be brought into the group when it is not part of the group. In either instance, what is clear is that the establishment of trust over time and in each session is essential. While this is true for any group, it is particularly so when distrust becomes the norm for the individual struggling with personal and/or familial substance abuse/addiction. In such families, feelings are often not valued or tolerated, and poor identification and labeling of feelings is a consequence of having little or no practice. The group provides an opportunity to practice these skills with the knowledge that no one will be physically or emotionally destroyed by violent or impulsive acts.

Group work provides people with places in which diversity is tolerated, difference is understood and respected, problems are universalized, and people depend upon one another and not only on the experts. To the extent that this occurs, group work becomes a protective factor in the lives of adolescents at risk.

EVALUATION

According to Muraskin (1993), evaluation for drug and alcohol prevention and treatment programs can be conducted for the following purposes:

> To determine the effectiveness of programs for the participants;
> To document that program objectives have been met;
> To provide information about service delivery that will be useful to program staff and other audiences; and
> To enable program staff to make changes that improve program effectiveness.

Categories of outcome measurement for individuals may include the following variables: use of alcohol and drugs, knowledge of alcohol and drugs, attitudes regarding the use of alcohol and drugs, ability to refuse using alcohol and drugs in the face of peer pressure, self-esteem, and a sense of hope. Pre- and posttests can be given to determine changes in attitude and habits. Surveys can be developed for this purpose (see Muraskin, 1993, for several examples). In the case of drug and alcohol use, many programs (e.g., in treatment-oriented and criminal justice settings) use the breathalizer and urine analysis to test for use. Changes in risk and protective status and in level of functioning over time are also variables that can be used to assess change.

Observations of the group members over time, reports from parents and school personnel, and monitoring of academic, social, and extracurricular progress are all important in the process of evaluation. Not to be underestimated is the self-evaluation of the individual, members' evaluations of one another, and the group's evaluation of itself, a standard part of the ending phase of group work.

According to Dryfoos (1993), "prevention programs seem to work best when they address the total life of the young person and focus on the factors that place him or her at risk" (p. 3). In this era of categorical funding for human services, it is not always easy to provide comprehensive services; therefore, collaboration between the various systems that serve youth is essential.

NATIONAL RESOURCES

Al-Anon Family Groups
World Service Office
P.O. Box 862
Midtown Station
New York, New York 10018
(800) 344-2666

Alcoholics Anonymous (AA)
World Service, Inc.
468 Park Ave. South
New York, NY 10016
(212) 870-3400

Institute on Black Chemical Abuse
   Resource Center
2616 Nicollet Ave. South
Minneapolis, MN 55408
(612) 871-7878

Johnson Institute
7205 Ohms Lane
Minneapolis, MN 55439-2159
(800) 231-5165

Join Together
441 Stuart Ave., 6th Floor
Boston, MA 02116
(617) 437-1500

Marin Institute for the Prevention
   of Alcohol and Other Drug
   Problems
24 Belvedere Street
San Rafael, CA 94901
(415) 456-5692

Nar-Anon Family Group
P.O. Box 2562
Palos Verdes Peninsula,
   CA 90274-0019
(310) 547-5800

Narcotics Anonymous (NA)
P. O. Box 9999
Van Nuys, CA 91409
(818) 773-9999

National Association for Children of
   Alcoholics (NACOA)
11426 Rockville Pike, #100
Rockville, MD 20852
(301) 468-0985

National Black Alcoholism Council
1629 K St. NW
Washington, DC 20006
(202) 296-2696

National Clearing House for Alcohol
   and Drug Information (NCADI)
P.O. Box 2345
Rockville, MD 20847-2345
(301) 468-2600 or (800) 729-6686

National Cocaine Hotline
c/o Phoenix House
164 West 74th St.
New York, NY 10021
(800) COCAINE

National Council on Alcoholism and
   Drug Dependence, Inc.
12 West 21st St.
New York, NY 10010
(212) 206-6770 or
   (800) NCA-CALL

National Institute on Drug Abuse
Drug Abuse Information and
   Treatment Referral Hotline
(800) 662-HELP

Parents' Resource Institute for
   Drug Education, Inc. (PRIDE)
50 Hurt Plaza
Atlanta, GA 30303
(800) 677-7433

EVALUATION RESOURCES

J. A. Linney and A. Wandersman
*Prevention Plus III, Assessing Alcohol
and Other Drug Prevention
Programs at the School and
Community Level*
Center for Substance Abuse
Prevention
U.S. Department of Health and
Human Services
5600 Fishers Lane
Rockville, MD 20857

Program Evaluation Handbook:
Drug Abuse Education
IOX Associates
P.O. Box 24095
Los Angeles, CA 90024-0095

REFERENCES

Bachman, J. G., Wallace, J. M., Jr., Kurth, C. L., Johnston, L. D., & O'Malley, P. M. (1991). *Drug use among black, white, Hispanic, Native American and Asian American high school seniors (1976–1989): Prevalence, trends and correlates* (pp. 1–63). Ann Arbor: Institute for Social Research, University of Michigan.

Bernard, B. (1991). *Fostering resiliency in kids: Protective factors in the family, school and community* (pp. 1–27). Portland, OR: Northwest Regional Training Laboratories.

Bilides, D. (1990). Race, color, ethnicity and class in school-based adolescent counseling groups. *Social Work with Groups, 13*(4), 43–58.

Bilides, D. (1992). Reaching inner city children: A group work program model for a public middle school. *Social Work with Groups, 15*(2/3), 129–144.

Black, C. (1979). Children of alcoholics. *Alcohol, Health and Research World, 1*(1), 23–27.

Brandeis University, Institute for Health Policy (1993). *Substance abuse: The nation's number one health problem; key indicators for policy.* Princeton, NJ: Robert Wood Johnson Foundation.

Breton, M. (1990). Learning from social group work traditions. *Social Work with Groups, 13*(1), 21–34.

Brown, M. E. (1993). Successful components of community and school prevention programs. *National Prevention Evaluation Research Collection, 1*(1), 3–5.

Catalano, R. F., Morrison, D. M., Wells, E. A., Gillmore, M. R., Iritani, B., & Hawkins, D. J. (1992). Ethnic differences in family factors related to early drug initiation. *Journal of Studies on Alcohol, 55*(3), 208–217.

Deckman, J., & Downs, D. (1982). A group treatment approach for adolescent children of alcoholic parents. *Social Work with Groups, 5*(1), 73–77.

De La Rosa, M. R., & Adrados, J. (1993). *Drug abuse among minority youth; advances in research and methodology.* NIDA Research Monograph 130. Washington, DC: U.S. Department of Health and Human Services.

Dryfoos, J. (1993). Lessons from evaluation of prevention programs. *National Prevention Evaluation Research Collection, 1*(1), 2–4.

Efron, D. (1987). Videotaping groups for children of substance abusers: A strategy for emotionally disturbed acting out children. *Alcoholism Treatment Quarterly, 4*(2), 71–85.

Emshoff, J. G. (1989). A preventive intervention with children of alcoholics. *Prevention in Human Services, 17*(1), 225–253.

Felner, R. D., Silverman, M. M. & Adix, R. (1991). Prevention of substance abuse and related disorders in childhood and adolescence: A developmental based, comprehensive ecological approach. *Family and Community Health, 14*(3), 12–22.

Friedman, A. S., & Utada, A. T. (1992). Effects of two group interaction models on substance using adjudicated adolescent males. *Journal of Community Psychology* (special issue: Programs for Change, Office of Substance Abuse Prevention), 106–117.

Garland, J., Jones, H., & Kolodny, R. (1965). A model for stages of development in social work with groups. In S. Bernstein (Ed.), *Explorations in group work: Essays in theory and practice* (pp. 21–30). Boston: Boston University School of Social Work.

Garmezy, N. (1991). Resiliency and vulnerability to adverse development outcomes associated with poverty. *American Behavioral Scientist, 34*(4), 416–430.

Garmezy, N., & Rutter, M. (1983). *Stress, coping and development in children.* New York: McGraw-Hill.

Goleman, D. (1987, October 13). Thriving despite hardship: Key childhood traits identified. *New York Times*, pp. C1, C11.

Gross, J., & McCane, M. (1992). An evaluation of a psychoeducational and substance abuse risk reduction intervention for children of substance abusers. *Journal of Community Psychology* (OSAP Special Issue). 75–87.

Hansen, W. B. (1992). School based substance abuse prevention: A review of the state of the art in curriculum, 1980–1990. *Health and Education Research: Theory and Practice, 7*(3), 403–430.

Hawkins, J. D., Catalano, R. F., Jr., and Associates (1992). *Communities that care: Action for drug abuse prevention.* San Francisco: Jossey-Bass.

Hawkins, D., Catalano, R., & Miller, J. (1992). Risk and protective factors for alcohol and other drug problems in adolescence and early adulthood: Implications for substance abuse prevention. *Psychological Bulletin, 112*(1), 64–105.

Hosang, M. (1995). Groupwork with children of substance abusers: Beyond the basics. In M. Feit, J. Ramey, J. Wodarski, & A. Mann (Eds.), *Capturing the power of diversity* (pp. 109–114). New York: Haworth.

Kantor, G., Candill, B., & Ungerleider, S. (1992). Project impact: Teaching the teachers to intervene in student substance abuse problems. *Journal of Alcohol and Drug Education, 38*(1), 11–29.

Knight, A., Vail-Smith, K., & Barnes, A. (1992). Children of alcoholics in the classroom: A survey of teacher perceptions and training needs. *Journal of School of Health, 62*(8), 367–371.

Kurland, R. (1980). Planning—the neglected component of group development. *Social Work with Groups, 1*(2), 173–178.

Kurland, R. (1982). *Group formation: A guide to the development of successful groups*. Albany, NY: Continuing Education Program, School of Social Welfare, State University of New York at Albany and Untied Neighborhood Centers of America.

Malekoff, A. (1984). Socializing preadolescents into the group culture. *Social Work with Groups, 7*(4), 7–19.

Malekoff, A. (1991). "What's goin' on in there?!?!": Alliance formation with parents whose children are in group treatment. *Social Work with Groups, 14*(1), 75–85.

Malekoff, A. (1994a). Action research: An approach to preventing substance abuse and promoting social competency. *Health and Social work, 19*(1), 46–53.

Malekoff, A. (1994b). A guideline for group work with adolescents. *Social Work with Groups, 17*(1/2), 5–19.

Middleman, R. & Wood, G. G. (1990). From social group work to social work with groups. *Social Work with groups, 13*(1), 3–20.

Muraskin, L. D. (1993). *Understanding evaluation: The way to better prevention programs*. Washington, DC: U.S. Department of Education.

National Institute of Alcohol Abuse and Alcoholism (1990). Children of alcoholics: Are they different? In *Alcohol Alert*, 9.

Northen, H. (1988). *Social work with groups*. New York: Columbia University Press.

Prothrow-Stith, D., & Weissman, M. (1991). *Deadly consequences*. New York: Harper Collins.

Redl, F., & Wineman, D. (1952). *Controls from within: Techniques for the treatment of the aggressive child*. New York: Free Press.

Rutter, M. (1979). Protective factors in children's responses to stress and disadvantage. In M. W. Kent & J. E. Rolf (Eds.), *Primary prevention of psychopathology: Social competence in children* (Vol. 3). Hanover NH: University Press of New England.

Rutter, M. (1984, March). Resilient children. *Psychology Today*, pp. 57–65.

Sameroff, A. (1988, June). The concept of the environtype: Integrating risk and protective factors in early development. Keynote address for North Shore Child and Family Guidance Center Conferences, Garden City, NY.

Schinke, S. P., Orlandi, M. A., & Cole, K. C., (1992). Boys and girls clubs in public housing developments: Prevention services for youth at risk. *Journal of Community Psychology* (OASP Special Issue), 118–128.

Schorr, L. B. (1989). *Within our reach: Breaking the cycle of disadvantage*. New York: Doubleday.

Shields, S. (1986). Busted and branded: Group work with substance abusing adolescents in schools. *Social Work with Groups, 8*(4), 61–81.

Smith, T. E. (1985). Group work with adolescent drug abusers. *Social Work with Groups, 8*(1), 55–64.

Treadway, D. C. (1989). *Before it's too late: Working with substance abuse in the family*. New York: W. W. Norton.

Vega, W. A., Zimmerman, R. S., Warheit, G. J., Apospori, E., & Gil, A. C. (1993). Risk factors for early adolescent drug use in four ethnic and racial groups. *American Journal of Public Health, 83*(2), 185–189.

Wallace, B. C. (1993). Cross cultural counseling with the chemically dependent: Preparing for service delivery within a culture of violence. *Journal of Psychoactive Drugs, 25*(1), 9–20.

Walthrust, N. (1992). Program description for Youth of Culture Drug Free Club (an edited and revised program concept derived from the 100% Drug Free Club, with permission from De. L. F. Brisbane). Roslyn Heights, NY: North Shore Child and Family Guidance Center.

Wegscheider, S. (1981). *Another chance: Hope and health for alcoholic family.* Palo Alto, CA: Science and Behavior Books.

Werner, E. (1986). Resilient offspring of alcoholics: A longitudinal study from birth to age 18. *Journal of Studies on Alcohol, 44*(1), 34–44.

Werner, E. (1989). High-risk children in young adulthood: A longitudinal study from birth to 32 years. *American Journal of Orthopsychiatry, 59*, 72–81.

Werner, E. (1990). Protective factors and individual resilience. In S. Meisels & J. Shonkoff (Eds.), *Handbook of early childhood intervention* (pp. 97–116). New York: Cambridge University Press.

17

Common Themes for Parents in a Methadone Maintenance Group

Geoffrey L. Greif

People with an addiction to heroin who enter methadone maintenance are often dealing not only with their addiction but also with their role as parents. Although treatment initially must focus on drug-related behavior, other issues may be raised once the patient has been stabilized. Otherwise, the continual stress that so often accompanies an addicted person's life may make maintenance and recovery doubtful. Parents who enter methadone maintenance often have realistic concerns about their children. A parents' group provides an opportunity to address these concerns. In addition, it affords them the chance to redefine themselves not as being drug addicted but rather as parents with drug problems who are getting help for their children. Such a redefinition can provide the basis for a healthier self-concept. This chapter describes some of the issues in working with a parents' group in a methadone maintenance program.

REVIEW OF THE LITERATURE

Perhaps one of the most misunderstood drug abuse treatment approaches, methadone maintenance has attracted new interest during the last 15 years with the spread of AIDS. Methadone maintenance offers the chance for people who share needles to cease their high-risk disease-spreading behavior. The benefits can go further. Effective methadone maintenance pro-

---

For an earlier version of this chapter, see G. L. Greif & M. Drechsler (1993). Common issues for parents in a methadone maintenance group. *Journal of Substance Abuse Treatment, 10*, 339–343.

grams have also been found to curb drug abuse, to reduce criminal activity, and to have potentially positive benefits for the members of the addicted person's family (Zweben & Sorensen, 1988).

When methadone is dispensed, it is usually coupled with some form of psychotherapy in most programs. Research on psychotherapy approaches has shown the potentially beneficial effects of limit setting in structured treatment (McCarthy & Borders, 1985), cognitive-behavioral therapy (Weiner & Fox, 1982), and contracting (Magura, Casriel, Goldsmith, & Lipton, 1987) in either reducing drug abuse or facilitating other useful behaviors. Numerous sources cited elsewhere in this book also describe the benefits of group therapy.

Despite some evidence of effective treatment, the children of addicts are often at risk for a variety of physical and emotional problems, particularly if they were conceived while the mother was on heroin or methadone (Hayford, Epps, & Dahl-Regis, 1988). These problems can begin prenatally, as the addicted mother is likely to neglect her health. Obstetrical complications are frequent (Deren, 1986; Hayford et al., 1988). At birth, these children's head circumferences are smaller and their birth weights are lower (Deren, 1986); neonatal drug withdrawal symptoms are more marked in children of methadone-maintained than heroin-addicted mothers (Hayford et al., 1988) The neonate's withdrawal from methadone or heroin may continue for up to 3 months (Hayford et al., 1988).

A range of symptoms may be present in the newborn. Marcus, Hans, and Jeremy (1984) found that very young children of methadone-maintained mothers exhibited poorer motor coordination and shorter attention spans than a comparison group. Similarly, Bernstein, Jeremy, Hans, and Marcus (1984) reported that a subgroup of the infants exposed to methadone in utero had worse social functioning and a higher level of tension than the comparison group who were not exposed to methadone. During withdrawal, sleep may be impaired (Hayward et al., 1988) and the infants may suffer from flu-like symptoms (West & Gossop, 1994), restless and irritable behavior (Barr & Jones, 1994), and sucking and feeding difficulties (Deren, 1986). While the focus here is on heroin, alcohol and cocaine, commonly used by heroin users, have also been found to have negative effects on infants pre- and postnatally (Scherling, 1994).

Symptoms in newborns can have a negative impact on the bonding that normally develops between a healthy newborn and a nonaddicted mother. The mother, seeking a bond and having little tolerance for rejection, may experience failure at her first attempt to connect with the newborn given the symptoms listed above. Unfortunately, the potential problems of these children do not necessarily cease in infancy. They have been known to continue until children reach to age of 6 or older, in part because of a lack of ability to attend to tasks (Deren, 1986). Recent research has begun to question how far-reaching the effects of neonatal addiction are, with some researchers finding that these effects do *not* last into middle childhood.

With the addicted mother (or father), adequate child-rearing behavior is sometimes minimal (Plasse, 1995). Thus, the child may be affected by both the residue of the drug and inadequate parenting (Johnson, Boney, & Brown, 1991). Mothers may exhibit low self-esteem, anxiety, and depression, and may not have adequate sources of social support for dealing with a difficult child and their own problems. They also are likely to feel inadequate and to use authoritarian and often ineffective means of parenting (Deren, 1986). Financial stability and safe housing may be issues. On measures of intelligence and personality these mothers, compared with non-drug-addicted mothers, have been found to be less adaptive (Bauman & Levine, 1986). In addition, they often come from dysfunctional families (Deren, 1986) where they had few adequate role models for how to parent.

Other problems that beset the often fragile child include erratic and unpredictable parental behavior and mood swings, absence of consistent parenting, and the shifting of parental responsibility to other adults in the family (often the mother of the addict). When the addicted mother has a low level of tolerance for the demands of parenting, the children may be placed at higher risk for child abuse (Deren, 1986; Hayward et al., 1988) and neglect and may not be given the structure needed to cope with their own deficits. The result is a parent with a host of problems attempting to raise a child with potential biological and emotional difficulties.

By treating these drug-dependent parents in a group, some of these issues can be addressed with success (Plasse, 1995). Group treatment can provide a supportive atmosphere where members can disclose their fears; gain information about normal developmental stages in children, as well as those that often accompany an addicted neonate: and learn how to cope with daily parenting demands, and where, perhaps for the first time, they can experience themselves constructively helping others (Yalom, 1995). Attachment to children is encouraged (Hayward et al., 1988). With this approach they are learning in vivo many of the give-and-take skills necessary for parenting.

Significant hurdles remain for the group members. They are subsisting on low incomes; often raising children with severe physical, emotional, and legal problems; and living in neighborhoods where drug use is rampant. Therefore, change, is measured in terms of years, not weeks or months.

PRACTICE PRINCIPLES

This group, which met from 1988 to 1993 and varied in size from four to six members, was racially mixed and had both male and female members. The members ranged in age from their mid-20s to their 40s. All were of the lower socioeconomic class. Members came and went as their status at the drug center changed. Some were removed from the program for noncompliance or drug abuse (as measured by a urine test or for displaying drug-induced or other noncompliant behavior). Others quit the program to try a different kind of treatment or no treatment at all. Some also moved to a different group because of scheduling conflicts. It was an involuntary group in that members had to attend or be reported to their individual counselors for non-compliance.

The members, most of whom had abused a variety of drugs for many years before entering treatment, specifically raised issues concerning their children, who ranged in age from birth to young adulthood. Teenagers, especially daughters, some of whom were being reared away from their mothers, caused the most conflict in the parents. The group met weekly and lasted for an hour (an agency policy), a period of time that occasionally seemed too short. Yet given the short attention span and child care demands of some of the parents, it may have been as long as was possible. A group member was allowed to miss four sessions every 6 months without a physician's note. If there were more absences or continued drug abuse, the member was dropped from the program and detoxified over a 1-month period.

The group leaders, the author and a full-time female social worker at the agency, used a multimethod approach that was guided by two types of family therapy: structural family therapy (Minuchin & Fishman, 1981) and Bowen family systems (Wylie, 1991). The structural school provided a framework for looking at the parent–child interactions that emphasized the maintenance of boundaries between the two. Families are viewed as dysfunctional when children are pulled into the parental sub-system or when parents are not maintaining a hierarchy in which they are in charge of the children. The focus of many of the interventions in this model is on the present. Group members were asked to review their behavior, with suggestions sometimes given by the leaders and others for possible behavioral changes to try at home during the week. In this way, work that began in the session could be continued throughout the week. This focus on the present provided a way of dealing with crises and emphasized for all parents that their behavior affected and was affected by others in the family.

Bowen's family systems theory provided a framework for teaching about the family of origin. By drawing genograms or family trees (Lewis, 1989), the members examined their own drug histories and behaviors in the context of a family history. The genograms also provided the leader with easy access to important information that might not have emerged during the group process. Members learned that their own behaviors and expectations for their children might have been the result of the family environment in which they were raised. Such an approach provided insight into feelings that might have impeded their attempts to parent. The genogram was also used to focus on strengths. After considering the devastating effect that drugs have had on families, we asked the group members whom they got their strength from in the family and wondered aloud with them how these family members survived when others of their generation were dead.

Contracting played an important part in the group process. The members were expected to follow the rules that had been established concerning confidentiality, supporting other members in the group, and coming to the group one final time before termination. The leaders encouraged group interaction, looked for ways to be supportive, and positively reinforced healthy behavior. The potential for assaultive behavior between members was low, in part because some of them took their methadone just prior to group meetings, which had a temporary narcotizing effect on them.

The group members were seen as having had deficient parenting themselves and as being in need of specific parenting skills. An attempt was made to present information in a way that did not undermine the self-esteem of these parents, who already felt incompetent. Thus, in this long-term group (some members had been attending for over 2 years and had remained abstinent from heroin and other drugs during this period), the emphasis was on accepting the member's behavior, confronting it, relating it to past experiences where appropriate, providing information about child development, and suggesting areas for change. This was done with the context never straying from drug treatment. The impact of long-term substance abuse on relationships was kept at or near the forefront of the discussions.

COMMON THEMES FOR THE MEMBERS

Throughout the course of the group, a number of common themes emerged. These themes fell into two groups: those relating to the behavior and personality traits of the addicted parent (points 1 through 4) and those associated with the challenges of raising children (points 5 through 7). They included (1) difficulty with being consistent and providing structure on a daily basis; (2) inability to parent because of deficiencies in their own upbringing; (3) inability to parent because of guilt from neglecting their children in the past; (4) difficulty in dealing with their own parents, who may have been blocking their attempts to establish parenting relationships with their children; (5) being verbally attacked by their children because of their drug histories; (6) raising adolescents; and (7) dealing with larger systems like the school system and child protective services.

Difficulty with Being Consistent and Providing Structure on a Daily Basis

Many group members lacked consistency and structure in their own lives. They often lived in chaotic households and neighborhoods where unpredictability and violence were the norm. Providing a predictable, caring environment for their children was difficult. Members came and went in their own homes at odd hours. Discipline was often too harsh or inappropriately lax. If restrictions were placed on the child that were unrealistically punitive, the parent backed away from them as they became difficult for the parent to enforce. At other times, parents forgot what the punishment was supposed to be. If the mother had been on drugs or methadone during pregnancy, the child's development may have been problematic in the early years, further burdening parent–child relationship.

Inability to Parent Because of Deficiencies in Their Own Upbringing

These drug addicts were often insufficiently parented themselves. Many may have turned to drugs as a result. When they became parents, they had few positive models to guide them in dealing with the normal ups and downs of child rearing. By looking at their family histories, as suggested by Bowen, the group members learned that their way of interacting with their own children might have been similar to how they were raised. One mother, who was abandoned by her father, learned to deal with difficult situations by cutting herself off from people, as her father had done with her. When she needed to intervene in her 14-year-old daughter's pregnancy, her tendency was to remove herself and say that her daughter had to handle it alone. Another parent, ill equipped to manage her own life, became overly responsible (Nelson-Zlupko, Kauffman, & Dore, 1995), trying to raise her own children and also those of a sister. She had difficulty saying no to outside obligations because that was never a role model for her.

Inability to Parent Because of Guilt from Neglecting Their Children in the Past

A number of theses parents neglected their children or turned them over to relatives to raise while they were addicted. The group members who regained custody, always had it, or were only peripherally involved with their children were often unable to follow through with punishment because of the guilt they felt about what their children had experienced at their hands or at the hands of others when they were addicted. As one mother in the group said, "Whenever I punish my daughter, I feel sorry for her because I wasn't there for her [when she was younger]."

Parents struggled with the issue of how involved to be in their children's lives, unsure of whether they were a positive influence and if their children wanted them to be involved. Many of these parents were immobilized when their child was angry at them, even though anger at one's parent is a normal part of growing up. As a reaction, the parents refrained from parenting and instead tried to establish a peer relationship, hoping to get love from the child through friendship.

Difficulty in Dealing with Their Own Parents, Who May Have Been Blocking Their Attempts to Establish Parenting Relationships with Their Children

Drug abuse has been cited as one of the primary reasons for the increase over the last few years in relatives, rather than parents, raising children (Minkler, Roe, & Robertson-Beckley, 1994). Often the mother of the addicted parent assumes the primary parenting responsibility if the parent abdicates it. As the parent enters treatment and begins methadone maintenance, he or she reaches a point where there may be a desire to resume parenting responsibilities. Attempts to do so are often blocked by the parent's mother, who does not trust the parent because of past indiscretions. In this situation, the grandmother may be attempting to protect the child. However, she may also have her own need to keep the parent in a dependent position and herself codependent, a family cycle that may have contributed to the parent's initial addiction.

In the group, it was not always a relative who was challenging the parenting abilities of the members. One group member, while abusing drugs, relinquished custody of her child to a friend to avoid having the child placed in foster care. The friend then refused to return the child after the member's status improved because, according to the group member, the friend could not afford to lose the welfare payment she received for the child.

Being Verbally Attacked by Their Children Because of Their Drug Histories

Some members experienced the verbal, and occasionally physical, wrath of their children because of their past histories of drug abuse. The children may have been responding solely to their own feelings or to feelings generated by their peers, who teased the children about their parent's drug abuse. Being called an addict by one's child often fed into a group member's own insecurity and heightened the imbalance in the parent–child hierarchy, placing the child in a position of greater power. One member stopped disciplining and nurturing her child because of these attacks. Another member (described earlier as having a pregnant 14-year-old daughter) reported that she was not going to advise her daughter to get an abortion even though she thought she should. "I can't tell her what to do," she told the group. "She already says I did stuff to her because of drugs, and I'm not going to be blamed by her later for telling her to kill her baby."

Raising Adolescents

Many addicted parents began taking drugs during their own adolescence. Their psychosocial development may have ceased at that point, resulting in their now responding to situations from an adolescent rather than adult perspective. When their own children reached adolescence, this began a particularly hard period for them for a number of reasons: (1) raising an adolescent may have cause any unresolved issues from their own adolescence to reemerge; (2) many thorny issues, such as sexuality, pregnancy, and sexually transmitted diseases, emerged for the first time in the parent–child relationship; and (3) the way the member handled issues focused on drug and alcohol abuse was important not only from a parent–child perspective but also from the perspective of that member's own abstinence. For example, if a parent tolerated any drug use in his or her own children, did that undermine a policy of abstinence that the parent may have been pursuing in treatment?

Dealing with Larger Systems: The School System and Child Protective Services

A few of the parents had ongoing contact with the school concerning their children's problems. These were usually behavioral concerns, with children exhibiting short attention spans and disruptive behavior, and sometimes academic concerns. These were naturally serious issues for the parents, who often saw their own histories of school failure being repeated in their children. Their ability to cope with these issues in partnership with the school was often severely compromised by their own histories. They tended to side with their children and to approach the school administration and teachers with an oppositional attitude rather than one of partnership. As a result, problems were often exacerbated when they could have been worked through.

Dealing with the Child Protective Services (CPS) System

Similar authority issues were raised by parents who complained that either their children threatened to call CPS if they disciplined them physically or that CPS was involved. In one situation, a mother started to beat her 15-year-old daughter for staying out past curfew but was forced to restrain herself when the daughter threatened to call CPS. Parents complained that they were no longer able to "do anything" with their children because of governmental interference.

When CPS was actually investigating a situation, the leaders were occasionally asked to write a letter for the group member attesting to his or her good parenting skills. While we could write that the member was in a group for parents, we could honestly say only that we had not seen the parent interact with the child often enough to make a sound determination as to the parent's ability. The parents were aware that reports of abusive behavior would have to be reported by us.

RECOMMENDED WAY OF WORKING

Teaching child development, particularly information relevant to a drug-addicted infant, is important (Edelstein, Kropenske, & Howard, 1990). The group leaders attempted to help the parents internalize structure by providing it themselves through consistent interactions with the members. The structural model was used in explaining to group members the need to act in a manner that reinforced their own competence as parents.

In helping parents deal with the ghosts from their own past, we attempted to show group members where their feelings about their parenting abilities originated. More difficult was the task of then convincing them that they were not tied to the past but had a choice as to how they wished to parent in the present and future.

As mentioned, parents felt guilty about the way they had previously treated their child. For the mother who had difficulty punishing her daughter, withdrawal of the punishment could be seen as engaging in enabling behavior and as a reflection of the relationship this mother had with her own mother. Focusing on the gains the parent has made in treatment can help the parent to incorporate a more beneficial self-image. Emphasizing the appropriate building of boundaries and examining past relationships the member had with responsible adults can assist similar parents in deciding where parental and child roles should be kept distinct.

For the parents who struggled with the involvement of other family members, the group leaders' interventions had a dual focus: (1) asserting the importance of avoiding all drugs, as any abuse reinforces the need for intrusion of the surrogate parent, and (2) asserting the importance of responsible behavior, particularly parenting behavior, in other areas of the member's life. Family work was assigned for the members to accomplish outside of the group. When warranted, the group member was asked to discuss with his or her mother (or responsible adult) what behaviors the group member would need before that responsible adult would relinquish more control of the child. For the group members, confronting their mothers or fathers on these issues was particularly difficult because of past unresolved conflicts.

Children in these situations are often angry but also frightened about their parents' potential return to drugs. One approach in the group had been for the leaders to reframe the verbal attacks by a child as a call for help or structure and that more, not less, parental involvement may be needed. This combatted the parent's tendency to withdraw, a pattern usually seen in other areas of their lives.

Because of the often overlapping developmental stage of the parent and the adolescent he or she is raising, adolescents pose particular problems. Insight assisted some of the parents here. Helping the group members recognize the overarching themes between their own adolescence and their children's provided them with tools to begin to deal more objectively with the difficulties of this development stage. This theme had to be reconsidered in every group session, as it was the parents with adolescents who tended to have the most severe crises.

Helping parents with school-related problems begins with pointing out to them the potential similarities between their own academic histories and that of their child. Introducing the notion of partnership or "teaming" with the school teacher can place the parent in an executive or parental role, which is more appropriate than reacting to school contacts as if the school is "picking on" their child.

Parents complained about not being able to raise their children the way they wanted to because their children threatened to call CPS. They were supported in their frustration but encouraged to find other ways to discipline that would avoid this potential source of conflict. This opened up an opportunity for discussing discipline in general and searching for alternative, less punitive measures.

Two illustrations show the often divergent reactions when authority systems become part of a parent's life.

> Carly felt unable to control her teenage daughter from the time the girl was quite young. She turned over her rearing to her own parents and assisted them in disciplining. But when the daughter reached her teens and became uncontrollable, Carly's parents called the Department of Social Services for help. The courts also became involved when the daughter committed several petty crimes. Carly supported her parents' decision, feeling that they needed more help with discipline than either she or they could offer.

More complicated is the situation in which intrusion is unwelcome:

> CPS was concerned about Nancy's sometimes neglectful and abusive behavior of her son. Nancy turned over custody of her 8-year old son to her neighbor, telling CPS that the neighbor was a cousin. She was trying to prevent the child's being placed in foster care, where she would not see him. The neighbor received foster care payments for the son but later refused to return him and lose the payments. Nancy also was frequently at school, fielding complaints about a second child's behavior, and indicated that she often stretched the truth when meeting with school officials.

> Nancy wanted the group leaders to testify at a custody hearing that she was fit to regain custody. Social workers are often asked to advocate for clients, but in this situation we did not feel comfortable representing her when we believed her to be unfit. To avoid any triangulation, we asked her whether she really wanted her son back.

For Carly and Nancy, their erratic, drug-induced behavior contributed to the intrusion of outside systems into their lives. But Carly welcomed it as a needed form of external control, while Nancy resisted it. Diagnostically, the outcomes of their treatment were perhaps predictable. Carly succeeded and Nancy was thrown out of the program for using other drugs.

EVALUATION AND SUMMARY

Measuring change is a matter of parental self-report in terms of both the child's reactions and the group member's parenting behavior, lack of substance abuse (also measured by urine screens), in-group behavior, and lack of trouble with the law. By these criteria, change was noted in some of the group members. For example, one long-term group member (Carly), who never spoke when she was in a previous group that focused on addiction-related problems, became the role model for other members. In this group, she said, she felt more competent. She was appropriately outspoken and established relationships with her children that consistently supported the parent–child boundaries that needed to be drawn. One specific issue she resolved involved her 19-year-old son and his girlfriend, who was pregnant. By role playing the different positions of each of these people (Carly was paying the rent and had the right to set the rules; the girlfriend was feeling unaccepted by Carly and was acting out inappropriately; the son was caught between trying to please the two women), Carly was able to clarify for herself how to approach future conflicts.

A second group member improved her relationship with her son (age 3) but still struggles with her 15-year-old daughter. What was most effective was teaching her to count to 10 before responding to what she considers the goading of both children. In addition, she was feeling pressured by her mother, in whose house she lived, to toilet train her son. After learning about the normal developmental stages and allowing for other possible deficits that might be related to having a child who was addicted at birth, the member was able to put less pressure on her son and to feel more competent herself.

A third member slowly opened up to the group after being guarded and defensive for the first 4 months of attendance. With her youngest son in a group home for delinquent boys, interventions focused on supporting her attempts to see him and following her to vent her frustration at trying to raise him alone. A fourth member showed little improvement and continued to be of great concern to the leaders. A fifth member (Nancy) entered the group as a continual abuser and was detoxed from the program 6 months later because she continued to abuse. A sixth member had to change groups because of child care conflicts.

Work with this difficult population requires a long-term commitment and the establishment of goals that consider the life history of the abuser. Change is slow and incremental. There are nearly as many setbacks as there are signs of positive change. Yet, in a supportive atmosphere, group members can be reparented and helped to be more effective in raising their children.

NATIONAL RESOURCES

National Institute of Drug Abuse
(NIDA)
5600 Fishers Lane
Rockville, MD 29857
(800) 662-HELP

Narcotics Anonymous
(800) 677-7282
(ask for sites in your area)

Narcotic Treatment Program
Directory
U.S. Department of Health and
Human Services
(has nationwide inventory of drug
programs)

National Directory of Drug Abuse
and Alcoholism Treatment and
Prevention Programs
Published by NIDA (see address
above)

Numerous professional journals are
also available on the topic, including:
Journal of Substance Abuse
*The American Journal of Drug
and Alcohol Abuse*
*International Journal of the
Addictions*
Journal of Drug Issues
Journal of Psychoactive Drugs

REFERENCES

Barr, G.A., & Jones, K. (1991). Opiate withdrawal in the infant. *Neurotoxicology and Teratology, 16,* 219–225.

Bauman, P.S., & Levine, S.A. (1986). The development of children of drug addicts. *International Journal of Addictions, 21,* 849–863.

Bernstein, V., Jeremy, R.J., Hans, S.L., & Marcus, J. (1984). A longitudinal study of offspring born to methadone-maintained women. II. Dyadic interaction and infant behavior at 4 months. *American Journal of Drug and Alcohol Abuse, 10,* 161–193.

Deren, S. (1986). Children of substance abusers: A review of the literature. *Journal of Substance Abuse Treatment, 3,* 77–94.

Edelstein, S., Kropenske, V., & Howard, J. (1990). Project T.E.A.M.S. *Social Work, 35,* 313–318.

Hayford, S.M., Epps, R. P., & Dahl-Regis, M. (1988). Behavior and development patterns in children born to heroin-addicted and methadone-addicted mothers. *Journal of the National Medical Association, 80,* 1197–1200.

Johnson, J. L., Boney, T. Y., & Brown, B. S. (1991). Evidence of depressive symptoms in children of substance abusers. *International Journal of the Addictions, 25*(4A), 465–479.

Lewis, K. G. (1989). The use of color-coded genograms in family therapy. *Journal of Marital and Family Therapy, 15,* 169–176.

Magura, S. Casriel, C., Goldsmith, D. S., & Lipton, D. S. (1987). Contracting with clients in methadone treatment. *Social Casework, 68*(8), 485–493.

Marcus, J., Hans, S. L., & Jeremy, R. J. (1984). A longitudinal study of offspring born to methadone-maintenance women. III. Effects of multiple risk factors on development at 4, 8, and 12 months. *American Journal of Drug and Alcohol Abuse, 10,* 195–207.

McCarthy, J. J., & Borders, O. T. (1985). Limit setting on drug abuse in methadone maintenance patients. *American Journal of Psychiatry, 142,* 1419–1423.

Minkler, M., Roe, K. M., & Robertson-Beckley, R. J. (1994). Raising grandchildren from crack-cocaine households: Effects on family and friendship ties of African-American women. *American Journal of Orthopsychiatry, 64,* 20–29.

Minuchin, S., & Fishman, C. (1981). *Family therapy techniques.* Cambridge, MA: Harvard University Press.

Nelson-Zlupko, L., Kauffman, E., & Dore, M. M. (1995). Gender differences in drug addiction and treatment: Implications for social work intervention with substance-abusing women. *Social Work, 40,* 45–54.

Plasse, B. R. (1995). Parenting groups for recoving addicts in a day treatment center. *Social Work, 40,* 65–74.

Scherling, D. (1994). Prenatal cocaine exposure and childhood psychopathology: A developmental analysis. *American Journal of Orthopsychiatry, 64,* 9–19.

Weiner, H., & Fox, S. (1982). Cognitive-behavioral therapy with substance abusers. *Social Casework, 63,* 564–567.

West, R., & Gossop, M. (1994). Overview: A comparison of withdrawal symptoms from different drug classes. *Addiction, 89,* 1483–1489.

Wylie, M. S. (1991). Family therapy's neglected prophet. *Family Therapy Networker, 15,* 24–37, 77.

Yalom, I. (1995). *The theory and practice of group psychotherapy* (4th ed.) New York: Basic Books.

Zweben, J. E., & Sorensen, J. L. (1988). Misunderstanding about methadone. Journal of Psychoactive *Drugs, 20,* 275–281.

V

GAY MEN AND LESBIAN ISSUES

18

Group Work with Gay Men

Steven Ball and Benjamin Lipton

In the history of social group work with gay men, as in the history of all
mental health services to this population, the past three decades have witnessed a dramatic shift from a pathological stance that once regarded
homosexuals as mentally ill to an affirmative model that assists gay men
and lesbians in asserting their equal, healthy, and ethical place in society
(Gonsiorek, 1985). Currently, gay affirmative psychotherapy regards
homophobia—anti-homosexual attitudes and behaviors (Maylon, 1982)—
rather than homosexuality as the major pathological variable affecting the
mental health of this population (Margolies, Becker, & Jackson-Brewer,
1987). Since the psychosocial issues facing all gay men are the result of
adapting to an environment that has denied them recognition and accept
ance, groups serving this population can provide a healing antidote to a
lifelong history of deprivation. The developmental process of growing up
in an environment hostile to homosexuality creates a stigmatized identity
for all gay men. As a result, it is essential that workers understand the
overriding psychosocial factors arising from homophobia that inform
individual responses to particular environmental stressors and life issues.
Societal homophobia, internalized homophobia, stigmatization, coming
out, gender role conflicts, familial relationships, and the impact of AIDS
inform the process of all group work with gay men, regardless of the specific commonalities around which these groups may be organized. While
the psychosocial needs and experiences of gay men are as diverse as those
of any other minority group, this chapter will provide essential clinical

information about the above issues that can inform practice with more specific subgroups of the population in a variety of social service settings.

REVIEW OF THE LITERATURE

Any overview of the social service and mental health literature on gay men must be understood within the rapidly changing social context of the past three decades (Abelove, 1993; Duberman, 1991; Isay, 1989; Stein & Cohen, 1986). The response of social workers to those with a same-sex orientation reflects a historical progression from pathology to ambivalence across all mental health professions. Prior to 1973, when the American Psychiatric Association officially declassified homosexuality as pathological, gay men were considered mentally ill or perverse because of their sexual object choice. While a small but dedicated group of influential practitioners to this day remain committed to labeling homosexuality an illness (Bieber, 1962; Nicolosi, 1991; Socarides, 1978), growing numbers of gay and lesbian mental health practitioners, including many social workers (Deyton & Lear, 1988), have united with an increasingly vocal and organized gay community in leading the way toward dismantling homophobic myths and creating a psychosocial model for healthy homosexuality. By openly challenging traditional models of pathology and exposing their lack of empirical support (Friedman, 1988), these men and women have paved the way toward developing an alternative, affirmative practice base for working with gay and lesbian clients.

Practitioners began developing a significant body of literature on the theory and practice of gay affirmative counseling and psychotherapy prior to the onset of AIDS in the early 1980s (Bell & Weinberg, 1978; Cass, 1979; Coleman, 1982; Gonsiorek, 1977). During this same period, psychotherapy groups for gay men primarily came out of the private practices and agency work of increasing numbers of openly gay mental health practitioners who were responding to the long-suppressed needs of their clients. As late as 1980, however, there was only one published article on generic group work with gay men, an outcome study of a short-term group conducted in Australia (Russell & Winkler, 1977). Subsequent reviews of the literature on group psychotherapy with this population by Conlin and Smith (1985) and by Schwartz and Hartstein (1986) reveal that they are the only articles of their kind that specifically address the role of group work in fostering psychosexual maturation in gay men rather than focusing on a particular psychosocial stressor affecting this population. Their articles document the process of groups designed to support, value, and integrate the gay identity by fostering disclosure of sexual orientation, providing opportunities for emotional intimacy, and confronting both external stigmatization and internalized homophobia.

How can we account for the paucity of literature on general group work with gay men over the past decade? We believe there are at least three related reasons. First, many social workers conventionally think of first contacts as individual, often relegating group treatment to a secondary or auxiliary position in treatment. Initial developments in gay affirmative psychotherapy seem to reflect this pattern. Second, at the historical moment when mental health agencies were beginning to sanction the use of affirmative models for group work with gay men, the biopsychosocial crisis of AIDS necessitated an immediate shift in treatment to this population (Caputo, 1985; de la Vega, 1990; Nichols, 1986; Shernoff, 1991). As clients and workers began to view the ongoing external and internal stressors of being self-identified as a gay man through the lens of the human immunodeficiency virus (HIV), the literature on practice with gay men focused on AIDS-related issues of immediate concern and provided a new context in which to understand gay identity development (Cadwell, Burnham, & Forstein, 1994; Isay, 1989; Odets, 1994). Third, self-help has always been a necessary and essential part of the gay experience in a heterosexist, homophobic environment and consistently filled the gap in social services long before mainstream professionals formally responded by incorporating services into their organizations and documenting their work with contributions to the literature (Eller & King, 1990). The most powerful example of this process was the rapid and comprehensive organization of the gay community in response to AIDS when their needs were not addressed by social service agencies.

While much remains to be written about groups for gay men that do not specifically focus on AIDS issues, the present literature on AIDS-related group work provides an invaluable resource not only for understanding HIV issues but also for understanding deeper conflicts about being gay that will inform the process of working with any group of gay men (Tunnell, 1994). Regardless of the particular focus of any group, whether related to AIDS or not, what is most crucial is the opportunity to build social supports and interpersonal connections. *Homosocialization*, defined as building relationships with other gay men, is essential to the healthy integration of a homosexual identity and the discovery of positive gay role models (Isay, 1989). In their work with gay populations, Hetrick and Martin (1987), Conlin and Smith (1985), and Schwartz and Hartstein (1986) all suggest that commonly shared issues arising from stigmatization such as social, cognitive, and emotional isolation — the negative outcomes of stigmatization—can best be coped with by creating opportunities for socialization with peers. Since gay men are one of the few minorities denied the opportunity to identify with others like them because of both the absence of identifying factors and the oppression of a homonegative environment, group work with this population takes on ever-increasing importance in the lives of its members.

PRACTICE PRINCIPLES

Based on the pervasive impact of stigmatization and homonegativity on gay male development, as well as the need for homosocialization to mitigate the influence of these factors, the following practice principles and procedures should guide a social worker in beginning group work with the population.

Level of Worker Activity Inside and Outside of the Group

The worker's role in any group for gay men extends far beyond facilitating the group process. When developing a group for gay men, the need for outreach and psychoeducation can be guaranteed. Those most in need of a gay men's group may be the hardest to reach, as they remain unaffiliated with the gay community or unacknowledged within it, as in the case of HIV-negative men (Odets, 1994). Outreach to the larger, nonspecifically gay environment away from traditional resources for membership such as community centers, bars, and social clubs may provide new awareness not only to those isolated men who could benefit from a gay group but also to the nongay community at large about issues confronting gay men.

While a secondary gain may be public education about the realities of gay life, an essential task of a social worker leading a gay men's group is to educate the staff of his or her social service agency about gay men. In-service training in addition to individual interactions will increase understanding about gay men and their particular issues as well as the potential for referrals. The combined acknowledgment of the community and the agency positively influences the functioning of the group, as potential members see the group as an acceptable and accepted source of support and a safe place to explore their concerns.

When the group process moves from the stage of pregroup formation to the beginning phase of group work, the social worker's role as an educator continues. Not only must the worker lend a vision and contribute data to the group as it begins to take shape, but throughout the life of the group he or she must continue to provide resources, conceptual frameworks, interpersonal modeling, and general education to counter the cognitive and experiential deficits that result from growing up in an environment void of gay role models and gay affirmative information. Implicit in a social worker's vision of the group must be the awareness that a gay person's stigmatization stems from a society—and a gay community—that often dictate a rigid repertoire of physical and social expressions that may impair healthy psychosocial development.

The Group as a Basic Resource

While the leader is initially responsible for guiding the development of group norms and modeling adaptive interpersonal relating, the goal of these interventions is to help group members see themselves as a source of support for each other and to develop a sense of belonging. Gay men enter groups with a legacy of isolation. Historically, societal groups have been sources of persecution for this population that reinforce a feeling of powerlessness rather than resources for affiliation and validation. When the group recognizes and employs their communal resources for support, group members can begin to counteract their collective history of disenfranchisement. Groups offer an opportunity to clarify emotional priorities and increase their capacity for building cohesive interpersonal networks. To this end, the social worker must consistently introduce, model, and reinforce group norms that invite the group to join with the leader as a basic resource for answers, empathy, and conflict resolution.

Boundaries and Confidentiality

A powerful effect of homophobia and stigmatization has been the internalization by many in the gay community of a narrow sense of identity organized around sex rather than sexual orientation. This reality makes group contracting around the issues of interacting both within and outside of the group of paramount importance in developing an environment of safety and trust. Often group members initially alternate between expressions of excitement and pleasure resulting from identification among members, and fear that the group will become yet another sexualized experience and lose its credibility as a safe space for exploring feelings. To foster and preserve a safe environment, the role of sex within the group process must be addressed from the outset. While setting limits for socialization always includes members' abstaining from having sex with each other, it is particularly important in a group where sexual identity is an essential commonality to help members explore how sexual involvement between them would affect the ability of the group to function successfully. A social worker's initial interventions must reflect and normalize sexualized interactions such as flirting among members while helping the group to identify the role of these interactions in defending against emotional intimacy. Modeling an inquisitive stance toward the role of sexuality in initiating relationships in the group empowers members to begin to question what modes of socializing will best fit their needs and help them to realize their treatment goals.

Since gay men have historically had to respond to rather than determine the social norms, boundaries, and limits established by a heterosexual culture, social workers must recognize the interplay between the opportunity for self-determination and the fear of acquiescing to the restrictive norms of a dominant culture. In the authors' experience that even in large cities that offer some sense of anonymity within the gay community, members may share some past or present social connection to other members. As a result, restricting socialization to the group may, on the one hand, not meet the needs of isolated gay men who would benefit from outside social support and, on the other hand, fail to mesh with the social reality of men already socialized within the gay community.

While the group may recognize the need for limits on sexual interactions among members, efforts to restrict outside socialization, a common guideline in many models of group work, need to be explored, contracted, and recontracted throughout the group process.

All of the principles discussed above must be founded on a firm commitment to the guiding group work principle of confidentiality. The leader must actively address the place of confidentiality in the group process and in outside contacts in order to establish a feeling of safety, particularly for those who have yet to speak openly about their sexual orientation. An ongoing exploration of this principle may provide a powerful opening to discussions of stigmatization and shame.

COMMON THEMES

While the themes discussed in this section will assume varying degrees of priority in groups organized around any number of commonalities, including coming out, substance abuse, sexual abuse, parenting, couples, bereavement, HIV status, aging, and socialization, they may also serve as the target issues for which groups for gay men are developed.

Homophobia

The socialization of every gay man involves exposure to homophobia. The literature refers to the subsequent internalization of the social animosity that a gay man experiences (Hetrick & Martin, 1987) as *internalized homophobia* and widely supports the view that the external and internal impacts of the resulting stigmatization must be addressed in treatment (Hetrick & Martin, 1987; Isay, 1989; Margolies et al., 1987; Silverstein, 1991; Tunnel, 1994). Homophobia frequently manifests itself alongside heterosexism, the culturally conditioned bias that heterosexuality is superior to other sexual orientations (Gonsiorek, 1985).

Homophobia manifests itself in a variety of ways, both blatant and subtle, internal and external, within the gay community and in society at large. It is essential to understand, first, that recognizing homophobia is not equal to eradicating it and, second, that one's some-sex orientation does not preclude homophobic beliefs and behaviors. Within the group process, homophobia may present as fear of disclosure in general; fear of disclosing one's sexual orientation; fear of commitment to the group; discomfort with more open group members or leaders; generalized rejection of heterosexuality; and denial of social differences between gay and heterosexual men. While some of these manifestations may on the surface seem far from homophobic, exploration of feelings will most often unearth negative attitudes and beliefs about what it means to be a gay man.

Stigmatization and Shame

As previously noted, stigmatization is the inevitable result of developing within a homophobic environment. Stigma is the precursor to shame in the psychosocial development of every gay man. As members begin to share life histories, whether anecdotally in support groups or more formally in psychotherapy groups, common themes of rejection, isolation, violence, and abuse will often surface. This retelling of the impact of stigmatization will frequently find its complement in the current group process. Isensee (1991) carefully outlines the process by which shame interferes with interpersonal relating and fosters the development of a false self. Since the legacy of shame leads gay men to embrace negative stereotypes about their potential for developing lasting and important relationships, members may initiate a self-fulfilling prophecy that often results in treating one another in the same hostile/rejecting ways in which they fear being treated themselves.

Coming Out

As a gay man begins to integrate his sexuality, the impact of homophobia and stigmatization on gay male development necessitates a process that the literature defines as coming out—an ongoing developmental process of gay identity formation organized around revealing and accepting one's sexual orientation. Of seminal importance to the coming-out literature have been Coleman's (1982) five-stage model, which describes a developmental process from before coming out to integration, and Cass's (1979) six-stage model, which leads from identity confusion to identity synthesis as the gay man works to synthesize his sexuality with his self-concept. For a recent review of the coming-out literature that also provides new insight into the impact of HIV on gay male development, see Linde (1994).

In order to understand the impact of any life crisis or stressor around which a group for gay men has been formulated, it is necessary to recognize the impact of coming out on each of the group members and on the group process as a whole (Cass, 1979). As stereotypes and dormant issues of homophobia, self-definition, and self-acceptance are activated by the diverse psychosocial issues and stages of members, a group organized around any task can offer a powerful experience on the coming-out continuum for those just beginning the process, as well as for those more openly identified as gay. Initial movements toward coming out in this society are often limited to sexual experimentation and sexualized socialization in bars, dance clubs, and parties. There are few opportunities to attend to the powerful emotions that generate and are generated by the coming-out experience. Whether beginning to come out or already identified as gay, gay men often arrive at a group with a lack of knowledge related to the diversity of gay lifestyles, range of social outlets, and ways of relating to others like themselves. A gay men's group can serve not only as an emotional anchor to explore turbulent feelings to self and others in regard to a specific common issue. It can also be a window on the diversity of the gay experience as one begins to identify more openly as a gay man and/or to expand one's understanding of what it means to be gay.

AIDS/HIV

In the second decade of the AIDS epidemic, HIV remains a central component of gay identity and a consistent stressor in the daily lives of gay men, regardless of their HIV status (Cadwell et al., see also Chapter 3, this volume). HIV is not only a health issue; it is a mental health issue that may further exacerbate existing stressors related to family, friends, relationships, life choices, and a sense of the future. Agencies may organize groups for gay men presenting with any number of HIV-related issues: HIV status, serodiscordant couples, care partners, safer sex, early adjustment, bereavement, or substance abuse. Social workers providing group services to gay men within social service organizations will likely find themselves leading AIDS-related groups.

Regardless of the particular task around which a social worker organizes a group for gay men, and regardless of whether or not the group task is itself specific to HIV, AIDS will undoubtedly appear as a recurring theme in the group process. Any gay man will have to redefine his sense of self in a world of ongoing AIDS-related trauma. Isensee (1991) outlines five areas in which AIDS continues to affect gay men: the trauma of life-threatening illness, hypervigilance, survivor guilt, effects on sexuality, and the impact of catastrophic loss. The uncertainty of both diagnosis and prognosis for all gay men, whether HIV positive or HIV negative, whether tested for HIV antibodies or untested, whether symptomatic or asymptomatic for AIDS, often leads to ongoing anxiety and depression. Such anxiety may manifest itself in hypervigilance—a preoccupation with any signs of illness at the expense of more productive and fulfilling activities of daily living. Anxiety may also manifest itself unconsciously as survivor guilt, a complex process through which one maladaptively manages overwhelming feelings of loss and abandonment by acting out a variety of more or less overtly self-destructive behaviors (Odets, 1994).

Emotional conflicts stemming from the trauma of HIV often affect the sexual behaviors of gay men. The legacy of homophobia and stigmatization prior to the AIDS epidemic already complicated their sex lives as feelings of shame frequently shrouded sexual behaviors in secrecy. With the emergence of AIDS, these shameful feelings may be traumatically reinforced as acts of sexual expression become linked to horrible visions of wasting, decay, and death. As gay men struggle with shame, survivor guilt, and internalized homophobia, they may play out feelings of self-loathing in unsafe sexual practices or feelings of fear in abstinence. In an environment in which the link between sex and survival has been turned upside down, groups for gay men may offer invaluable forums for normalizing fears, clarifying values, disseminating information, and building a community of concern to mitigate against overwhelming feelings of loss and isolation that might otherwise lead to self-destructive behavior. To this end, social workers must be willing to take on a psychoeducational role on the issue of safer sex. Workers must not only respond to requests for information and discussion but also initiate them. When necessary, they must be prepared to make direct interventions to clarify and confront maladaptive defense structures of members.

Family Issues

As in group work with any population, the group process recapitulates for each gay member the family dynamics that he brings to the group (Yalom, 1995). For gay men who have most often grown up hiding their true selves from their families of origin, this aspect of the group process can prove either particularly traumatizing or extremely empowering. Even in families that appear to function well and attend to the psychosocial needs of all members, apparent attunement can mask underlying, unintentional emotional abuse. As the family fails even to consider the possibility that a son, brother, or father may be gay, the gay member remains silenced by shame, guilt, and secretiveness. If the group process recreates this experience for its members by failing to reach for and affirm self-disclosure and self-reflection about being gay, then the group will perpetuate emotional trauma. If, on the other hand, members are made aware of the dynamic of familial recapitulation in the group process and helped to use it to create new scripts of acceptance and affirmation, then the group can be an important place for developing and consolidating feelings of empowerment.

For many gay men, particularly those who came of age in the period preceding public debate about the place of gay men within social structures, their definition of family has been expanded to include families of choice in addition to families of biological origin. Families of choice often develop during the initial stages of the coming-out process, as gay men have had to look outside of their families for acceptance and affirmation, as well as for affiliation with other gay men. Interdependent groups of gay men develop out of this search and provide each other with the physical and emotional caring that heterosexuals can usually expect from their families of origin. For some gay men, families of choice may even replace their families of origin as the primary reservoirs of emotional security. When working with gay men, it is essential to value and respect the place of these families within the lives of group members and to assess the roles that a member may play within his family of choice. Often these roles coincide with earlier roles played out in a member's family of origin and provide helpful information toward understanding the interpersonal dynamics that a member may bring to the group. A social worker must also be alert to the devastating impact of multiple losses and continual grieving on this system of psychosocial support since the beginning of the AIDS epidemic.

Gender Roles

Popular gay culture seems to have evolved, at least in part, in reaction to the collective childhood trauma of gender role nonconformity (Friedman, 1988). Literature on gay male development (Isay, 1989; Schwartz &

Hartstein, 1986) suggests that such trauma may begin with a prehomo-sexual boy's relationship with his father. Emotional distance and unavailability of fathers often develop out of the father's conscious or unconscious homophobia and contribute to poor relations between these men and their gay children. Early negative relationships with fathers then are reinforced as developing gay men continue to interact with heterosexual males in larger social circles. Teased and ostracized for not taking part in traditionally masculine social and sexual pursuits, gay adolescents and younger men often develop feelings of shame and insecurity for failing to fit into heterosexual definitions of masculinity. In keeping with theories of oppressed populations, gay men may defend against these feelings by identifying with the same stereotypical images of traditional masculinity that oppress them. Unfortunately, identification with traditional masculine gender roles creates significant problems with building intimacy, trust, and a willingness to depend on other men.

Since many gay men come to groups with scarred self-images and difficulty relating openly to other men, an important task of any social worker will be to foster interdependence and group cohesion by exploring and normalizing an expansive, inclusive definition of masculinity unimpaired by traditional limitations. The group leader can employ basic, supportive social work skills to help members identify their feelings and learn to hear each other in increasingly empathic ways. The particular tasks of any group for gay men may allow members to peel away layers of maladaptive, rigid identifications in search of more fluid, emotionally responsive, true selves.

Relationships and Intimacy

Men who choose membership in a gay men's group desire relationships with other gay men. Often men may want to use the group either to find a romantic partner or to explore difficulties in their already existing partnerships. While the impulse to fall in love and partner exists for heterosexual as well as gay men, a social worker must be sensitive to the particular difficulties confronting single and coupled group members. Living within a homophobic society excludes gay men from the legal, religious, financial, and social structures that affirm and sanctify heterosexual coupling. Nevertheless, surveys of gay men demonstrate that more than half of them are involved in ongoing partnerships (Peplau & Cochran, 1990).

To provide help in this area of psychosocial development, social workers must come to understand the ways in which both societal oppression and the characteristics of same-sex relationships impact on gay male couples and on gay men looking for a partner. For example, in contrast to the accepted heterosexual model of monogamy, many male couples in durable, committed relationships distinguish between emotional and sexual fidelity. As members of a culture steeped in heterosexual norms, social workers must reflect carefully on their heterosexist biases and strive not to assign pathology or dysfunction to gay couples. A group leader must transfer these challenges to group members as well, reinforcing hope by presenting the group as a model for the potential in each member to build intimate relationships. At the same time, the social worker must identify the negative impact of internalized homophobia, heterosexist assumptions, and misleading stereotypes on the process of building intimacy in the group and help the group to reflect on how each of these affects external partnerships or efforts to establish them.

Ethnocultural Diversity

Contrary to prevalent stereotypes, racial, cultural, and ethnic diversity impact on the development and functioning of individual gay men. Just as the white, middle-class male does not represent all of American society, a social worker must recognize that the most easily identifiable gay men do not represent the population in all of its complexity. Since the majority of the literature on gay men is based on samples of white, middle-class men, neither the theory nor research that has resulted is necessarily relevant to all subgroups of the gay population. The marginalized place of ethnic and racial minorities within the literature on gay men parallels the social realities of minority populations not only within society at large but also within the gay community. Being gay does not preclude one from experiencing or fomenting ethnocultural prejudice. It is imperative for a group leader to recognize the additional stigmas of discrimination based on race, gender, age, or ethnicity that many men must carry.

Social workers must help group members to articulate and validate their particular ethnocultural experiences and conflicts in relation to their sexual orientation. For example, African-American gay men may experience identity conflicts as they search for a healthy place amid two problematic environments: their homophobic African-American heritage, on the one hand, and the racist white gay culture, on the other (Loiacano, 1989). Carballo-Dieguez (1989) and Chan (1989) explore similar difficulties that arise from the interplay of race, ethnicity, and sexual orientation for Latino and Asian-American gay men. A group leader can help clients develop effective coping strategies for traversing seemingly exclusive cultures and provide a safe place for ventilating painful feelings of alienation from one or both groups.

In addition to ethnocultural factors, age affects one's identity as a gay man. Since AIDS began to take its toll on the lives of gay men, the concept of longevity has undergone radical redefinition. After the deaths of hundreds of thousands of gay men from AIDS, men in their 40s and 50s are joining those in their 60s, 70s, and 80s in the developmental tasks of survivorship as they work through issues of loss and strive for regeneration. As they tackle these difficult tasks, older gay men must develop an identity outside of a mainstream gay culture that lauds youth and pays little regard to its older members or to the realities of aging. It is ironic that so many younger members in groups for gay men lament the scarcity of role models, while the culture in which these men are trying to find a place continues to marginalize older gay men. These men, the first generation to have had the possibility of living as openly gay for most of their adult lives, are invaluable and overlooked resources for the younger generation. Their ability to continue to thrive in the face of tremendous cumulative stressors indicates a resilience that workers must recognize and validate whenever possible while providing all of the services that a social worker would provide to any older person.

RECOMMENDED WAYS OF WORKING

The authors' clinical and anecdotal experiences reveal that many gay men continue to mistrust the intentions of their mental health providers, particularly in nongay settings. Such mistrust underscores the marginalized place of gay men within the mental health system, the need for outreach to the gay community, and the ways in which unattuned social work agencies and workers might reinforce injurious feelings of difference, isolation, and invisibility among gay people. To this end, the following section will provide information on effective ways of addressing the needs of this population through group work.

Pregroup Interview

The pregroup interview, an essential procedure for composing all groups, is particularly charged for gay men. It must initiate a process of attunement. For an individual whose identity and way of relating to his environment rest on anticipated rejection, the pregroup interview must set a tone of acceptance as the social worker actively normalizes a gay identity. As social workers attend to the psychosocial assessment of a prospective group member, including a determination of his developmental stage in the coming-out process, the worker must demonstrate real knowledge and awareness of gay issues and the gay community. At the same time, the worker who is less informed about these subjects must acknowledge his ignorance and demonstrate a willingness to learn more about them from sources *outside* of the group so as not to reinforce or repeat negative experiences of members requiring them to confront homophobic misinformation from the group leader (Kus, 1990). Clients must be informed about the diversity of membership and told that the group will not focus on labels or definitions, but instead on their own needs regarding their concerns about being gay and how it may relate to the specific focus of the group.

Member Selection

Groups for gay men must affirm inclusion. As a social worker evaluates an interviewee's appropriateness for group membership, he or she must guard vigilantly against recapitulating a lifelong process of rejection and exclusion from social group participation. Excluding gay men from groups designed specifically for them may not only perpetuate feelings of isolation but may actually leave the client isolated from specific gay services, particularly in geographic areas where there are few alternative resources for this population. Since many agencies do not offer a wide variety of group services to gay men, social workers may find themselves leading groups that must address myriad divergent needs. As a result, the major criteria for membership should be an expressed desire to be a group member and a willingness to commit to the group process. For groups that do not require specific inclusion criteria, only those who are unable to acknowledge consciously that they are attracted primarily to other men to satisfy their sexual and affectional needs, or who are actively psychotic or antisocial in personality, should be excluded (Gonsiorek, 1985).

The question of whether or not to include bisexual clients in groups for gay men often depends on the specific focus and setting of the group. If the group is a more general therapy group, then including bisexual men may prove very helpful in fostering acceptance of diversity and recognition of the complexity of sexual identity. Similarly, in a coming-out group, one could include bisexual men because they share issues with gay men regarding accepting their desire for members of the same sex. In fact, many men who later identify as gay prefer to label themselves bisexual when they first begin to integrate their same-sex object choice (Isay, 1989). If, however, group cohesion is organized around a particular issue or theme not focused on identity formation, then including bisexual men may prove counterproductive to the group task. In an HIV-negative men's group, for example, including bisexual men may create scapegoating and divert the group's process away from the established group focus. At the same time, the limitations of agency provisions and geographic realities may require the group leader to adjust inclusion criteria for the needs of a bisexual client.

Self-Disclosure and Modeling

The social worker's disclosure of his or her own sexual orientation is essential to creating an affirmative environment in which clients can explore their sexuality. Isay (1989) and Frommer (1994) suggest that clients enter treatment with an inherently nonneutral, heterosexist assumption of a social worker's orientation. As a result, they believe a gay social worker should disclose this information when asked by the client and after a careful exploration to determine its meaning for the client in treatment. They contend that gay leaders provide invaluable opportunities for positive gay role models in a world where too few exist (Isay, 1989). Failure to self-disclose as a gay leader at the beginning of the group experience forsakes an invaluable opportunity to model an affirmative stance toward homosexuality in the service of establishing a trusting environment and building cohesion. Conlin and Smith (1985) believe that gay social workers leading groups for gay men should be in the late stage of their coming-out process. Such leaders may be more able to tolerate the often powerful and ambivalent feelings of those members who remain at earlier stages in the process and reflect to the group more subtle manifestations of homophobia in the group process.

The issue of self-disclosure for heterosexual social workers leading groups for gay men has not been adequately addressed in the literature. Gay affirmative theory seems to be moving toward asserting the value of gay clients receiving treatment from gay practitioners (Isay, 1989). However, the reality of human resources within social service agencies requires that heterosexual social workers also provide services to gay clients. The question of self-disclosure remains for heterosexual leaders, but the dynamics are significantly different. Particularly in short-term, problem-focused, and support groups, persistent focusing on the group leader who does not disclose may well sidetrack or derail the necessary tasks of the group and permit the development of maladaptive defenses against group affiliation and intimacy. In any group, a heterosexual social worker must have become a social anthropologist prior to beginning work with the group. He or she must not only identify his or her own homonegative attitudes, beliefs, and behaviors, but also must develop a firm understanding of and belief in the complexity of gay culture and life experiences.

While self-disclosure is important, how one handles disclosure is as important as the act of disclosing itself. The tension between offering a supportive, positive environment for self-exploration, on the one hand, and impinging on a client's ability to verbalize any and all feelings of shame and self-doubt, on the other, must inform the social worker's process of disclosing his or her sexual orientation to group members. The social worker who does not remain keenly aware of his or her own internalized homophobia may shut the door on more helpful explorations of shame and guilt and the healthy desire of members to identify with the gay group leader as a positive role model or a heterosexual leader as a genuinely informed and nurturing influence.

Case

A heterosexual female social worker experienced in group work with gay men was assigned to lead a coming-out group in the absence of openly gay staff at the university counseling service where she worked. After the second group session, the group fell into several weeks of very little activity in spite of the worker's skilled efforts to elicit participation. Long periods of silence were followed by occasional bickering and apologies between members. After 5 weeks, two members had dropped out of the group and those remaining began to express feelings of hopelessness. The worker's supervisor stated that these dynamics were not unusual in the beginning stages of group work and focused on processing the worker's anxiety about her difference from group members. Nonetheless, after reviewing the group process of the preceding weeks, the social worker suggested to the group in the next session that their disappointment and difficulty in moving forward was related not only to her gender difference but also to her perceived sexual orientation as heterosexual.

The group immediately responded. Several members finally expressed feelings of mistrust, anger, and disappointment that the leader was not a gay man. The social worker validated their concerns and managed to redirect the group's anger away from each other and toward her. Her ability to remain supportive and empathic during this period in the group process helped move the group to a new level of openness, understanding, and cohesion.

After many weeks, group members expressed idealized feelings toward the social worker and expressed surprise that they could experience her as particularly nurturing. One client joked, "You must be a lesbian." The group immediately picked up on this theme and demanded an answer, which the leader agreed to provide after the group explored their thoughts and fantasies on the subject. When the social worker finally acknowledged her heterosexuality, the members were able to explore more fully both their hetero-phobia and their homophobia within a safe environment.

Group Prospectus

A social worker, and sometimes an agency or another sponsoring organization, must decide whether a group should be open or closed and short or long term, based on the group's task and setting. To hasten acceptance within an nongay identified agency that has not previously had a gay-related group, a worker should structure the group to imitate the prevailing model for group work in the agency in order to integrate and normalize the group within the agency culture. These efforts not only elicit acceptance by staff and administration, but also suggest to gay clients that the agency provides a safe place to discuss and explore their sexual orientation.

Case

An openly gay social worker in a continuing day treatment program recognized the need for a gay men's group after several clients confided feeling isolated and unable to express themselves openly in groups, the primary treatment modality at the agency. The worker confronted agency homophobia by educating the staff about the needs of gay and lesbian clients and documenting clients' concerns. The executive director ultimately overrode the worker's immediate supervisor and sanctioned the group.

Initially, the group was composed of clients who had been attending the treatment program for some time. The group process seemed to parallel long-standing institutional beliefs that the group did not belong in the treatment program. Members projected powerful feelings of internalized homophobia onto each other and prevented group cohesion by verbally attacking each for coming out to community members outside of the group. One member stated, "I didn't come to this place to work on my sexual orientation or identity stuff I came here to deal with my psychiatric problems."

As some of the more hostile, intensely homophobic clients left the group, new clients who had entered treatment after the gay group had already been integrated into the agency began contributing more to the process. Members developed greater social relatedness as they began to see themselves not only as part of an affirming gay subgroup, but also as people integrated and accepted by the rehabilitative community. To date, the group has been ongoing for 4 years.

Whether homosexual or heterosexual, a social worker leading groups for gay men must be gay affirmative; cognizant of the powerful impact of homophobia on oneself and on one's clients and willing to address the issue directly; sensitive to the diverse experiences of gay and bisexual men; vigilant against subscribing to destructive stereotypes; and open to exploring both heterosexuality and homosexuality without permitting personal ideology or identity to contaminate professional explorations. In the authors' experience, coming out professionally not only enhances one's self-esteem and professional identity, but also may be a primary step toward helping an agency respond to the emotional needs of its gay, lesbian, and bisexual clients and staff. Hiring motivated, openly gay social workers may increase interest in and attention to the particular needs of gay men while providing essential role models for an all too often silenced, shamed, and ignored population. Armed with awareness, acceptance, and a genuine desire to be helpful, social workers working with gay men can create precious spaces in which these individuals can work toward developing self-esteem, integrating their sexuality, and building emotionally intimate relationships with their peers.

EVALUATION APPROACHES

Outcome measures for clients in gay men's groups remain anecdotal. To date, no instruments directly addressing the outcomes of work with this population in groups have been developed for public use, although instruments for addressing individual problems such as low self-esteem or homophobia could certainly be incorporated into an outcome study of group work with gay men. As in most group work, eliciting outcome information is an essential component of termination. Statements about improved psychosocial functioning seem to be the best barometer for determining the effectiveness of the group. Desire for continued affiliation with other gay men; a sense of belonging both within the gay community and within the larger social environment; improved social and intimate relationships; and diminished homophobic statements and behaviors all would testify to positive outcomes. As men in these groups learn to celebrate their everyday heroism and hard-earned strengths in living as openly gay, hopefully they will carry their resilience outside of their groups, use it to expand on previous roles, and adopt a more affirmative sense of themselves.

NATIONAL RESOURCES

For the most part, mental health services for this population are provided at the local and regional levels. To locate these services in a particular region, we suggest consulting the Gay Yellow Pages, which can be found in many bookstores and libraries.

American Civil Liberties Union/
Lesbian and Gay Rights Project
132 West 43rd St.
New York, NY 10036
(212) 944-9800

Gay and Lesbian Alliance Against
Defamation (GLAAD)
150 West 26th St.
New York, NY 10011
(212) 627-1398

The Hetrick Martin Institute
2 Astor Place
New York, NY 10003
(212) 674-2400

Lambda Legal Defense and
Education Fund
666 Broadway
New York, NY 10012
(212) 995-8585

National Gay and Lesbian Task
Force (NGLTF)
1734 14th St. NW
Washington, DC 20009
(202) 332-6483

Parents and Friends of Lesbians
and Gays (P-FLAG)
P.O. Box 96519
Washington DC 20090
(202) 638-4200

Pride Institute Hotline
(800) 54-PRIDE
(612) 934-7554 (within Minnesota)

Senior Action in a Gay Environment
(SAGE)
208 West 13th St.
New York, NY 10011
(212) 741-2247

REFERENCES

Abelove, H. (1993). Freud, male homosexuality and the Americans. In H. Abelove, M. Aina-Barale, & D. M. Halperin (Eds.), *The lesbian and gay studies reader* (pp. 381–393). New York: Routledge.

Ball, S. (1994). A group model for gay and lesbian clients with chronic mental illness. *Social Work, 39*(1), 109–115.

Bell, A. P., & Weinberg, M. S. (1978). *Homosexualities: A study of diversity among men and women.* New York: Simon & Schuster.

Bieber, I. (1962). *Homosexuality: A psychoanalytic study.* New York: Basic Books.

Cadwell, S. A., Burnham, R. A., & Forstein, M. (Eds.). (1994). *Therapists on the front line: Psychotherapy with gay men in the age of AIDS* (pp. 453–471). Washington, DC: American Psychiatric Press.

Caputo, L. (1985). Dual diagnosis: AIDS and addiction. *Social Work, 30*(4), 361–363.

Carballo-Dieguez, A. (1989). Hispanic culture, gay male culture, and AIDS: Counseling implications. *Journal of Counseling and Development, 68*(1), 26–30.

Cass, V. (1979). Homosexual identity formation: A theoretical model. *Journal of Homosexuality, 4,* 219–235.

Chan, C. (1989). Issues of identity development among Asian-American lesbians and gay men. *Journal of Counseling and Development, 68*(1), 16–20.

Coleman, E. (1982). The developmental stages of the coming out process. In J. C. Gonsiorek (Ed.), *Homosexuality and psychotherapy: A practitioner's handbook of affirmative models* (pp. 31–43). New York: Haworth Press.

Conlin, D., & Smith, J. (1985). Group psychotherapy for gay men. In J. Gonsiorek (Ed.), *A guide to psychotherapy with gay and lesbian clients* (pp. 105–112). New York: Harrington Park Press.

De la Vega, E. (1990). Considerations for reaching the Latino population with sexuality and HIV/AIDS information and education. *SIECUS Report, 18*(3), 1–8.

Deyton, B., & Lear, W. (1988). A brief history of the gay/lesbian health movement in the U.S.A. In M. Shernoff & W. Scott (Eds.), *The sourcebook of lesbian/gay healthcare* (2nd ed., pp. 15–19). Washington, DC: National Lesbian/Gay Health Foundation.

Eller, M., & King, D. (1990). Self help groups for gays, lesbians and their loved ones. In R. Kus (Ed.), *Keys to caring* (pp. 330–339). Boston: Alyson Publications.

Friedman, R. C. (1988). *Male homosexuality: A contemporary psychoanalytic perspective.* New Haven, CT: Yale University Press.

Frommer, M. S. (1994). Homosexuality and psychoanalysis: Technical considerations revisited. *Psychoanalytic Dialogues, 4.*

Gonsiorek, J. (1985). *A guide to psychotherapy with gay and lesbian clients.* New York: Harrington Park Press.

Gonsiorek, J. (1977). Psychological adjustment and homosexuality. *JSAS Catalog of Selected Documents in Psychology, 7,* 45 (MS No. 1478).

Hetrick, E. S., & Martin, A. D. (1987). Developmental issues and their resolution for gay and lesbian adolescents. In E. Coleman (Ed.), *Integrated identity for gay men and lesbians* (pp. 25–43). New York: Harrington Park Press.

Isay, R. (1989). *Being homosexual.* New York: Avon Books.

Isensee, R. (1991). *Growing up gay in a dysfunctional family.* New York: Prentice Hall.

Kus, R. (1990). *Keys to caring.* Boston: Alyson Publications.

Lewes, K. (1988). *The psychoanalytic theory of male homosexuality.* New York: Simon & Schuster.

Linde, R. (1994). Impact of AIDS on adult gay male development: Implications for psychotherapy. In S. A. Cadwell, R. A. Burnham, Jr. & M. Forstein

(Eds.), *Therapists on the front line: Psychotherapy with gay men in the age of AIDS* (pp. 453–471). Washington, DC: American Psychiatric Press.

Loiacano, D. (1989). Gay identity issues among black Americans: Racism, homophobia, and the need for validation. *Journal of Counseling and Development, 68*(1), 21–25.

Margolies, L., Becker, M. R., & Jackson-Brewer, (1987). Internalized homophobia: Identifying and treating the oppressor within. In Boston Lesbian Psychologies Collective (Eds.), *Lesbian psychologies: Explorations and challenges* (pp. 229–241). Chicago: University of Illinois Press.

Maylon, A. (1985). Psychotherapeutic implications of internalized homophobia in gay men. In J. Gonsiorek (Ed.), *A guide to psychotherapy with gay and lesbian clients* (pp. 105–112). New York: Harrington Park Press.

Nichols, S. E. (1986). Psychotherapy and AIDS. In T. S. Stein & C. J. Cohen (Eds.), *Contemporary perspectives on psychotherapy with lesbians and gay men* (pp. 209–239). New York: Plenum Press.

Nicolosi, J. (1991). *The reparative therapy of male homosexuality: A new clinical approach.* Northvale, NJ: Jason Aronson.

Odets, W. (1994). Survivor guilt in seronegative gay men. In S. A. Cadwell, R. A. Burnham, Jr. & M. Forstein (Eds.), *Therapists on the front line: Psychotherapy with gay men in the age of AIDS* (pp. 453–471). Washington, DC: American Psychiatric Press.

Peplau, L. A., & Cochran, S. D. (1990). A relational perspective on homosexuality. In D. McWhirter, S. Sanders, & J. Reinisch, (Eds.), *Homosexuality/heterosexuality* (pp. 321–349). New York: Oxford University Press.

Russell, A. & Winkler, R. (1977). Evaluation of assertiveness training and homosexual guidance service groups designed to improve homosexual functioning. *Journal of Consulting and Clinical Psychology, 45*(1), 1–13.

Schwartz, R., & Hartstein, N. (1986). Group psychotherapy with gay men. In T. Stein & C. Cohen (Eds.), *Contemporary perspectives on psychotherapy with lesbians and gay men* (pp. 157–177). New York: Plenum Press.

Shernoff, M. (1991). Eight years of working with people with HIV: The impact upon a therapist. In C. Silverstein (Ed.), *Gays, lesbians, and their therapists* (pp. 227–239). New York: W. W. Norton.

Silverstein, C. (Ed.). (1991). *Gays, lesbians, and their therapists.* New York: W. W. Norton.

Socarides, C. (1978). *Homosexuality.* New York: Jason Aronson.

Stein, T. S., & Cohen, C. J. (Eds.). (1986). *Psychotherapy with lesbians and gay men.* New York: Plenum Press.

Tunnel, G. (1994). Special issues in group psychotherapy for gay men with AIDS. In S. A. Cadwell, R. A. Burnham, Jr., & M. Forstein (Eds.), *Therapists on the front line: Psychotherapy with gay men in the age of AIDS* (pp. 453–471). Washington, DC: American Psychiatric Press.

Yalom, I. (1995). *The theory and practice of group psychotherapy* (4th ed.). New York: Basic Books.

19

Group Work with Lesbians

Bonnie J. Engelhardt

The purpose of this chapter is to acquaint social workers with the important issues facing lesbian women and to promote social group work as the primary modality offered to the lesbian client. Lesbians are at risk in our heterosexist, misogynist, homophobic society. They cannot participate fully in our societal institutions and are denied social acceptance. It is therefore imperative to include this chapter in a social work textbook focusing on at-risk populations. Previously, little nonheterosexist material was available for new workers. An *Annotated Bibliography of Gay and Lesbian Readings*, edited by Judith A. B. Lee, under the sponsorship of the Commission on Lesbian Women and Gay Men of the Council on Social Work Education, was published in 1991. It was developed out of the Council's mandate "to build knowledge about diversity and its commitment to oppressed groups"(p. i). The introduction of this second edition states, "it represents approximately a twenty-year survey and review of the literature with an eye toward what is genuinely helpful to minorities of sexual orientation" (p. v), noting that previously articles had been written in "medical language with words like 'deviance,' 'perversion,' 'ego dystonic homosexuality,' 'developmental arrest,'" and other pejorative terminology.

As clinical social workers, we cannot support any implication that the primary cause of lesbians' difficulties in adjusting to their sexual identity is intrapsychic. The primary obstacles for any minority group today originate in the dominant culture and interaction with it. Social workers have written about the experience of racism, classism, sexism, and ageism on our clientele, but this chapter deals with homophobia stemming from our heterosexist society. Herek (1986), looking at the social psychology of homophobia, defined heterosexism "as a world-view, a value system that prizes heterosexuality, assumes it is the only appropriate manifestation of love and sexuality, and devalues homosexuality" (p. 924). Homophobia is defined as the "prejudice, discrimination, and hostility directed at gay men and lesbian women because of their sexual orientation" (Ellis & Murphy, 1994, p. 50). It should be noted that the experience of homophobia linked with sexism is unique to the lesbian culture and that lesbians of color often experience the triple threat of racism, sexism, and homophobia.

As social group workers, we favor group work as the primary modality offered to the lesbian client, whether or not the leader is a lesbian. Group work provides a connection with other lesbians in a safe, partially controlled environment and places responsibility for the evolution of the content and process on the members, not the leader. This allows the diversity needed for individual lesbians, who might be lost in their own identity crises, to appreciate that there are many right choices about how to live one's life as a lesbian. It diffuses the power of the leader and clarifies the need for variety in the role modeling available to women entering the lesbian community. It is an invaluable experience to be in the company of lesbian women talking about their lives because, for all of us, the *invisibility* of the lesbian lifestyle is prominent. In groups, lesbians can gain a perspective on how their choices are similar to or different from those of other lesbians, thereby acquiring more knowledge of what is the norm of lesbian life.

It is important to understand that there is no unified lesbian community, only many distinct lesbian communities. There is no typical lesbian, but rather many unique lesbian women who have developed individually into the type of lesbian that they are today. Good social work practice entails getting the particulars from any lesbian about her own development as a lesbian without making *any* assumptions. It is empowering to an individual to experience her own experience as being a valid developmental process without trying to impose a societal stereotype, a social work definition, or a lesbian community mandate. Having established that no one person, process, or experience is typical, we can then proceed to look for the commonalities. There are no universal paths to lesbian identity development, but coming out or disclosure stages have been noted in the literature (Lehman, 1978; Roth, 1985; Roth & Murphy, 1986). Five or six stages are usually noted including disclosure to self, significant family members, and intimate others, disclosure at the workplace and in social networks, and identification with the lesbian label and community.

Social workers must be cognizant of the lesbian client's intrapsychic and sociopolitical issues in order to help her decide whether her presenting problems are primarily:

- intrapsychic issues, and a therapy group is needed;
- related to her coming-out process, and a group focused on self-acceptance and disclosure strategies is appropriate;
- isolation-based issues so that a support group is needed to connect her to the lesbian subculture;
- issues of oppression and discrimination, so that an action-oriented empowerment group would be helpful;
- a combination of these situations requiring more than one type of group intervention.

Social workers need to provide opportunities for women to find their natural processes of self-disclosure and disclosure to others without stigmatization. We need to be able to differentiate the more vulnerable women who could become marginalized during the coming-out process. Even though there is debate about whether lesbianism is caused or created—predetermined genetically or chosen as a preference—everyone does agree that the lesbian woman has to continue to make the choice of self-disclosure or disclosure to others every day. A safe group environment is especially helpful for this process. A group may be composed entirely of lesbian women and formed with this awareness in mind or it may contain lesbians, with or without the knowledge of the nonlesbian members.

The phrase *lesbian women* is used by Murphy (1992) "to affirm the use of the terms gay and lesbian as *adjectives* rather than as *nouns* to highlight that sexual orientation is only one aspect of an individual's life AND to emphasize that lesbian women may have more in common with heterosexual women than with gay men" (p. 242). As noted above, only for the lesbian is the experience of homophobia linked with sexism. While this double identity may allow some lesbians to feel comfortable in all-women's groups or in all-gay groups, in my experience this does not work for all lesbian women. For example, it is not uncommon for lesbian feminists to feel alienated in a group of heterosexual women even though they identify with the women's movement. Similarly, women who identify strongly with the gay rights movement may resent having to deal with gender differences with their male brothers.

LesBiGay is a new term used to affirm the range of possible gay individuals including gay men, bisexual women and men, and lesbians. The understanding that coming out is a process and is on a spectrum is only now being written and codified so that all persons can be informed of the various life issues affecting lesbians. It should be noted that until recently, the mainstream culture's understanding of the lesbian experience has been gained primarily through observation of the gay male lifestyle.

There have always been lesbians who identified with a wide spectrum of the lesbian community and those who identified with only a small part. The paths of many subcommunities never cross; the sadomasochistic community, the radical lesbian socialists, the bar crowd, the study group women, the feminist woman–identified lesbians who may or may not have had sexual relations with a woman. Oppression and the resultant invisibility keep these communities separate and isolated. Social group work is the best vehicle to help an individual find her place in this possibly confusing spectrum of options.

COMMON THEMES

The themes that regularly arise in groups designed for lesbian women will now be considered.

Management of Oppression, Stigma, and Difference

> Gay adults often describe themselves as having felt "different" from other children. The factors leading to a sense of difference are diverse. . . . In boys these tend to be aesthetic and intellectual; in girls, they are athletic. Beginning in children, many gay and lesbian people have feelings of shame at being considered deviant, as well as feelings of self-hatred because they identify with those who devalue them. Such feelings arise from identification with the aggressor, a mental mechanism experienced by many victims of abuse. (Friedman & Downey, 1994, p. 926)

The management of shame, self-hatred, and internalized homophobia is required for every lesbian. Internalized homophobia is experienced as internalizing the prejudicial, pejorative views of the homosexual held by the dominant society. Marginalized lesbian women are especially vulnerable because they lack a positive gay identity. Psychologically vulnerable women, teenage girls, and elderly women may resort to alcohol and drug abuse, and there is a higher tendency toward suicide, especially for teenagers (Friedman & Downey, 1994, p. 926). Work performance and career advancement can be seriously impaired by internal and external dilemmas with the development of a lesbian identity. Social group workers must be prepared to deal with despair, alienation, rage, loss, anger, and hostility and to help clients turn these feelings appropriately outward to injustices in the dominant culture.

Invisibility of the Lesbian Woman's Experience

The reality of oppression leads to the invisibility of the identified lesbian woman in our society today. In the lesbian community, the formation of an identity is much more difficult when subcommunities are divided and invisible to each other. Because of the limited number of visible role models, the lesbian subculture has had difficulty developing a nonstigmatized identity. In the dominant culture, confusion can develop and stereotypes can prevail. Lesbians themselves tend to underestimate the complexities of the invisibility factor and the toll it takes on their psychological development.

Safety and Vigilance Issues

Many lesbians have experienced gay bashing ranging from verbal harassment to physical assault. The threat of physical and emotional harm is a powerful determinant of lesbian women's mental health. The actual experience or the veiled threat can dictate constrictiveness, hiddenness, and paranoia or a reactive, self-conscious, or overexpressive behavior pattern. Sometimes mental health professionals have judged these behaviors to be adolescent and acting out rather than seeing them as coping mechanisms for dealing with harassment, assault, and persecution.

It should be noted that the humiliation, shame, and lack of empowerment that physical and sexual abuse survivors experience prevents them from easily acknowledging their difficulties with their own safety. The social group worker needs to create a structure that acknowledges the appropriateness of their dilemma and a language for the entire group to use in negotiating trust and emotional closeness.

Lesbian Relationships and Sexual Expression

Lesbian sexuality and sexual behavior in long-term relationships are more frequently written about than perhaps other aspects of lesbian life. Loulan observed that "frequency of sex among lesbian couples drops off dramatically after the first year" and that "it's so much easier to become passionate about the things we don't like about each other. But who would want to have sex with someone who is critical?" (1987, pp. 103, 117). There appears to be a high correlation between a lesbian's satisfaction with her relationship and satisfaction with her sex life. "Even with infrequent sex, it seems that a woman remains satisfied with her sex life because she feels loved" (Loulan, 1987, p. 202). Murphy hypothesized that "although internalized homophobia affects the sexual relationships of both gay and lesbian couples, the differences in amount of sexual activity and sexual exclusivity may be seen as reflections of gender socialization" (1994, p. 21). "Lesbian women report that they are happy with their amount of sexual activity and that they have more affectionate and non-genital sexual contact than heterosexual and gay male couples" (Murphy, 1994, p. 22).

The goal of the social group worker is to reduce the stigma of discussing lesbian sexuality and to increase the ability of the client to develop her own norms. In groups the worker must take an active stance, leading conversation and providing information on sex. Bibliotherapy and structured group exercises can help reduce anxiety for everyone.

The value of lesbian couples' groups is immeasurable; because there is little visible role modeling, however, the fear of being seen as "abnormal," "not good enough," or an "immature couple" is great. Good preparation is needed, and a focused educational format with enough time for telling the couple's "story" is optimal.

Living with Dignity as a Declared Lesbian Women

No one can deny the stress of living as a member of a minority group in an oppressed subculture; physical, psychological, emotional, and spiritual stressors continually occur. Managing conflictual inner and outer messages is the accepted reality for all lesbians.

By the time one goes through the coming-out stages, makes peace with one's losses and gains, and accepts a lesbian identity usually a very strong personal sense of self has developed. The lesbian woman today has gifts to give to the general culture, especially in the area of building self-esteem. Brown, a lesbian ethicist, states: "three intertwined themes I see as defining, cross-situationally, the experience of being lesbian and gay: *biculturalism*, with its requirements of juggling, balance and living in and with ambiguity; *marginality*, with its perspective that is both outside and from within; and *normative creativity*, the ability to create boundaries that will work where none exist or may be only partially suited to the task" (1990, p. 2). Examples of courage and perseverance are found particularly in multiply-oppressed lesbians. "A number of clinicians have suggested that the cultural expectations of Asian, African-American, Latino/Latin and Jewish gay men and lesbian women present them (and the couples in which they are members) with unique stress. . . . Although each community offers some support, each has its own expectations and demands which often conflict with each other. The tension of living in these three communities, in all of which one feels marginalized, adds to identity difficulties" (Murphy, 1994, p. 25).

Although it is not always clear to a lesbian woman whether it is better for her physical health (raises risk to assault and harassment) or her economic health (creates the risk of job discrimination, eviction, and loss of family support) to disclose fully her sexual orientation, living as a declared lesbian has may advantages. One's psychological well-being is greatly enhanced by a reduction of ambivalence and inner anxiety. Removing from one's mind and emotions the constant quandary of when to "come out" frees a significant amount of life energy for other purposes.

PRACTICE PRINCIPLES

Sensitize Your Organization as Well as Yourself

The Council on Social Work Education Curriculum Policy statement states:

> Special Populations: The social work profession, by virtue of its system of ethics, its traditional value commitments, and its long history of work in the whole range of human services, is committed to preparing students to understand and appreciate cultural and social diversity. The profession has also been concerned about the consequences of oppression. . . . The curriculum . . . should include content on other special population group . . . in particular, groups that have been consistently affected by social, economic and legal bias or oppression. Such groups include those distinguished by age, religions, disablement, *sexual orientation*, and culture. (Council on Social Work Education, 1982, cited in Gochros, 1984, p. 154; emphasis added)

This policy statement means that your social work agency and your social work training/placement should be sensitive to the issues of gay and lesbian populations and that you will not be alone in trying to create opportunities to serve these populations in your agency. Do not be surprised, however, if that is not so. There are many inherent difficulties even in discovering these populations in your caseload. Although it is always supportive to provide opportunities for clients to come out on intake forms or management information systems (MIS) data sheets, do not underestimate the fear of discrimination and homophobia that might prevent a client from choosing to be open early in the intake process.

Develop Comfort with Learning from Group Members

Do not overstate your knowledge or competencies to your clients or supervisors. It is important, when appropriate, to be a beginner about subculture issues, to ask thoughtful questions, and to seek advise about how to prepare for your role as group leader. You may also need to be prepared to clarify to the group your own sexual preferences, or to talk about sexual practices or ask questions that might imply sexual practices. Don't let feelings of shame or embarrassment stop you. Consult with a knowledgeable person and reveal your lack of knowledge of the lesbian woman's experience. Be direct and share concerns that you feel might be limiting your effectiveness with your clients. Do not rely on the clients as your primary source of information; our work is a partnership, and you must supply your own knowledge and experience.

Communicate Your Positions on Issues

For the most part, lesbians appreciate heterosexuals taking the initiative to bring up the subject of gayness, especially in positions that have a possibly negative effect on the status of the lesbian (job or work settings, authority settings like schools, physicians' offices, etc.). A gay-positive atmosphere or environment can be created in which diversity and differences are affirmed. Taking definite stands on antigay jokes and antigay literature is noticed especially in the workplace. Many persons have come to understand gayness through a family member, a close business/work relationship, or a homosexual encounter. While social workers should be encouraged to work with lesbians in groups, I believe that specialized knowledge, training, and empathetic connection are vital for building trust and being effective.

Lesbians come in every size, shape, and color; variety is the norm. Many women defy the lesbian stereotype. The social group worker's responsibility is to program opportunities to discuss discrimination, stereotypes, and prejudice. Encouraging group interaction and direct feedback to each other is invaluable helping the individual lesbian understand how she is perceived by others.

Because lesbians are a hidden minority, it is very important to always assume that someone in your group is a lesbian; has a lesbian mother, sister, aunt, or child; or could be developing any of these options. It is equally important to assume that your boss, your secretary, or your mail carrier is possibly a lesbian or has a lesbian relative. In this way, you will open your eyes to the difficulties or knowing who is actually a lesbian. You will hear antigay jokes and know that someone who is listening is unable to speak out against the ignorance being displayed because of fear of declaring her identity. As you take the subject of lesbianism seriously, you will begin to experience the internal struggles of trying to decide when and where to tackle persons on their homophobia.

You must appreciate the burden of managing the dominant culture's constant and intrusive influence on the lesbian's life. An excerpt from an anxiety reduction group for lesbians follows:

> *Beth*: You don't know what is real or not; are you being paranoid or would my supervisor tell our boss that I'm gay just to further her career? I can't take the chance; I change all of my pronouns, don't let my lover call me at work, and I don't know what I will do when the baby is born. I run out at break and call her because her workplace is much more accepting; they know that she is a lesbian and pregnant. But she doesn't want me to come to her work parties because she thinks that I look too "butch" and that her staff might be uncomfortable with me or with us both present and acting like a couple.
>
> *Yvonne*: Do you think that you look too butch? Could you grow your hair a little longer and that might help? You probably wouldn't be wearing your work boots at the party either, right?
>
> *Beth:* I don't think that I look butch at work. Most of the workers in my department are men, and we all dress casual; my supervisor is almost the only one in the entire company that wears a dress. I'm afraid that I can't really change how I look that much—sort of androgynous, I hope. To try and change my looks and personality—now that would really make anxious. Do I really have to look different to feel less anxious?
>
> *Group worker*: How have others in the group dealt with these issues? Do you sometimes wonder if you are being paranoid? The presence of homophobia in our workplace is very real, but I would like us to focus here on sharing your tips and strategies for managing this multidimensional dilemma.

By acknowledging both the reality of the homophobia/heterosexism and the need to be proactive, the group worker encourages members and emphasizes the need to be proactive. Thus, the group worker encourages members to develop resilient behaviors. Be aware, however, that as some group members share examples of courageous behaviors, some clients are inspired but others may feel depression and anxiety.

Set Clear Guidelines and Contract for Them

A common experience in lesbian group life is having couples begin to form sexual relationships (subgroups) and the difficulties that occur for those who are being left out, that is, not chosen. Although group workers usually develop 'rules' at the beginning of groups against involvement with a member of the group, this continues to occur. The experience of intimacy and closeness in the company of other lesbians in a safe setting is almost overwhelming for some women, and no amount of discussion in advance will deter from them acting on their sexual feelings. The author has found it useful to encourage the group to articulate these issues in the first two sessions, focusing on the experience of being in the group and eliciting feelings about both situations: getting sexually involved and not getting sexually involved. Role playing can be a useful tool, utilizing warmups of inclusion/exclusion or "what if" scenarios—What would happen to our group if sexual feelings are acted upon by _____ and _____? Encouraging women to get together in small groups only outside the group can also act as a deterrent. Making agreements to share all contacts outside the group immediately, including phone calls, will make the information available to all members of the group and avoid surprises. It is the group's responsibility, along with the worker, to manage the balance of intimacy, intensity, sexuality, and appropriate boundaries.

RECOMMENDED WAYS OF WORKING

Use of Time and the Program

Due to a lack of "visibility" and "role modeling" within the dominant culture for lesbians, it is very important to create opportunities within group structures to provide remedial experiences.

The importance of allowing sufficient time for women to tell their stories cannot be underestimated; to share with other lesbian women and with other lesbian-affirmative women the secret experiences of everyday life is very empowering. Groups often provide a way to have the first contact with a declared lesbian or with the lesbian community; often individuals are encouraged by case workers to sign up for a coming-out group or an informational lesbian consciousness group. The worker may have assessed with her client that she is ready to begin contact with other lesbians in the process of clarifying her sexual identity. It is very important for the group leader to screen potential group members to determine what phase of the process they are in; if possible, it is best for the group worker to know the range of experiences that members have had so that all aspects can be included within the norm. Examples include a 50-year-old woman, married, with three children, who has had a 48-year-old lover, married, with two children, for 12 years; a 27-year-old woman who has never had a sexual relationship with anyone but has had a best friend since college whom she loves and lives with; an 18-year-old woman who has had three short-term relationships with women, but none of whom call themselves lesbian. The program would need to be structured to discuss choice of partners, labels to be considered for oneself, the role of children in the woman's life, and the struggle between the sexual self (perhaps just flowering) and the parental and career roles. Because of the nature of some of the issues involved, I believe that coming-out groups need to be run by lesbian group workers. More needs to be known about the special role of a worker who shares the characteristics of the group being served. Perhaps more could be learned by looking to the substance abuse field, the sexual abuse field, or the disability field. Any group leaders, however, might find themselves in a position to help a client engage in these dilemmas; therefore, I consider it important to discuss them. Any worker can support the healthy aspects of the choice and look for any dysfunctional responses (always looking through the lens of oppression and prejudice).

In the author's experience, short-term groups work best when the purpose is educational or when everyone in the group has one or two pivotal life experiences in common (e.g., being Hispanic, being a mother, being an executive). The formation of a long-term group lends itself to the inclusion of more differences and allows interests to evolve as cohesion is built as part of the group process. The use of program materials can always be used to add variety; for example, an all-white able-bodied mothers' group can learn from a videotape featuring Asian women, disabled women, or gay men in nurturing or mothering roles. Books, videotapes, and audiotapes are wonderful resources for showing healthy role models and helping lesbian women to visualize how their behavior might change. These resources are available from gay and lesbian organizations locally and nationally; catalogs are also available if you live in an inaccessible area.

The use of activities to enhance communication nonverbally and to focus communication verbally has been documented by Middleman (1980) and Lynn and Nisivoccia (1992). Creating a genogram, especially noting to whom one has disclosed one's lesbianism, provides a rapid connection for most people to their problems with the coming-out process and to the issue of shame. By adapting anxiety and depression scales, as well as attitude and fear surveys that have been used to help focus symptoms and to show change, you can help group members focus on how much of their current anxiety and depression appears to be rooted in homophobia. Sometimes it is especially useful to have the group create the instrument together. Collages of society's view of the lesbian lifestyle, created by clients at home and presented to the group, can be very evocative.

Coleadership is never my first choice of leadership model for women's groups. Although traditionally it has been used in special circumstances where it has served a particular purpose (e.g., to allow a trainee to gain experience with a difficult population, to provide male–female balance), I have not found the usefulness of the method to outweigh the difficulties of trying to coordinate two leadership styles into one leadership role for a group. The primary exception that I have encountered concerns groups where physical safety and controls are needed and where emotional expressions of the group (sexual abuse or domestic violence) are best shared by two leaders.

Ethical Behaviors and Boundaries

These are expected from all social group workers working with groups but are especially important in working with an invisible and marginalized community group. Relationships that meet the worker's needs and are not focused on those of the lesbian client are inappropriate and harmful. More has been written recently about female sexual abuse perpetrators (Gartrell, 1994) and lesbian domestic violence (Morrow & Hawhurst, 1989). More attention is needed to these issues because of many lesbians' and professionals' denial and avoidance. Sexual behavior and a sexual relationship is never appropriate between member and group worker; it can be especially destructive in group situations when a secret is being kept by one member of the group and the worker. Sexualizing and flirtatious behavior is destructive in group situations because of the power imbalance between worker and member; it also creates specialness and competition among members. Supervision and consultation should always be sought for help in tricky multiple relationship areas, especially if you have any doubts about whether your behavior is in the best interests of the member and the group.

Initial Screening Session

If possible, an initial individual screening session is always useful. Gathering data on the following is useful:

- The individual's knowledge of the coming-out process and where she is currently on the continuum.
- Her current coping skills and social support network.
- How shame and internalized homophobia have been addressed. Ask directly: "How have you handled your internalized homophobia and your experiences of shame?"
- Whether alcohol and substance abuse have been part of the client's life and the family history in regard to alcohol, drugs, violence, and neglect.
- How the client is managing the balance between privacy, disclosure to self, and disclosure to others. This question should always be asked.

In addition, be conscious of the complexities of multiple oppressions. If you are working with a disabled lesbian woman, you may need to get additional information through self-help groups or disability literature. If you are working with a member of another culture, knowing the customs of dealing with privacy and sexuality will help the communication.

Aligning Yourself with the Member's Perspective

It is crucial to assume that the client is doing the best she can in the coming-out process. It is not wise to push a client to come out, both because the outcome can be so variable and because the choice is better made when the client feels ready and able. With a client who says that she is being persecuted or could be persecuted, always start by believing the statement because so little validation is available for her position within the dominant culture. Even liberal colleagues and the social work community can do harm at times by not believing the client's experience.

Help with Planning

An important practice principle is to help members realize that they need a *plan* to deal with their families of origin and with their created families. Too often clients sink into despair because they feel they have to take care and be supportive of their families while their families are processing their losses and expressing dismay about the client's lesbian identity. The members of the group can give reasons for the correctness of the decision and can also reflect on how difficult it is to hear about anger and emotional turmoil when the woman wants her family of origin to be happy and eager to meet her new lover. Having definite plans for holidays that work for the lesbian woman is crucial. Holidays can be traumatic for lesbians, whether they have declared their status to their families or not. For example:

> *Member:* Even though my mother knows that I am in a relationship now, she still hasn't asked Judy to come to our house for Thanksgiving dinner yet. How long should I wait before I say something? I asked my sister, Kate, and she said that probably since this is the first Thanksgiving since Dad's death, I shouldn't push it. I feel confused because I don't want to upset my mother's holiday, but it is my life, too, and we [she and her lover] have so little time together that I would hate to spend the holiday apart. We have been together for five years, and we have spent the last year coming out in many more places and feeling good about our relationship, and it feels like a step backward.
>
> *Worker:* Could anyone else share how you planned their first few family encounters with your new partner? Did you involve your siblings and friends in the planning or did you do it primarily alone?

Talking about all of the possibilities in a group of individuals who have experienced many of these options is invaluable to the lesbian woman's learning experience of herself and her motives. Understanding that a range of options is available may be new information for her. It is more effective to have members describe how they have handled or would handle this situation than to have the individual social worker work through this with the lesbian client.

EVALUATION MEASURES

One positive outcome of the managed-care movement in mental health has been the emphasis on outcomes and outcome research. At first, it was difficult to change my language and perceptions from intuitions and feelings to numbers and points on a scale. My evaluative expressions of the individual's experience in the group used to be that "she is stuck," "making progress," "having a hard time," and "feeling safe enough to work on her issues." The group evaluative statements used to include "group is stuck," "group is developing leadership," and "group went well tonight." Now I am able to change most of the language on goals, progress, and stuckness into scales for the individual in the group. More techniques are needed to help us evaluate group progress.

It is helpful to utilize specific behavioral terms for goals, group activities, and homework or activities that clients do outside the group. We attempt to develop statements for how they will know when they have reached their goals before the group begins. Group feedback and anecdotal evidence are still the primary tools used to evaluate effectiveness. I often use the next to the last session to evaluate and encourage members to give each other feedback as well. We compare the pregroup goals and the postgroup evaluation, and members are often extremely insightful about the changes made during the life of the group.

Readings

For up-to-date information, see Journal of Gay and Lebian Psychotherapy, published by Haworth Press. Also look for the Gay Yellow Pages.

NATIONAL RESOURCES

Children of Lesbians and Gays
　Everywhere (COLAGE)
2300 Market St.
P.O. Box 165
San Francisco, CA 94114
(415) 861-5437

Disabled Womyn's Educational
　Project—Dykes, Disability and
　Stuff
P.O. Box 8773
Madison, WI 53708

Gay and Lesbian Parents Coalition
　International (GLPCI)
P.O. Box 50360
Washington, DC 20091
(202) 583-8029

Lesbian Connection
Helen Diner Memorial Women's
　Center
Ambitious Amazons
P.O. Box 811
East Lansing, MI 48826
(517) 371-5257

Lesbian/Gay Bisexual Committees
　(NASW)
750 First St. NW
Washington, DC 20005
(202) 408-8600 ext. 276

Parents and Friends of Lesbians and
    Gays (P-FLAG)
P.O. Box 96519
Washington, DC 20090
(202) 638-4200

Senior Action in a Gay Environment
    (SAGE)
208 West 13th Street
New York, NY 10011
(212) 741-2247

REFERENCES

Brown, L. S. (1990). *Making psychology safe for gays and lesbians.* Paper presented at the 98th Annual Convention of the American Psychological Association, Boston.

Ellis, P., & Murphy, B. C. (1994). The impact of misogyny and homophobia on therapy with women. In M. Merkin (Ed.), *Women in context: Toward a feminist reconstruction of psychology* (pp. 48–73). New York: Guilford Press.

Friedman, R. & Downey, J. (1994). Homosexuality. *New England Journal of Medicine, 331* (14), 923–930.

Gartrell, N. (1994). Boundaries in lesbian therapist-client relationships. In B. Greene & G. Hereck (Eds.), *Lesbian and gay psychology* (Vol. 1, pp. 98–117). Thousand Oaks, CA: Sage Publications.

Gochros, H. L. (1984). Teaching social workers to meet the needs of the homosexually oriented. *Journal of Social Work and Human Sexuality, 2*(2/3), 137–156.

Herek, G. (1986). The social psychology of homophobia: Toward a practical theory. *Review of Law and Social Change, 14*(4), 923–934.

Lee, J. A. B. (Ed.) (1991). *An annotated bibiliography of gay and lesbian readings,* New York: Cummings & Hathaway.

Lehman, J. L. (1978). What it means to love another woman. In G. Vida (Ed.), *Our right to love* (p. 25). Englewood Cliffs, NJ: Prentice-Hall.

Loulan, J. (1987). *Lesbian passion.* San Francisco: Spinsters, Inc.

Lynn, M. & Nisivoccia, D. (1992). *Activity groups: Integrating the "doing" with special populations.* Paper presented at the 14th Annual Symposium of the Association for the Advancement of Social Work with Groups, Atlanta.

Middleman, R. (1980). *The non-verbal method in working with groups: The use of activity in teaching, counseling and therapy.* Bloomfield, CT: Practitioner Press.

Morrow, S. L., & Hawhurst, D. M. (1989). Lesbian partner abuse—implications for therapists. *Journal of Counseling and Development, 68*(1), 58–62.

Murphy, B. C. (1991). Coming out of the classroom closet. In K. Harbeck (Ed.), *Educating mental health professionals about gay and lesbian issues* (pp. 229–246). New York: Haworth Press.

Murphy, B. C. (1994). Difference and diversity: Gay and lesbian couples. *Journal of Gay and Lesbian Social Services, 1*(2), 5–31.

Roth, S. (1985). Psychotherapy with lesbian couples: Individual issues, female socialization and the social context. *Journal of Marital and Family Therapy, 11*(3), 273–286.

Roth, S., & Murphy, B. C. (1986). Therapeutic work with lesbian clients: A systemic therapy view. In M. Ault-Riche (Ed.), *Women and family therapy* (pp. 78–89). Rockville, MD: Aspen Press.

VI

SCHOOLS AND THE
WORKPLACE

20

Group Work with Urban African-American Parents in Their Neighborhood Schools

Geoffrey L. Greif

It is well known that inner-city youth, particularly minority youth, are an at-risk population. Poverty, inadequate housing (Halpern, 1990), and racism (Taylor, Chatters, Tucker, & Lewis, 1990), when combined with an environment rife with drugs, crime, and teenage pregnancy, make life a difficult trek in the early years. The school systems, often underfunded in major cities due to a shrinking or static tax base, can be ill equipped to meet the educational, much less the emotional, needs of children. Parents and parent figures are also affected by these problems, as well as by the high unemployment rate. Their own resources are sorely depleted. A feeling of powerlessness, a traditional target of social work practice (Parsons, 1991), abounds. A cycle is maintained in which parents with diminished resources are raising children in great need. Finally, traditional attempts to assist minority clients often fall short because of a lack of understanding of the culture (Boyd-Franklin, 1989), their overwhelming needs, and a lack of resources.

This chapter describes a parenting support group in three different Baltimore city public schools in a neighborhood that has historically been underserved. Dominated by housing projects and young families, the area

Versions of this chapter appear in G. L. Greif (1993). A school-based support group for urban African American parents. *Social Work in Education*, *15*, 133–139; G. L. Greif (1994). Using family therapy ideas with parenting groups in schools. *Journal of Family Therapy*, *16*, 199–207; and J. Mackey & G. L. Greif (1994). Using rituals to help parents in the school setting: Lessons from family therapy. *Social Work in Education*, *16*, 171–178.

is frequently described as one of the worst in Baltimore in terms of crime rate and poverty. This chapter describes the group and the parenting issues that members bring to the group. Discussion of how these issues are handled is included.

REVIEW OF THE LITERATURE

As low-income African-American families have historically received few or no services (Kalyanpur & Rao, 1991), group work, based on the concept of mutual aid (Shulman, 1992), provides a forum for parents to join together and help each other. Here the suggestions emanating from the group will be consistent with the neighborhood's and culture's style of parenting. Group work also has the potential to reduce the isolation so often felt by these parents while providing education and support (Gitterman, 1989). The benefits of groups also include experiences of universality, the instillation of hope, and the feeling of greater strength in numbers. Rehearsal of new parenting behaviors can be attempted, and parents may gain insight into their own approaches to the children they are raising (Shulman, 1992; Yalom, 1995).

The social worker as a partner in the school setting is a well-established role, whether functioning as an employee or as a consultant. Leading parent groups to provide both intervention and prevention (see, e.g., O'Donnell, Hawkins, Catalano, Abbott, & Day, 1995) is clearly part of the social work function. Not much has been written, though, about group work specifically with African-American parents. Literature on work with the African-American family in general has suggested the importance of relationship building, focusing on strengths, keeping interventions concrete, and gathering information about who is considered part of the family (Boyd-Franklin, 1989; Hines, 1989).

The notion of family, particularly for a white worker, often needs to be broadened to include those living in the home rather than only those related by blood. In addition, as Proctor and Davis (1994) indicate, if the worker is of a different race (as is the case with this group leader and these parents), issues of difference cannot be ignored and the worker must show his or her skill, concern, and ability to offer meaningful help during the group meetings.

PRACTICE PRINCIPLES

This group is given the name "Help! My Kids Are Driving Me Crazy!" The title was picked to convey with humor what parents frequently experience while raising their children. A more straightforward title might have been more threatening. The group is held in several public elementary schools in downtown Baltimore. The attendees are usually mothers and occasionally grandmothers, great-grandmothers, and fathers. It is a 60-minute drop-in group set up to provide mutual aid (see Shulman,

1992), with parents encouraged to help each other. In addition, it functions as a socioeducational group. As Radin (1985) states, such groups can be educative in format, place the worker on a more equal footing with the clients, and are based on nonpathological assumptions. Philosophically, the group is driven by the notion that parenting is a developmental process, that each new stage of a child's growth may pose difficulty for both the child and the parent. The group can help ease that transition by providing support and education about normal stages of development. These parents are also buffeted by the stresses inherent in their environment and by larger social institutions, like Child Protective Services, the Housing Authority, or the Department of Social Services. While these institutions are designed to benefit the parents, they are often perceived as unresponsive and intrusive. Thus the group also deals with issues impinging on the family from the outside.

While long-term supportive work is the major purpose of the group, some parents attend only one or two sessions. For this reason, each group should be a learning and supportive experience in itself. Some sessions address a specific topic that is planned in advance, while others have an open format. The members are encouraged to share concerns about their children and are asked to keep confidential all information they hear from other members.

The leader's level of participation is an important component, particularly when working with a client population from a different racial and economic background. Too much input too early in the group process might be construed as controlling. Yet it is also standard practice for a leader to be active at the beginning of a group in order to establish group structure and allay normal anxiety. There was a beginning period at the first school when the members and worker sized each other up. An African-American coleader from the parent body, a key person in the success of that particular group, was more active at the beginning. With the parents (the author is white), once the worker was accepted by the group, it was important to be active, as he had been incorporated into the group as a parent and as a person with expertise, the "doctor" from the university. The danger of taking a peripheral role during the middle phase of group work, a role often suggested in the literature on group therapy, is that the leader is perceived as withholding or rejecting. The standard approach was modified. Once the leader was accepted, an active role was assumed and parent issues were both discussed by the leader *and* turned back on the group. It became possible to be active during all phases. The leader also met occasionally outside of the group for consultation with parents who did not feel comfortable using the group to discuss their issues. While this approach theoretically might have undermined the work of the group, given the drop-in nature of the group it was seen to accommodate the needs of the parents.

The groups, which have been conducted for different lengths of time since they started in 1990, were set up to meet weekly or monthly (depending on the school). The parents and leader agreed to meet for a certain period of time, and then stop and determine if they wished to continue. This held the parents and worker to a joint commitment and, depending on the culture of the school, proved effective most of the time. Occasionally, groups ran out of steam because the school administration failed to provide a meeting place and refreshments.

COMMON THEMES

A number of issues have surfaced at various schools during the years the groups have been in existence. These tend to center on the following themes: disciplining the difficult child; dealing with the noncustodial parent who visits sporadically (usually the father and sometimes the mother if a grandmother was attending the group); managing intrusive grandparents; being triangulated between a child and Child Protective Services; keeping children safe in the neighborhood; enhancing self-esteem; dealing with stress; and how to give a child what he wants when there is little money.

Disciplining the Difficult Child

Perhaps foremost in concern among the parents is unhappiness with the behavior of their children. It is this problem that initially drives parents to attend these groups. Complaints range from the mundane to the extraordinary, from normal developmental concerns to examples of extreme behaviors and exposure to traumatic events that strain the limits of current social work thinking.

Parents raise routine concerns about children who will not sit still during dinner, who do not finish their homework, who balk at doing chores, and who ignore them. They raise more troublesome complaints about teenagers feeling unsafe in schools and getting into fights, dropping out of school, and of running the streets until late at night. Occasionally, striking concerns are brought up. One parent worried about what to tell her 5-year-old daughter who had seen a dead body in a dumpster. She also wanted assistance in dealing with the same daughter following sexual abuse by a 7-year-old neighborhood boy. The question of how to handle the parent of the boy after the boy was reported to the police was also raised. One great-grandmother did not know what to do about her great-grandson, who, at the age of 10, often stayed out all night without her knowing his whereabouts.

Underlying these concerns and, in some cases, instigating them is a sense the parents have of feeling totally overwhelmed by their environment. Poverty, unsafe housing, unsafe neighborhoods, inadequate resources, and sometimes their own history of school failure and having been inadequately parented combine to drain the parents of the ability to cope with the vagaries of life their children display. Their own needs are so great that marshalling strength to cope with the environmental pressures on their children is nearly impossible.

Dealing with the Noncustodial Parent Who Visits Occasionally

Many parents (usually mothers) are raising children alone. As such, their lives often remain entwined with those of the father or fathers of their children, particularly if the father shows an interest in his offspring. Visits pose a problem for two reasons: Some fathers say they will visit and do not. When they do visit, they often have more control over the children than the mother.

As with many separations and divorces, the logistics of contact between the noncustodial parent and the child can be problematic. Even in the best of situations, schedules get lost, communication is confused, and last-minute cancellations wreak havoc on long-standing plans. In these families, where some children have been the product of brief relationships, commitments are kept less often. Thus, promises to visit end up being hollow, leaving the custodial parent to deal with the upset child whose father did not stop by to take the child for a ride he had promised.

Group members also raise the problem of having less control over the child than the father seems to have. Whether married or single parents, mothers complain that their attempts to discipline fall short, while all the father has to do is "raise his voice," "stamp his feet," or "shout once" and the children fall into line. The seeming power of the father poses a triple threat to the mother: making her feel incompetent, reinforcing the importance of men over women in her community, and angering her, as she is the one who usually spends most time with the child.

Occasionally it is the grandmother raising her daughter's child who discusses this issue. In these situations, the grandmother may complain about her daughter's lack of concern and sporadic involvement or, as just discussed with regard to fathers' visits, that when the daughter does visit, she spoils the child.

Managing Intrusive Grandparents

Many group members live with their parents due to financial constraints and the unavailability of child care. These situations lead easily to disagreements over how to parent. Group members sometimes feel undercut by their parents, who invoke certain rules because it is their home. The members, having few options about where else to live, are caught between succumbing to their parents' suggestions about how their grandchildren should be raised and wishing to follow their own rules.

Being Caught Between a Child and Child Protective Services

Parents of older children often feel undermined in their attempts to discipline their child when the child threatens to call 911 or Child Protective Services if the parent is on the verge of physically punishing the child. At times this may be appropriate from the child's perspective. As indicated by the parents, though, it is used even for minor acts of discipline. For the parents, this tips the balance of power in the home and is an example of the state intruding on their family. For some parents, it creates the feeling that life has changed from the time when they were young and parents were in charge of their children.

Keeping Children Safe in the Neighborhood

One of the larger problems in these neighborhoods is the safety of the streets. Members often lament that they were able to play outside until nighttime when they were young, whereas their own children cannot. Yet keeping the children inside in a small apartment or house, especially on a hot evening, poses other problems and adds to the general level of stress in the home.

Enhancing Self-Esteem

Some parents have been exposed to other parent education efforts in the schools. Chief among their goals is the enhancement of self-esteem. A few group members are able to relate their feelings as parents to their feelings about themselves as people and raise this as a topic for discussion in the groups.

Dealing with Stress

Parents are constantly bombarded by the chaos in their neighborhoods. They complain that they are stressed out and unable to meet the continuing needs of their children. An ongoing theme is the request for information about how to deal with this stress.

How to Give a Child What He Wants When There Is Little Money

Parents on limited incomes are often scraping the barrel by the end of the month to make ends meet. Giving a child even a small bonus for good behavior or a good school performance can be a financial stretch. Finding enjoyable family activities like a visit to a fast food restaurant or a movie is frequently out of a parent's range. As a result, chances to celebrate in a way that is meaningful for a child are few. This makes the parent feel incompetent as a provider and nurturer.

RECOMMENDED WAYS OF WORKING

The approaches used with these group members must be consistent with their culture and cognizant of their inherent strengths. Suggestions for interventions that are outside their resources will not be successful or accepted and may well be experienced as destructive.

Giving instruction about child development is the first stage in help-ing parents to discipline more effectively. Parents of very young children often interpret rambunctious behavior as disobedience rather than normal exuberance and get into battles with their children. For example, the 18-month-old who looks at the parent and then throws food on the floor is not trying to anger the parent. Messy rooms are not meant to be dis-respectful but rather are a reflection of the child's feelings about himself or herself and a lack of interest in cleanliness. In most cases, the instruc-tion comes from the group members themselves, and not from the lead-ers. For some members, depending on their acceptance or rejection of authority, this may make the information more palatable. It also gives a sense of competence to the provider of the information.

More serious discipline issues are usually handled in two ways. First, the group provides specific suggestions. If these fall short, as they often do, or if the group is put off by the difficulty of the issue, the leader and coleader step in. If a diagnostic assessment of the parent has not been made in advance, a few questions about the context of the problem (e.g., who is in the family and who is affected by the problem) sometimes clar-ify the picture. Family system strengths are often the focus of the ques-tioning. The questions asked include "What has worked for you in the past?" and "Give me other examples of successful coping." Ideas from structural family therapy (Minuchin, 1974; Simon, 1995) are often applied. In addition, rituals are prescribed that are intended to enhance enduring family patterns and build closeness (Mackey & Greif, 1994). Encouraging parents to read to their children every night, have a special pizza night once a week, or have a "choose a TV show" night introduces structure to families that often live in chaos. While these rituals do not deal specifically with the discipline problem, they do build family strength and set the stage for solving the problem. Concepts underpinning short-term therapy are also applied (Nickerson, 1995), with an eye toward pro-viding a different view of the problem. The role of the leader tends to become more central the more serious the problem. Yet the group, when it is working well, provides support around these intractable problems that can touch a reserve of strength in the parent.

Inadvertently, the timing of some disciplinary interventions may be fortuitous. Something that failed once may work again a year later. The parent who comes occasionally, gets a little information, and does not come back is reminded of that information when he or she sees a sign advertising the group, even if the parent chooses not to return. Over the course of many years of working in the same school, the mere presence of the group, even for one-time attendees, becomes a reminder of sugges-tions for change.

Dealing with the noncustodial parent, particularly a man, requires an acknowledgment of the differential status men hold in this community, where women so frequently are in the majority. While ventilation is help-ful, unless a context and limits for group discussion are set, members tend to spiral off into diatribes about men that are ultimately unproductive. Helping to set the context can include leading discussions about the role of men in the parents' lives when they were younger and focusing on the current precarious position that men occupy in many communities.

Group members often believe that the visiting father should be treated harshly, perhaps reflecting the members' own feelings of anger and helplessness. Ideally, the group can be helped to reach the conclusion that, for most fathers, involvement is a positive experience when it is regulated. If the father visits and undermines the authority of the mother, both parents should be encouraged to work together on setting rules for the child. Often this does not work, though, and the influence of the outside father becomes something that the custodial parent and her children have to learn to live with. In that case, the mother is assisted to view the father's involvement in a way that does not get her so upset. This can include discussing what other behaviors surround the visit that the mother can better understand and change. For example, the mother who finds herself screaming at the father the minute he walks in will be asked to anticipate his visit with a different reaction. The purpose is to handle the visit in a way that makes her feel more in control.

In dealing with intrusive grandparents, we return to the ideas of structural family theory. Boundary issues are emphasized at the same time that group members are asked to explore any unresolved problems they may have with their own parents that affect how they themselves parent. The advantage of the group is that grandmothers caring for grandchildren are also present, giving an intergenerational perspective to the discussion. Sometimes when a mother or grandmother sees the conflict from the other's perspective, change can occur.

When group members believe that their attempts to parent are being impeded by a child's threat to call Child Protective Services, we sympathize with them by saying, "It must be hard to be unable to parent the way you want to." The underlying interventions must speak to two themes: helping the members find a way of parenting that will work for them (i.e., increasing their sense of competence) and acknowledging the interference of other institutions in their lives. The first theme is approached by returning the question to the group of what solutions they have found for the particular problem. Then the discussion can turn to other ways in which the members feel that outsiders are interfering, including referring to the group leader as a potential outsider. This sometimes opens up issues about being referred by the school principal to the parenting group and the members' reactions to that suggestion.

When safety concerns keep children cooped up in their homes, suggestions about alternative modes of entertainment in Baltimore are usually given by other group members. The discussion then evolves into how life has changed since the members were young. By broadening the question, members can then be asked to discuss how they can recapture part of their past that they enjoyed. These discussions usually occur as parents exchange ideas about how to improve their position on public housing lists so that they can move to a safer neighborhood sooner. For some, a move is the best intervention.

Self-esteem is built within the group process. By supporting the parents' effective attempts to parent and by parents finding ways to help other group members, self-esteem does increase. Breaking down parenting into small steps helps the parents gain a sense of control. If the group provides helpful suggestions that are put into action, the members often feel better. Some parents are unreachable through the group. The task here is to prevent them from discouraging members working toward change.

Stress is handled the same way. Parents are encouraged to find a small thing they can accomplish that will make their lives more pleasurable. Stress often seems to loom over these parents as a mountain that they can never scale. Telling parents that they have the right to have time for themselves, by asking a trusted neighbor to watch their children one day in exchange for their watching the neighbor's children the next, and stating that they should be allowed to take a shower or bath without interruption provides solace to some parents.

Stress is also handled by helping the parent feel more competent, an issue related to self-esteem.

> One parent whose young daughter was sexually abused by another neighbor's child had also observed a dead body in a trash dumpster adjacent to their high-rise development. As the child was significantly traumatized and then retraumatized by the second event, the mother wanted assistance in dealing with the child's nightmares and increasingly uncontrollable behavior.
>
> Borrowing from structural family theory, we tried to place the mother in charge of the situation by increasing her feeling of competence. The belief was that if the mother felt more competent, the child would feel less upset. (The child was also in occasional individual treatment related to the sexual trauma.)
>
> We asked the mother to read to her child at bedtime. If she could find books about children successfully coping, so much the better. We also asked her to involve her daughter in other activities where the mother was clearly the expert, like cooking and game playing. The hope was that such activities would enhance the role of the mother and show the child that the mother was competent. The intervention succeeded in reducing the child's nightmares but was less successful with the discipline problem.

Finally, we try to help parents discuss money management. Groups whose members receive welfare do not meet when checks arrive. Such groups are often poorly attended because parents go on buying sprees. By the end of the month, little money is left. Parents who can begin to use money more effectively are not bereft the final week of the month when the child wants change for a candy bar. Money management also shows the child that the parent will be consistent in meeting the child's needs, a message that all children need to hear.

EVALUATION AND CONCLUSION

It must be noted that despite the examples given of successful group interventions, some problems presented by the group members are unsolvable in the group context. They push the limits of social work practice because of the extreme nature of the situation and the extent to which the family is embedded in our society, which affords little sustenance. Some members with intractable problems drop out of the group, perhaps believing that another attempt to help them has failed. Unfortunately, the net result is to reinforce their sense of helplessness.

The success of the drop-in group is judged by the answers to three questions: (1) Do parents return?, (2) Do the parents who attend even one session appear to get something out of it (a subjective assessment, as paper-and-pencil tests appear to scare off potential attendees)? and (3) Does the principal think it is working? Some parents do return, depending in part on the culture of the school. In two of the three schools, the group has been successful with returning parents; in the third school, where attendance is low, the parent–school liaison reports that the parents still request the group. Parents do tend to leave after each session, saying that they enjoyed the meeting. For some principals, the mere presence of the group is a statement that the school is trying to meet parents' needs. As long as the group may be constructive, the principals of all three schools are happy to sponsor it, though support from one school to the next tends to vary.

Empowering disadvantaged parents through group work can be a key element in any plan to improve the situations of at-risk children. By assisting those who want help and building on their strengths, greater parenting competence may develop throughout the community.

NATIONAL RESOURCES

Home and School Institute
1500 Massachusetts Ave. NW
Washington, DC 20002
(202) 466-3633

Parents Without Partners
401 N. Michigan Ave.
Chicago, IL 60611
(312) 644-6610

The journal *Social Work in Education*, published by the National Association of Social Workers, often has relevant articles.

REFERENCES

Boyd-Franklin, N. (1989). *Black families in therapy: A multisystems approach.* New York: Guilford Press.

Gitterman, A. (1989). Building mutual support in groups. *Social Work with Groups, 12*(2), 5–21.

Halpern, R. (1990). Poverty and early childhood parenting: Toward a framework for intervention. *American Journal of Orthopsychiatry, 60*, 6–18.

Hines, P. M. (1989). The family life cycle of poor black families. In B. Carter & M. McGoldrick (Eds.), *The changing family life cycle: A framework for family therapy* (2nd ed., pp. 513–544). Boston: Allyn & Bacon.

Kalyanpur, M., & Rao, S. S. (1991). Empowering low-income black families of handicapped children. *American Journal of Orthopsychiatry, 61*, 523–532.

Mackey, J., & Greif, G. L. (1994). Using rituals to help parents in the school setting: Lessons from family therapy. *Social Work in Education, 16*, 171–178.

Minuchin, S. (1974). *Families and family therapy*. Cambridge, MA: Harvard University Press.

Nickerson, P. R. (1995). Solution-focused group therapy. *Social Work, 40*, 132–133.

O'Donnell, J., Hawkins, D., Catalano, R. F., Abbott, R. D., & Day, L. E. (1995). Preventing school failure, drug use, and delinquency among low-income children: Long-term intervention in elementary schools. *American Journal of Orthopsychiatry, 65*, 87–100.

Parsons, R. J. (1991). Empowerment: Purpose and practice principle in social work. *Social Work with Groups, 14*(2), 7–21.

Proctor, E. K., & Davis, L. E. (1994). The challenge of racial difference: Skills for clinical practice. *Social Work, 39*, 314–323.

Radin, N. (1985). Socioeducation groups. In M. Sundel, P. Glasser, & R. Vintner (Eds.), *Individual change through small groups* (2nd ed., pp. 101–116). New York: Free Press.

Shulman, L. (1992). *The skills of helping individuals, families and groups* (3rd ed.). Itasca, IL: F. E. Peacock.

Simon, G. M. (1995). A revisionist rendering of structural family therapy. *Journal of Marital and Family Therapy, 21*, 17–26.

Taylor, J. T., Chatters, L. M., Tucker, M. B., & Lewis, E. (1990). Developments in research on black families: A decade review. *Journal of Marriage and the Family, 52*, 993–1014.

Yalom, I. (1995). *The theory and practice of group psychotherapy* (4th ed.). New York: Basic Books.

21

Group Work with Unemployed People

Jane E. Lytle-Vieira

The traditional social work focus on the person in the situation underscores the intimate connection between a client's psychosocial status and environment. If the personal situation of a particular client includes unemployment, a social worker is particularly well trained to understand the many layers of the client's life on which this impacts.

REVIEW OF THE LITERATURE

The recent literature is replete with documentation of the link between unemployment and a variety of mental health problems (see, e.g., Crouter & Manke, 1994; Vosler, 1994). In 1984, Keefe used modern research on stress to examine unemployment and to suggest that alienation theory is relevant for understanding unemployment. Whereas workers in preindustrial societies had a strong sense of identification with and control over the products they produced, contemporary jobs usually offer little opportunity for meaningful impact on the products produced. Rather, the worker becomes the "commodity," whose main function is to earn a certain salary. This then permits some freedom (which is lacking on the job) to be exercised in purchasing other commodities outside of work. Loss of one's commodity status can be devastating, not only in the workplace but in one's ability to continue to function in our consumer society.

That unemployment is problematic for the family of the unemployed as well is documented by Fleuridas (1987), among others, who lists five areas where the unemployed person and family experience "psychological stress":

1. "Daily structure": whereas the employed worker was out of the house on a regular schedule, the unemployed person may be at home, either all the time or for unpredictable periods. While this may not be the most devastating aspect of unemployment, it can destroy a family's heretofore predictable routine and may raise new questions about responsibility for child care and discipline, household tasks, and so on.

2. "Shared experiences and social interaction": Not only does the unemployed person lose access to his or her previous social contacts in the workplace, but the fund of workplace stories or anecdotes that used to enliven the dinner table, for instance, suddenly dries up. In addition, the family may lose access to company picnics or networks of important social contacts.

3. "Economics": The financial implications for a family may be profound, as unemployment can lead to a dramatically altered lifestyle, including uncertainty about the ability to continue to live in the current residence or to continuing funding a child already in college.

4. "Status, identity and purpose": If the breadwinner's status in the community is dramatically altered, this may affect the real or perceived standing of the family in the community and raise critical questions for all family members about how much the future can be trusted and how much one can believe that hard work and loyalty to a particular company or profession will be rewarded.

5. "Opportunity to develop skills, creativity, and productivity": Unemployment may dramatically arrest an individual's or family's hopes and dreams for self-improvement, a more affluent future, and/or recreational or avocational pursuits that were goals of a planned, comfortable retirement.

Another, more recent source of information on the negative implications for families dealing with unemployment is Price's article (1992), which summarizes the psychological strain, the effect on the family, and the "double burden" of coping with the stress of job seeking at a time when one is already vulnerable because of the crisis of job loss. Even the threat of job loss can be stressful. Larson, Wilson, and Beley (1994), investigating 111 couples in which one or both members was threatened with job loss, found significant family and marital dysfunction.

Two articles by House, Kessler, and Turner focus on mental health issues among involuntarily unemployed workers in southeastern Michigan. While theirs is not a representative sample, because they studied primarily blue-collar workers in the automotive industry, some interesting points are raised. In the first paper (Kessler, Turner, & House, 1987), the authors point out that, at least among this more economically vulnerable population, the connection between unemployment and health has two parts: (1) the financial strain is a critical variable, and an unemployed worker who is not suffering financial hardship reduces by 50% his or her chances of developing health problems caused by stress; (2) an unemployed person, already with weakened emotional resources, is much more vulnerable to unrelated life crises that previously could have been handled more effectively. The second paper (Turner, Kessler, & House, 1991) explores which factors act as buffers against mental health deterioration and suggests that supportive networks, both in the individual's personal environment and in a planned mental health intervention, are important. They also raise a subtle, interesting question: whether damage to self-esteem during unemployment may possibly be related to class, professional identity versus blue-collar status, and financial vulnerability, rather than being a broad problem affecting all the unemployed.

Three more papers from the Institute for Social Research at the University of Michigan (Price, Van Ryn, & Vinokur, 1992; Vinokur, Price, & Caplan, 1991; Vinokur, Van Ryn, Gramlich, & Price, 1991) explore the cost-benefit ratio in prevention programs that aim to maintain mental health and coping skills and to support timely reemployment in productive jobs. Together these articles document the benefits—both financially, in terms of eventual job satisfaction and earning power, and emotionally, in terms of symptom reduction—of offering intervention to the unemployed population.

Two recently published books are valuable resources for the social worker seeking more understanding of the clinical and policy issues involved in work with the unemployed (Kates, Greif, & Hagen, 1990; Maida, Gordon, & Farberow, 1989). Several detailed clinical case studies are provided, and Kates et al. offer a very nice, modified psychiatric history, with emphasis on the individual's work history and interpersonal dynamics on the job. Both books also address the systemic solutions that need to be pursued at a policy and governmental level to meet the needs of the unemployed.

Wide-ranging as the above literature is, the author was unable to locate anything that dealt extensively with the application of group work methods to this particular population. This chapter is one of the first attempts to do so.

PRACTICE PRINCIPLES

The basic tenets of group composition and commitment apply to the targeted population of unemployed persons if the leaders have some control over the selection of group members and if members must commit for a specific period of time. If, however, it is an open-ended group, with regular movement into and out of the group as some participants attend a few meetings and drop out or become employed and others become regular long-term members, then the role of the social worker shifts. (The author's experience is with the latter type of group, and it is to this kind of mixed therapy/support group that these remarks apply.) Such a group, with an open door policy and a shifting membership, is probably the most appropriate vehicle for this population, as its structure supports the hopeful notion that group membership is temporary and that participants can eventually return to full-time employment. However, while this is logically the best format, the inevitable transiency raises questions about the group's identity, cohesiveness, and development of trust.

There are several classic studies of the stages of group development, which, in this kind of open-ended group, are always going on simultaneously (Bennis & Shepard, 1956; Garland, Jones, & Kolodny, 1973; Yalom, 1995). Whereas a closed group may progress along a more or less discernible path, an open group is always in flux around certain core themes, such as authority, dependence versus interdependence, and problem-solving styles.

Budman and Bennett (1983) have written about the specific differences between short-term therapies and more classical long-term groups. The social worker who leads an unemployed group is faced with the challenge of integrating senior group members who may be facing both long-term unemployment and long-term group membership with people who may attend only briefly, in the immediate post-layoff crisis, and then leave the group by succeeding in their employment search. Thus, the social worker is always balancing different levels of attachment to the group and to the leader, different stages of the process of grief and mourning over job loss, and radically different expectations of what the group can provide. Recently laid off workers often need to express their anger at and sense of betrayal by former employers, as well as their anxiety and uncertainty about the group itself. More long-term members who are comfortable in the group and clear about how to use it to meet their needs may be more focused on the integrity of the group process and on preventing perceived distractions.

Social workers, no strangers to operating on several levels at the same time, can return confidently to the old social work adage to "start where the client is" as a guiding principle in dealing with these multiple needs. To integrate individuals at varying stages into the group, it is helpful to have enough structure to ensure that some time is allocated to newcomers, as well as "check-in" time that allows more experienced members to discuss their past week, their morale, and any specific concerns or thoughts.

The social worker must also maintain a delicate balance between running an educational support group and a psychotherapeutic group. Inevitably, issues surface with dynamic meaning, and it is the social worker's task to provide appropriate intervention and to redirect the group or individual members when they veer in the direction of emotional issues not directly related to unemployment. Since group membership is transient and since participants' adjustment to unemployment and to the group vary immensely, the social worker must help the group maintain the common issue of coping with unemployment as a central, unifying theme.

COMMON THEMES
Anger

However the job loss has occurred, there is almost always anger at the boss, the company, colleagues, and/or the self. A particular individual, like the former boss, may be targeted as the sole cause of one's unemployment and the aggression may focus there, with intrusive thoughts about fantasied acts of revenge against this individual. In other cases, the larger company, often thought of formerly as a benevolent parent who would reward dedication and hard work, may now be seen as a callous, money-hungry entity that encouraged the worker's idealization and then cruelly discarded him or her when it was expedient to do so. In some individuals, the aggression is turned against the self, with self-recriminations of "Why did I hang on so long?" or "Why didn't I see this coming?"

Depression

Internalized rage or relatively normal mourning over a job loss can lead to depression. Depending on the particular personality, life circumstances of the person, and genetic makeup, the depression may become more or less severe. Obviously, the more debilitating forms of depression become major obstacles to healthy coping and eventual reemployment and may necessitate medication.

Loss of Self-Esteem and Confidence

Loss of a job, with all that is included in that role, is almost always a severe blow to one's ego and sense of well-being. The blow may be lessened somewhat if one is part of a large group laid off due to bad economic conditions rather than one of a very few people laid off in a company. Nonetheless, losing one's job represents a major challenge to one's role in society, sense of competence and control, and belief in one's abilities. A common refrain is "What's wrong with me? Why me?" as if the path to unemployment always followed a rational, predictable course. Obviously, self-esteem is particularly at risk when the job is a major source of self-fulfillment and/or economic survival.

Stress

The unemployed person may suffer all the classic physiological and emotional signs of stress in which the demands on the organism exceed its ability to respond. Stress-related illnesses are common, as are disturbed sleep, intrusive thoughts, irritability with the family or other loved ones, and constant ruminations on the bleak future.

Paralysis

Any or all of the above factors may result in temporary paralysis of the individual. He or she may be unable to apply for unemployment compensation and, at the same time, unable to get organized to job hunt. Networking opportunities are passed up as the person is overwhelmed with massive anxiety and possibly by demands from family and friends to "do something."

Shame

Particularly in Western societies, unemployment carries with it a sense of personal responsibility for not having a job. There is still a capitalistic ethic that suggests that there is a job for anyone willing to work, and therefore that anyone without a job is either shiftless or incompetent. Repeatedly, group members have quoted well-meaning family members and friends who generalize optimistically about certain areas or professions: "Anyone can get a job in sales." There are also relatives or associates who tout the unemployed person's qualifications, thus asking, by implication, "What's wrong with *you* that you can't get a job?" when the person has a particular degree or a desirable background in a certain field. In essence, an unemployed person who is well qualified must deal with the emotional problem of this dilemma. Group members can often remember clearly the first time they told neighbors or friends that they were unemployed.

Isolation

Employment usually is associated with a host of formal and informal relationships, all of which are lost through unemployment. The casual socialization at lunch or conversations in a carpool are both casualties of job loss. The depressed, immobilized person sees his or her world rapidly shrinking and, with it, the opportunities for stimulation and reinforcement.

Financial Crisis

Clearly, the impact of job loss is somewhat less if finances aren't a major concern, but for the majority of unemployed persons, the necessity of working for a living is a fact of life. In addition to struggling to pay current bills for basic needs and dealing with aggressive creditors, the person who is out of work more than briefly may also face the loss of future hopes and dreams. The middle-aged person may have to use retirement savings for basic daily survival and faces the very real question of how he or she will survive in old age with no assets. Whereas earlier the person may have been helping adult children with education or first home purchases, he or she may now confront a dramatic role reversal whereby the adult child is relied on for loans or cash gifts to allow the unemployed parent to survive. Similarly, young families and single persons are faced with basic daily decisions that are critical to their health and welfare. Questions about bankruptcy, continuing to survive by charging one's food bills and/or applying for food stamps and public assistance become real.

Conflict with Family and Friends

Stress, depression, financial pressures, and other problems all conspire to create a situation ripe for marital breakdown, parent–child conflict, loss of close supportive relationships, and often substance abuse or other forms of acting out. Family members, roommates, or domestic partners are also threatened as they see their emotional and economic security jeopardized by unemployment by extension. They may pressure the person and often, quite legitimately, expect to have their own needs put into the equation. Even the most well-timed, supportive, loving comment can lead to sparks if the jobless person feels undeserving of such acceptance.

RECOMMENDED WAYS OF WORKING

The author coleads a weekly 90-minute group for unemployed workers that is funded by the county Department of Employment and Training. The agency setting is a nonprofit community mental health center, and the target population is persons who have been in stable employment and have lost their jobs through plant closings or reduction in the workforce. (However, we inevitably have some participants who are among the chronically unemployed, which will be discussed below.) There is no charge, and although people are asked to make a commitment to attend for at least 6 weeks, the reality is that members come and go on a much more irregular basis. The stated purpose of the group is to focus on the social and emotional impact of loss of work in such a way that future reemployment is facilitated. (Other possible sites for such a group could include the employment office itself, a church or temple, or a community center.)

The format is not rigid but usually begins with a brief introduction of the leaders and the purposes of the group. At this time, it is emphasized that this is not a "how to get a job" group. That is, discussions about resume writing, interviewing techniques, and so on are discouraged, although these topics inevitably crop up. First-time participants are given an orientation sheet that expands on the purposes of the group and the group's norms, and a registration sheet with minimal identifying information. At this point, a list is also given out about other unemployment resources in the hope of familiarizing the newcomer with the agencies and programs that do focus on the "how to" of finding a job so that this group can remain more therapeutically focused.

Usually, the next step is a "check in" whereby regular members share activities of the past week that caused distress or joy and ask for group feedback or support about any pending emotional issue related to unemployment. The two social workers leading the group attempt to empower the members by conveying the notion that this is their group and, as such, is to be used by them as they wish. This often means that a formal check in is abandoned when a member is in particular pain and the group process focuses on him or her. Common topics that may emerge are disappointment when one doesn't get a hoped-for interview or an offer after one or two interviews. Periodically, all the common themes in the grief process are revisited by different members at different stages.

The social workers provide psychoeducational content on stress reduction, anger management, coping with depression, and so on, although more experienced group members may have internalized enough of this information to offer it to others when needed.

Group dynamics emerge in all the predictable ways. Certain personalities thrive in the spotlight, either challenging the leaders or other members or focusing on their own uniquely terrible situation, with minimal empathy for others. This process sometimes takes on class overtones as needy, narcissistic professionals may unconsciously lord it over blue-collar workers by describing their generous severance packages, IRAs, and savings, which cushion the financial impact of unemployment. Other members, unable to tolerate their own pain or that of others, become "rescuers" who have a perfect answer to every existential question posed and cut off members' attempts to share painful emotions.

More of the burden for intervention falls on the leaders when there is no cohesive, stable group of core members at any one time, either because of successful reemployment or an influx of new members who haven't yet been socialized into the group norms. Ideally, some of the more problematic individuals described above are handled by the group itself through confrontation, redirection, and so on. Indeed, in the author's experience, this is usually the case. There is normally an extraordinarily positive identification with the group, which some members have referred to as "my family." Just as in a healthy family, where dysfunctional behavior is addressed when it threatens the well-being of the individual or of the unit, so too, in the group, committed members speak up to clarify, interpret, emphasize the importance of the group in their lives, and confront members whose behavior is inimical to the group process.

Identification with the group is fostered by the regularity of the sessions, by telephone outreach by the social workers during the week to members who seem particularly at risk, and by an informal agreement whereby "old" members buddy up with "new" members, often including them in the core group that usually adjourns after the meeting to a nearby bagel shop. A sense of continuity and hope is encouraged by a bulletin board on which letters are posted from former group members who are now employed. (In two cases, these former members wrote to tell the group of job opportunities at their new workplace.) A fair amount of bartering for goods and services has sprung up, entirely at the initiative of the members. A dentist offered free or reduced dental care in return for yard work, and another person offered free consultations, outside of the group, on resume writing and interviewing.

The benefits of this group cohesiveness and loyalty include a sense of common ground where members can find purpose in giving and receiving help. The group engenders a sense of universality, conveying the idea that people are not alone, even if they are unemployed, and that feelings can become less formidable when shared with others. There is a strength in numbers ethos that tends to reduce feelings of isolation and impotence.

Cases

A middle-aged, single white professional woman was fighting off despair as bills mounted and nothing seemed to break for her in her chosen field. When the group identified the need for specialized services for family members or friends affected indirectly by the unemployment, this talented woman volunteered to write a proposal to fund services for this group. Not only was the new group funded, which brought well-deserved kudos to this member, but she was then able to list this particular accomplishment on her resume. This resulted in a significant boost in her self-esteem and energy level and secured her an esteemed place in the group.

Another group member was so depressed at his first session that he was unable to take his eyes off the floor. This middle-aged African-American man had been employed in a specialty technical field that had suffered significant layoffs and cutbacks in recent years. This was not his first experience of unemployment, but it was his longest to date. In addition to the financial strain, he questioned his future in this field, and it was obvious that his severe depression was interfering with his ability to job hunt. Compounding these problems were marital tensions, behavioral problems of his two teenage children and a pervasive sense of shame at being unemployed. Once he started to explore some of these issues, he began to lift his eyes a bit and agreed to the social worker's suggestion that medication and individual therapy could be helpful. The real turning point came in a group session where he was exploring the pros and cons of accepting part-time governmental work at a much lower salary than he felt he deserved. His pride was wounded at considering a job so far below his professional level and previous salary. But the group provided a "reality check," stating that some salary and activity were better than none and by reassuring him that his professionalism wasn't being undermined by settling temporarily for a lower-status job. On the strength of the group process, he did accept the job and became a role model for the group in terms of developing a creative alternative method of handling unemployment. Once his medication and newfound job combined to alleviate his depression, he began to report enthusiastically on the benefits of his new job, which rapidly became a three-quarter-time job with benefits. Buoyed by this success and by his newfound role in the group, he resumed an active job search in his field and quickly accepted a good full-time job. The last we knew, he wrote back to his old colleagues in the group to pass on a job lead and to say that he had retained the part-time job, in addition to his new full-time job, because of its great benefits and flexible hours. He became an important example to other members, particularly men, who felt that their pride and self-worth were already so damaged that they couldn't allow themselves to consider any position they regarded as beneath them.

PROBLEMS

An unanticipated problem concerns the number of chronically unemployed people whom the group has attracted. Although most group members are either actively looking for work or are using the group to mobilize them to begin a job search, another subgroup appear more attracted to the group for its camaraderie, free refreshments, and something to do. These are people who are basically unemployable because of a major psychiatric disorder or who have long since dropped out of the job market due to ambivalence about working at all. In one such case, it became apparent that the member had no intention of ever going back to work and actually refused to return phone calls from potential employers who sought him out. In most cases, the group itself has been able to confront such persons, and with the social worker's help, to indicate that their needs would best be met in other settings. In several cases, the social workers have spoken individually to such chronically unemployed people who are inappropriate for the group and arranged for individual therapy, psychiatric evaluation, and/or a support group for the chronically mentally ill.

EVALUATION APPROACHES

When a member is reemployed in a satisfactory position, there is always a shared sense of success between the member and the group. Something has worked, a logjam has been broken, and the person leaves the ranks of the unemployed. Employment is obviously the most easily measured and the most clearly stated goal for the group.

However, less tangible factors are evaluated in a questionnaire that is sent to every former group participant. He or she is asked to rank areas of the group that were or were not helpful and to identify themes, topics, or experiences that were particularly relevant. The results of the questionnaires are reviewed by the social workers and passed on to the funder. Annually, the executive director of the agency visits the group without the social workers for a formal evaluation of the group.

It would be worthwhile to design and validate an instrument that measured over time the impact of the group experience on longevity and satisfaction in the new job, level of self-esteem, degree of long-term disruption to the family situation, and other factors.

NATIONAL RESOURCES

Institute for Social Research
University of Michigan
426 Thompson St.
Ann, Arbor, MI 48106-1248
(313) 747-2402

In addition, social workers can contact state and county government agencies for possible additional training funds and/or research on the relationship between mental health issues and unemployment. As happened in the group described here, participants themselves can compile a list of local resources helpful to the job search. In this local community, the list includes governmental agencies that deal with retraining, mental health agencies, job clubs that focus on the nuts and bolts of finding a job, and a local church group that offers a free luncheon and speaker series to unemployed workers.

REFERENCES

Bennis, W. G., & Shepard, H. A. (1956). A theory of group development. *Human Relations, 9*, 415–457.

Budman, S. H., & Bennett, M. J. (1983). Short-term group psychotherapy. In *Comprehensive group psychotherapy* (pp. 138–144). Baltimore: Williams & Williams.

Crouter, A. C. & Manke, B. (1994). The changing American workplace: Implications for individuals and families. *Family Relations, 43*, 117–124.

Fleuridas, C. (1987). The stress of unemployment: Its effects on the family. *The Family Therapy Collections, 22*, 112–122.

Garland, J. A., Jones, H., & Kolodny, R. L. (1973). A model for stages of development in social work groups. In S. Bernstein (Ed.), *Explorations in group work* (pp. 12–53). Boston: Milford House.

Kates, N., Greif, B., & Hagen, D. (1990). *The psychosocial impact of job loss.* Washington, DC: American Psychiatric Press.

Keefe, T. (1984). The stresses of unemployment, *Social Work, 29*, 264–268.

Kessler, R., Turner, J., & House, J. (1987). Intervening processes in the relationship between unemployment and health. *Psychological Medicine, 17*, 949–961.

Larson, J. H., Wilson, S. M., & Beley, R. (1994). The impact of job insecurity on marital and family relationships. *Family Relations, 43*, 138–143.

Maida, C., Gordon, N., & Farberow, N. (1989). *The crisis of competence: Transitional stress and the displaced worker.* New York: Brunner/Mazel.

Price, R. (1992). Psychosocial impact of job loss on individuals and families. *Current Directions in Psychological Science, 1*, 9–11.

Price, R., Van Ryn, M., & Vinokur, A. (1992). Impact of a preventive job search intervention on the likelihood of depression among the unemployed. *Journal of Health and Social Behavior, 33*, 158–167.

Turner, J., Kessler, R., & House, J. (1991). Factors facilitating adjustment to unemployment: Implications for intervention. *American Journal of Community Psychology, 19*, 521–541.

Vinokur, A., Price, R., & Caplan, R. (1991). From field experiments to program implementation: Assessing the potential outcomes of an experimental intervention program for unemployed persons. *American Journal of Community Psychology, 19,* 543–561.

Vinokur, A., Van Ryn, M., Gramlich, E., & Price, R. (1991). Long-term follow-up and benefit cost analysis of the jobs program: A preventive intervention for the unemployed. *Journal of Applied Psychology, 76,* 213–219.

Vosler, N. R. (1994). Displaced manufacturing workers and their families: A research-based practice model. *Families in Society, 75,* 105–115.

Yalom, I. D. (1995). *The theory and practice of group psychotherapy* (4th ed.). New York: Basic Books.

22

Group Work with Employee-Related Issues

Muriel Gray

Issues of the workplace are of interest, in large part, because of the role of work in shaping the lives and identities of individuals and the impact of the nature of work on shaping the identities of nations. The workplace and its workers become increasingly important as the economies of nations become more interdependent and more dependent on work products and services.

From the worker's perspective, Studs Terkel (1974) considers the paradox of work by acknowledging that it is integral to personal identity but can also be degrading to the spirit. He quotes William Faulkner: "You can't eat for eight hours a day nor drink for eight hours a day nor make love for eight hours a day—all you can do for eight hours is work. Which is the reason why man makes himself and everybody else so miserable and unhappy" (p. xi).

Social workers have traditionally worked in a variety of host settings with a variety of populations; however, only recently has the workplace emerged as an appropriate practice setting for social workers (Gray & Barrow, 1993; Kurzman & Akabas, 1993). As a result, there has been a proliferation of creative efforts to use social work skills (Resnick & King, 1985). This field of practice is commonly referred to as *occupational social work*.

According to Kurzman and Akabas (1993), the practice of occupational social work is different from more traditional fields of practice because "the auspices of this field-trade unions and employing organizations—are new, uncommon host settings . . . outside the social service arena and not part of the formal human service tradition" (p. 3). Therefore, social work services in the workplace are typically provided by one or a very few social workers, who are likely to be the only human service professionals at the work site trained to deal with workers' psychosocial issues. Hence, they may be called on to address anything that does not appear to be a personnel issue. While social work skills equip social workers to perform many functions in the workplace, social workers function primarily in assistance programs (Gray & Barrow, 1993).

Assistance programs are commonly identified by the populations they serve. They are typically employee assistance programs (EAPs) when sponsored by management; member or labor assistance programs when sponsored by labor alone; worker assistance programs when sponsored jointly by labor and management; faculty and staff assistance programs when sponsored by colleges and universities to serve those populations; and student assistance programs when sponsored by schools to serve students.

THE SETTING

While basic social work principles and values are the cornerstone of such practice, there are many nuances that make this setting different from the more traditional social work practice settings. These nuances are often reflected in the nature of the populations being served, the philosophy of the programs, the manner of problem identification, and the types of issues being addressed. For instance, in this setting the social worker may have multiple clients: individual workers, groups of workers, the work organization, and the labor union. Being effective requires an understanding of the broader cultural context of the workplace in order to address both the needs of the worker and the needs of the organization. In some instances, these needs may conflict with each other. At those times, Kurzman (1993) notes, occupational social work may present unique ethical dilemmas and challenges. As in other settings, confidentiality is the cornerstone of clinical practice; however, in the occupational setting, the *perception* of confidentiality is also critical. This can be quite a challenge when resolution of a particular problem may require collaboration with other systems within the workplace or when the worker has been referred to the EAP by a supervisor who expects to collaborate with the EAP social worker.

The philosophy guiding the programs may also differ from that of traditional social work practice settings. The philosophy of most assistance programs sees work as the goal of functional performance. These programs typically assume that when workers have personal problems, these problems may affect job performance, and that job performance will improve as personal problems are resolved. Hence, work-related issues may be identified by the workplace and/or by workers. In some instances, individual workers may not be able to articulate a problem and may be unfamiliar with the assistance process because they may never have utilized the services of a professional helper. Moreover, since the services offered through assistance programs are not limited to a particular type of problem (such as mental health, substance use disorders, family), workers seek assistance for a variety of problems. Social workers in this setting have no idea what kind of assistance may be requested. Therefore, occupational social workers need to know enough about many concerns to perform a differential assessment. As in other settings, the assessment considers the person in the environment. In this instance, the environment is the workplace. Therefore, the assessment must consider the interaction between worker and work.

The types of problems or issues presented may also be different from those in the more traditional social work settings. In other words, many presenting issues may be those of the workplace and may require collaboration between supervisors, human resource managers, and occupational social workers.

Traditional approaches to human resource management utilized by U.S. corporations have focused on *individual* worker productivity; however, a global economy has resulted in management approaches focusing on work *group* productivity. Hence, many employee issues that were formerly defined as individual worker problems and addressed by social casework approaches may now be redefined as workplace problems and addressed by social group work strategies. Not only has there been a change in the approach used in managing human resources, there has also been a change in the nature and types of issues the workplace considers important to address. For instance, the editor of *American Business 2000* (1992) indicates that employers must adapt to the changing nature of work by replacing adversarial labor relations with a cooperative approach that recognizes the clash between workers' status as employees and their needs as individuals.

Hence, occupational social workers need to be mindful of the history of work groups and how the acceptance of group work may be associated with increased worker power and the resultant political ramifications (Bramel & Friend, 1987). Social workers need to be aware of the cultural context, political environment, and political implications when developing and applying group work strategies in the workplace. Of utmost importance is the role of labor (Molloy & Kurzman, 1993) and the nature of the labor–management relationship.

Finally, occupational social workers need to recognize that they are practicing in a culture that is primarily composed of groups but a culture that may not recognize that its day-to-day decisions (should) utilize basic group work principles. In other words, workers are so accustomed to working in an office or on a team that these work situations are rarely thought of as groups that require the application of group work principles.

These themes are a few examples of the nuances that may be unique to the workplace that social workers must be knowledgeable of if they are to be effective. In fact, Googins (1993) perceives social work's lack of familiarity with the operations and culture of the workplace as a deficit that must be overcome if social workers are to gain wider access to corporate management and labor.

The social and health issues of the employed population, and the tension of balancing the roles of worker and individual, have long been part of the social welfare tradition; however, contemporary assistance programs are characterized by a much broader array of services (Kurzman & Akabas, 1993). Increasingly, interventions are utilizing group methodologies.

The remainder of this chapter consists of an overview of selected work-related issues typically addressed by social group work interventions: brown bag seminar groups addressing life cycle development issues; post-trauma debriefing groups (also referred to as *critical incident stress debriefing*) addressing workplace violence; support and mutual help groups addressing issues of multiculturalism and diversity; and self-help and treatment groups addressing recovery from substance use disorders.

Note that in this chapter the term *worker* refers to an individual employee who may be employed by an organization or an individual worker who identifies himself or herself as a member of labor. *Worker* is therefore distinguished from *social worker*.

REVIEW OF THE LITERATURE

A review of the literature found that supervisor training and consultation (Akabas & Hanson, 1990; Googins & Casey, 1990; Resnick & King, 1985), cultural diversity education (Gray, 1992; Gray & Barrow, 1993; Van Den Bergh, 1991), drug use disorder recovery counseling (Gray, 1993), critical incident stress debriefing (Braverman, 1993; Michael, Russell, & Unger, 1985), conflict management (Bargal, 1992; Mondros, Woodrow, & Weinstein, 1992), and a variety of problems in living (Schopler & Galinsky, 1993; Sussal, 1985) are among the critical issues affecting employees that utilize social group work interventions. However, just as there are nuances in the workplace that require sensitivity, there are nuances that need to be taken into account when attempting to retrieve data on employee-related issues. For instance, the literature on employee-related issues is stored in several different databases under several different headings: employee assistance programs, human resource management, labor relations, business, social work, psychology, education, and training. In the workplace, the term *group work* is seldom used; however, the work group has long been recognized as an integral part of the workplace. Therefore, *work group* is a category that may result in an expanded computerized literature search.

While the study of work groups has long been of interest to scholars and practitioners of industrial psychology, industrial relations, and administration, it has not directly been the terrain of occupational social workers. However, with the presence of occupational social workers, the workplace has an increased expectation that these social workers are a resource to address directly the social dynamics that evolve within the work group. As a result, more information on practice in the workplace is appearing in social work literature and databases.

GROUP WORK IN THE WORKPLACE

In addition to working with individual workers and/or their families, occupational social work increasingly reflects various forms of practice in which the primary unit of intervention is the work organization itself (Smith & Gould, 1993) or special groups of workers (Mondros et al., 1992; Norman, 1991; Pettigrew, 1987; Resnick & King, 1985; Sussal, 1985).

To form groups in the workplace, the occupational social worker will need to be sensitive to resistance from workers who perceive themselves as self-sufficient and functionally capable. Therefore, promotional strategies that acknowledge self-sufficiency as a strength are often very effective.

While interventions with individuals may include clinical treatment, the purposes of most workplace groups generally include information exchange, training and consultation, self-help, mutual aid, support, and problem solving (Sussal, 1985). Only in rare instances is providing treatment the focus.

Workplace groups have been conceptualized according to their focus (Sussal, 1985; Wegener, 1992) and may be generally categorized as

- groups formed to meet developmental needs or life transitions;
- groups formed in response to work-related needs;
- groups formed to address environmental pressures; and
- treatment groups.

The following section describes these workplace groups.

Groups to Meet Developmental Needs

Brown bag seminars offered during lunch hour are the most common types of information exchange groups. They are designed for special groups of workers to address issues in living and topics identified by workers as being of special interest (Vigilante, 1993). These groups may be offered as a series on family life education. Examples of topics include financial and legal planning, problems of adult children of alcoholics, parenting issues, elder care, child care, AIDS, and children of divorce. Most of these groups utilize a structured approach that includes a presentation on a specific topic, opportunities for questions and answers, information regarding additional resources to address the topic, and promotion of the EAP as a resource. These seminars may be conducted by the occupational social worker, or the latter may introduce a presenter with the needed expertise. Whether conducted by the occupational social worker or the informational expert, the purpose is to impart information that may (1) empower employees to address aspects of a personal issue of concern; (2) promote the EAP as a resource to help resolve a personal issue of concern; and (3) identify organizational problems.

Groups Formed in Response to Work-Related Needs

The focus of groups in this category is work related and addresses issues of the workplace or the individual as worker.

Social workers in the workplace may be called on to address a variety of work-related issues that are amenable to social group work approaches. These groups are typically self-help/mutual help groups, support groups, focus groups, training groups, or groups that have all of the aforementioned characteristics.

Self-Help/Mutual Help Groups   Self-help groups may or may not be developed by a professional. The focus is on the shared personal experiences of the participants. The group intervention is usually a standardized format with general procedures for sharing.

Such work-related groups are typically used in response to worker trauma (on or off-site) resulting from announcements of mass layoffs, corporate mergers, environmental accidents, natural or social disasters, or suicidal or homicidal violence. Following a crisis readiness plan should be the typical workplace response to such crises. Defusing groups, deescalating groups, and debriefing groups are components of such a plan. Since the debriefing group is widely used, this chapter will highlight its format and content.

Posttrauma Debriefing Groups   The debriefing group, as previously mentioned, is one component in a larger crisis readiness plan designed to respond rapidly to a disastrous event. According to Michael et al. (1985), it is designed "to deal with the aftermath of a social crisis by focusing on the community of sufferers created" (p. 245). The crisis readiness plan is typically developed by management and a team of human service professionals that may include the occupational social worker. Following a traumatic event, the occupational social worker in conjunction with management, labor, and a crisis consultant identifies individuals who may be particularly affected by the event because of their connection to the event or their closeness to those directly involved in it (Braverman, 1993). Workplace trauma practitioners agree with Ephross and Vassil (1987) that experience is a good teacher when composing groups, and they have found it best *not* to include children or family members of trauma victims (Braverman, 1993).

Critical incident stress debriefing (CISD) groups are designed to assist individuals with their emotional reactions to involvement in traumatic events such as suicides, homicides, robberies, assaults, and traumas associated with losses incurred during natural disasters. These groups are typically led by a trained team of professionals. At the very least, there should be a management representative who is familiar with the event, the EAP social worker who is trained in posttrauma stress and familiar with the specific workplace culture, and the crisis consultant, who may be an external consultant. In some instances, the EAP social worker may also be the consultant. In other instances where the occupational social worker is external to the workplace, another workplace representative may be included. The main objective of the CISD group is to prevent post-trauma disorders.

To that end, debriefings should occur as soon as possible after the event but certainly within 24–72 hours in order to be most effective. Debriefing groups are very structured and may last for 2–6 hours, depending on the nature of the incident and its emotional impact on the group participants.

There needs to be a confidential, nonevaluative discussion of individual involvement, reactions, and feelings resulting from the incident (Boriskin, 1994). While debriefings have psychological and educational components, they are not therapy or treatment groups. They are often followed by individual counseling for those who have been identified in the group as needing additional help.

The Case of the Fast Food Restaurant

Following a robbery and murder of two employees while opening this fast food restaurant, the contractual EAP company was called for consultation regarding how to help the employees. In the plan that was developed, management scheduled debriefing groups the next day and assigned workers according to their work group shifts. Groups of 10 people were scheduled during nonwork shifts. They remembered that the father of one of the victims was also an employee and offered him individual help instead of the group. The EAP social worker, the district manager (of the food chain), and the store manager coordinated and introduced the team, described the event, and stated the purpose of the meeting. The managers described their feelings about the incident. They also gave updates regarding the investigation and addressed issues of safety, security, handling the media, and handling customers' reactions and inquiries. Following the question-and-answer period, the store manager joined the group as a participant. The district manager left. The EAP social worker began group facilitation by acknowledging to the group the change in the managers' role. The social worker again introduced herself, briefly described what would take place, and provided trauma education by reviewing the natural human response to trauma and some of the expected signs and symptoms. Ground rules were set, and each group member was afforded the opportunity to share his or her reactions, thoughts, feelings, and concerns. The social worker asked each member to prepare mentally to answer specific questions, such as these: What were you doing when you first heard of the incident? What was your first thought? What was it like for you? How did this incident affect you personally? How did you feel immediately afterward? Last night? How are you now? How has the incident changed you? The social worker responded with empathy and validated reactions throughout this sharing phase. During the wrapup, the social worker presented an opportunity for persons to say anything they had not said or to restate something already said. She also described how the EAP could help and gave the phone number. The manager resumed her role as manager and helped the group develop a plan of action. Following the formal debriefing, the manager and the social worker remained to talk informally to participants. They met later to "debrief" the debriefing and to develop any necessary follow-up plans.

Evaluation Approaches A study of strategies for coping with exposure to violent death (McCarroll, Ursano, Wright, & Fullerton, 1993) found that support systems in the work group seemed to facilitate effective coping in the short term, but the long-term results are unclear. Evaluation of CISD effectiveness raises the same questions as other primary prevention interventions regarding the extent to which the phenomenon would have occurred without the intervention. Therefore, it is difficult to determine the true impact of primary prevention interventions.

Groups Formed in Response to Environmental Pressures Many workplace environmental pressures are experienced by workers. However, the U.S. Department of Labor (1988) cites the changing demographics of the workforce as a major challenge to the workplace and to its workers. Due to the compelling nature of this challenge, the use of groups to address cultural and ethnic diversity and to resolve interethnic conflict will be the focus of this section.

The emerging cultural diversity of the workplace creates an environment in which workers of various ethnic and cultural backgrounds need help in adjusting to and succeeding in the workplace and managers need help in creating an environment that is receptive to understanding and affirming differences among a diverse workforce (Gray & Barrow, 1993). Successful interventions result in a workplace that affirms diversity; however, conflict and the skills to resolve it are often part of this transformation process. While the conflict literature focuses mainly on intergroup conflict, Van Den Bergh (1991) notes that if diversity is affirmed, it is necessary for workers to be knowledgeable about many cultures and to be bicultural in individual transactions with each other.

For the most part, the traditional workplace has inadvertently used the work group for worker socialization; however, the progressive workplace *strategically* utilizes group work approaches for socialization. Gray and Barrow (1993) and Van Den Bergh (1991) identified the following foci as organizing principles of workplace groups addressing cultural diversity and multiculturalism:

- assisting employees in adapting to the workplace culture;
- assisting the workplace in affirming differences;
- assisting employees in acquiring workplace opportunities and rewards;

- helping to develop formal and informal networks and linkages among and between groups of employees;
- educating the workforce to cultural differences;
- reinforcing racial, cultural, and ethnic pride;
- protecting and advocating for group rights and concerns; and
- providing a vehicle for the resolution of intercultural and interethnic conflict.

Specific practice principles are determined by the focus of the group. For instance, Mondros et al. (1992) found that successful groups dealing with conflict must be structured, encourage a lot of participation, be coled by individuals who model the nature of the diversity in the workplace, and be contracted to focus on substantive issues rather than merely the ventilation of grievances. On the other hand, groups focusing on facilitating cultural and ethnic consciousness may utilize an educational approach while providing support and mutual aid for their members. Van Den Bergh (1991) points out that such groups may include topics dealing with strategies "for getting promoted and/or how to maintain sanity" (p. 79). The occupational social worker may actually facilitate the group, or may broker or coordinate the planning of the group.

The Case of the African-American Managers

The EAP social worker for a large, predominantly white accounting firm observed that several African-American clients had utilized the EAP due to feelings of professional isolation and frustration because younger, more recently hired African-Americans were not receiving the professional training and mentoring that would allow them to be considered for future positions with the potential for advancement to the manager and partner levels. This observation led to the formation of a support group for all African-American employees who had an interest in career development and informal mentoring. The social worker served as the coordinator. In that role, he collaborated with the human resources manager to identify all African-American employees. A questionnaire was sent to all of these employees inquiring (1) about their interest in attending regularly scheduled group meetings focused on supporting and helping African-American employees develop strategies for career enhancement and promotion and (2) about convenient meeting times if interested. Twenty African-American employees indicated an interest. The social worker contacted his original clients, who agreed to facilitate these self-help support group meetings. The social worker scheduled the meeting place and time and notified all who had indicated an interest. He attended the first meeting, but only to market the EAP and to provide a brief program orientation.

Treatment Groups In the workplace, treatment groups typically focus on recovery from an addictive disorder and prevention of relapse. They may have a support focus, a monitoring focus, an educational focus, or various combinations thereof. The most prevelant groups associated with relapse prevention are 12-step groups such as Alcoholics Anonymous and Narcotics Anonymous. While some workplaces may have 12-step groups on the work site, they are typically under the auspices of the group members, not the workplace.

The Substance Abuse Recovery Monitoring Group

The substance abuse monitoring group is another group that the occupational social worker may be asked to colead with a management representative. Monitoring groups are typically used by management for monitoring treatment plan compliance, identifying signs and symptoms of relapse, and determining the nature and quality of recovery. Membership is comprised of employees who have been diagnosed as having a substance use disorder and whose employment, or whose license to perform a particular type of work, is contingent on a contract of abstinence from alcohol and other drugs as regulated by external governmental agencies, licensing boards, or workplace policy. For instance, monitoring the recovery of airline pilots, drivers of vehicles carrying hazardous materials, physicians, nuclear power plant workers, and other groups of workers who perform safety-sensitive work is the responsibility of the employer.

In the organized workplace, this monitoring role typically involves collaboration between labor and management. Labor usually takes an active role because it has a stake in ensuring the continued employment of its members, whose job may be in jeopardy. In the labor assistance program, this group is part of the service delivery system offered by the union for its members with substance use disorders, although it may not necessarily be related to employment (Molloy & Kurzman, 1993).

The role of the occupational social worker varies according to the situation and setting. For instance, the on-site social worker employed by management or labor is likely to be the actual group coleader or the person responsible for contracting for the monitoring service; by contrast, the external social worker employed by an outside EAP company providing EAP services by contract is more likely to broker such services or to provide the services using a casework approach. In either event, this is a politically sensitive role that is expected to be performed in a neutral manner, respecting the concerns of both management and labor while ensuring that the focus remains on substance abuse recovery. This issue is also sensitive because in most instances group participants enter the group involuntarily.

In addition to group work skills, occupational social workers (as group leaders or as brokers of the service) are expected to be knowledgeable about substance use disorders, recovery, and relapse prevention models that recognize the importance of identifying factors associated with relapse (Lewis, Dana, & Blevins, 1994).

The monitoring group is a structured, open-ended group comprised of members in different phases of recovery. Its purpose is to maintain the positive changes that have occurred during a previous intensive treatment phase by

- encouraging compliance with the recovery plan;
- providing direct support;
- helping members explore other environmental supports; and
- assessing behavioral, cognitive, and affective coping strategies.

Most groups expect participation and provide an educational component based on shared experiences. Support and education are also components of the self-efficacy training that is the cornerstone of the meetings. This training helps group members identify their own high-risk situations of substance use and develop a strategy for addressing these situations before they are encountered. Members remain in the group until the group is certain that they are complying with the recovery plan and are not at great risk for relapse. In some instances, regulatory agencies may mandate participation for a minimum of 2–4 years, in addition to continued evidence of recovery. Often members voluntarily remain in the group to offer support to new members.

The Case of the Airline Pilot Monitoring Group

This ongoing group was co-led by the EAP social worker, the company physician, and the pilot union's EAP representative. The members were all pilots who had been "grounded" by the Federal Aviation Administration pending treatment and evidence of recovery from a substance abuse disorder. The group of 4–10 people met once a month for approximately 2 hours. After they were seated in a circle, each participant was asked to state the components of his recovery plan and to provide an update of his recovery activities. Using the Checklist for Relapse Preventing Monitoring (Gray, 1990), the leaders asked questions to assess each member's cognitive, behavioral, and affective reactions to daily living situations, to being abstinent, and to the recovery plan. Other members offered supportive suggestions and comments on how they handled similar situations. After all members shared, the leaders asked what strategies each member had for handling upcoming holiday family gettogethers that might include alcohol.

SUMMARY

Occupational social workers may be expected to help address a variety of anticipated and unanticipated needs in the workplace. Effective social work helps the workplace identify organizational as well as employee problems. The use of groups is helpful in identifying workplace issues of which management may not be aware. In this regard, the social worker may initiate the development of specific groups as a result of information about employee issues that may have been assessed from casework with clients or information derived from the ongoing process of assessing the organization. To this end, various types of groups may be used in addressing employee-related and organizational issues. The skills needed to address these issues may require continuing education and consultation. The resources listed below may be helpful.

NATIONAL RESOURCES

American Institute for Managing
Diversity
830 Westview Drive
Morehouse College
Atlanta, GA 30314
(404) 524 7316

American Management Association
135 West Fiftieth St.
New York, N.Y. 10020
(212) 586-8100

Employee Assistance Professionals
Association (EAPA)
4601 North Fairfax Drive
Arlington, VA 22203
(703) 522-6272

National Association of Alcoholism
and Drug Abuse Counselors
(NAADAC)
3717 Columbia Pike
Arlington, VA 22204
(703) 741-7686

National Clearinghouse on Alcohol
& Drug Information (NCADI)
11426 Rockville Pike
Besthesda, MD
(301) 468-2600

National Foundation for the Study
of Employment Policy
1015 Fifteenth St. NW
Washington, DC 20005
(202) 789-8685

Society for Human Resource
Management
606 North Washington St.
Alexandria, VA 22314
(703) 548 3440

Society for Intercultural Education,
Training and Research
733 Fifteenth St. NW
Washington, DC 22314
(202) 737-5000

REFERENCES

Akabas, S. (1993). Introduction. In P. Kurzman & S. Akabas (Eds.), *Work and well-being: The occupational social work advantage* (pp. iii–v). Washington, DC: National Association of Social Workers Press.

Akabas, S., & Hanson, M. (1990). Organizational implications of drug abuse programming. In USDHHS (Ed.), *Drug abuse curriculum for employee assistance professionals* (Module III, pp. 1–57). Rockville, MD: National Clearinghouse on Alcohol and Drug Information.

American Business 2000. (1992). The changing nature of work. June 23, 66–77.

Annis, H., & Davis, C. (1989). Relapse prevention. In R. Hester & W. Miller (Eds.), *Handbook of alcoholism treatment approaches: Effective alternatives* (pp. 170–182). New York: Pergamon Press.

Bargal, D. (1992). Conflict management workshops for Arab Palestinian and Jewish youth—a framework for planning, intervention and evaluation. *Social Work with Groups, 15*, 51–68.

Boriskin, J. (1994, February). On the front lines: EAPs battle workplace violence. *Employee Assistance*, pp. 14–18.

Bramel, D., & Friend, R. (1987). The work group and its vicissitudes in social and industrial psychology. *Journal of Applied Behavioral Science, 23*(2), 233–253.

Braverman, M. (1993, Spring). Coping with trauma in the workplace. *Compensation and Benefits Management*, 58–63.

Ephross, P., & Vassil, T. (1987). Towards a model of working groups. *Social Work with Groups, 10*, 13–23.

Googins, B., & Casey, J. (1990). Supervisor training. In USDHHS (Ed.), *Drug abuse curriculum for employee assistance program professionals*, (pp. 1–46). Rockville, MD: National Clearinghouse on Alcohol and Drug Information.

Googins, B. (1993). Work-site research: Challenges and opportunities for social work. In P. Kurzman & S. Akabas (Eds.), *Work and well-being: The occupational social work advantage* (pp. 61–78). Washington, DC: National Association of Social Workers Press.

Gray, M. (1990). Case management. In USDHHS (Ed.), *Drug abuse curriculum for employee assistance program professionals*. Rockville, MD: National Clearinghouse on Alcohol and Drug Information.

Gray, M. (1992). Cultural diversity. In D. Masi (Ed.), *The AMA handbook for developing employee assistance and counseling programs* (pp. 303–320). New York: AMACOM.

Gray, M., & Barrow, F. (1993). Ethnic, cultural, and racial diversity in the workplace. In P. Kurzman & S. Akabas (Eds.), *Work and well-being: The occupational social work advantage* (pp. 138–152). Washington, DC: National Association of Social Workers Press.

Lewis, J., Dana, R., & Blevins, G. (1994). *Substance abuse counseling: An individualized approach* (pp. 169–190). Pacific Grove, CA: Brooks/Cole.

Kurzman, P., & Akabas, S. (Eds.). (1993). *Work and well-being: The occupational social work advantage*. Washington, DC: National Association of Social Workers Press.

Lieberman, M. (1990). A group therapist perspective on self-help groups. *International Journal of Group Psychotherapy, 40*, 251–278.

McCarroll, J., Ursano, R., Wright, K., & Fullerton, C. (1993). Handling bodies after violent death: Strategies for coping. *American Journal of Orthopsychiatry, 63*, 209–214.

Michael, L. E., Russell, N., & Unger, L. (1985). Rapid response mutual aid groups: A new response to social crises and natural disasters. *Social Work, 30*, 245–252.

Molloy, D., & Kurzman, P. (1993). Practice with unions: Collaborating toward an empowerment model. In P. Kurzman & S. Akabas (Eds.), *Work and well-being: The occupational social work advantage* (pp. 46–60). Washington, DC: National Association of Social Workers Press.

Mondros, J., Woodrow, R., & Weinstein, L. (1992). The use of groups to manage conflict. *Social Work with Groups, 15*, 43–57.

Norman, A. (1991). The use of the group and group work techniques in resolving interethnic conflict. In A. Vinik & M. Levin (Eds.), *Social action in group work: Principles and practice* (pp. 175–186). New York: Haworth Press.

Pettigrew, T. (1987). Shaping the organizational context for black American inclusion. *Journal of Social Issues, 43,* 41–78.

Resnick, H., & King, J. (1985). Shadow consultation: Intervention in industry. *Social Work, 30,* 447–450.

Schopler, J., & Galinsky, M. (1993). Support groups as open systems: A model for practice and research. *Health and Social Work, 18,* 195–207.

Smith, M., & Gould, G. (1993). A profession at the crossroads: Occupational social work—present and future. In P. Kurzman & S. Akabas (Eds.), *Work and well-being: The occupational social work advantage* (pp. 7–25). Washington, DC: National Association of Social Workers Press.

Sussal, C. (1985). Group work with federal employees. *Social Work with Groups, 8,* 71–79.

Terkel, S. (1974). *Working.* New York: Avon Books.

U.S. Department of Labor. (1988). *Opportunity 2000.* Washington, DC: U.S. Government Printing Office.

Van Den Bergh, N. (1991). Managing biculturalism at the workplace: A group approach. *Social Work with Groups, 13,* 71–84.

Vigilante, F. (1993). Work. In P. Kurzman & S. Akabas (Eds.), *Work and well-being: The occupational social work advantage* (pp. 179–199). Washington, DC: National Association of Social Workers Press.

Wegener, N. (1992). Supportive group services in the workplace: The practice and the potential. In J. Garland (Ed.). *Group work reaching out: People, places and power* (pp. 207–221). New York: Haworth Press.

Name Index

Subject Index